D0990006

大中华文库

汉英对照

LIBRARY OF CHINESE CLASSICS

Chinese-English

荀 子

Xunzi

II

［美］约翰·诺布洛克　英译

张　觉　今译

Translated into English by John Knoblock

Translated into Modern Chinese by Zhang Jue

湖南人民出版社

Hunan People's Publishing House

外文出版社

Foreign Languages Press

目　录

CONTENTS

强国第十六

【原文】

16.1 刑范正，金锡美，工冶巧，火齐得，剖刑而莫邪已。然而不剥脱，不砥厉，则不可以断绳；剥脱之，砥厉之，则劙盘盂、刎牛马忽然耳。彼国者，亦强国之“剖刑”已。然而不教诲，不调一，则入不可以守，出不可以战；教诲之，调一之，则兵劲城固，敌国不敢婴也。彼国者亦有“砥厉”，礼义、节奏是也。故人之命在天，国之命在礼。人君者，隆礼、尊贤而王，重法、爱民而霸，好利、多诈而

【今译】

16.1 模子平正，铜、锡的质量好，冶炼工人技艺高明，火候和配料得当，那么打开模子，莫邪宝剑就铸成了。但是如果不除去它表面的硬皮，不磨砺它，就不能用它来斩断绳子；除去了它的硬皮，磨砺它，那么用它切割铜器、宰杀牛马就很轻快了。一个国家，也像“刚出模时的毛坯”，只是一个强国的基础，但如果不进行教育，不使人民协调一致，那么在国内就不能依靠他们来守卫，到国外就不能用他们去作战；如果教育他们，使他们协调一致，那就会兵力强劲，城防牢固，敌国不敢来冒犯。国家也有“磨刀石”，礼义法度就是这种“磨刀石”。所以人的命运取决于上天，国家的命运取决于礼义。作为君主，推崇礼义，尊重贤人，就能称王天下；注重法治，爱护人民，就能称霸诸侯；喜欢财

Book 16

On Strengthening the State

16. 1

When the mold is exact, the copper and tin have their proper virtue, the workmanship and casting are skillful, and the fire and alloying successfully controlled, then one has only to break open the mold to have a Moye. Nonetheless, if one has not stripped away the outer debris and sharpened the sword with a whetstone, then it could not cut even a marking-line. But if it has been stripped and sharpened, then the sword will slice a metal pan or bowl in two and will cut the throat of a cow or horse in a flash.

In regard to the state,there is also a "breaking the mold" for a strong state. Nonetheless, if one does not teach and instruct and does not harmonize and unify, then on the one hand one cannot maintain his position and on the other hand one cannot wage war. But if one teaches and instructs the population and harmonizes and unifies them, then the army will be powerful, the city walls stoutly defended, and rival states will not venture to press an advantage.

In regard to the state, there is moreover a "sharpening with the whetstone"consisting of ritual and moral principles, the handling of emergencies, and the making of reports. Thus, just as the fate of men lies with Heaven, so too the fate of the state lies with its rituals.

A lord of men who exalts ritual principles and honors worthy men will become a True King; one who stresses law and loves the people will become lord-protector; one who is fond of profit and is much given to

【原文】

危，权谋、倾覆、幽险而亡。

16.2 威有三：有道德之威者，有暴察之威者，有狂妄之威者。此三威者，不可不孰察也。

礼乐则修，分义则明，举错则时，爱利则形。如是，百姓贵之如帝，高之如天，亲之如父母，畏之如神明。故赏不用而民劝，罚不用而威行。夫是之谓道德之威。

礼乐则不修，分义则不明，举错则不时，爱利则不形，然而其禁暴也察，其诛不服也审，其刑罚重而信，其诛杀猛而必，黭然而雷击

【今译】

利，多搞欺诈，就会危险；玩弄权术，坑人害人，阴暗险恶，就会灭亡。

16.2 威严有三种：有道德的威严，有严酷督察的威严，有放肆妄为的威严。这三种威严，是不可不仔细考察的。

礼制音乐完善，名分道义明确，采取措施切合时宜，爱护人民、造福人民能具体表现出来。像这样，百姓就会像对待上帝那样尊重他，像对待上天那样景仰他，像对待父母那样亲近他，像对待神灵那样敬畏他。所以奖赏不用而民众就能卖力，刑罚不用而威力就能扩展。这就叫做道德的威严。

礼制音乐不完善，名分道义不明确，采取措施不合时宜，爱护人民、造福人民不能落实，但是他禁止暴乱很明察，他惩处不服的人很

dissimulation will be imperiled; and one who schemes after power, plots revolution, and risks secret intrigues will perish.

16. 2

Of awesome authority, there are three varieties: that instilled by the influence of the Way and its Power; that instilled by harsh and cruel judicial investigations; and that instilled by deranged madness. In regard to these types of awesomeness, it would be wrong to be superficial in one's investigations.

When rites and music are reformed and cultivated, when social divisions and the obligations congruent with them are kept clear, when promotions and demotions are timely, when a love for the people and a desire to benefit them is given visible form—when all these conditions obtain, the Hundred Clans will esteem their ruler as they do a Di Ancestor, will exalt him as they do Heaven, will cherish him as they do their own parents, and will stand in awe of him as they do of the Spiritual Intelligences.

Thus, although incentives are not offered, the people will be stimulated to action and although punishments are not used, an awesome authority will hold sway.

This deserves to be described as the awesome authority of the Way and its Power.

Rites and music are not kept in good order; social divisions and their inherent obligations are not kept clear; promotions and demotions are not timely; a love for the people and a desire to benefit them is not given visible form. Nonetheless, harsh applications of the prohibitions are the product of "judicial inquiry" and executions even for [minor] disobedi-

【原文】

之，如墙厌之。如是，百姓劫则致畏，嬴则敖上，执拘则聚，得间则散，敌中则夺，非劫之以形势，非振之以诛杀，则无以有其下。夫是之谓暴察之威。

无爱人之心，无利人之事，而日为乱人之道，百姓讙敖，则从而执缚之，刑灼之，不和人心。如是，下比周贲溃以离上矣，倾覆灭亡，可立而待也。夫是之谓狂妄之威。

此三威者，不可不孰察也。道德之威成乎安强，暴察之威成乎危

【今译】

审慎，他施行刑罚从重而守信用，他处决犯人严厉而坚决，突然地就像雷电闪击他们一样，就像墙壁倒塌压死他们一样。像这样，百姓一受到胁迫就会产生畏惧，一放松就会傲视君主，强行集中就聚在一起，一得到机会就四散逃跑，敌人一进攻就会被敌人争取过去，君主如果不是用权势地位去胁迫他们，不是用惩罚杀戮去震慑他们，那就无法控制臣民。这就叫做严酷督察的威严。

没有爱护人民的心肠，不做有益于人民的事情，而天天搞那些扰乱人民的歪门邪道，百姓如果怨声沸腾，就跟着逮捕他们，对他们用刑烧灼，而不去调解民心。像这样，臣民就会结伙逃散而离开君主。他的垮台灭亡，就可以立刻等到。这就叫做放肆妄为的威严。

这三种威严，是不可不仔细考察的。道德的威严终结于安定强

ence are the product of "judicial examinations."Punishments and penalties are numerous and dependable as though a sudden clap of thunder rolled across the land, and executions and death sentences are fierce and inevitable as though a wall were collapsing on top of the people. In such cases, as long as the Hundred Clans are under compulsion, they will show the utmost dread of authority, but whenever it is relaxed, they will be arrogant toward their superiors; as long as they are held by force, they will assemble, but whenever they find a weak point, they will scatter; and whenever enemies are in the vicinity, they will abscond. If they are not placed under the compulsion of punishments and authority and if they are not scared of punishment and public executions, there will be no means of holding them as subjects. This may indeed be described as the awesome authority of harsh and cruel judicial investigations.

There is no disposition to love mankind, no undertaking to bring benefit to the people, but rather the ruler daily acts so as to create chaos in the Way of Man. If the Hundred Clans should shout in protest, he would in consequence seize and bind them or punish them with burning so that he disquiets the hearts of men. In such a situation, subjects become partisans, and intimates are filled with dissatisfaction and violent turbulence through alienation from their superiors.

One has only to stand by and await his imminent overthrow and destruction.

This may indeed be described as the awesome authority of a deranged madman.

In regard to these three types of awesome authority, it is impermissible to be superficial in one's investigations, for the awesome authority that comes from the Way and its Power finds its culmination in tranquillity and strength, that of harsh and cruel investigations culminates in peril

【原文】

弱，狂妄之威成乎灭亡也。

16.3 公孙子曰："子发将西伐蔡，克蔡，获蔡侯，归致命曰：'蔡侯奉其社稷而归之楚，舍属二三子而治其地。'既，楚发其赏，子发辞曰：'发诫布令而敌退，是主威也；徙举相攻而敌退，是将威也；合战用力而敌退，是众威也。臣舍不宜以众威受赏。'"

讥之曰："子发之致命也恭，其辞赏也固。夫尚贤使能，赏有功，罚有罪，非独一人为之也，彼先王之道也，一人之本也，善善、恶恶之应也，治必由之，古今一也。古者明王之举大事、立大功也，大事

【今译】

盛，严酷督察的威严终结于危险衰弱，放肆妄为的威严终结于灭亡。

16.3 公孙先生说："子发带兵向西讨伐蔡国，攻克了蔡国，俘获了蔡圣侯，回来后向楚宣王汇报执行命令的情况说：'蔡侯献出他的国家而把它送给楚国，我景舍已委派了几个人去治理他的领土。'过后不久，楚宣王向他颁发奖赏，子发推辞说：'一发出警告，一颁布命令，敌人就退却，这是君主的威力；一调发军队去攻打，敌人就退却，这是将领的威力；交战用力后敌人才退却，这是战士们的威力。我景舍不该凭战士们的威力受到奖赏。'"

荀卿指责此事说："子发汇报执行命令的情况倒是谦恭有礼的，他推辞奖赏却鄙陋无知。那推崇贤人，使用能人，奖赏有功的，惩罚有罪的，这不单单是某一个人这样做的，那是古代圣王的政治原则啊，是使人民行动一致的根本措施，是赞美善行、憎恨邪恶的反应，治国一定得遵循这一原则，古代和现在都是一样的。古时候英明的帝王在举办大事、建立大功的时候，大事已经完成，大功已经建立，那么君

and weakness, and that of deranged madness in utter destruction.

16. 3

The *Gongsun [Ni]zi* says:

Prince Fa commanded an expedition westward to invade[Gao]cai, which he overcame, taking the Marquis of [Gao]cai prisoner. On his return he reported his accomplishment, saying: "The Marquis of [Gao] cai has offered up his altars of soil and grain to be presented to Chu. I have entrusted a few men with governing his territory."When Chu was about to declare his reward, Prince Fa declined, saying: "To issue warnings and promulgate edicts so the enemy will withdraw—such is the awesome authority of the ruler. To advance, maneuver, and attack so that the enemy withdraws—such is the awesome authority of a general. To join the enemy in battle with all their strength is the awesome power of the troops. Your servant, She, considers it inappropriate to make use of the awesome power of his soldiers to receive a personal reward."

In criticism of this, I say: In carrying out his charge, Prince Fa was properly respectful, but in refusing to accept the reward for doing so he was obstinate. Indeed "to honor the worthy and employ the able" and "to reward where there is achievement and punish where there is fault"are not the idiosyncratic views of a single individual. Such was the Way of the Ancient Kings, and such is the foundation of the unity of mankind. It is the natural response of treating well what is good and of despising what is evil, out of which the principles of government necessarily grow and concerning which both antiquity and today are in total accord. In antiquity enlightened kings set up the great tasks and established great achievements so that when these great tasks had been accomplished and

【原文】

已博，大功已立，则君享其成，群臣享其功，士大夫益爵，官人益秩，庶人益禄。是以为善者劝，为不善者沮，上下一心，三军同力，是以百事成而功名大也。今子发独不然，反先王之道，乱楚国之法，堕兴功之臣，耻受赏之属，无僇乎族党而抑卑其后世，案独以为私廉，岂不过甚矣哉？故曰：子发之致命也恭，其辞赏也固。”

16.4 荀卿子说齐相曰：

“处胜人之势，行胜人之道，天下莫忿，汤、武是也；处胜人之势，不以胜人之道，厚于有天下之势，索为匹夫不可得也，桀、纣是

【今译】

主就享有它的成果，群臣就分享它的功劳，士大夫晋升爵位，官吏增加俸禄，普通士兵增加粮饷。因此，做好事的受到鼓励，做坏事的受到制止，上下团结一心，三军共同努力，因此各种事情能办成而功业名声伟大卓著。现在子发偏偏不是这样，他违反古代圣王的政治原则，扰乱楚国的法令，使建功立业的臣子懈怠，使受到奖赏的人惭愧，即使没有使家族蒙受羞辱，也已压低了他的后代，还独自把这当作是个人的廉洁，难道不是错得很厉害了吗？所以说：子发汇报执行命令的情况时谦恭有礼，他推辞奖赏却显得鄙陋无知。”

16.4 荀卿劝说齐国的相国道：

“处在制服别人的地位，实施制服别人的办法，而天下没有人怨恨，商汤、周武王就是这样；处在制服别人的地位，不采用制服别人的办法，富裕得拥有统治天下的权势，但要求做一个平民百姓也不可

these great achievements realized, the lord could take pleasure in their completion and his ministers in the accomplishment, knights and grand officers could receive ennoblement, minor officers promotions in rank, and commoners salaries. In this way, those who acted on behalf of the good would be encouraged and those who acted in the interests of what was not good would be stymied. When the ruler and his subjects are of one mind and the three armies make a common effort, it will result in the Hundred Tasks being perfected and in solid accomplishments famed for their greatness. Now Prince Fa alone would not grant this, but rather would turn away from the Way of the Ancient Kings and bring confusion to the laws of the state of Chu. He would bring to naught the flourishing accomplishments of ministers and would put to shame subordinates who would accept rewards. Although he brought no disgrace to his family, yet the prestige of his posterity was diminished and reduced. He based himself on a single individual's private view of what constitutes integrity, so how indeed could it be expected that he did not greatly transgress? It is for this reason that I say Prince Fa in carrying out his charge was properly respectful, but in refusing to accept the reward for doing so was obstinate.

16. 4

Master Xun Qing persuaded the prime minister of Qi, saying: To obtain a position of power that allows one to dominate others and so to carry out the way of domination that no one in the whole world feels resentment—such were Tang and Wu.

To obtain a position of power that allows one to dominate others and not avail oneself of the way to domination and,although one's position of

【原文】

也。然则得胜人之势者，其不如胜人之道远矣。

“夫主相者，胜人以势也。是为是，非为非，能为能，不能为不能，并己之私欲，必以道夫公道通义之可以相兼容者，是胜人之道也。今相国上则得专主，下则得专国，相国之于胜人之势，亶有之矣。然则胡不驱此胜人之势，赴胜人之道，求仁厚明通之君子而托王焉？与之参国政，正是非，如是，则国孰敢不为义矣？君臣上下、贵贱长少，至于庶人，莫不为义，则天下孰不欲合义矣？贤士愿相国之朝，能士愿相国之官，好利之民莫不愿以齐为归，是一天下也。相国

【今译】

能办到，夏桀、商纣王就是这样。这样看来，那么得到制服别人的权势地位，远远及不上实施制服别人的办法。

“那君主和相国，是用权势来制服别人的。对的就认为对，错的就认为错，有才能的就认为有才能，没有才能的就认为没有才能，屏弃自己的个人欲望，一定使自己遵行那些可以互相并存而没有抵触的公正原则和普遍适用的道理，这就是制服别人的办法。现在您相国上能独得君主的宠信，下能独揽国家的大权，相国对于制服别人的权势地位，的确已拥有它了。既然这样，那么为什么不驾驭这制服别人的权势，实行制服别人的办法，寻觅仁慈忠厚明智通达的君子而把他推荐给皇上呢？您和他一起参与国家政事，端正是非，如果像这样，国内还有谁敢不遵行道义呢？君主与臣子，上级与下级，高贵的与卑贱的，年长的与年幼的，以至于平民百姓，没有谁不遵行道义，那么天下还有谁不想会聚到我们这个遵行道义的国家来呢？贤德的人士向往相国所在的朝廷，有才能的人士仰慕相国管理下的官职，好利的民众没有谁不愿意把齐国作为自己的归宿，这就是统一天下了。相国如果

power is more substantial than that possessed by any other position in the world, to be unable even to find a place as a desolated poor wretch—such were Jie and Zhou Xin. This being the case, it is far better to possess the way of domination than to win a position of power that permits one to dominate others. The position of a ruler or that of a prime minister can be a position with the power to dominate. Treat right as right, wrong as wrong, the capable as capable, and the incapable as incapable, so as to preclude entirely personal wishes. To guarantee that a common, public way and comprehensive moral principles guide everything and that they are properly combined with generous tolerance is the way of domination.

Now since the prime minister of a state enjoys exclusively the confidence of his ruler above and has exclusive access to the entire country below, he occupies a position of power that can dominate, provided he truly exercises the power inherent in his position. This being the case, why do you not hasten to exercise the power inherent in a dominant position and betake yourself to the way of domination? Seek out humane and liberal gentlemen who are intelligent and universally learned to whom you can entrust the king's affairs. Join them in examining the administration of the state and in putting aright matters of right and wrong. In this circumstance, then, who in the whole nation would presume not to act according to the requirements of justice and morality? If among lord and subject, superior and inferior, noble and base, old and young, even down to the lowest commoner, none fail to act according to the requirements of justice and morality, who in the whole world would not desire to join in doing what is right? Worthy scholars will long to attend the court of such a prime minister's state, able scholars will long to hold office in his country, but none of those commoners who are fond of profit will want to consider Qi as his home. This would be to unite the whole world.

【原文】

舍是而不为，案直为是世俗之所以为，则女主乱之宫，诈臣乱之朝，贪吏乱之官，众庶百姓皆以贪利争夺为俗，曷若是而可以持国乎？今巨楚县吾前，大燕鳅吾后，劲魏钩吾右，西壤之不绝若绳，楚人则乃有襄贲、开阳以临吾左。是一国作谋，则三国必起而乘我。如是，则齐必断而为四三，国若假城然耳，必为天下大笑。曷若？两者孰足为也？

“夫桀、纣，圣王之后子孙也，有天下者之世也，势籍之所存，天下之宗室也；土地之大，封内千里；人之众，数以亿万；俄而天下倜然举去桀、纣而奔汤、武，反然举恶桀、纣而贵汤、武。是何也？夫桀、纣何失而汤、武何得也？曰：是无它故焉，桀、纣者，善为人

【今译】

舍弃了这些办法不干，而只是采用那些世俗之人所采用的办法，那么王后太后就会在后宫捣乱，奸诈之臣就会在朝廷捣乱，贪官污吏就会在官府捣乱，群众百姓都会把贪图私利互相争夺作为习俗，难道像这样就可以维持国家了吗？现在庞大的楚国摆在我们的前面，强大的燕国紧逼在我们的后面，强劲的魏国牵制了我们的西面，西面的领土虽然没有断送，也危险得像根细绳一样了，楚国则还有襄贲、开阳两个城监视着我们的东面。在这种形势下，如果有个国家出谋划策，那么这三个国家就必然会一同起来欺凌我们。如果这样，那么齐国一定会被分割成三四块，国土将像借来的城池一样而不属于自己了，这就一定会被天下人大大地嘲笑一番了。你觉得怎么样？上面所说的这两种办法哪一种可行呢？

“那夏桀、商纣，是圣明帝王的后裔子孙，是拥有天下统治权的天子的继承人，是权势帝位的占有者，是天下人所尊崇的帝王之家；领土那么广大，境内方圆上千里；人口那么众多，要用亿万来计数；但没有多久天下人便远远地都离开了夏桀、商纣而投奔商汤、周武王了，很快地都憎恶夏桀、商纣而尊崇商汤、周武王了。这是为什么呢？那夏桀、商纣为什么失败而商汤、周武王为什么成功呢？回答说：这并没有其他的缘故，而是因为夏桀、商纣这种人，好做人们所

When the prime minister of a country abandons this goal and does not act in its behalf, is he not acting in accord with the vulgar customs of his age? Then the ruler's women will bring confusion to the palace, deceitful ministers will bring chaos to the court, avaricious officers will bring confusion to the bureaus, and the common masses of the Hundred Clans will all come to consider a rapacious appetite for profit and contentious plundering to be the norms of society. In this situation, how can he retain his hold on the state?

Today vast Chu stretches out before you, great Yan presses at your rear, mighty Wei is a sickle aimed at your right side, and all along your western territory is an unbroken band [of small states]. Furthermore, the men of Chu also possess Xiangfei and Kaiyang from which they can look down on your flank. If even one of these countries should formulate a stratagem, then all three countries are sure to raise their armies to press their advantage. In such a case, Qi will surely be sliced up and partitioned into three or four sections. It would be as though [Qi] had but borrowed its own cities: it would certainly become the object of great hilarity for the whole world. Which of these two principles would you approve as deserving enactment?

Jie and Zhou Xin were the descendants of sage kings. Each belonged to a ruling family that possessed the empire. In them lay power and position: they were the spiritual authority of the whole world; their land was a fief extending a thousand *li*; and the mass of population inhabiting it numbered into the millions. Yet suddenly the whole world abandoned Jie and Zhou and rushed to Tang and Wu, changing their attitudes to hatred for Jie and Zhou Xin and admiration for Tang and Wu. How did this happen? Why did Jie and Zhou Xin lose? Why did Tang and Wu succeed?

I say that it was due to no other cause than that Jie and Zhou Xin

【原文】

之所恶也；而汤、武者，善为人之所好也。人之所恶何也？曰：污漫、争夺、贪利是也。人之所好者何也？曰：礼义、辞让、忠信是也。今君人者，辟称比方，则欲自并乎汤、武；若其所以统之，则无以异于桀、纣；而求有汤、武之功名，可乎？

“故凡得胜者，必与人也；凡得人者，必与道也。道也者，何也？曰：礼义辞让忠信是也。故自四五万而往者，强胜，非众之力也，隆在信矣；自数百里而往者，安固，非大之力也，隆在修政矣。今已有数万之众者也，陶诞比周以争与；已有数百里之国者也，污漫突盗以争地。然则是弃己之所安强，而争己之所以危弱也；损己之所不足，

【今译】

厌恶的事情；而商汤、周武王这种人，好做人们所喜欢的事情。人们所厌恶的是什么呢？回答说：污秽卑鄙、争抢夺取、贪图私利。人们所喜欢的是什么呢？回答说：礼制道义、推辞谦让、忠诚守信。现在统治人民的君主，打个比方，就是想把自己和商汤、周武王并列；至于他们统治人民的方法，却和夏桀、商纣没有什么不同；像这样而要求取得商汤、周武王那样的功业名望，可能么？

“所以凡是获得胜利的，一定是因为依顺了人民；凡是得到人民拥护的，一定是因为遵从了正确的政治原则。这正确的政治原则是什么呢？回答说：礼制道义、推辞谦让、忠诚守信便是。所以，拥有的人口在四五万以上的国家，能够强大取胜，并不是靠了人口众多的力量，重要的在于守信啊；拥有的领土在方圆几百里以上的国家，能够安定稳固，并不是靠了国土宽广的力量，重要的在于搞好政治啊。现在已经拥有了几万人的国家，却还是用招摇撞骗、拉拢勾结的办法去争取盟国；已经拥有了方圆几百里土地的国家，却还是用肮脏卑鄙、强取豪夺的办法去争夺土地。这样的话，那就是抛弃了使自己安定强盛的办法，而采取了使自己危险衰弱的办法；是在减损自己所缺少的

were adept at doing what men hate whereas Tang and Wu were adept at doing what men like. What do I mean by what men hate? Baseness and recklessness, contention and plundering, and a rapacious appetite for profit are such. What do I mean by what men like? Ritual and moral principles, polite refusals and deference to others, and loyalty and trustworthiness are such. Consider the rulers of the present. If we compare them, we find, for instance, a desire on their part to be ranked with Tang and Wu. But if we look at their guiding principles, then we find them to be no different from those of a Jie or a Zhou Xin. How then is it possible that they seek to have the reputation and accomplishments of a Tang or a Wu?

Therefore, as a general principle, one who would obtain ascendancy must gain the adherence of mankind. As a general rule, to obtain mankind one must adhere to the Way. What then is this Way? I say that it is just ritual and moral principles, polite refusals and deference to others, and loyalty and trustworthiness. Thus, that a state with forty to fifty thousand or so inhabitants is strong and enjoys ascendancy is due not to the strength of its population but to its exalting trustworthiness. That a state of several hundred *li* square is peaceful and secure is due not to the strength of its great size but to its exalting a reformed governmental administration.

Now your country has a population of several tens of thousands, but it is given to spreading false rumors and boasting, and it has cliques and parties that contend among themselves. Your country has an area of several hundred *li* square, yet it acts basely and recklessly and it plunders and robs in order to contend over land. By acting in this way, it casts away what makes it strong and secure, contending within over what makes it weak and endangered. You slight what you already have in insufficient

【原文】

以重己之所有余。若是其悖缪也，而求有汤、武之功名，可乎？辟之，是犹伏而咶天、救经而引其足也，说必不行矣，愈务而愈远。

“为人臣者，不恤己行之不行，苟得利而已矣，是渠冲入穴而求利也，是仁人之所羞而不为也。故人莫贵乎生，莫乐乎安，所以养生安乐者，莫大乎礼义。人知贵生乐安而弃礼义，辟之，是犹欲寿而殇颈也，愚莫大焉。

“故君人者，爱民而安，好士而荣，两者无一焉而亡。《诗》曰：‘价人维藩，大师维垣。’此之谓也。”

16.5“力术止，义术行。曷谓也？”

【今译】

东西，而在增加自己所多余的东西。他们的错乱荒谬竟像这样，却还要求取得商汤、周武王那样的功业名望，可能么？拿它打个比方，这就好像是趴在地上去舔天，挽救上吊的人却拉他的脚，这种主张一定行不通，越是用力从事就离目标越远。

“做臣子的，不顾自己的德行不像德行，只要得到利益就行了，这就等于是用大冲车或钻地道去攻城来求取利益一样，这是讲求仁德的人感到羞耻而不去做的事情。对于人来说，没有什么比生命更宝贵，没有什么比安定更快乐，但用来保养生命、取得安乐的途径，没有比遵行礼义更重要的了。人们如果只知道珍重生命，喜欢安定而抛弃了礼义，拿它打个比方，这就好像是想长寿而割断脖子一样，愚蠢没有比这更厉害的了。

“所以统治人民的君主，爱护人民就能安宁，喜欢士人就会荣耀，这两者一样都没有就会灭亡。《诗》云：‘贤士就是那屏障，大众就是那围墙。’说的就是这个道理。”

16.5“强力的方法行不通，礼义的方法行得通。这说的是什

quantities and give importance to what you have in excess. In this fashion you are foolishly unreasonable and perversely false. How then is it possible that you seek to have the solid accomplishments of a Tang or a Wu? This is analogous to lying down flat on one's face and trying to lick the sky or trying to rescue a man who has hanged himself by pulling at his feet. A doctrine like this certainly cannot be put into practice, and the more intent one is on doing so, the further away one gets from one's goal.If in serving the people, a minister does not care whether his actions are proper, but is concerned only with personal benefit whatever the cost, then his conduct is a case of "using assault machines to go into a cave after treasure." Such behavior is a veritable taboo to the humane man, and he will not act in this fashion.

Thus men prize nothing so highly as life and enjoy nothing more than peace. Among the things used to nurture life and bring about the enjoyment of peace, they consider nothing as important as ritual and moral principles. Although men still know to prize life and to enjoy peace, yet they will cast aside ritual and moral principles. This is analogous to "desiring old age and slitting one's throat." No stupidity could be greater! Accordingly, a lord of men who loves his people will be secure, and one who is fond of scholars will be honored. One who lacks either characteristic will perish. An *Ode* says:

> The great men are a fence,
> the great host a wall.

This expresses my meaning.

16. 5

When the techniques of power have reached their end, put into prac-

【原文】

曰："秦之谓也。威强乎汤、武，广大乎舜、禹，然而忧患不可胜校也，諰諰然常恐天下之一合而轧己也，此所谓力术止也。"

"曷谓乎威强乎汤、武？"

"汤、武也者，乃能使说已者使耳。今楚父死焉，国举焉，负三王之庙而辟于陈、蔡之间，视可、伺间，案欲剡其胫而以蹈秦之腹；然而秦使左案左，使右案右，是能使仇人役也。此所谓威强乎汤、武也。"

"曷谓广大乎舜、禹也？"

曰："古者百王之一天下、臣诸侯也，未有过封内千里者也。今秦，南乃有沙羡与俱，是乃江南也；北与胡、貉为邻；西有巴、戎；

【今译】

么呢？"

回答说："说的是秦国。它的兵力比商汤、周武王还要威武强大，它的领土比舜、禹还要广大，但是忧虑祸患多得不可胜数，提心吊胆地经常怕天下各国团结一致来颠覆自己，这就是我所说的强力的方法行不通。"

"为什么说比商汤、周武王还要威武强大？"

回答说："商汤、周武王，只能使喜爱自己的人听使唤罢了。而现在楚王的父亲死在秦国，国都被秦国攻克，楚王背着三个先王的神主牌位躲避在陈、蔡两地之间，观察适宜之时，窥测可乘之机，想抬起他的脚去践踏秦国的腹地；但是秦国让他向左他就向左，让他向右他就向右，这是能使仇敌为自己服役啊。这就是我所说的比商汤、周武王还要威武强大。"

"怎么说是比舜、禹还要广大？"

回答说："古时候各代帝王统一天下，臣服诸侯，境内从没有超过方圆上千里的。现在的秦国，南边便占有了沙羡及其周围一带，这是长江的南面了；北边与胡、貉相邻；西边占有了巴、戎；东边，在楚

tice the arts of justice. What does this mean? I say that it refers to Qin. The might of Qin is more awe-inspiring than was that of Tang or Wu. Its lands are broader and vaster than were those belonging to Shun or Yu. Nonetheless, it is distressed and seized with anxiety that it might not be able to overcome its opposition. It is constantly seized with fear and apprehension lest the whole world unite together in a concerted action to crush Qin with their collective power. This is what it means to say the techniques of power have failed.

Why do I say that its awe-inspiring might is greater than was that of Tang or Wu? Tang and Wu were able to take into their service only those who were personally devoted to them. Consider now the circumstances of the death of the Father of the House of Chu, when Qin overran the whole country, forcing Chu to physically carry away the ancestral temples of three kings and to remove its capital to the region of the old states of Chen and Cai. Chu still keeps on the lookout in the expectation of espying some opening through which it can realize its desire to lift high its truncated legs to stomp the belly of Qin. Nonetheless, when Qin orders Chu to move left, it is constrained to move left, and when Qin orders it to move right, it is constrained to move right. To such a degree has Qin made a lackey of its adversary. This is what it means to say "the might of Qin is more awe-inspiring than was that of Tang or Wu."

Why do I say that its lands are broader and vaster than were those belonging to Shun or Yu? It is said that in antiquity the Hundred Kings in uniting the world and making servants of the feudal lords never possessed fiefs with an area in excess of a thousand *li*. Today Qin to the south possesses Shaxian with all the lands in between, including even the area south of the Yangtze. In the north its borders neighbor on the lands of the Hu and Mo tribes. To the west, it has Ba and the Rong tribes. In

【原文】

东，在楚者乃界于齐，在韩者逾常山乃有临虑，在魏者乃据圉津——即去大梁百有二十里耳，其在赵者剡然有苓而据松柏之塞，负西海而固常山：是地遍天下也。威动海内，强殆中国，然而忧患不可胜校也，諰諰然常恐天下之一合而轧己也。此所谓广大乎舜、禹也。"

"然则奈何？"

曰："节威反文，案用夫端诚信全之君子治天下焉，因与之参国政，正是非，治曲直，听咸阳，顺者错之，不顺者而后诛之。若是，则兵不复出于塞外而令行于天下矣；若是，则虽为之筑明堂于塞外而朝诸侯，殆可矣。假今之世，益地不如益信之务也。"

【今译】

国，其所占领的土地已和齐国交界，在韩国的军队已经越过了常山而占有了临虑，在魏国的军队占据了圉津——即距离大梁只有一百二十里了，它在赵国的军队大刀阔斧地占有了灵丘而盘踞在松柏丛中的要塞上，背靠着西海而把常山作为险阻：这是领土遍及天下啊。这就是我所说的比舜、禹还要广大。它的威武震撼了天下，它的强大打败了中原各国，但是忧虑祸患多得不可胜数，提心吊胆地经常怕天下各国团结一致来颠覆自己啊。"

"这样的话，那怎么办呢？"

回答说："节制武力而回到文治上来，任用那些正直忠诚、守信完美的君子来治理天下，并同他们一起参与国家的政事，端正是非，治理曲直，听政于咸阳，顺从的国家就放在一边不去管它，不顺从的国家才去讨伐它。如果能这样，那么秦国的军队不再出动到边塞以外的地方去而政令就能在天下实行了；如果能这样，那么即使在边关以外的地方给秦王建造了明堂而使诸侯来朝拜，也差不多可以办到了。当今这个时世，致力于增加领土实不如致力于增加信用啊。"

the east there is Chu, through which it has an effective border with Qi. There is Han, where Qin has leaped across the Chang Mountains to hold Linlü. There is Wei, where Qin has seized the Yu Ford,so that it has now advanced to within 120 *li* of Wei's capital Daliang. It has gradually encroached on Zhao to hold Ling and now has control over the Fir and Cypress Barrier. To its rear is the Western Ocean, and its line of defense is the Chang Mountains. These territories stretch across the whole world. Their awesomeness shakes all within the seas; their strength imperils the Central States. This is what it means to say "its lands are broader and vaster than were those belonging to Shun or Yu." Despite all this, it is distressed and seized with anxiety that it might not be able to overcome its opposition. It is constantly seized with fear and apprehension lest the whole world unite together in a concerted action to crush Qin under their collective power.

Well, what then should be done in such a case? I say that Qin should moderate its emphasis on overawing and instead should emphasize civilian matters. Use of gentlemen who are correct, sincere, trustworthy, and complete is required to govern the whole world. Collaborating with them in administration of the state, Qin should rectify the distinction between right and wrong, control the crooked and straight, and adjudicate from its capital Xianyang. Those who are obedient should be established; those who are not should subsequently be executed. If things are done in this way, then although the army is not sent out from the passes ever again, Qin can issue commands and the world will do its bidding. If it should do all this, then even if it should construct a Bright Hall and summon the feudal lords to pay court there, it would almost be proper. For our present generation, augmenting territory is not so important as increasing the attention we devote to becoming trustworthy.

【原文】

16.6应侯问孙卿子曰："入秦何见？"

孙卿子曰："其固塞险，形势便，山林川谷美，天材之利多，是形胜也。入境，观其风俗，其百姓朴，其声乐不流污，其服不挑，甚畏有司而顺，古之民也。及都邑官府，其百吏肃然，莫不恭俭、敦敬、忠信而不楛，古之吏也。入其国，观其士大夫，出于其门，入于公门，出于公门，归于其家，无有私事也；不比周，不朋党，倜然莫不明通而公也，古之士大夫也。观其朝廷，其朝间，听决百事不留，恬

【今译】

16.6应侯问荀卿说："到秦国看见了什么？"

荀卿说："它的边塞险峻，地势有利，山林河流美好，自然资源带来的好处很多，这是地形上的优越。踏进国境，观察它的习俗，那里的百姓质朴淳厚，那里的音乐不淫荡卑污，那里的服装不轻薄妖艳，人们非常害怕官吏而十分顺从，真像是古代圣王统治下的人民啊。到了大小城镇的官府，那里的各种官吏都是严肃认真的样子，无不谦恭节俭、敦厚谨慎、忠诚守信而不粗疏草率，真像是古代圣王统治下的官吏啊。进入它的国都，观察那里的士大夫，发现他们走出自己的家门，就走进公家的衙门，走出公家的衙门，就回到自己的家里，没有私下的事务，不互相勾结，不拉党结派，卓然超群地没有谁不明智通达而廉洁奉公，真像是古代圣王统治下的士大夫啊。观察它的朝廷，当它的君主主持朝政告一段落时，处理决定各种政事从无遗漏，安闲得好像没

16. 6

The Marquis of Ying questioned Master Xun Qing, saying: What have you observed since you entered Qin?

Master Xun Qing replied: Its defenses at the border barriers have a natural strength of position. Its topographical features are inherently advantageous. Its mountains, forests, streams, and valleys are magnificent. The benefits of its natural resources are manifold. Such are the inherent strengths of its topography. When I passed across the border, I noted that the customs and mores of the Hundred Clans were unspoiled, that their music and dances were neither dissipated nor filthy, that their clothing was not frivolous, that they were exceedingly deferential to the authorities and obedient—just as were the people of antiquity. When I reached the bureaus and agencies of the towns and cities, I saw the Hundred Officials sternly attend to their functions, none failing to be respectful, temperate, earnest, scrupulously reverential, loyal, and trustworthy, and never being deficient in the execution of their duties—just as were the officers of antiquity. When I entered the capital, I noticed how when knights and grand officers left their house gates, they entered the gate of their office, and when they left their office gate, they returned to their homes without conducting any private matters; how they do not form cliques and parties; and how they do not associate in exclusive friendships; but rather how in an exalted manner none fail to be intelligent, comprehensive, and public-spirited—just as were the knights and grand officers of antiquity. I noted how in the operation of your court adjudications, the Hundred Tasks of government are decided without delay and so serenely it seems as though there were no government at all—just as

【原文】

然如无治者，古之朝也。故四世有胜，非幸也，数也。是所见也。故曰：佚而治，约而详，不烦而功，治之至也。秦类之矣。虽然，则有其諰矣。兼是数具者而尽有之，然而县之以王者之功名，则倜倜然，其不及远矣。"

"是何也？"

"则其殆无儒邪! 故曰：'粹而王，驳而霸，无一焉而亡。'此亦秦之所短也。"

16.7 积微，月不胜日，时不胜月，岁不胜时。凡人好敖慢小事，大事至，然后兴之务之。如是，则常不胜夫敦比于小事者矣。是何也? 则小事之至也数，其县日也博，其为积也大；大事之至也希，其

【今译】

有什么需要治理似的，真像是古代圣王治理的朝廷啊。所以秦国四代都有胜利的战果，并不是因为侥幸，而是有其必然性的。这就是我所见到的。所以说：自身安逸却治理得好，政令简要却详尽，政事不繁杂却有成效，这是政治的最高境界。秦国类似这样了。即使如此，却仍有它的忧惧啊。上面所说的这几个条件全都具有了，但是用称王天下者的功绩名声去衡量它，那简直是天南海北，相差得还很远哩。"

"这是为什么呢？"

"那是他们大概没有儒者吧。所以说：'纯粹地崇尚道义、任用贤人的就能称王天下，驳杂地义利兼顾、贤人亲信并用的就能称霸诸侯，这两者一样也做不到的就灭亡。'这也是秦国的短处啊。"

16.7 积累微小的成果，每个月积累不如每天积累，每个季度积累不如每个月积累，每年积累不如每个季度积累。一般人喜欢轻视怠慢小事，等大事来了，然后才把它提到议事日程上努力去做它。像这样，就常常不如那些认真办理小事的人了。这是为什么呢？因为小事来得频繁，它牵扯的时间多，它积累起来的成果大；大事来得稀少，

were the courts of antiquity. Hence, that for four consecutive generations there have been victories is due not to mere chance good luck but to method and calculation. This is what I have observed. Anciently it was said:

> Undertaken with ease, yet well ordered; restricted to essentials, yet carried out in full detail; not involving trouble, yet resulting in real achievement—these are the perfection of government.

Qin belongs to this category. Yet even though all this is so, Qin is filled with trepidation. Despite its complete and simultaneous possession of all these numerous attributes, if one weighs Qin by the standard of the solid achievements of True Kingship, then the vast degree to which it fails to reach the ideal is manifest. Why is that? It is that it is dangerously lacking in Ru scholars. Thus, it is said:

> Those who possess the pure form are True Kings; those who have the mixed form are lords-protector;those who lack any at all are annihilated.

This is precisely the shortcoming of Qin.

16. 7

The Accumulation of Minutiae

The month is not more important than the day; nor the season than the month; nor the year more than the season. As a general rule, men prefer to neglect minor matters, which they despise. When a major matter comes along, they are roused to action and devote themselves to it, but they invariably fail to arrange minor matters.

Why is this? It is that as minor matters come along, they are numerous. Only as they are strung together day by day do they become of

【原文】

县日也浅，其为积也小。故善日者王，善时者霸，补漏者危，大荒者亡。故王者敬日，霸者敬时，仅存之国危而后戚之，亡国至亡而后知亡，至死而后知死。亡国之祸败，不可胜悔也；霸者之善著焉，可以时托也；王者之功名，不可胜日志也。财物货宝以大为重，政教功名反是，能积微者速成。《诗》曰："德輶如毛，民鲜克举之。"此之谓也。

16.8 凡奸人之所以起者，以上之不贵义、不敬义也。夫义者，

【今译】

它牵扯的时间少，它积累起来的成果小。所以珍惜每一天的君主就能称王天下，珍惜每一季度的君主就能称霸诸侯，出了漏洞再去补救的君主就危险了，一切时间都荒废掉的君主就会灭亡。所以称王天下的君主慎重地对待每一天，称霸诸侯的君主重视每一个季度，勉强存在的国家陷入危险以后君主才为它担忧，亡国的君主到了国家灭亡以后才知道会灭亡，临死的时候才知道要死。亡国的君主造成的祸害和破坏，多到悔不胜悔。称霸诸侯的君主的善政显著，可以按季度来记录；称王天下的君主的功绩名誉，就是每天记录也不可能全部记下来。财物宝贝以大为贵，政教功名却与此相反，能积累微小成果的君主才能迅速成功。《诗》云："道德轻得像毛发，民众很少能举它。"说的就是这个道理。

16.8 大致说来，奸邪的人之所以会产生，是因为君主不推崇道

wider significance. As they accumulate, they become of great importance. Major matters come along but rarely. As they continue on day after day, they become of narrower significance. As they accumulate, they become of less importance. Therefore, one who is good at day-to-day matters will become a True King. One who is good at seasonal matters will become a lord-protector. One who confines himself to repairing leaks will be endangered. But one who is utterly negligent will perish. Accordingly, a king will take scrupulously reverent care to attend to the tasks of the day; a lord-protector will take scrupulously reverent care to attend to the tasks of the season; but a country that is barely surviving will be endangered before it feels any distress. A doomed country will reach its doom before it realizes that it is doomed, and it will be dead before it realizes that it has died, for the calamitous ruination of a doomed state cannot be overcome with mere regrets. The excellence of the lord-protector is manifest, and it can be attributed to him by the season. The solid achievements of the king are such that even day-by-day records cannot fully encompass their merit. In property and goods, wealth and treasure, large quantities are important; in government and instruction, accomplishment and reputation, the opposite is true. The ability to accumulate minutiae is the quickest route to completion. An *Ode* says:

> Inner power is light as a hair,
> but among the people few can lift it.

This expresses my point.

16. 8

As a general rule, the reason there are wicked men is that superiors do not prize moral principles and do not take care to uphold justice with

【原文】

所以限禁人之为恶与奸者也。今上不贵义、不敬义，如是，则下之人百姓皆有弃义之志而有趋奸之心矣，此奸人之所以起也。且上者，下之师也。夫下之和上，譬之，犹响之应声、影之像形也。故为人上者，不可不顺也。夫义者，内节于人而外节于万物者也，上安于主而下调于民者也。内外上下节者，义之情也。然则凡为天下之要，义为本，而信次之。古者禹、汤本义务信而天下治；桀、纣弃义背信而天下乱。故为人上者，必将慎礼义、务忠信，然后可。此君人者之大本也。

【今译】

义，不尊重道义。道义这种东西，是用来限制人们为非作歹和施行奸诈的。现在君主不推崇道义，不尊重道义，像这样，下面的老百姓就都会有背弃道义的思想而有趋附奸邪的心情了，这就是奸邪之人产生的原因。况且，君主是臣民的师表。臣民附和君主，打个比方，就好像是回声应和声音，影子类似形体一样。所以做君主的，不可不慎重地对待道义。道义，是内能调节人而外能调节万物的，是上能使君主安定而下能使民众协调的东西，内外上下都能调节，这是道义的实质啊。这样看来，所有治理天下的要领，道义是最根本的，而守信用在其次。古时候夏禹、商汤立足于道义，致力于守信而天下大治；夏桀、商纣抛弃了道义，违背了信用而天下大乱。所以做君主的，一定要慎重地对待礼义，致力于忠诚守信，然后才行。这是做君主的最大根本。

strict reverence. Moral principles and a sense for what is just are what must be used to prevent men from acting in an evil and wicked manner. When superiors do not prize morality and do not revere justice, subordinates as well as the Hundred Clans will be motivated to abandon the requirements of morality and justice and be of a mind to hasten after wicked pursuits. This is just the reason there are wicked men.

Furthermore, since the superior is the example to his subordinates, his subordinates will be in harmony with their superior, just as ,for example, an echo responds to the sound and as the shadow has the shape of the form. Accordingly, it is impossible to act as a superior to others and not to be obedient to the dictates of morality and justice.

Having moral principles and a sense for what is just moderates the person within and the myriad things without. Above they produce peace for the ruler, and below they create a fine-tuned balance for the people. Within and without, above and below, moderation is the essential quality of moral principles and of justice. This being the case, then as a general rule, as the essential consideration for governing the world, morality and justice constitute the basic principle and good faith follows close behind.

In antiquity when Yu and Tang founded their conduct on morality and justice and devoted themselves to showing good faith, the world became well ordered. When Jie and Zhou Xin abandoned morality and justice and turned their back on good faith, the world became chaotic. Accordingly, a superior must realize that this is possible only when he is sedulous about matters of ritual and moral principles and when he is earnestly devoted to loyalty and good faith. This is the great basic principle for all lords of men.

【原文】

16.9 堂上不粪，则郊草不瞻旷芸；白刃扞乎胸，则目不见流矢；拔戟加乎首，则十指不辞断。非不以此为务也，疾养缓急之有相先者也。

【今译】

16.9 厅堂上面还没有打扫，那么郊外的野草就没有足够的余暇去铲除了；雪白的刀锋刺到胸口，那么眼睛就看不到飞来的暗箭了；带旁刃的戟加到头上，那么十只手指就会不回避被砍断而去抵挡了。这并不是不把郊外的杂草、暗箭、手指当回事，而是因为痛痒缓急之间有个先顾及什么的问题。

16. 9

If the trash has not been cleared from before the pavilion, then you will not notice whether the grass on the suburban altar is growing. If the naked blade strikes your chest, then your eye will not notice the fleeting arrows. If the lance is about to strike your head, then you will not notice your ten fingers' being cut off. None of this is attributable to inattention, but to the pain and agony or to the urgency and gravity of the situation, which have priority.

天论第十七

【原文】

17.1 天行有常，不为尧存，不为桀亡。应之以治则吉，应之以乱则凶。强本而节用，则天不能贫；养备而动时，则天不能病；循道而不忒，则天不能祸。故水旱不能使之饥，寒暑不能使之疾，袄怪不能使之凶。本荒而用侈，则天不能使之富；养略而动罕，则天不能使之全；倍道而妄行，则天不能使之吉。故水旱未至而饥，寒暑未薄而疾，袄怪未至而凶。受时与治世同，而殃祸与治世异，不可以怨天，

【今译】

17.1 大自然的规律永恒不变，它不为尧而存在，不为桀而灭亡。用导致安定的措施去适应它就吉利，用导致混乱的措施去适应它就凶险。加强农业这个根本并节约费用，那么天就不能使他贫穷；衣食给养齐备而活动适时，那么天就不能使他生病；遵循规律而不出差错，那么天就不能使他遭殃。所以水涝旱灾不能使他挨饿，严寒酷暑不能使他生病，自然界的反常变异不能使他遭殃。农业这个根本荒废而用度奢侈，那么天就不能使他富裕；衣食给养不足而活动又少，那么天就不能使他保全健康；违背规律而恣意妄为，那么天就不能使他吉利。所以水涝旱灾还没有来到他就挨饿了，严寒酷暑还没有迫近他就生病了，自然界的反常变异还没有出现他就遭殃了。他遇到的天时和社会安定时期相同，而灾祸却与社会安定时期不同，这不可以埋怨上

Book 17

Discource on Nature

17. 1

The course of Nature is constant: it does not survive because of the actions of a Yao; it does not perish because of the actions of a Jie. If you respond to the constancy of Nature's course with good government, there will be good fortune; if you respond to it with disorder, there will be misfortune. If you strengthen the basic undertakings and moderate expenditures, Nature cannot impoverish you. If your nourishment is complete and your movements accord with the season, then Nature cannot afflict you with illness. If you conform to the Way and are not of two minds, then Nature cannot bring about calamity. Accordingly, flood and drought cannot cause famine, cold and heat cannot cause sickness, and inauspicious and freak events cannot cause misfortune.

If you ignore the basic undertakings and spend extravagantly, then Nature cannot enrich you. If your nourishment lacks essential elements and your movements accord with rare events, then Nature cannot make you whole. If you turn your back on the Way and behave with foolish recklessness, then Nature cannot bring good fortune. Accordingly, there will be famine when neither flood nor drought has come, there will be sickness when neither heat nor cold has reached you, and there will be misfortune even though inauspicious and freak events have not occurred. Although the seasons are received just the same as in an orderly age, the catastrophes and calamities will be of a different order [of magnitude] from those of an orderly age; yet you can have no cause to curse Nature,

【原文】

其道然也。故明于天人之分，则可谓至人矣。

17.2 不为而成，不求而得，夫是之谓天职。如是者，虽深，其人不加虑焉；虽大，不加能焉；虽精，不加察焉；夫是之谓不与天争职。天有其时，地有其财，人有其治，夫是之谓能参。舍其所以参，而愿其所参，则惑矣！

17.3 列星随旋，日月递照，四时代御，阴阳大化，风雨博施。万物各得其和以生，各得其养以成。不见其事而见其功，夫是之谓神。皆知其所以成，莫知其无形，夫是之谓天。唯圣人为不求知天。

【今译】

天，这是他所采取的措施造成的。所以明白了大自然与人类社会的区分的人，就可以称作是思想修养达到了最高境界的人了。

17.2 不做就能成功，不求就能得到，这叫做自然的职能。像这种情况，即使意义深远，那思想修养达到了最高境界的人对它也不加以思考；即使影响广大，那思想修养达到了最高境界的人对它也不加以干预；即使道理精妙，那思想修养达到了最高境界的人对它也不加以审察，这叫做不和自然争职能。上天有自己的时令季节，大地有自己的材料资源，人类有自己的治理方法，这叫做能够互相并列。人如果舍弃了自身用来与天、地相并列的治理方法，而只期望于与自己相并列的天与地，那就糊涂了。

17.3 布列于天空的恒星互相伴随着旋转，太阳月亮交替照耀，四季轮流控制着节气，阴阳二气大量地化生万物，风雨普遍地施加于万物。万物各自得到了阴阳形成的和气而产生，各自得到了风雨的滋养而成长。看不见阴阳化生万物的工作过程而只见到它化生万物的成果，这就叫做神妙。人们都知道阴阳已经生成的万物，却没有人知道它那无形无踪的生成过程，这就叫做天。只有圣人是不致力于了解天的。

for these things are the consequences of the way that you have followed. Accordingly, if you understand the division between Nature and mankind, then you can properly be called a "Perfect Man."

17. 2

Not to act, yet bring to completion; not to seek, yet to obtain—this indeed may be described as the work of Nature. In such a situation, the [Perfect] Man, however profound, does not apply any thought to the work of Nature; however great, does not apply his abilities to it; and however shrewd, does not apply his acumen for inquiry to it. This indeed may be described as "not competing with Nature in its work." Heaven has its seasons; Earth its resources; and Man his government. This, of course, is why it is said that they "can form a Triad." When man abandons what he should use to form the Triad yet longs for the [benefits that result from] the Triad, he suffers from delusion!

17. 3

The constellations follow their revolutions; the sun and moon alternately shine; the four seasons present themselves in succession; the Yin and Yang enlarge and transform; and the wind and rain spread out everywhere. Each of the myriad things must be in a harmonious relation with Nature in order to grow, and each must obtain from Nature the proper nurture in order to become complete. We do not perceive the process, but we perceive the result—this indeed is why we call it "divine." All realize that Nature has brought completion, but none realize its formlessness—this indeed is why we call it "Nature." Only the sage acts not

【原文】

17.4 天职既立，天功既成，形具而神生，好恶、喜怒、哀乐臧焉，夫是之谓天情。耳、目、鼻、口、形，能各有接而不相能也，夫是之谓天官。心居中虚，以治五官，夫是之谓天君。财非其类，以养其类，夫是之谓天养。顺其类者谓之福，逆其类者谓之祸，夫是之谓天政。暗其天君，乱其天官，弃其天养，逆其天政，背其天情，以丧天功，夫是之谓大凶。圣人清其天君，正其天官，备其天养，顺其天政，养其天情，以全其天功。如是，则知其所为、知其所不为矣，则天地官而万物役矣，其行曲治，其养曲适，其生不伤，夫是之谓知天。

【今译】

17.4 自然的职能已经确立，天生的功绩已经成就，人的形体也就具备而精神也就产生了，爱好与厌恶、高兴与愤怒、悲哀与欢乐等蕴藏在人的形体和精神里面，这些叫做天生的情感。耳朵、眼睛、鼻子、嘴巴、身体，就其功能来说，它们各有自己的感受对象而不能互相替代，这些叫做天生的感官。心处于身体中部空虚的胸腔内，用来管理这五种感官，这叫做天生的主宰。人类能够控制安排好与自己不是同类的万物，用它们来供养自己的同类，这叫做天然的供养。能使自己的同类顺从自己叫做福，使自己的同类反对自己叫做祸，这叫做天然的政治原则。搞昏了那天生的主宰，扰乱了那天生的感官，抛弃了那天然的供养，违反了那天然的政治原则，背离了那天生的情感，以至丧失了天生的功绩，这叫做大凶。圣人清醒自己那天生的主宰，管理好自己那天生的感官，完备那天然的供养，顺应那天然的政治原则，保养那天生的情感，从而成全了天生的功绩。像这样，就是明白自己应该做的事和不应该做的事了，天地就能被利用而万物就能被操纵了，他的行动就能处处有条理，他的保养就能处处恰当，他的生命就能不受到伤害，这就叫做了解了天。

seeking to know Nature.

17. 4

When the work of Nature has been established and its achievements perfected,the physical form becomes whole and the spirit is born. Love and hate, delight and anger, sorrow and joy, are stored within—these are described as "the emotions given us by nature." The eye, ear, nose, mouth, and body each have the capacity to provide sense contact, but their capacities are not interchangeable—these are termed "the faculties given us by nature." The heart/mind that dwells within the central cavity is used to control the five faculties—it is called "the lord provided by nature." The mind takes advantage of things not belonging to the human species and uses them for the nourishment of humans—these are termed "the nourishment provided by nature." The mind calls what conforms to the properties of its category "fortunate" and what rebels against the properties of its category "cursed"—this is called the "rule of order in nature."

To darken one's natural lord, bring confusion to the natural faculties, reject one's natural nourishment, rebel against the natural rule of order,turn one's back on the natural emotions, and thereby destroy the achievement of nature —this indeed is called the "Great Calamity." The sage purifies his natural lord, rectifies his natural faculties, completes his natural nourishment, is obedient to the natural rule of order, and nourishes his natural emotions and thereby completes nature's achievement. If this situation obtains, then he knows what is his to do and what is not his to do. Then Heaven and Earth perform the work of officers, and the myriad things serve him as foot soldiers. When his conduct is minutely controlled, his nourishment minutely moderated, and his life suffers no injury—this

【原文】

17.5 故大巧在所不为，大智在所不虑。所志于天者，已其见象之可以期者矣；所志于地者，已其见宜之可以息者矣；所志于四时者，已其见数之可以事者矣；所志于阴阳者，已其见知之可以治者矣。官人守天而自为守道也。

17.6 治乱，天邪？曰：日月、星辰、瑞历，是禹、桀之所同也；禹以治，桀以乱；治乱非天也。时邪？曰：繁启、蕃长于春夏，畜积、收臧于秋冬，是又禹、桀之所同也；禹以治，桀以乱；治乱非时也。地邪？曰：得地则生，失地则死，是又禹、桀之所同也；禹以

【今译】

17.5 所以最大的技巧在于有些事情不去做，最大的智慧在于有些事情不去考虑。对于上天所要了解的，不过是它所显现的天象中那些可以测定气候变化的天文资料罢了；对于大地所要了解的，不过是它所显现的适宜条件中那些可以便利种植庄稼的地况资料罢了；对于四季所要了解的，不过是它们所显现的规律中可以安排农业生产的节气罢了；对于阴阳所要了解的，不过是它们所显现的和气中可以治理事物的因素罢了。圣人任用别人来掌握这些自然现象而自己所做的只是去掌握治理国家的原则。

17.6 社会的安定或混乱，是由上天决定的吗？回答说：太阳月亮、行星恒星、祥瑞的历书，这在禹与桀是相同的；禹使天下安定，桀使天下混乱；可见社会的安定或混乱并不是由上天决定的。那么，是季节造成的吗？回答说：庄稼在春季、夏季纷纷发芽，茂盛地生长，在秋季、冬季积蓄、收藏，这在禹与桀又是相同的；禹使天下安定，桀使天下混乱；可见社会的安定或混乱并不是季节造成的。那么，是大地造成的吗？回答说：庄稼得到了大地就生长，失去了大地

indeed is called "understanding nature."

17. 5

Thus, [for the ruler] the greatest skill consists in what is not done; the greatest wisdom lies in what is not pondered. The [officials] charged with recording the events of Heaven simply observe that its configurations can be fixed by regular periods. Those charged with recording the affairs of Earth simply observe how its suitability for crops can foster yields. Those charged with recording the events of the four seasons simply observe how their sequence can give order to the tasks of life. Those charged with recording the Yin and Yang simply observe how their harmonious interaction can bring about order. These expert officers should attend to matters of Nature; the ruler himself should maintain the Way.

17. 6

What is the relation of order and chaos to Heaven? I say: the revolutions of the sun and moon and the stars and celestial points that mark off the divisions of time by which the calendar is calculated were the same in the time of Yu as in the time of Jie. Since Yu achieved order and Jie brought chaos, order and chaos are not due to Heaven.

What about the Seasons? I say that crops germinate and grow to maturity in the course of spring and summer and are harvested and gathered for storage during autumn and winter. This also was the same in the time of Yu and in the time of Jie. Since Yu achieved order and Jie brought chaos, order and chaos are not due to the seasons.

What about Earth? I say that if something obtains land on which to

【原文】

治，桀以乱，治乱非地也。《诗》曰："天作高山，大王荒之；彼作矣，文王康之。"此之谓也。

17.7 天不为人之恶寒也辍冬，地不为人之恶辽远也辍广，君子不为小人之匈匈也辍行。天有常道矣，地有常数矣，君子有常体矣。君子道其常，而小人计其功。《诗》曰："礼义之不愆，何恤人之言兮？"此之谓也。

17.8 楚王后车千乘，非知也；君子啜菽饮水，非愚也；是节然也。若夫心意修，德行厚，知虑明，生于今而志乎古，则是其在我者

【今译】

就死亡，这在禹与桀又是相同的；禹使天下安定，桀使天下混乱，可见社会的安定或混乱并不是大地造成的。《诗》云："天生高大的岐山，太王使它大发展；太王已经造此都，文王使它长平安。"说的就是这个道理。

17.7 上天并不因为人们厌恶寒冷就取消冬季，大地并不因为人们厌恶辽远就废除宽广，君子并不因为小人的叽哩呱啦就中止行动。上天有经久不变的规律，大地有经久不变的法则，君子有经久不变的规矩。君子遵行那常规，而小人计较那功利。《诗》云："礼义上我错误不犯，何必担忧人说长道短？"说的就是这个道理。

17.8 楚王外出时随从的车子有上千辆，并不是因为他聪明；君子吃豆叶，喝白水，并不是因为他愚蠢；这种情况是时势命运的制约造成的。至于思想美好，德行敦厚，谋虑精明，生在今天而能知道古

grow it will live and if it loses that land then it will die, and that this as well was the same for both Yu and Jie. Since Yu achieved order and Jie brought chaos, order and chaos are not due to Earth. An *Ode* expresses my meaning:

Heaven created the high mountain
and King Tai found it grand.
It was he who felled the trees,
and King Wen made it secure.

17. 7

Heaven does not suspend the winter because men dislike cold weather. Earth does not reduce its broad expanse because men dislike long distances. The gentleman does not interrupt his pattern of conduct because petty men rant and rail. Heaven possesses a constant Way; Earth has an invariable size; the gentleman has constancy of deportment. The gentleman is guided by what is constant; the ordinary man calculates what might be achieved. An *Ode* expresses this point:

{If I do not err in ritual and morality},
why be distressed over what men say?

17. 8

That the King of Chu has a retinue of a thousand chariots is not due to his wisdom. That the gentleman must eat pulse and drink water is not due to his stupidity. Both are accidents of circumstance. As for being developed in will and purpose, substantial in behavior springing from inner power, lucid in wisdom and thought,and, though born in the present generation, to

【原文】

也。故君子敬其在己者，而不慕其在天者；小人错其在己者，而慕其在天者。君子敬其在己者，而不慕其在天者，是以日进也；小人错其在己者，而慕其在天者，是以日退也。故君子之所以日进与小人之所以日退，一也。君子、小人之所以相县者，在此耳!

17.9 星队木鸣，国人皆恐，曰：是何也？曰：无何也。是天地之变、阴阳之化、物之罕至者也。怪之，可也；而畏之，非也。夫日月之有蚀，风雨之不时，怪星之党见，是无世而不常有之。上明而政平，则是虽并世起，无伤也；上暗而政险，则是虽无一至者，无益也。夫星之队、木之鸣，是天地之变，阴阳之化，物之罕至者也。怪之，可也；而畏之，非也。

【今译】

代，这些就是那取决于我们自己的事情了。所以，君子慎重地对待那些取决于自己的事情，而不去羡慕那些取决于上天的东西；小人丢下那些取决于自己的事情，而指望那些取决于上天的东西。君子慎重对待那些取决于自己的事情，而不去羡慕那些取决于上天的东西，因此天天进步；小人丢下那些取决于自己的事情，而指望那些取决于上天的东西，因此天天退步。所以君子天天进步的原因与小人天天退步的原因，道理是一样的。君子、小人相差悬殊的原因，就在这里。

17.9 流星坠落，树木发响，国内的人都害怕，说：这是为什么呢？回答说：这没有什么啊。这是自然界的变异、阴阳二气的变化、事物中很少出现的现象啊。觉得它奇怪，是可以的，但害怕它，就错了。那太阳、月亮发生日食、月食，旋风暴雨不合时节地突然袭击，奇怪的星星偶然出现，这些现象没有哪个时代不曾有过。君主英明而政治清明，那么这些现象即使在同一时代都出现，也没有什么妨害；君主愚昧而政治黑暗，那么这些现象即使一样都没出现，也毫无裨益。那流星的坠落，树木的发响，这是自然界的变异、阴阳二气的变化，事物中很少出现的现象啊。觉得它奇怪，是可以的，但害怕它，就错了。

fix the mind on the ancients—all these are within our power. Thus, the gentleman reveres what lies within his power and does not long for what lies with Heaven. The petty man forsakes what lies within his power and longs for what lies with Heaven. Because the gentleman reveres what lies within his power and does not long for what lies with Heaven, he progresses day by day. Because the petty man lays aside what lies within his power and longs for what lies with Heaven, he day by day retrogresses. Thus what impels the gentleman daily to progress and forces the petty man daily to retrogress is one and the same principle. What distinguishes the gentleman from the petty man lies precisely in this.

17. 9

When stars fall or trees groan, the whole state is terrified. They ask what caused this to happen. I reply that there was no specific reason. When there is a modification of the relation of Heaven and Earth or a transmutation of the Yin and Yang, such unusual events occur. We may marvel at them, but we should not fear them. As for the sun and moon being eclipsed, winds and rain occurring unseasonably, and the sudden appearance of a marvelous new star, there has been no age that has not occasionally had them. If the ruler is enlightened and his governmental regulations equitable, then although all these should occur within a generation, it would cause no harm. If the superior is benighted and his governmental regulations harsh, then although not one of them occurs, it would be of no advantage. For indeed the falling of stars and the groaning of trees—these are unusual events that occur because of a modification of the relation of Heaven and Earth or a transmutation of the Yin and Yang. We may marvel at them, but we should not fear them.

【原文】

17.10 物之已至者，人祆则可畏也。楛耕伤稼，枯耘伤岁，政险失民，田薉稼恶，籴贵民饥，道路有死人，夫是之谓人祆；政令不明，举错不时，本事不理，夫是之谓人祆；礼义不修，内外无别，男女淫乱，则父子相疑，上下乖离，寇难并至，夫是之谓人祆。祆是生于乱。三者错，无安国。其说甚迩，其菑甚惨。勉力不时，则牛马相

【今译】

17.10 在已经出现的事情中，人事上的反常现象才是可怕的。粗放地耕种而伤害了庄稼，粗放地锄草而妨害了年成，政治险恶而失去了民心，田地荒芜而庄稼长不好，米价昂贵而百姓挨饿，道路上有饿死的人，这些叫做人事上的反常现象；政策法令不明确，采取措施不合时宜，具有根本意义的农业生产不加管理，这叫做人事上的反常现象；礼义不加整顿，内外没有分别，男女淫荡混乱，而父子互相猜疑，君臣离心离德，外寇内乱同时到来，这叫做人事上的反常现象。人事上的反常现象实产生于昏乱。上述这三类反常现象交错发生，就不会有安宁的国家了。这种人事上的反常现象解说起来道理很浅显，但它造成的灾难却很惨重。发动劳役不顾农时，那么牛就会生出像马似的怪胎，马就会生出像牛似的怪胎，六畜就会出现怪异的现象，这

17. 10

Among the things that have occurred, the most fearful are monstrosities among men. {Someone asks what are called monstrosities among men? I say:} Plowing so badly done that the grain crop is damaged; weeding so poorly carried out that the harvest is lost; governmental regulations so unfair that the people are lost; fields so overgrown with weeds that the grain crops are bad; and grain so expensive and the people so hungry that the bodies of the dead lie along the roads—these are called monstrosities among men.

When governmental regulations and commands are unclear, public works are initiated or halted in an untimely way, <corvée labor is unseasonal,> and the fundamental undertakings are not properly administered—these are called monstrosities among men. <When armies and internal difficulties arise simultaneously, when superiors and inferiors are at odds and estranged,>{when neighbors behave violently toward one another and those whose gates face each other steal from each other,} when ritual and moral principles are not cultivated,<when cows and horses interbreed and the Six Domestic Animals produce monsters,>{when servants and subordinates assassinate their superiors,} when fathers and sons are suspicious of each other, when internal and external matters are licentious and disorderly, and when the duties of men and women are not kept separate—these are called monstrosities among men. It is just such monstrosities that are born of anarchy, when all three types of monstrosities occur simultaneously, there will be no safety for the state. The explanation of them is near at hand, and the injury they cause is grave. They can be

【原文】

生，六畜作袄。可怪也，而不可畏也。传曰：“万物之怪，书不说。”无用之辩，不急之察，弃而不治。若夫君臣之义，父子之亲，夫妇之别，则日切瑳而不舍也。

17.11 雩而雨，何也？曰：无何也，犹不雩而雨也。日月食而救之，天旱而雩，卜筮然后决大事，非以为得求也，以文之也。故君子以为文，而百姓以为神。以为文则吉，以为神则凶也。

【今译】

是可怕的，但不值得奇怪。古代解释经文的书上说：“各种事物的怪现象，经书上不作解说。”没有用处的辩说，不切需要的考察，应该抛弃而不加研究。至于那君臣之间的道义，父子之间的相亲，夫妻之间的区别，那是应该每天切磋琢磨而不能丢掉的啊。

17.11 祭神求雨就下雨了，为什么呢？回答说：这没有什么，这就像不去祭神求雨而下雨一样。太阳、月亮发生了日食、月食，人们敲鼓击盘去营救，天气干旱了就祭神求雨，占卜算卦然后决定大事，古人并不是认为这些做法能得到所祈求的东西，而只是用它们来文饰政事罢了。所以君子把这些活动看作为一种文饰，但老百姓却把它们看得神乎其神。把它们看作为一种文饰就吉祥，把它们看得神乎其神就凶险了。

marveled at, and they should be feared as well. A tradition says: {The calamities of Heaven and Earth are hidden in their coming.} Prodigies among the myriad things are documented but not explained. Argumentation with formal discriminations that have no use and exacting investigations into matters of no vital importance can be set aside and not dealt with. But when it comes to matters like the proper congruity between ruler and subject, the proper affection between father and son, and the proper separation of duties between husband and wife—these must day by day be "cut" and "polished" and never neglected.{An *Ode* says:

> Like bone cut, like horn polished,
> like jade carved, like stone ground.}

[This expresses my meaning.]

17. 11

If you pray for rain and there is rain, what of that? I say there is no special relationship—as when you do not pray for rain and there is rain. When the sun and moon are eclipsed, we attempt to save them; when Heaven sends drought, we pray for rain; and before we decide any important undertaking, we divine with bone and milfoil. We do these things not because we believe that such ceremonies will produce the results we seek, but because we want to embellish such occasions with ceremony. Thus, the gentleman considers such ceremonies as embellishments, but the Hundred Clans consider them supernatural. To consider them embellishments is fortunate; to consider them supernatural is unfortunate.

【原文】

17.12 在天者莫明于日月，在地者莫明于水火，在物者莫明于珠玉，在人者莫明于礼义。故日月不高，则光晖不赫；水火不积，则晖润不博；珠玉不睹乎外，则王公不以为宝；礼义不加于国家，则功名不白。故人之命在天，国之命在礼。君人者，隆礼、尊贤而王，重法、爱民而霸，好利、多诈而危，权谋、倾覆、幽险而尽亡矣。

17.13 大天而思之，孰与物畜而制之？从天而颂之，孰与制天命而用之？望时而待之，孰与应时而使之？因物而多之，孰与骋能而化

【今译】

17.12 在天上的东西没有什么比太阳、月亮更明亮的了，在地上的东西没有什么比水、火更明亮的了，在物品之中没有什么比珍珠、宝玉更明亮的了，在人类社会中没有什么比礼义更灿烂的了。太阳、月亮如果不高挂空中，那么它们的光辉就不显著；水、火如果不积聚，那么火的光辉、水的光泽就不大；珍珠、宝玉的光彩不显露于外，那么天子、诸侯就不会把它们当作宝贝；礼义不在国内施行，那么功业和名声就不会显著。所以人的命运在天，国家的命运在礼义。统治人民的君主，推崇礼义，尊重贤人，就能称王天下；注重法治，爱护人民，就能称霸诸侯；喜欢财利，多搞欺诈，就会危险；玩弄权术，坑人害人，阴暗险恶，那就会彻底灭亡了。

17.13 认为大自然伟大而思慕它，哪里及得上把它当作物资积蓄起来而控制它？顺从自然而颂扬它，哪里及得上掌握自然规律而利用它？盼望时令而等待它，哪里及得上因时制宜而使它为我所用？依靠万物的自然增殖，哪里及得上施展人的才能而使它们根据人的需要来

17. 12

Of the things of the heavens, none is brighter than the sun and moon; of the things of the earth, none is as bright as fire and water; of external things, none is brighter than pearls and jade; and of human things none is as bright as ritual and moral principles.

Accordingly, if the sun and moon did not rise high, their brilliant splendor would not have its fiery brightness. If fire and water did not collect together, their glow and moisture would not spread out. If pearls and jade did not shine on the outside, kings and dukes would not consider them precious. If ritual and moral principles are not applied in a nation, its meritorious accomplishments and the fame due it will not be plainly evident. Thus, just as the fate of men lies with Heaven, so too the fate of the state lies with its ritual. A lord of men who exalts ritual principles and honors worthy men will become a True King; one who stresses law and loves the people will become lord-protector; one who is fond of profit and is much given to dissimulation will be imperiled; and one who schemes after power, plots revolution, and risks secret intrigues will perish.

17. 13

How can glorifying Heaven and contemplating it, be as good as tending its creatures and regulating them? How can obeying Heaven and singing it hymns of praise be better than regulating what Heaven has mandated and using it? How can anxiously watching for the season and awaiting what it brings, be as good as responding to the season and exploiting it? How can depending on things to increase naturally be better than developing their natural capacities so as to transform them? How

【原文】

之？思物而物之，孰与理物而勿失之也？愿于物之所以生，孰与有物之所以成？故错人而思天，则失万物之情。

17.14 百王之无变，足以为道贯。一废一起，应之以贯。理贯不乱。不知贯，不知应变。贯之大体未尝亡也。乱生其差，治尽其详。故道之所善，中则可从，畸则不可为，匿则大惑。水行者表深，表不明，则陷；治民者表道，表不明，则乱。礼者，表也。非礼，昏世也；昏世，大乱也。故道无不明，外内异表，隐显有常，民陷乃去。

【今译】

变化？思慕万物而把它们当作与己无关的外物，哪里及得上管理好万物而不失去它们？希望了解万物产生的原因，哪里及得上占有那已经生成的万物？所以放弃了人的努力而寄希望于天，那就违背了万物的实际情况。

17.14 各代帝王都没有改变的东西，完全可以用来作为政治原则的常规惯例。国家有时衰微有时兴盛，但君主都凭这种常规惯例去应付它。把握好这种常规惯例，国家就不会混乱。如果不了解这种常规惯例，就不知道如何应付变化。这种常规惯例的主要内容从来没有消失过。社会的混乱，产生于这种常规惯例的实施出了差错；社会安定，全在于这种常规惯例的实施十分周详。所以，政治原则中那些被一般人看作为好的东西，如果符合这种常规惯例，就可以依从；如果偏离了这种常规惯例，就不可以实行；如果违反了这种常规惯例，就会造成极大的迷惑。在水中跋涉的人用标志来表明深度，如果这种标志不明确，就会使人陷入深水淹死；治理民众的君主用标准来表明政治原则，如果这种标准不明确，就会造成混乱。礼制就是治理民众的标准。违反了礼制，就是昏暗的社会；昏暗的社会，就会大乱。所以，政治原则没有照不亮的地方，它对外对内都有不同的标准，对隐蔽之

can contemplating things and expecting them to serve you be as good as administering them so that you do not miss the opportunities they present? How can brooding over for the origins of things be better than assisting what perfects them?

Accordingly if you cast aside the concerns proper to Man in order to speculate about what belongs to Heaven, you will miss the essential nature of the myriad things.

17. 14

What has remained unchanged through the Hundred Kings is sufficient to be regarded as the connecting thread of the Way. With each rise and fall, respond with this connecting thread; apply the connecting thread with reason, and there will be no disorder. If you do not know the connecting thread, you will not know how to respond to changing circumstances. The great, essential matter of this connecting thread has never ceased to be. Thus, disorder is produced by mistakes concerning it; order by exhaustive application of its every detail.

Hence, with regard to what is good when judged by the standard of the Way, follow what perfectly coincides with the Way; what departs from it by bits and fractions should not be done; and what is utterly contrary to it should be treated as the gravest of errors. When men cross the water at fords, they mark the deep places; but if their markers are unclear, those who come after will drown. Those who govern the people mark out the Way, but if the markers are not clear, then the people will fall into disorder. Ritual principles are such markers. To condemn ritual principles is to blind the world; to blind the world is to produce the greatest of disorders. Hence, if nothing is left unclear about the Way, if the

【原文】

17.15 万物为道一偏，一物为万物一偏。愚者为一物一偏，而自以为知道，无知也。慎子有见于后，无见于先；老子有见于诎，无见于信；墨子有见于齐，无见于畸；宋子有见于少，无见于多。有后而无先，则群众无门；有诎而无信，则贵贱不分；有齐而无畸，则政令不施；有少而无多，则群众不化。《书》曰：“无有作好，遵王之道；无有作恶，遵王之路。”此之谓也。

【今译】

事或显露之事都有永久不变的规定，那么民众的陷阱就可以除去了。

17.15 万事万物只体现了自然规律的一部分，某一种事物只是万事万物的一部分。愚昧的人只认识了某一种事物的一个方面，就自以为知道了自然规律，实在是无知。慎子对在后服从的一面有所认识，但对在前引导的一面却毫无认识；老子对委曲忍让的一面有所认识，但对积极进取的一面却毫无认识；墨子对齐同平等的一面有所认识，但对等级差别的一面却毫无认识；宋子对寡欲的一面有所认识，但对多欲的一面却毫无认识。只在后服从而不在前引导，那么群众就没有继续前进的门径；只委曲忍让而不积极进取，那么高贵和卑贱就不会有分别；只有齐同平等而没有等级差别，那么政策法令就不能贯彻实施；只求寡欲而不见多欲，那么群众就不易被感化。《尚书》上说：“不要任凭个人的爱好，要遵循君主确定的正道；不要任凭个人的厌恶，要遵循君主确定的正路。”说的就是这个道理。

inner and outer have different markers, and if light and dark have regularity, the pitfalls that cause the people to drown can thereby be eliminated.

17. 15

The myriad things constitute one aspect of the Way, and a single thing constitutes one aspect of the myriad things. The stupid who act on the basis of one aspect of one thing, considering that therein they know the Way, are ignorant. Shen Dao had insight into "holding back," but none into "leading the way." Laozi had insight into " bending down," but none into "straightening up." Mozi had insight into "uniformity," but none into "individuation." Song Xing had insight into "reducing," but none into "increasing." If there is only "holding back" and no "leading the way," then the masses will have no gate to opportunity. If there is only "bending down" and no "straightening up," then the noble and base cannot be distinguished. If there is only "uniformity" and no "individuation," then governmental regulations and commands will not be carried out. If there is only "reducing" and never "increasing," then the masses cannot be transformed. One of the *Documents* expresses this point:

> Have no predilections, follow the way of the king; have no aversions, follow the king's road.

正论第十八

【原文】

18.1 世俗之为说者曰："主道利周。"是不然。

主者，民之唱也；上者，下之仪也。彼将听唱而应，视仪而动。唱默则民无应也，仪隐则下无动也。不应不动，则上下无以相有也。若是，则与无上同也，不祥莫大焉。故上者，下之本也。上宣明，则下治辨矣；上端诚，则下愿悫矣；上公正，则下易直矣。治辨则易一，愿悫则易使，易直则易知。易一则强，易使则功，易知则明：是

【今译】

18.1 社会上那些庸俗的创立学说的人说："君主的统治措施以周密隐蔽为有利。"这种说法不对。

君主，好比是民众的领唱；帝王，好比是臣下的标杆。那臣民们将听着领唱来应和，看着标杆来行动。领唱沉默，那么民众就无从应和；标杆隐蔽，那么臣下就无从行动。臣民不应和，不行动，那么君主和臣民就无法相亲善了。像这样，那就和没有君主一样，不吉利的事没有比这更大的了。所以君主，是臣民的根基。君主公开明朗，那么臣民就能治理好了；君主端正诚实，那么臣民就老实忠厚了；君主公正无私，那么臣民就坦荡正直了。臣民治理得好就容易统一，老实忠厚就容易役使，坦荡正直就容易了解。臣民容易统一，国家就会强盛；臣民容易役使，君主就能建立功业；臣民容易了解，君主就会明

Book 18

Rectifying Theses

18. 1

In accord with popular opinion, persuaders offer the thesis:"For the Way of the ruler secrecy is beneficial."

This is not so. The ruler is to the people as a singing master who provides the tune; the superior is to his subordinates as the gnomon that provides the standard. They will listen to the tune of the singing master and respond to it; they will observe the standard of the gnomon and act accordingly. If the tune of the singing master is inaudible, then the people have nothing to respond to. If the gnomon is shrouded in darkness, then subordinates have nothing to act in accordance with. If they do not respond and do not act according to the gnomon, then superior and inferior will have no means of relying upon each other. If such a situation should obtain, it would be equivalent to having no ruler at all, and no harbinger of disaster could be greater than this. Thus the superior is the root and foundation for his subordinates.

If the superior exhibits and elucidates the standard, his subordinates will be orderly and manageable. If the superior is correct and sincere, his subordinates will be attentive and diligent. If the superior is impartial and right, his subordinates will be amenable and honest. If they are orderly and manageable, they are easily unified. If they are attentive and diligent, they are easily employed. If they are amenable and honest, they are easily understood. When the people are easily unified, there is strength; when they are easily employed, there is accomplishment; when they are

【原文】

治之所由生也。上周密，则下疑玄矣；上幽险，则下渐诈矣；上偏曲，则下比周矣。疑玄则难一，渐诈则难使，比周则难知。难一则不强，难使则不功，难知则不明：是乱之所由作也。故主道利明不利幽，利宣不利周。故主道明，则下安；主道幽，则下危。故下安，则贵上；下危，则贱上。故上易知，则下亲上矣；上难知，则下畏上矣。下亲上，则上安；下畏上，则上危。故主道莫恶乎难知，莫危乎使下畏己。传曰："恶之者众则危。"《书》曰："克明明德。"《诗》曰：

【今译】

白清楚。这是安定得以产生的缘由。君主隐蔽不露，那么臣民就疑惑迷乱了；君主阴暗险恶，那么臣民就虚伪欺诈了；君主偏私不公正，那么臣民就私相勾结了。臣民疑惑迷乱就难以统一，虚伪欺诈就难以役使，私相勾结就难以了解。臣民难以统一，那么国家就不会强盛；臣民难以役使，那么君主就不能建立功业；臣民难以了解，那么君主就不清楚。这是祸乱产生的根源。所以君主的统治措施以明朗为有利而以阴暗为不利，以公开为有利而以隐蔽为不利。君主的统治措施公开明朗，那么臣民就安逸；君主的统治措施阴暗不明，那么臣民就危险。臣民安逸，就会尊重君主；臣民危险，就会鄙视君主。君主的措施容易被了解，那么臣民就亲爱君主了；君主的措施难以被了解，那么臣民就害怕君主了。臣民亲爱君主，那么君主就安逸；臣民害怕君主，那么君主就危险。所以君主的统治措施没有比难以被了解更坏的了，没有比使臣民害怕自己更危险的了。古书上说："憎恨他的人众多，他就危险了。"《尚书》说："能够彰明贤明的德行。"《诗》云："彰

easily understood, there is an atmosphere of openness and forthrightness—and this is what produces order.

If the superior is secretive and mysterious, his subordinates will be suspicious and confused. If he is obscure and inaccessible, his subordinates will be furtive and treacherous. If the superior is biased and one-sided, his subordinates will form parties and cliques. If they are suspicious and confused, they are difficult to unify. If they are furtive and treacherous, they are difficult to employ. If they form parties and cliques, they are difficult to know. When the people are difficult to unify, there is no strength; when they are difficult to employ, there is no accomplishment; and when they are difficult to know, there is no atmosphere of openness and forthrightness—and this is what creates chaos.

Accordingly, the way of the ruler benefits from clarity and not from obscurity; it benefits from exhibiting [the standard] and not from secrecy.

Thus, if the way of the ruler is clear, his subjects will be calm and feel secure; if the Way is obscure, then his subjects will be uneasy and feel threatened. If his subjects are calm and feel secure, they will esteem their superior; if they are uneasy and feel threatened, they will despise their superior. Thus if the superior is easy to know, his subordinates will feel kinship with him; if he is difficult to know, they will fear him. If subordinates feel close to their superior, the superior is secure; if they fear him, he is threatened. Thus, no way of the ruler is so fraught with evil as that of being difficult to know; none is more perilous than causing his subordinates to fear him.

A tradition says:

When those who hate him are a multitude, he is in danger.

One of the *Documents* says:

He was able to make bright his illustrious inner power.

【原文】

"明明在下。"故先王明之，岂特玄之耳哉？

18.2 世俗之为说者曰："桀、纣有天下，汤、武篡而夺之。"是不然，以桀、纣为常有天下之籍，则然；亲有天下之籍，则不然；天下谓在桀、纣，则不然。

古者天子千官，诸侯百官。以是千官也，令行于诸夏之国，谓之王；以是百官也，令行于境内，国虽不安，不至于废易遂亡，谓之君。圣王之子也，有天下之后也，势籍之所在也，天下之宗室也，然而不材不中，内则百姓疾之，外则诸侯叛之，近者境内不一，遥者诸

【今译】

明美德在天下。"古代的圣王也彰明自己，难道只是使自己幽深难知就算了吗？

18.2 社会上那些庸俗的创立学说的人说："夏桀、商纣拥有天下，商汤、周武王把它篡夺了。"这种说法不对。认为夏桀、商纣曾经占有天子的权位，那是对的；认为他们亲自占有过统治天下的势位，那就不对了；以为天下都掌握在夏桀、商纣手中，那也是不对的。

古代天子有上千个官吏，诸侯有上百个官吏。依靠这上千个官吏，政令能推行到中原各诸侯国，就可称作为统治天下的帝王；依靠这上百个官吏，政令能推行到国境之内，国家即使不安定，还不至于被废黜撤换垮台灭亡，就可称作为诸侯国的国君。圣明帝王的子孙，是拥有天下的后代，是权势的占有者，是天下人所尊崇的帝王之家，但是如果没有才能又不公正，内则百姓怨恨他，外则诸侯背叛他，近

An *Ode* says:

Open and forthright are those below.

Thus, the Ancient Kings made themselves plain. Surely this was the result of their openness and nothing else.

18. 2

In accord with popular opinion, persuaders offer the thesis:"Jie and Zhou Xin truly possessed the empire; Tang and Wu usurped it and stole the throne."

This is not so. If one means that by the normal rule Jie and Zhou Xin would have possessed formal title to the empire, then it would be so. If one means that by right of inheritance they personally possessed formal title to the empire, then it would not be so. If "empire" refers to the fact that the world was with Jie and Zhou Xin, then it would not be so.

In antiquity, the Son of Heaven had a thousand offices in his government and the feudal lords each had a hundred. To use these thousand offices to execute orders in all the countries of the Xia Chinese traditions is what is meant by being "King". To use these hundred offices to execute orders within the boundaries of the state so that although there might be unrest in the state, it does not reach the point where the lord might be displaced, or destroyed—this is what is meant by being a lord. In the descendants of sage kings who inherited the empire in later generations is vested the position of political power and authority and in them is contained spiritual authority over the empire. Although all this is so, when a descendant is untalented and does not "hit the mark," the Hundred Clans, on the one hand, will loathe him, and the feudal lords,on the other, will desert him. Nearby those within his own borders will not be united;

【原文】

侯不听，令不行于境内，甚者诸侯侵削之，攻伐之。若是，则虽未亡，吾谓之无天下矣。

圣王没，有势籍者罢，不足以县天下，天下无君。诸侯有能德明威积，海内之民莫不愿得以为君师。然而暴国独侈，安能诛之，必不伤害无罪之民，诛暴国之君若诛独夫。若是，则可谓能用天下矣。能用天下之谓王。

汤、武非取天下也，修其道，行其义，兴天下之同利，除天下之同害，而天下归之也。桀、纣非去天下也，反禹、汤之德，乱礼义之分，禽兽之行，积其凶，全其恶，而天下去之也。天下归之之谓王，天下去之之谓亡。故桀、纣无天下，而汤、武不弑君，由此效之也。

【今译】

处是境内不统一，远处是诸侯不听从，政令不能在境内实行，甚至于诸侯侵略分割他，攻打讨伐他。像这样，那么他即使还没有灭亡，我也要说他已经失去天下了。

圣明的帝王死了，那些拥有权势的后代没有德才，无法掌握天下，天下等于没有了君主。诸侯中如果有人能够德行贤明威信崇高，那么天下的人民就无不愿意得到他让他做自己的君长。然而暴君统治的国家偏偏奢侈放纵，怎么能杀掉暴君呢?不要去伤害没有罪过的民众，那么杀掉暴虐之国的君主就像杀掉一个孤独无依的人一样。像这样，就可以称为善于治理天下了。善于治理天下的就叫做天子。

商汤、周武王并不是夺取天下，而是遵行那正确的政治原则，奉行那合宜的道义，兴办天下人的共同福利，除去天下人的共同祸害，因而天下人归顺他们。夏桀、商纣并不是丢了天下，而是违背了夏禹、商汤的德行，扰乱了礼义的名分，干出了禽兽般的行为，不断行凶，无恶不作，因而天下人抛弃了他们。天下人归顺他就叫做称王，天下人抛弃他就叫做灭亡。所以夏桀、商纣王并没有拥有天下，而商

far away the feudal lords will not heed him. His commands are not carried out even within his own borders, and in the worst case the feudal lords first encroach on him, slicing off territory, then they openly attack and invade. Given such a situation, although he might not yet have perished, I would say that he no longer really possessed the empire.

When the sage kings died, those who inherited their power and authority were so dissipated that they were incapable of holding the world to themselves. Since the world had come to have no real lord, were one of the feudal lords to have real ability, were he to make illustrious his moral power and gather up his majestic authority, none of the people within the seas would fail to long to gain him as their own lord and master. This being so, should he go on to seek out the isolated and extravagant tyrant for execution, it is certain that [this feudal lord] would have inflicted no injury nor done any harm, and that he would remain a blameless subject. For to execute a tyrannical lord is like executing a "solitary individual." In such circumstances it is proper to speak of his being "able to wield the empire," which is precisely what is meant by being "King."

Tang and Wu did not seize the whole world. Rather, they cultivated the Way, carried out their moral duty, caused whatever benefited the empire in common to flourish, and removed whatever did harm to the whole world, so that the empire offered allegiance to them. Jie and Zhou Xin did not abandon the world. Rather, they turned against the inner power of [their forebears] Yu and Tang, brought chaos to the divisions of social functions inherent in ritual and moral principles, behaved like wild beasts, gathered up their own ultimate catastrophe, completed their own evil, so that the world abandoned them. "The empire offering allegiance to you" is what is meant by "King." The "whole world abandoning you" is what is meant by "ruination." Thus, that Jie and Zhou Xin did not possess the

【原文】

汤、武者，民之父母也；桀、纣者，民之怨贼也。今世俗之为说者，以桀、纣为君，而以汤、武为弑，然则是诛民之父母，而师民之怨贼也，不祥莫大焉。以天下之合为君，则天下未尝合于桀、纣也，然则以汤、武为弑，则天下未尝有说也，直隳之耳！

故天子唯其人。天下者，至重也，非至强莫之能任；至大也，非至辨莫之能分；至众也，非至明莫之能和。此三至者，非圣人莫之能尽，故非圣人莫之能王。圣人，备道全美者也，是县天下之权称也。

桀、纣者，其知虑至险也，其至意至暗也，其行之为至乱也。亲者疏之，贤者贱之，生民怨之，禹、汤之后也而不得一人之与。刳比

【今译】

汤、周武王并没有杀掉君主，从这个角度就能证明它。商汤、周武王，是人民的父母，夏桀、商纣王，是人民的仇敌。现在社会上那些庸俗的创立学说的人，把夏桀、商纣王当作君主，而认为商汤、周武王是杀君，这样的话，那就是在谴责人民的父母，而把人民的仇敌当作君长，不吉利的事没有比这个更大的了。如果认为天下归附的人才是君主，那么天下人从来没有归附过夏桀、商纣王，这样的话，那么认为商汤、周武王是杀君，就是天下人从来没有过的说法了，这只不过是在毁谤他们罢了！

所以天子只有像汤、武这样的人才能胜任。治理天下，那任务是极其繁重的，不是最强劲有力的人是不能够担负它的；那范围是极其广大的，不是最明辨的人是不能够分辨它的；那人民是极其众多的，不是最英明的人是不能够协调他们的。这三个最，不是圣人没有谁能具备，所以不是圣人就没有谁能称王天下。圣人，是道德完备、十全十美的人，他就像挂在天下的一杆秤。

夏桀、商纣王，他们的谋虑极其险恶，他们的思想极其愚昧，他们的行为极其昏乱。亲近的人疏远他们，贤能的人鄙视他们，人民怨恨他们，他们虽然是夏禹、商汤的后代却得不到一个人的帮助。商纣

world and that Tang and Wu did not murder their sovereigns are by this argument demonstrated.

Tang and Wu were considered as the father and mother of the people. Jie and Zhou Xin were hated as predators of the people. Now the commonplace persuader's thesis that Jie and Zhou Xin were the true lords and that Tang and Wu were assassins is equivalent to advocating that "the father and mother of the people" be executed and that "the hated predator of the people" be made their masters. No misfortune could be greater than such a situation. If one considers that he who unites the empire is the true lord, then the empire was no longer held in unity by Jie or Zhou Xin. If this is given, then the thesis that Tang and Wu were assassins is no longer sustainable and is nothing more than out-and-out slander. Thus whether a man is truly a Son of Heaven depends entirely on what kind of man he is.

Since the world is the weightiest burden, only the strongest person will be able to bear it. Since it is the largest thing, only the most discriminating will be able to allocate social responsibilities properly. Since it is the most populous entity, only the most enlightened will be able to make it harmonious. Only a sage is capable of fully meeting these three conditions. Thus, only a sage is capable of being a True King. A sage thoroughly perfects himself in the Way and is a person of complete refinement, so he can be the balance scale of judgment for the whole world.

The thoughts and reflections of Jie and Zhou Xin were extremely dangerous; their goals and purposes benighted in the extreme; and their conduct and actions produced extreme chaos. Their own kin kept their distance; the worthy despised them; and their own people hated them. Although they were descendants of Yu and Tang, they did not gain the adherence of even one man. Zhou Xin disemboweled Bigan and impri-

【原文】

干，囚箕子，身死国亡，为天下之大僇，后世之言恶者必稽焉。是不容妻子之数也。故至贤畴四海，汤、武是也；至罢不容妻子，桀、纣是也。今世俗之为说者，以桀、纣为有天下而臣汤、武，岂不过甚矣哉？譬之，是犹伛巫跛匡大自以为有知也。

故可以有夺人国，不可以有夺人天下；可以有窃国，不可以有窃天下也。可以夺之者可以有国，而不可以有天下；窃可以得国，而不可以得天下。是何也？曰：国，小具也，可以小人有也，可以小道得也，可以小力持也；天下者，大具也，不可以小人有也，不可以小道得也，不可以小力持也。国者，小人可以有之，然而未必不亡也；天下者，至大也，非圣人莫之能有也。

【今译】

王将比干剖腹挖心，囚禁箕子，结果自身被杀，国家灭亡，成为天下最可耻的人，后世说到坏人，就一定要拿他作例证。这就是他们不能保住妻子儿女的道理。所以极有德才的人能囊括天下，商汤、周武王就是；极无德才的人不能庇护妻子儿女，夏桀、商纣就是。现在社会上那些庸俗的创立学说的人，认为夏桀、商纣王拥有了天下而把商汤、周武王作为他们的臣子，难道不是错得很厉害了吗？拿它打个比方，这就好像是驼背的巫婆、瘸了腿的残疾人狂妄地自以为有见解一样。

所以可以有夺取别人国家的事，却不可能有夺取别人天下的事；可以有窃取国家政权的事，却不可能有窃取天下统治权的事。夺取政权的人可能拥有一个国家，却不可能拥有整个天下；窃取政权可以得到一个国家，却不可能得到整个天下。这是为什么呢？回答说：国家是个小器具，可以让德才低劣的小人占有，可以依靠歪门邪道来取得，可以凭借较小的力量来维持；天下是个大器具，不可能让德才低劣的小人占有，不可能依靠歪门邪道来取得，不可能凭借较小的力量来维护。国家，小人可以拥有它，但是不一定就不灭亡；天下，是极其庞大的，不是圣人没有谁能占有它。

soned the Viscount of Ji. Both, having lost their own lives and destroyed their countries, became the greatest objects of scorn in the whole world. Those who in later generations discussed the problem of evil have had to examine the case of these two men closely, for they were unable even to protect their own wives and children.

Therefore, the worthiest of men could embrace all within the four seas—such were Tang and Wu. The most dissipated of men were not able to protect their own family—such were Jie and Zhou Xin. Now, to accord with popular opinion, persuaders' theses make Jie and Zhou Xin the real possessors of the empire and Tang and Wu their servants—what utter nonsense this is! It is analogous to a hunchbacked shaman or emaciated cripple pulling himself up to magnify himself in order to exaggerate his wisdom!

Accordingly, although it is possible for a state to be taken by force, it is impossible for the whole empire to be taken by force. Although it is possible to take over a state by stealth, it is impossible to take over the whole empire by stealth. A man who resorts to force may possess a state, but he cannot by means of force possess the empire; by stealth he can succeed in taking over a state, but he cannot gain control over the whole empire—why is this? I say that a state, being a small thing, can be possessed by a petty man, can be obtained by the way of a petty man, and can be held with the strength of a petty man. The empire is a great entity, so it is impossible for a petty man to possess it, the way of a petty man to obtain it, and the strength of a petty man to hold it. Although a state is something a petty man can possess, nonetheless it is inevitable that he will lose it. The empire is the greatest of all, and only a sage can possess it.

【原文】

18.3世俗之为说者曰:“治古无肉刑,而有象刑。墨黥;慅婴;共,艾毕;菲,对屦;杀,赭衣而不纯。治古如是。”是不然。

以为治邪?则人固莫触罪,非独不用肉刑,亦不用象刑矣。以为人或触罪矣而直轻其刑?然则是杀人者不死,伤人者不刑也。罪至重而刑至轻,庸人不知恶矣,乱莫大焉。凡刑人之本,禁暴恶恶,且征其未也。杀人者不死,而伤人者不刑,是谓惠暴而宽贼也,非恶恶也。故象刑殆非生于治古,并起于乱今也。治古不然。凡爵列、官

【今译】

18.3社会上那些庸俗的创立学说的人说:“治理得很好的古代社会没有肉刑,而只有象征性的刑罚。用黑墨画脸来代替脸上刺字的黥刑;割鼻子的劓刑,用系上草制的帽带来代替;阉割生殖器的宫刑,用割去衣服的前襟或蔽膝来代替;砍掉脚的剕刑,用穿麻鞋来代替;杀头的死刑,用穿上红褐色的衣服而不做衣领来代替。治理得很好的古代社会就像这样。”这种说法不对。

以为当时已经治理好了么?如果当时的人根本就没有谁再会犯罪,那就不但用不着肉刑,而且也用不着象征性的刑罚了。以为当时的人有的还是犯罪了而只是减轻他们的刑罚么?这样的话,那就是杀人的不会被处死,伤人的不会被惩罚。罪行极重而刑罚极轻,平常人就不知道憎恨犯罪了,而祸乱没有比这更大的了。大凡惩罚人的根本目的,是禁止暴行,反对作恶,而且防范那未来。杀人的不被处死,而伤害人的不受刑罚,这叫做优惠暴徒而宽恕强盗,不是反对作恶。所以象征性的刑罚恐怕并非产生于治理得很好的古代,而都是产生于混乱的现代。治理得好的古代并不是这样的。凡是爵位、官职、奖赏、

18. 3

In accord with popular opinion, persuaders offer the thesis:"In well-ordered periods of antiquity corporal punishments were not employed; rather, there were only symbolic punishments. For black-branding they had the offender wear a black hood over his face; for cutting off the nose, he wore bleached cap-strings; for amputation of the feet, he wore hemp sandals; for castration, he wore an apron with a piece cut off; and for the death penalty, he wore collarless garments dyed with red ocher. Such were the punishments during well-ordered periods of antiquity."

This is not so. Could one consider such practices indicative of good order? If one were to suppose that of old no one gave offense or committed a crime, then not only would there have been no need for physical punishments, there would have been no cause to use symbolic ones. [What if one] supposed that [punishments should be lightened]? If someone then did give offense or commit a crime and his due punishment were lightened, then murderers would not die and those who injured others would not be punished. The greatest of crimes would result in the lightest of punishments, so that commoners would perceive nothing to hate [in the prospect of punishment] and nothing would create greater chaos than that!

As a general rule the fundamental reason for punishment is the need to prohibit acts of violence, to instill hatred of evil acts, and further to warn men against committing them in the future. When murderers are not killed and those who assault others are not punished, this should be called "generosity to the violent and liberality with predators." It is not hatred of evil. Accordingly, symbolic punishments surely did not develop in well-governed periods of antiquity, but arise rather out of the chaos of the present. The mode of order in antiquity was not at all like this.

【原文】

职、赏庆、刑罚皆报也，以类相从者也。一物失称，乱之端也。夫德不称位，能不称官，赏不当功，罚不当罪，不祥莫大焉。昔者武王伐有商，诛纣，断其首，县之赤旆。夫征暴诛悍，治之盛也。杀人者死，伤人者刑，是百王之所同也，未有知其所由来者也。刑称罪则治，不称罪则乱。故治则刑重，乱则刑轻；犯治之罪固重，犯乱之罪固轻也。《书》曰："刑罚世轻世重。"此之谓也。

18.4 世俗之为说者曰："汤、武不能禁令。"是何也？曰："楚、越

【今译】

刑罚都是一种回报，与行为的类别相应的。一件事情赏罚失当，那就是祸乱的开端。德行和地位不相称，能力和官职不相称，奖赏和功劳不相当，刑罚和罪过不相当，不吉利的事没有比这更大的了。从前周武王讨伐商王朝，惩罚商纣王，砍下了他的头，把它挂在大红旗的飘带上。这征伐暴君惩治元凶，是政治上的丰功伟绩。杀人的被处死，伤人的被惩罚，这是历代帝王所相同的，没有人知道它是从什么时代传下来的。刑罚和罪行相当，社会才能治理好；刑罚和罪行不相当，社会就会混乱。所以社会治理得好，刑罚就重；社会混乱，刑罚才轻。因为在治理得好的时代犯的罪，本来就重；在混乱的时代犯的罪，本来就轻。《尚书》上说："刑罚有的时代轻，有的时代重。"说的就是这种情况。

18.4 社会上那些庸俗的创立学说的人说："商汤、周武王不能实

As a general principle, every rank and official responsibility, and each reward or punishment, was given as a recompense that accorded with the nature of the conduct involved. Even one action not having proper recompense in this balanced scheme would be the beginning of chaos. Nothing could be more inauspicious than moral worth not being matched by a suitable position, or ability not being matched by appropriate office, or rewards not corresponding to achievement, or penalties not corresponding to offenses. In the past when King Wu attacked the "possessor of Shang" and condemned Zhou Xin to execution, he had his head cut off and suspended from a crimson banner. To correct violent behavior with punishment and rebuke the cruel is the fulfillment of good government. That murderers should be put to death and that those who injure others should be punished—this has been the same for the Hundred Kings, although we do not know how the practice originated. If punishment is balanced against offense, then there is order; if it is not so balanced, then there is chaos. Accordingly, if there is to be order, then punishments must be heavy, and if there is to be chaos, then punishments must be light. The treatment of criminal offenders in a period of good government is sternly harsh, and their treatment in a chaotic age is exceedingly light. One of the *Documents* expresses this point: The punishments and penalties are in some ages lenient and in some harsh. {The phrase "symbolic punishments make clear" refers to the fact that punishments were created to symbolize the Way of Heaven. How could they have been merely a question of "hemp sandals" and "garments dyed with red ocher"!}

18. 4

In accord with popular opinion, persuaders offer the thesis:"Tang and

【原文】

不受制。"是不然。

汤、武者，至天下之善禁令者也。汤居亳，武王居鄗，皆百里之地也，天下为一，诸侯为臣，通达之属，莫不振动从服以化顺之，曷为楚、越独不受制也？彼王者之制也，视形势而制械用，称远迩而等贡献，岂必齐哉？故鲁人以糖，卫人用柯，齐人用一革。土地形制不同者，械用备饰不可不异也。故诸夏之国同服同仪，蛮、夷、戎、狄之国同服不同制。封内甸服，封外侯服，侯、卫宾服，蛮、夷要服，

【今译】

施禁令。"这种说法的根据是什么呢？他们说："因为楚国、越国不受他们的制约。"这种说法不对。

商汤、周武王，是普天下最善于实施禁令的人。商汤居住在亳邑，周武王居住在鄗京，都不过是方圆百里的地方，但天下被他们统一了，诸侯做了他们的臣子，凡交通能到达的地方，人们无不惊恐颤动听从归服以至于被感化而依顺他们，为什么楚国、越国偏偏不受他们的制约呢？那些王者的制度，根据各地的情形来制造器械用具，衡量远近来规定进贡的等级差别，哪里一定要整齐划一呢？所以鲁国人用碗，卫国人用盂，齐国人用整块皮制作的器皿。土地环境风俗习惯不同的地方，器械用具设备服饰不能不有差别。所以中原各国同样服事天子而礼节规范相同。南蛮、东夷、西戎、北狄等国家同样服事天子而习俗不同。天子直接管辖的领地内以交纳农作物来服事天子，天子直接管辖的地区外围以守候放哨来服事天子，再向外负责守望保卫的地区则以宾客的身份按时进贡来服事天子，南蛮、东夷等少数民族

Wu were incapable of effecting their prohibitions and commands." How is that? We say:"Chu and Yue would not receive their ordinances."

This is not so. Tang and Wu were the most skillful men in the world at putting their prohibitions and commands in effect.

Tang resided at Bo and King Wu lived at Hao, both territories only a hundred *li* square. Yet they unified the world, made the feudal lords their servants, so that wherever news of them reached and wherever it penetrated, there were none who were not stirred and moved to submit and follow after them, thereby to be transformed and made obedient to them.

How is it that Chu and Yue alone should not have received their ordinances?

The ordinances of those two kings observed the qualities inherent in the land forms and regulated with ordinances the vessels and implements. They judged the various distances and so differentiated grades of tribute and offerings.

Why should it be necessary that they all be uniform? Thus, the people of Lu use cups as tribute, the people of Wei use vats, and the people of Qi use containers made of hide. When the soils, lands, and inherent qualities of the topography are not the same, it is impossible that their vessels and implements should not be differently prepared and ornamented. Accordingly, all the states of Xia Chinese have identical obligations for service to the king and have identical standards of conduct. The countries of the Man, Yi, Rong, and Di barbarians perform the same obligatory services to the king, but the regulations governing them are not the same.

Those who are enfeoffed within [the royal domain] do royal service. Those who are enfeoffed without [the royal domain] do feudal service. Those who are in the feudal marches zone do guest service. The Man

【原文】

戎、狄荒服。甸服者祭，侯服者祀，宾服者享，要服者贡，荒服者王。日祭，月祀，时享，岁贡，终王。夫是之谓视形势而制械用，称远近而等贡献，是王者之至也。彼楚、越者，且时享、岁贡，终王之属也，必齐之日祭、月祀之属然后曰"受制"邪？是规磨之说也。沟中之瘠也，则未足与及王者之制也。语曰："浅不足与测深，愚不足与谋知，坎井之蛙不可与语东海之乐。"此之谓也。

【今译】

地区以接受约束来服事天子，西戎、北狄等少数民族地区以不固定的进贡来服事天子。以交纳农作物来服事天子的地区负责供给祭祀祖父、父亲的物品，以守候放哨来服事天子的地区负责供给祭祀曾祖、高祖的物品，以宾客身份按时进贡来服事天子的地区负责供给祭祀远祖、始祖的物品，以接受约束来服事天子的地区负责供给祭祀天神的物品，以不固定的进贡来服事天子的地区要承认天子的统治地位。这些地区有的供给天子每天祭祀的物品，有的供给天子每月祭祀的物品，有的供给天子每季祭祀的物品，有的每年向天子进贡，有的崇敬天子，老的天子死后，就要去朝见新的天子以承认他的统治地位。这就是所谓的根据各地的情形来制造器械用具，衡量远近来规定进贡的等级差别，这就是王者的制度。那楚国、越国，不过是进贡每季祭祀、每年祭祀的祭品以及一代天子死了以后要来承认新天子一类的国家，难道一定要使他们与那些供给每天祭祀、每月祭祀的祭品一类的国家一样，然后才说他们"受制约"了吗？这是有差错的说法啊。这种人真像山沟中的僵尸，不值得和他谈及圣王的制度。俗话说："肤浅的东西是测量不出深刻的东西的，愚蠢的人不值得和他商量智巧的事，废井中的青蛙不能和它谈论东海中的乐趣。"说的就是这种情况。

and Yi nations do service according to treaty obligations. The Rong and Di do irregular service. Those who do royal service provide offerings for the sacrifices of thanks; those who do feudal service provide offerings for the cult sacrifices; those who do guest service provide for the drinking ceremonies; those who do service according to treaty present tribute offerings; and those who do irregular service come to pay their respects at the succession of the new king. Each day, offerings of thanks must be provided; each month, cult sacrificial offerings are made; each season, there is the drinking ceremony; each year, tribute is offered;{and once a generation there is the succession of the new king}. This is just what is meant by they observed the qualities inherent in the land forms and regulated with ordinances the vessels and implements; they judged the various distances and so differentiated grades of tribute and offerings—for such is the perfection of true kingship.

Further, Chu and Yue were of the class of states that made the seasonal presentation of offerings, the yearly tribute, and came at the succession of the new king. Why must one compare them only with the class of states that provided for the daily offering of thanks or monthly cult sacrifices in order to contend that they "received the ordinances"? Such would be a case of the "compass for grindstone" theory. [···] A saying goes:

> The shallow are inadequate to participate in fathoming the depths; the stupid are unable to join in dealing with the wise. It is impossible for a frog from the well pit to join in discussing the happiness of the Eastern Sea. Starvelings lying in drainage ditches will never be adequate to share in reaching up to the ordinances of true kingship.

This expresses my point.

【原文】

18.5 世俗之为说者曰:“尧、舜擅让。”是不然。

天子者，势位至尊，无敌于天下，夫有谁与让矣？道德纯备，智慧甚明，南面而听天下，生民之属，莫不振动从服以化顺之，天下无隐士，无遗善，同焉者是也，异焉者非也，夫有恶擅天下矣？

曰:“死而擅之。”是又不然。

圣王在上，图德而定次，量能而授官，皆使民载其事而各得其宜。不能以义制利，不能以伪饰性，则兼以为民。圣王已没，天下无圣，则固莫足以擅天下矣。天下有圣而在后者，则天下不离，朝不易

【今译】

18.5 社会上那些庸俗的创立学说的人说：“尧、舜把王位禅让给别人。”这种说法不对。

天子权势地位至高无上，在天下无与伦比，他又和谁推让呢？尧、舜道德美好完备，智慧非常发达，朝南坐着治理天下，所有的民众，都惊恐颤动听从归服以至于被感化而依顺他们，天下没有被埋没的人才，没有被遗忘的好人好事，和尧、舜相同的言行才是正确的，和他们不同的言行就是错误的，他们又为什么要把天下让掉呢？

有人说：“是等他们死了以后再把王位禅让给别人的。”这又不对。

圣明的帝王处在君位上，考虑德行来确定等级，衡量才能来授予官职，使人们全都能担负起自己的职事而各人又都能得到适宜的安排。那些不能用道义来制约私利，不能通过人为的努力来改造本性的人，就统统让他们当老百姓。圣明的帝王已经死了，天下如果没有圣人，那么根本就没有人能够接受禅让了。天下如果有圣人而又出在圣明帝王的后代之中，那么天下人就不会离心离德，朝廷上就不会改变

18. 5

In accord with popular opinion, persuaders offer the thesis:"Yao and Shun abdicated and yielded their thrones."

This is not so. Consider the Son of Heaven: his position of power and authority is the most honorable in the empire, having no match whatever. Further, to whom should they yield? Since their Way and its Power are pure and complete, since their wisdom and intelligence are exceedingly perspicacious, they had only "to face south and adjudicate the affairs of the empire." Every class of living people, each and all, would be stirred up and moved to follow after them and submit in order to be transformed and made obedient to them. The world had no "hidden scholars," and there was no "lost goodness." What was identical with them would be right, and what was different from them would be wrong. Again, why would they abdicate the empire?

They say:"At death, they relinquished all claims."

This as well is not so. Both sage kings, in occupying the supreme position, fixed precedence of rank by determining the moral worth of the person and filled offices by measuring his capability.

Both assigned the people their allotted duties so that "each received those tasks that best suited him." Those who were unable to control personal cupidity with a sense of propriety or whose natures could not be refined with the application of conscious effort were in every case made subjects. If the sage kings had already died, and there was no other sage in the empire, then most assuredly there was no one of sufficient stature to whom the empire should be yielded. Given the situation that there is a sage in the empire who is his descendant, then the empire is not interrupted, the dynasty does not change in status, the various states do not

【原文】

位，国不更制，天下厌然与乡无以异也；以尧继尧，夫又何变之有矣？圣不在后子而在三公，则天下如归，犹复而振之矣，天下厌然与乡无以异也；以尧继尧，夫又何变之有矣？唯其徙朝改制为难。故天子生，则天下一隆，致顺而治，论德而定次；死，则能任天下者必有之矣。夫礼义之分尽矣，擅让恶用矣哉？

曰："老衰而擅。"是又不然。

血气筋力则有衰，若夫智虑取舍则无衰。

曰："老者不堪其劳而休也。"是又畏事者之议也。

天子者，势至重而形至佚，心至愉而志无所诎，而形不为劳，尊

【今译】

各人的官位，国家也不会改变制度，天下就安安稳稳地和过去没有什么不同；这是用尧一样的圣王来继承尧，那又会有什么改变呢？如果圣人不出在圣明帝王的后代子孙之中而出在辅佐大臣之中，那么天下人随从归附他，就像恢复国家而振兴它一样了，天下也会安安稳稳地和过去没有什么不同；这是用尧一样的圣王来继承尧，那又会有什么改变呢？只有那改朝换代、变更制度才是困难的。所以圣明的天子活着，那么天下人就专一地尊崇他，极其顺从而有秩序，评定德行来确定各自的等级位次；圣明的天子死了，那么能够担负起治理天下重任的继承人，一定会有的。礼义的名分全部落实了，哪里还用得着禅让呢？

有人说："是他们年老体衰才把王位禅让给别人的。"这又不对。

人的血脉气色、筋骨体力倒是有衰退的，至于那智慧、思考能力、判断决择能力却是不会衰退的。

有人说："年老的人不能忍受那劳累才退下来休息的。"这又是怕做事者的议论。

天子权势极大而身体极安逸，心情极愉快而志向没有不能实现

alter their regulations, and the whole empire is contented. There is no difference between the new situation and that of a short time before. If a Yao continues after a Yao, what change can be said to have taken place? Given the situation in which there is no sage among his descendants, but there is one among the Three Dukes, then the empire will turn to him naturally as though he were restoring and reviving it. (With the whole empire contented, with there being no difference between the new and old situations, and with a Yao succeeding a Yao, again what change can be said to have taken place?) Only when there is the removal of a dynasty and the creation of new regulations are difficulties engendered. Thus, while the Son of Heaven lives, in thc whole world only one person is exalted. The height of obedience has led to order, and the assessment of moral worth has fixed the precedence of rank. When he dies, then there will certainly be someone who is able to carry the responsibility for the empire. Where the distinctions of ritual and moral principles have been systematically carried out, what need indeed would there be for abdication and relinquishing?

They say: "The Son of Heaven should abdicate because of old age and infirmity."

This too is not so. Although in terms of his blood humours and physical vigor, there may be decay, if one refers to his wisdom, his ability to think, or his power to choose or reject, then there is no decay.

They answer: "Because he is aged, he is not equal to the burdens of his high estate and should be given rest."

This as well is but the contention of one who is afraid of work. Although the position of the Son of Heaven is the most significant position of power, his body enjoys the most perfect leisure. His heart is filled with the purest pleasures, for his will is never thwarted; and his physical body

【原文】

无上矣。衣被，则服五采，杂间色，重文绣，加饰之以珠玉。食饮，则重大牢而备珍怪，期臭味，曼而馈，代睪而食，《雍》而彻乎五祀，执荐者百人侍西房。居，则设张容，负依而坐，诸侯趋走乎堂下。出户而巫觋有事，出门而宗祀有事，乘大路、趋越席以养安，侧载睪芷以养鼻，前有错衡以养目，和鸾之声步中《武》《象》、驺中《韶》《护》以养耳，三公奉轭持纳，诸侯持轮挟舆先马，大侯编后，大

【今译】

的，所以身体不会因为当了天子而劳累，而他的尊贵则是至高无上的了。穿着嘛，便是穿五色的上衣，再配上杂色的下衣，加上有花纹的刺绣，再用珠玉加以装饰。吃喝嘛，便是牛、羊、猪齐全的宴会一个连一个，珍贵奇异的佳肴样样具备，各种香气美味应有尽有，在音乐声中送上食物，在击鼓声中进餐，奏起《雍》曲而把宴席撤回到灶上祭祀灶神，端菜的人有上百个侍候在西厢房。呆在天子的位置上听政，就设置了帷帐和小屏风，背靠大屏风而坐，诸侯在堂下有礼貌地奔走前来朝见。要出宫门，巫觋就有事情了，要出王城大门，大宗伯、大祝就有事情了；坐上宽阔的大车，踩着柔软的蒲席来保持身体的安稳，旁边放置湖岸上生长的香草来调养鼻子，车前有画着交错花纹的横木来调养眼睛，车铃的声音在车子慢行时合乎《武》、《象》的节奏，在车子奔驰时合乎《韶》、《护》的节奏来调养耳朵，三公扶着车轭，握着缰绳，诸侯有的扶着车轮，有的护在车厢两侧，有的在马前引路，大国诸侯排列在车后，大夫跟在他们的后面，小国诸侯与

is not subjected to toiling labor since he has in honor no superior. The clothes and garments he wears are of the five basic colors with every gradation of shade in between. They are covered with repeated patterns and embroidered designs with ornaments of pearl and jade. His food and drink include abundant servings of the meat from sacrificial animals, replete with rare and exotic delicacies, and with the most refined aromas and tastes. With an array of dancers the food is presented, at the beating of the great drum the feast begins, to the strains of the *Yong* music, food for presentation in the Five Sacrifices is taken away, and a hundred attendants lay out the dishes for informal presentation in the Western Antechamber.

When he has to be present at court, curtains and protective screens are set up; when he takes his position standing with his back to the ornamented screen, feudal lords hasten with quickened steps to their positions at the lower end of the audience hall. When he goes out the inner door, shamanesses and shamans busy themselves. When he leaves the gate, the master of sacrifices and the invocators busy themselves. When he is to ride in the Great Chariot, they place rush mats to care for his comfort. On either side they place fragrant marsh angelica to nurture his sense of smell. In front there is the ornamented yoke shaft to nurture his sense of sight. There are the harmonious sounds of the tinkling bells on the horse's trappings; the chariot moves along in time with the *Martial* and *Imitation* music and [the horses] gallop in time with the *Succession* and *Guarding* music—all to nurture his sense of hearing. The Three Dukes hold the yoke bow in their hands and hold the inner reins of the outside horses. The feudal lords hold on to the wheel, steady the carriage body, and lead the horses along. The great marquises arrange themselves in rows behind, with the grand officers arrayed behind them. The lesser marquises and

【原文】

夫次之，小侯、元士次之，庶士介而夹道，庶人隐窜莫敢视望。居如大神，动如天帝，持老养衰，犹有善于是者与不？老者，休也，休犹有安乐恬愉如是者乎？故曰：诸侯有老，天子无老；有擅国，无擅天下。古今一也。

夫曰"尧、舜擅让"，是虚言也，是浅者之传，陋者之说也。不知逆顺之理，小大、至不至之变者也，未可与及天下之大理者也。

18.6 世俗之为说者曰："尧、舜不能教化。"是何也？曰："朱、象不化。"是不然也。

尧、舜，至天下之善教化者也，南面而听天下，生民之属莫不振动从服以化顺之。然而朱、象独不化，是非尧、舜之过，朱、象之罪也。尧、舜者，天下之英也；朱、象者，天下之嵬、一时之琐也。今世俗之为说者，不怪朱、象而非尧、舜，岂不过甚矣哉？夫是之谓嵬

【今译】

天子的高级文官再跟在大夫的后面，士兵们穿着铠甲而在道路两旁警卫，百姓们隐藏躲避而没有人敢观望。天子坐着像大神一样尊严，行动像天帝一样自如，扶持老年的生活，保养衰退的身体，还有比这更好的吗？老年人要休息，那休息还有像这样安定快乐宁静愉悦的吗？所以说：诸侯有告老退休的，天子没有告老退休的；有诸侯传让国家的，没有天子禅让天下的。这是古今都一样的。

所谓"尧、舜把王位禅让给别人"，这是不符合事实的假话，是知识肤浅者的传闻，是孤陋寡闻者的胡说。他们是一些不懂得是否违背世道人情的道理，不懂得国家与天下、至高无上与不至高无上之间的不同的人，是一些还不能和他们谈论天下的大道理的人啊。

18.6 社会上那些庸俗的创立学说的人说："尧、舜不能教育、感化人。"这种说法的根据是什么呢？他们说："因为丹朱、象都没有被感化。"这种说法不对。

尧、舜，是普天下最善于进行教育感化的人，他们朝南坐着治理天下，所有的民众无不惊恐颤动听从归服以至于被感化而依顺他们。然而惟独丹朱、象不能被感化，这不是尧、舜的过错，而是丹朱、象的罪过。尧、舜是天下的英杰，丹朱、象是天下的怪物、一代

the principal knights follow afterward. The ordinary knights decked out in armor protect both sides of the route. Commoners hide in secret places, for none dares witness the event. At rest, he is like one of the great spirits; in motion, he is like one of the heavenly ancestors.

Supported in old age and nurtured in infirmity, could anything be better than this? The aged require rest, and what rest has such peace and enjoyment, such tranquillity and pleasure as this? Therefore it is said: The feudal lords get old, but the Son of Heaven does not. That there have been cases of abdicating a state, but no case of abdicating the empire—in regard to this antiquity and today are one. To say that "Yao and Shun abdicated and yielded the throne" is to make a vacuous statement. It is the received tradition of shallow minds and the theory of rude provincials; it is a principle of the ignorant and those who rebel against obedience. It transmogrifies the small into the large, the perfect into the imperfect; it will never be possible with such a doctrine to reach up to the Great Principle of the world.

18. 6

A persuader's thesis common in the world today says: "Yao and Shun were incapable of teaching and transforming." How is this? They say: "[Dan] Zhu and Xiang were not transformed."

This is not so. Yao and Shun were the most expert in the whole world at teaching and transforming. When they faced south and adjudicated the affairs of the world, all living people were moved and stirred to follow and submit in order to be transformed and obey them. This being so, that Zhu and Xiang alone were not transformed is not the fault of Yao and Shun; rather, it is the crime of Zhu and Xiang. Yao and Shun were the heroes of the empire; Zhu and Xiang were perverse figures, the pettiest men of their

【原文】

说。羿、蜂门者，天下之善射者也，不能以拨弓曲矢中；王梁、造父者，天下之善驭者也，不能以辟马毁舆致远；尧、舜者，天下之善教化者也，不能使嵬琐化。何世而无嵬？何时而无琐？自太皞、燧人莫不有也。故作者不祥，学者受其殃，非者有庆。《诗》曰："下民之孽，匪降自天；噂沓背憎，职竞由人。"此之谓也。

18.7 世俗之为说者曰："太古薄葬，棺厚三寸，衣衾三领，葬田不妨田，故不掘也。乱今厚葬饰棺，故掘也。"是不及知治道而不

【今译】

庸人。现在社会上那些庸俗的创立学说的人，不责怪丹朱、象而非议尧、舜，岂不是错得很厉害了吗？这叫做奇谈怪论。羿、逢蒙，是天下善于射箭的人，但不能用别扭的弓和弯曲的箭去射中微小的目标；王良、造父，是天下善于驾驭马车的人，但不能依靠瘸腿的马和坏车子到达远方的目的地；尧、舜，是天下善于进行教育感化的人，但不能使怪僻鄙陋的人转化。哪个社会没有怪僻的人？哪个时代没有鄙陋的人？从太皞氏、燧人氏以来没有什么时代没有过。所以那些创立学说的人不善，学习的人就受到了他们的毒害，反对他们的人才值得庆幸。《诗》云："民众的灾难与不幸，并非从天来降临；当面唠叨背后恨，主要作祟在于人。"说的就是这种情况。

18.7 社会上那些庸俗的创立学说的人说："远古时代葬礼节俭，棺材板只有三寸厚，衣服只有三套，被子只有三条，埋在田底下而不妨碍种田，所以不会被挖掘。混乱的今天葬礼奢侈，用珍宝来装饰棺材，所以会被盗挖。"这是对治国的道理还没有达到通晓的程度而对

day. As the persuader's thesis common in the world today does not blame Zhu and Xiang, but rather condemns Yao and Shun, how could it not greatly transgress the truth! It is indeed truly to be called a perverse theory.

Though Yi and Pengmen were the best archers in the world, they could not hit the bull's-eye with a bent bow and crooked arrows. Although Wang Liang and Zaofu were the best charioteers in the world, they could not cover great distances with lame horses and a broken chariot. Although Yao and Shun were the best at instructing and transforming, they were unable to cause perverse and petty men to be transformed. What age has had no perverse men, and what time has had no petty fellows? From the time of Taihao and Suiren, all ages have had them. Accordingly, those who create such doctrines are harbingers of doom; those who study them meet with calamity; but those who condemn them will have their reward. An *Ode* expresses this point:

> The evils of the lower people,
> are not sent down from Heaven.
> They chatter and babble and backbite with hatred;
> such quarrels simply come from men themselves.

18. 7

A persuader's thesis common today claims:"In highest antiquity burials were meager with an inner coffin only three inches thick and only three thicknesses of grave cloth covering the corpse. Because burials did not impede cultivation of the land, they were not dug up. In the disorderly present, sumptuous burials with ornamented coffins are the cause of graves being violated."

This thesis does not attain to true knowledge of the Way of good

【原文】

察于扣不扣者之所言也。

凡人之盗也，必以有为，不以备不足，足则以重有余也。而圣王之生民也，皆使当厚优犹不知足，而不得以有余过度。故盗不窃，贼不刺，狗豕吐菽粟，而农贾皆能以货财让。风俗之美，男女自不取于涂，而百姓羞拾遗。故孔子曰："天下有道，盗其先变乎！"虽珠玉满体，文绣充棺，黄金充椁，加之以丹矸，重之以曾青，犀、象以为树，琅玕、龙兹、华觐以为实，人犹且莫之扣也。是何也？则求利之诡缓，而犯分之羞大也。

夫乱今然后反是。上以无法使，下以无度行，知者不得虑，能者不得治，贤者不得使。若是，则上失天性，下失地利，中失人和；故

【今译】

盗墓不盗墓的原因又不清楚的人所说的话。

大凡人们的盗窃，一定是有原因的，不是为了使自己不足的东西能齐备，就是为了使自己绰绰有余的东西进一步富余。而圣明的帝王养育民众，使他们都富足宽裕而懂得满足，不可以有多余的财物，不可以超过规定的标准。所以窃贼不会来偷窃，强盗不会杀人抢劫，狗猪会不吃粮食，而农夫商人都能把财物让给别人。风俗是那样的美好，男女自然不在路上相会，而百姓都以拾取别人遗失的东西为羞耻。所以孔子说："社会政治清明，盗贼大概会首先转变吧！"像这样，即使珍珠宝玉挂满了尸体，绣有彩色花纹的丝织品塞满了内棺，黄金塞满了外棺，用朱砂涂刷它，用曾青粉饰它，在墓穴中用犀牛角和象牙雕刻成树，用琅玕、龙兹、华觐做成树上的果实，人们仍就没有去盗挖它的。这是为什么呢？是因为人们求取私利的诡诈之心退隐了，而违犯道义的羞耻感增强了。

混乱的当今世道正与古代相反。君主不根据法度役使人民，臣民不根据法度办事，有才智的人不能去谋划国家大事，有能力的人不能去治理国家，有德行的人不能在位役使人。像这样，那么上面就会错

government. It is a proposition not based on inquiry into the reason men decide to violate graves.

As a general rule, men who take to robbing have some reason for their actions. If it is not to provide against shortages, then it is to ensure that they have a surplus. But since under the sage kings everyone was prosperous, was provided a generous living, and was content from knowing full sufficiency; none tried to obtain surpluses in excess of what was needed. Thus, robbers did not steal and thieves did not break in; dogs and pigs would turn up their noses at beans and millet; and both farmers and traders were able to give away some of their products and goods. So refined were customs and mores that "men and women would not congregate along the paths besides canals" and "the Hundred Clans were ashamed to pick up lost articles." Therefore Confucius said: When the world possesses the Way, robbers are the first to be changed.

[In these ancient times,] the body was covered with pearls and jades, the inner coffin was filled with beautifully ornamented embroideries, and the outer coffin was filled with yellow gold and decorated with cinnabar with added layers of laminar verdite. [In the outer tomb chamber were] rhinoceros and elephant ivory fashioned into trees, with precious rubies, magnetite lodestones, and flowering aconite for their fruit. Despite all this, men still did not violate them. Why is that? It is because the people found tricks in the pursuit of profits were ineffective and that the shame of offending against their proper social station was great.

It is only the chaotic present age that has turned against this example. Superiors, by acting without regard for the law, cause their subordinates to act without regard for prescribed rules. The wise have no opportunity to think through matters, the able none to achieve order, and the worthy none to obtain employment. Given this situation, then, we lose the natural

【原文】

百事废，财物诎，而祸乱起。王公则病不足于上，庶人则冻餧羸瘠于下。于是焉桀、纣群居，而盗贼击夺以危上矣。安禽兽行，虎狼贪，故脯巨人而炙婴儿矣。若是，则有何尤扣人之墓、抉人之口而求利矣哉？虽此裸而薶之，犹且必扣也，安得葬薶哉？彼乃将食其肉而龁其骨也。夫曰“太古薄葬，故不扣也；乱今厚葬，故扣也”，是特奸人之误于乱说，以欺愚者而潮陷之以偷取利焉，夫是之谓大奸。传曰：“危人而自安，害人而自利。”此之谓也。

18.8 子宋子曰：“明见侮之不辱，使人不斗。人皆以见侮为辱，

【今译】

失农时，下面就会丧失土地所产生的利益，中间就会失掉人民的同心合力。所以各种事情被废弃，财物紧缺，而祸乱也就产生了。天子诸侯在上面忧虑财物不足，老百姓则在下面受冻挨饿疲弱消瘦。于是桀、纣似的暴君成群地占据在各国的君位上，而盗贼也就打家劫舍以至于危害到他们的君主了。于是人们像禽兽一样横行，像虎狼一样贪婪，所以也就把大人做成肉干来吃而把婴儿做成烤肉来吃了。像这样，那么又为什么要指责盗掘死人的坟墓、挖死人的嘴巴来求取利益的行为呢？像这样，即使是赤身裸体来埋葬死人，也一定会被挖掘的，哪能埋葬呢？因为他们将会吃死人的肉而啃死人的骨头。所谓“远古时代葬礼节俭，所以不会被挖掘；混乱的今天葬礼奢侈，所以会被盗挖”，这只是奸邪的人被谬论所迷惑了，却又用它来欺骗愚蠢的人而坑害他们，以便从中苟且捞取好处，这叫做最大的奸邪。古书上说：“使别人危险以便使自己安全，使别人受害以便使自己得利。”说的就是这种人。

18.8 宋钘先生说：“明白了受到欺侮并不是耻辱的道理，就能使人们

endowments Heaven above has given us, we lose the benefits Earth below provides, and in the middle realm we lose harmonious relations in society. For this reason the hundred tasks are frustrated in their execution, wealth and resources dwindle, and calamity and confusion appear. Kings and dukes suffer from insufficiencies; commoners freeze and starve. It is in just such a situation that would-be Jies and would-be Zhou Xins throng together and robbers so openly plunder as to endanger the upper classes. How bestial is their conduct, and their avarice is like tigers and wolves! Thus, they will "make dried meat out of great men" and "roast infants on spits." When matters have come to this, why then should we still be surprised to find men violating graves and tearing open the mouth of the dead in search of profit! Even if a man had been buried stark naked, it would still be inevitable that his grave should be violated. How could he hope to have a peaceful burial! Those kind of men would eat his flesh and gnaw on his bones with their teeth.

The theory that "in highest antiquity burials were meager, which is why they were not violated" and that "in the present burials are sumptuous, which is why they are violated" is just the deception of wicked men. It is a theory born of confusion, which hoodwinks the stupid so that they will sink into the mire of thievery to secure illicit profits. This is what is called the "Great Wickedness." A tradition records:

> They imperil others to make secure themselves; they harm others to profit themselves.

This expresses my meaning.

18. 8

Your Master Song said: "Clearly understanding that to suffer insult is

【原文】

故斗也；知见侮之为不辱，则不斗矣。”

应之曰：“然则亦以人之情为不恶侮乎？”

曰：“恶而不辱也。”

曰：“若是，则必不得所求焉。凡人之斗也，必以其恶之为说，非以其辱之为故也。今俳优、侏儒、狎徒詈侮而不斗者，是岂钜知见侮之为不辱哉？然而不斗者，不恶故也。今人或入其央渎，窃其猪彘，则援剑戟而逐之，不避死伤，是岂以丧猪为辱也哉？然而不惮斗者，恶之故也。虽以见侮为辱也，不恶则不斗；虽知见侮为不辱，恶之则必斗。然则斗与不斗邪，亡于辱之与不辱也，乃在于恶之与不恶也。夫今子宋子不能解人之恶侮，而务说人以勿辱也，岂不过甚矣哉？金

【今译】

不争斗。人们都把被侮辱当作为耻辱，所以会争斗；如果懂得了被侮辱算不上是一种耻辱，就不会争斗了。”

回复他说：“这样的话，那么先生也以为人之常情是不憎恶被人侮辱的吗？”

他说：“虽然憎恶被人侮辱，但并不把被侮辱当作是耻辱。”

回复他说：“像这样，那就一定达不到先生所追求的目标了。大凡人们的争斗，一定是把自己憎恶受侮辱当作辩解，而不是把自己感到耻辱作为理由。现在那些滑稽演员和唱戏的优伶、供人取乐的矮子、被人戏弄的奴仆，受到辱骂欺侮却不争斗，这哪里是因为他们懂得了被人侮辱算不上是一种耻辱的道理呢？然而他们不争斗，是因为他们不憎恶被人侮辱的缘故啊。现在如果有人进入人家的沟中，偷了人家的猪，那么失主就会拿起剑戟去追赶窃贼，甚至不避死伤，这哪里是因为他把丢失猪看作为耻辱呢？然而他不怕争斗，是因为憎恶窃贼啊。所以，即使把被侮辱看作为一种耻辱，但如果不憎恶它，就不会争斗；即使懂得了被侮辱算不上是一种耻辱的道理，但如果憎恶它，就一定会争斗。这样看来，争斗不争斗，不在于感到耻辱还是不感到耻辱，而在于憎恶还是不憎恶。现在宋先生不能消除人们对被人侮辱

no disgrace will cause men to cease fighting. All men consider that to suffer insult is to be disgraced, hence they fight. If they knew that to suffer insult does not disgrace a person, then they would not fight."

I reply to this: If that were so, then would a person not also have to consider the essential nature of man such that he does not hate being insulted?

They rejoin: "You may hate insults, but you should not consider them a disgrace."

I say: If that is granted, then it is certain that your search [for a way to make men stop fighting] will be in vain. As a general principle, the explanation of why men fight must be found in what they hate; the cause is not to be found in what they consider to be a disgrace. Consider the case of court jesters, buffoons, dwarfs, and fools who are treated contemptuously, like a menial, and are vilified and insulted, yet do not fight—would this be due to their realization that it is no disgrace to suffer insult? Those who do not fight in such cases do so because they do not hate being insulted.

Now consider this example: a man enters a place by way of the sewers and pilfers another man's pigs and hogs. The owner takes up arms to pursue him at the risk of serious injury or death. Would this happen because he considers the loss of his pigs to be a disgrace! Men do not shrink from a fight in such cases because of what they hate. Although a man might consider receiving an insult a disgrace, if he does not hate being disgraced, then he will not fight. Although a man knows that to suffer insult is no disgrace, if he hates the disgrace, then he will surely fight. That being the case, then the reason he fights lies not in whether he is disgraced, but rather in whether he hates it.

Now your Master Song is unable to explain the fact of men's hatred of insult and so he devotes his attention to persuading men that they

【原文】

舌弊口，犹将无益也。不知其无益，则不知；知其无益也，直以欺人，则不仁。不仁不知。辱莫大焉。将以为有益于人耶？则与无益于人也，则得大辱而退耳！说莫病是矣。”

18.9 子宋子曰：“见侮不辱。”

应之曰：“凡议，必将立隆正然后可也，无隆正，则是非不分而辨讼不决。故所闻曰：‘天下之大隆，是非之封界，分职名象之所起，王制是也。’故凡言议期命，是非以圣王为师；而圣王之分，荣辱是也。是有两端矣，有义荣者，有势荣者，有义辱者，有势辱者。志意修，

【今译】

的憎恶，而致力于劝说人们别把受侮辱看作为耻辱，岂不是错得很厉害了吗？即使是能言善辩的铁嘴巴把嘴皮都磨破了，仍将毫无裨益。不懂得这种劝说毫无裨益，那就是不明智；知道它毫无裨益，却故意要用它来骗人，那就是不仁慈。不仁慈不明智，耻辱没有比这更大的了。要认为宋先生的说法有益于人吗？但全都无益于人，只落得个极大的耻辱而退场罢了！学说没有比这更糟的了。”

18.9 宋钘先生说：“被侮辱而不以为耻辱。”

回复他说：“凡是议论，一定要树立一个最高的准则才行，没有一个最高准则，那么是非就不能区分而争辩也无法解决。我过去听到的话说：‘天下最大最高的准则，判断是非的界线，分掌职务、名物制度的起源，就是古代圣王的制度。’所以，凡是发言立论或约定事物的名称，它们的是非标准都要以圣王作为榜样；而圣王的道德原则，是看重光荣耻辱的。这光荣耻辱各有两个方面，有道义方面的光荣，有

should not consider it a disgrace—is he not utterly wrong! Although he had a metal tongue that destroyed his mouth, it would be to no advantage. Not realizing that it is of no advantage is ignorance; and, to know that it is of no advantage and yet simply to deceive others is not humane. No behavior is more disgraceful than to be both inhumane and ignorant. If what he takes to be of advantage to others is no advantage, he will be forced to withdraw in great disgrace. No theory could be more defective than this!

18. 9

Your Master Song says:"To suffer insult is no disgrace."

I reply to this: As a matter of general principle, in deliberations it is necessary to establish high standards of correctness, for only then may the validity of an argument be determined. If there are no such high standards of correctness, then truth and falsity cannot be separated and discriminations and disputes cannot be settled. Thus, what we have been taught says:

> The highest standards are those that establish the boundary between truth and falsity and that give rise to social class distinctions, to the offices of government, and to their names and symbols—these are the regulations of the True King.

Thus, as a general rule discussions and deliberations on definitions and terms of right and wrong should take the sages and kings as guide and master. And among the distinctions made by the sages and kings is the distinction between honor and disgrace.

In these there are two principles: there is the honor that derives from moral principles and that which derives from the force of circumstances;

【原文】

德行厚，知虑明，是荣之由中出者也，夫是之谓义荣。爵列尊，贡禄厚，形势胜，上为天子诸侯，下为卿相士大夫，是荣之从外至者也，夫是之谓势荣。流淫污僈，犯分乱理，骄暴贪利，是辱之由中出者也，夫是之谓义辱。詈侮捽搏，捶笞膑脚，斩断枯磔，藉靡舌绁，是辱之由外至者也，夫是之谓势辱。是荣辱之两端也。故君子可以有势辱而不可以有义辱，小人可以有势荣而不可以有义荣。

【今译】

势位方面的光荣，有道义方面的耻辱，有势位方面的耻辱。志向美好，德行淳厚，智虑精明，这是从内心产生出来的光荣，这叫做道义方面的光荣。爵位尊贵，贡品俸禄优厚，权势地位优越，高一点的做了天子诸侯，低一点的做了卿相士大夫，这是从外部得到的光荣，这叫做势位方面的光荣。行为放荡丑恶，违犯道义，扰乱伦理，骄横凶暴，惟利是图，这是从内心产生出来的耻辱，这叫做道义方面的耻辱。受人责骂侮辱，被揪住头发挨打，受杖刑被鞭打，受膑刑被剔去膝盖骨，被砍头断手、五马分尸并弃市，被五花大绑，被反绑吊起，这是从外部得到的耻辱，这叫做势位方面的耻辱。这些就是光荣耻辱的两个方面。所以君子可能有势位方面的耻辱而不可能有道义方面的耻辱，小人可能有势位方面的光荣却不可能有道义方面的光荣。有势

there is the disgrace that derives from considerations of morality and that which derives from the force of circumstances. When a person is developed in will and purpose, substantial in conduct springing from inner power, and lucid in wisdom and thought,then there arises from within the cause of honor, and this is what is meant by honor that derives from considerations of morality.

Holding exalted rank and distinction, receiving substantial tribute or emolument, holding a position of overwhelming power and influence, being at the highest Son of Heaven or a feudal lord or at the lowest a minister or prime minister, knight or grand officer—these are honors that arrive from without, and precisely these are what is meant by honors that derive from a person's circumstances.

When a person is wayward and abandoned, base and reckless, when he offends against the divisions of society and brings chaos to rational order, when he is proudly arrogant and cruel with a rapacious appetite for profits—these are disgraces that come from within, and precisely these are what is meant by disgraces that derive from a person's morality.

Vilified and insulted, dragged about by the hair and beaten, whipped and cudgeled, kneecaps shattered or legs amputated, decapitated, quartered or hacked apart and made into diced dried meat, chained and fettered, with tongue split in two—these are disgraces that come from without, and precisely these are what is meant by disgraces that derive from a person's circumstances. Such are the two principles of honor and disgrace.

Thus, although it is possible that the gentleman should incur disgrace through personal circumstances, it is not possible that he should incur disgrace from what derives from personal morality. Although it is possible that the petty man should possess honors deriving from personal

【原文】

有势辱无害为尧，有势荣无害为桀。义荣、势荣，唯君子然后兼有之；义辱、势辱，唯小人然后兼有之。是荣辱之分也。圣王以为法，士大夫以为道，官人以为守，百姓以成俗，万世不能易也。

"今子宋子案不然，独诎容为己，虑一朝而改之，说必不行矣。譬之，是犹以抟涂塞江海也，以焦侥而戴太山也，蹎跌碎折不待顷矣。二三子之善于子宋子者，殆不若止之，将恐得伤其体也。"

18.10 子宋子曰："人之情，欲寡，而皆以己之情为欲多，是过

【今译】

位方面的耻辱不妨碍他成为尧，有势位方面的光荣不妨碍他成为桀。道义方面的光荣、势位方面的光荣，只有君子才能同时拥有它们；道义方面的耻辱、势位方面的耻辱，只有小人才会同时占有它们。这就是光荣和耻辱方面的道理。圣王把它当作法度，士大夫把它当作原则，一般官吏把它当作守则，老百姓根据它形成习俗，这是千秋万代也不会改变的。

"现在宋先生却不是这样，他独自用委曲容忍来整饬自己，想一个早晨改变历来的道德原则，他的学说一定行不通。拿它打个比方，这就好像是用捏成团的泥巴去填塞江海，让三尺长的矮人去驮泰山，跌倒在地粉身碎骨也就用不着等待片刻了。诸位中与宋先生相好的，恐怕还不如去制止他，否则，将来恐怕会伤害自己身体的。"

18.10 宋钘先生说："人的本性是少欲的。但现在的人却都认为

circumstances, it is not possible that he should possess honors deriving from moral principles. Incurring disgrace through the force of circumstances will not hinder one's becoming a Yao; having the honors that derive from the force of circumstances will not hinder one's becoming a Jie. As for the honor that derives from personal morality and that which derives from circumstances, only the gentleman may possess both at the same time. As for the disgrace that derives from morality and that which derives from circumstances, only the petty man may possess both at the same time. Such is the distinction between honor and disgrace. Sages and kings used this distinction in their laws, the knights and grand officers used it as their way, the various petty bureaucrats considered that they should safeguard it, and the Hundred Clans viewed it as established custom. For a myriad generations it has been impossible to alter the distinction.

Now your Master Song believes that this is not so, for he distorts things and admits facts on his own and as he chooses. With no more than a single morning's thought he would change the nature of the distinction between honor and disgrace. It is certain that his theories could never be put into practice. They are an example of using balls of mud to dam up rivers and oceans. They are like using the Jiao pygmies to lift up Mount Tai; one need only wait a moment and they will stumble and let it break in two. The two or three masters who take delight in the doctrines of your Master Song stand the risk, I fear, of suffering grave injury to their own persons if they do not cease this admiration.

18. 10

Your Master Song says:"It is the essential nature of man that his

【原文】

也。”故率其群徒，辨其谈说，明其譬称，将使人知情欲之寡也。

应之曰：“然则亦以人之情为欲目不欲綦色，耳不欲綦声，口不欲綦味，鼻不欲綦臭，形不欲綦佚？此五綦者，亦以人之情为不欲乎？”

曰：“人之情，欲是已。”

曰：“若是，则说必不行矣。以人之情为欲此五綦者而不欲多，譬之，是犹以人之情为欲富贵而不欲货也，好美而恶西施也。

“古之人为之不然。以人之情为欲多而不欲寡，故赏以富厚，而罚以杀损也，是百王之所同也。故上贤禄天下，次贤禄一国，下贤禄

【今译】

自己的本性是多欲的，这是错误的。”所以他率领他的弟子们，把他的言论学说说得动听有理，把他的比喻称引说得明白清楚，想要使人们懂得人的本性是少欲的。

回复他说：“这样的话，那么先生也认为人的本性是眼睛不想看最美丽的颜色，耳朵不想听最悦耳的音乐，嘴巴不想吃最好的美味佳肴，鼻子不想闻最好的气味，身体不想追求最大的安逸？这五种极好的享受，先生也认为人们的本性是不想要的吗？”

他说：“人的本性，是想要这些享受的。”

回复他说：“如果这样，那么先生的说法就一定行不通了。认为人的本性是想要这五种极好的享受而又并不想要很多，拿它打个比方，这就好像认为人的本性是想富贵的但又不要钱财，是喜爱美色的但又讨厌西施一样。

“古代的人做事就不是这样。他们认为人的本性是想要多而不希望少，所以用财富来奖赏，用减少财富来处罚，这是各代帝王所相同的。所以上等的贤才以天下的税收作为俸禄，次一等的贤才以一国的

desires are few, yet everyone believes in his own case that the desires of his essential nature are numerous. This is an error." Accordingly, he leads his numerous disciples, offers discriminations in defense of his contentions and theories, and elucidates his examples and judgments that he might cause men to realize that the desires inherent in their essential nature are but few.

In response to this I say: Given that assumption, then one must also consider that it is the essential nature of man that the eye does not desire the full range of colors, the ear does not desire the full range of sounds, the mouth does not desire the full range of tastes, the nose does not desire the full range of smells, and the body does not desire the full range of leisure. In regard to these five "full sensory ranges" can it indeed be also considered that the essential nature of man is such that they are not desired?

Master Song admits: The desires inherent in the essential nature of man are in truth as you say.

I say: If you grant that they are such, then your theory is certainly impractical. It grants that the desires inherent in the essential nature of men have these five "full sensory ranges," yet it denies that such desires are numerous. This is like, for example, considering it a part of man's essential nature to desire wealth and prestige, yet denying that men desire property, or considering that they desire sex and beauty, yet despise Xi Shi.

The ancients thought otherwise:they considered that from his essential nature man's desires were numerous, not few. Accordingly, they rewarded men with wealth and plenty and penalized them with reduction and deprivation. In this respect the Hundred Kings have all been the same. Accordingly, the supremely worthy man received the world as his

【原文】

田邑，愿悫之民完衣食。今子宋子以是之情为欲寡而不欲多也，然则先王以人之所不欲者赏而以人之所欲者罚邪？乱莫大焉。今子宋子严然而好说，聚人徒，立师学，成文曲，然而说不免于以至治为至乱也，岂不过甚矣哉？”

【今译】

税收作为俸禄，下等的贤才以封地内的税收作为俸禄，忠厚老实的百姓能保全穿的吃的。现在如果宋先生认为古代这些人的本性也是想要少而不想要多，那么古代的圣王是用人们所不想要的东西来奖赏而用人们想要的东西来处罚吗？混乱没有比这更大的了。现在宋先生一本正经地珍爱自己的学说，聚集门徒，建立了师生教学关系，写成了文章，但是他的学说不免把治理得最好的情况看成是最混乱的情况，岂不是错得很厉害了吗？”

emolument, those next in worth received a single state, those of lesser worth received fields and cities, and the attentive and diligent among the common people had the full complement of clothing and food. Now your Master Song considers man's essential nature to be that desires are few and not that they are numerous. If this were so, then would it not be equivalent to the ancient kings' employing what men do not desire as their reward and what men do desire as their punishment? No confusion could be greater than this!

Now your Master Song has a commanding presence and is fond of persuasions. He gathers men about him as disciples, he establishes himself as a master of learning, and he perfects, polishes, and documents his essays. Yet, despite all this, his theories do not avoid the mistake of considering the perfection of order the height of chaos. Indeed, does he not greatly transgress the truth!

礼论第十九

【原文】

19.1 礼起于何也？曰：人生而有欲，欲而不得，则不能无求；求而无度量分界，则不能不争；争则乱，乱则穷。先王恶其乱也，故制礼义以分之，以养人之欲，给人之求，使欲必不穷乎物，物必不屈于欲，两者相持而长。是礼之所起也。

19.2 故礼者，养也。刍豢稻粱，五味调香，所以养口也；椒兰芬苾，所以养鼻也；雕琢刻镂，黼黻文章，所以养目也；钟鼓、管

【今译】

19.1 礼是在什么情况下产生的呢？回答说：人生来就有欲望，如果想要什么而不能得到，就不能没有追求；如果一味追求而没有个标准限度，就不能不发生争夺；一发生争夺就会有祸乱，一有祸乱就会陷入困境。古代的圣王厌恶那祸乱，所以制定了礼义来确定人们的名分，以此来调节人们的欲望，满足人们的要求，使人们的欲望决不会由于物资的原因而不得满足，物资决不会因为人们的欲望而枯竭，使物资和欲望两者在互相制约中增长。这就是礼的起源。

19.2 所以礼这种东西，是调养人们欲望的。牛羊猪狗等肉食和稻米谷子等细粮，五味调和的佳肴，是用来调养嘴巴的；椒树、兰草香气芬芳，是用来调养鼻子的；在器具上雕图案，在礼服上绘彩色花

Book 19

Discourse on Ritual Principles

19.1

How did ritual principles arise? I say that men are born with desires which, if not satisfied, cannot but lead men to seek to satisfy them. If in seeking to satisfy their desires men observe no measure and apportion things without limits, then it would be impossible for them not to contend over the means to satisfy their desires. Such contention leads to disorder. Disorder leads to poverty. The Ancient Kings abhorred such disorder; so they established the regulations contained within ritual and moral principles in order to apportion things, to nurture the desires of men, and to supply the means for their satisfaction. They so fashioned their regulations that desires should not want for the things which satisfy them and goods would not be exhausted by the desires. In this way the two of them, desires and goods, sustained each other over the course of time. This is the origin of ritual principles.

19. 2

Thus, the meaning of ritual is to nurture.

The meat of pastured and grain-fed animals, rice and millet, blends and combinations of the five flavors, are what nurture the mouth. The fragrances of peppercorns and orchids, aromas and bouquets, are what nurture the nose. Carved and polished [jade], incised and inlaid [metals], and [fabrics] embroidered with the white and black axe emblem, the

【原文】

磬、琴瑟、竽笙，所以养耳也；疏房、檖貌、越席、床笫、几筵，所以养体也。故礼者，养也。

19.3 君子既得其养，又好其别。曷谓别？曰：贵贱有等，长幼有差，贫富轻重皆有称者也。故天子大路越席，所以养体也；侧载睪芷，所以养鼻也；前有错衡，所以养目也；和鸾之声，步中《武》、《象》，趋中《韶》、《护》，所以养耳也；龙旗九斿，所以养信也；寝兕、持虎、蛟韅、丝末、弥龙，所以养威也；故大路之马，必信至教

【今译】

纹，是用来调养眼睛的；钟、鼓、管、磬、琴、瑟、竽、笙等乐器，是用来调养耳朵的；窗户通明的房间、深邃的朝堂、柔软的蒲席、床上的竹铺、矮桌与垫席，是用来调养躯体的。所以礼这种东西，是调养人们欲望的。

19.3 君子已经得到了礼的调养，又喜爱礼的区别。什么叫做区别？回答说：就是高贵的和卑贱的有不同的等级，年长的和年幼的有一定的差别，贫穷的和富裕的、权轻势微的和权重势大的都各有相宜的规定。所以天子乘坐那宽阔的大车，铺垫那柔软的蒲席，是用来保养身体的；旁边放置湖岸上生长的香草，是用来调养鼻子的；车前有画着交错花纹的横木，是用来调养眼睛的；车铃的声音，在车子慢行时合乎《武》、《象》的节奏，在车子奔驰时合乎《韶》、《护》的节奏，这是用来调养耳朵的；画着龙的旗帜下边有九条飘带，是用来保养身份信号的；车子上画着横卧的犀牛和蹲着的老虎，马系着用沙鱼皮制成的腹带，车前挂着丝织的车帘，车耳刻成龙形，这是用来保养威严的；天子的大车上所用的马，一定要真正训练得十分驯服，然后

azure and black notched-stripe, the azure and crimson stripe, the white and crimson blazon, are what nurture the eye. Bells and drums, flutes and chime-stone, lutes and zithers, reed pipes and reed organs, are what nurture the ear. Spacious rooms, secluded chambers, mats of plaited rushes, couches and bed mats, armrests and cushions, are what nurture the body.

Thus, rituals are what nurtures.

19. 3

When the gentleman has been nurtured by these things, he will also be fond of ritual distinctions. What is meant by "distinctions"? I say that these refer to the gradations of rank according to nobility or baseness, disparities between the privileges of old and young, and modes of identification to match these with poverty or wealth, insignificance or importance. Thus, the Son of Heaven has the Great Chariot and rush mats to care for his comfort. On either side of the chariot fragrant marsh angelica is placed to care for his sense of smell. In front of him there is the inlaid yoke shaft to nurture his sense of sight. There are the harmonious sounds of the tinkling bells on the horse's trappings; the chariot moves along in time with the *Martial* and *Imitation* music; and the horses gallop in time with the *Succession* and *Guarding* music—all in order to nurture his sense of hearing.

There is the dragon banner with nine scallops to nurture a sense of sacredness about him. There are the recumbent rhinoceros, the crouching tiger, back harnesses with scaly dragon patterns, the silken carriage coverings, and yoke-ends with dragons to nurture his majestic authority.

Thus, the horse for the Grand Chariot must be thoroughly reliable and perfectly trained before it is harnessed, to nurture a sense of security

【原文】

顺，然后乘之，所以养安也。孰知夫出死要节之所以养生也？孰知夫出费用之所以养财也？孰知夫恭敬辞让之所以养安也？孰知夫礼义文理之所以养情也？故人苟生之为见，若者必死；苟利之为见，若者必害；苟怠惰偷懦之为安，若者必危；苟情说之为乐，若者必灭。故人一之于礼义，则两得之矣；一之于情性，则两丧之矣。故儒者将使人两得之者也，墨者将使人两丧之者也，是儒、墨之分也。

19.4 礼有三本：天地者，生之本也；先祖者，类之本也；君师者，治之本也。无天地，恶生？无先祖，恶出？无君师，恶治？三者偏亡，焉无安人。故礼，上事天，下事地，尊先祖而隆君师。是礼之三本也。

【今译】

才用它拉车，这是用来保持安全的。谁懂得那献出生命坚守节操是用来保养生命的呢？谁懂得那花费钱财是用来保养钱财的呢？谁懂得那恭敬谦让是用来保住安逸的呢？谁懂得那礼义仪式是用来调养情操的呢？所以人如果只看见生，这样的人就一定会死；如果只看见利，这样的人就一定会受到损害；如果只是喜欢懈怠懒惰苟且偷安，这样的人就一定会遇到危难；如果只是喜欢纵情作乐，这样的人就一定会灭亡。所以人如果专门把心思放在讲究礼义上，那么礼义情性两方面就都能保全了；如果专门把心思放在满足情性上，那么礼义性情两方面就都保不住了。儒家要使人们双双保全它们，墨家要使人们双双丧失它们，这就是儒家和墨家的区别。

19.4 礼有三个根本：天地是生存的根本，祖先是种族的根本，君长是政治的根本。没有天地，怎么生存？没有祖先，种族从哪里产生？没有君长，怎么能使天下太平？这三样即使部分地缺失了，也不会有安宁的人民。所以礼，上事奉天，下事奉地，尊重祖先而推崇君长。这是礼的三个根本。

about him.

Who understands that risking death in carrying out a commission is how an officer cares for his life? Who understands that producing and supplying goods are how to nurture resources? Who knows that reverence and courtesy are how to nurture his security? Who knows that acting in accordance with ritual and moral principles and observing good form and reason are how to nurture his emotions?

Accordingly, if one acts with only the preservation of his own life in view, death is inevitable. If one acts with only profit in mind, loss is certain. If one is indolent and timorous, thinking thereby he will be safe, danger is certain. If he seeks happiness through self-gratification, destruction is certain. Thus, if a man concentrates single-mindedly on ritual and moral principles, then both his desires and ritual will be fulfilled; but if he concentrates solely on his inborn desires and emotions, then both will be lost. Hence, Ru practices will cause a man to fulfill both ritual and desires, whereas Mohist practices will cause him to lose both. Such is the distinction between the Ru and the Mohists.

19. 4

Ritual principles have three roots. Heaven and Earth are the root of life. Forebears are the root of kinship. Lords and teachers are the root of order. Were there no Heaven and no Earth, how could there be life? Were there no forebears, how could there be issue? Were there no lords and no teachers, how could there be order? Were even one of these three lost, there would be no peace and security for man. Thus, rituals serve Heaven above and Earth below, pay honor to one's forebears, and exalt rulers and teachers, for these are the three roots of ritual principles.

【原文】

19.5 故王者天太祖，诸侯不敢怀，大夫、士有常宗，所以别贵始。贵始，得之本也。郊止乎天子，而社止于诸侯，道及士、大夫，所以别尊者事尊、卑者事卑、宜大者巨、宜小者小也。故有天下者事七世，有一国者事五世，有五乘之地者事三世，有三乘之地者事二世，持手而食者不得立宗庙，所以别积厚者流泽广，积薄者流泽狭也。

19.6 大飨，尚玄尊，俎生鱼，先大羹，贵食饮之本也。飨，尚

【今译】

19.5 所以，称王天下的天子可以把创建国家的始祖当作天来祭祀，诸侯则不敢有这个想法，大夫和士有百世不迁的大宗，这种宗法祭祀制度是用来区别各自所尊奉的始祖的。尊重始祖，是道德的根本。到郊外祭天神仅限于天子，而祭土地神则从天子开始到诸侯为止，祭路神则向下延及到士和大夫，这是用来区别：尊贵的人才能事奉尊贵的，卑贱的人只能事奉卑贱的；适宜做大事的就做大事，适宜做小事的就做小事。所以拥有天下的天子祭祀七代祖先，拥有一个国家的诸侯祭祀五代祖先，拥有五个六里见方的土地的大夫祭祀三代祖先，有三个六里见方的土地的士可以祭祀两代祖先，依靠双手来糊口的百姓不准建立祖庙，这是用来区别：功绩大的人传布的恩德应该广远，功绩小的人传布的恩德应该狭窄。

19.6 在太庙合祭历代祖先时，以盛着清水的酒器以及小盘里盛着

19. 5

Accordingly, the king associates his Founding Patriarch with Heaven in his sacrifices. The feudal lords do not allow [the temple of their first ancestor] to go to ruin. Grand officers and knights have sacrifices to the Constant Progenitor. These are the ways they distinguish their eminent beginnings. These eminent beginnings are the root of their moral authority. Performance of sacrifice at the Suburban Altar stops with the Son of Heaven. Performance of sacrifice at the Altar of the Soil stops with the feudal lords. But the sacrifice at the end of mourning extends even to the knights and grand officers. These serve to distinguish between the noble who should serve the noble and the base who should serve the base, between the greatness of those who should be great and the smallness of those who should be small.

Hence, the ruler of the empire serves seven generations in his sacrifices; the ruler of a single state serves five generations; one who has territory to furnish five chariots serves three generations; and one who has territory to furnish three chariots serves two generations. Those who eat by the labor of their hands are not permitted to establish a temple to their progenitor. These practices serve to distinguish between substantial accomplishment that yields abundant beneficial influences and slight accomplishment from which flow but meager beneficial results.

19. 6

At the Grand Xiang sacrifice, the *zun* goblet holding the dark liquid is offered up, raw fish is placed on the *zu* offering table, and the grand

【原文】

玄尊而用酒醴，先黍稷而饭稻粱。祭，齐大羹而饱庶羞，贵本而亲用也。贵本之谓文，亲用之谓理，两者合而成文，以归大一，夫是之谓大隆。故尊之尚玄酒也，俎之尚生鱼也，豆之先大羹也，一也。利爵之不醮也，成事之俎不尝也，三侑之不食也，一也。大昏之未发齐也，太庙之未入尸也，始卒之未小敛也，一也。大路之素幭也，郊之麻绕也，丧服之先散麻也，一也。三年之丧，哭之不反也，《清庙》

【今译】

的生鱼为上等祭品，首先献上不加调味品的肉汁，这是为了尊重饮食的本源。四季祭祀远祖时，以盛着清水的酒器为上等祭品，酌献甜酒，首先献上黍、稷，再陈供稻粱；每月祭祀近祖时，先进献未加调味品的肉汁，再盛陈各种美味的食物。这些都是为了尊重饮食的本源而又接近实际的食用。尊重饮食的本源叫做形式上的修饰，接近实际的食用叫做内容上的合理，这两者结合起来就形成了礼仪制度，然而又使它趋向于远古的质朴状态，这才叫做对礼的最大尊崇。所以酒杯中以替代酒的清水为上等祭品，小盘中以生的鱼为上等祭品，豆中先盛不加调味品的肉汁，这三种做法与远古的质朴是一致的。代替死者受祭的人不把佐食的人所献的酒喝光，祭礼完毕时小盘中的祭品留下不吃，劝受祭者饮食的三次劝食而不食，这三种做法与远古的质朴是一致的。婚礼中还没有进行喝交杯酒的时候，祭祀太庙而尚未使代表死者受祭的人进庙的时候，人刚死还没有换上寿衣的时候，这三种情况与远古的质朴是一致的。天子祭天的大车用未染色的丝绸做车帘，在郊外祭天时头戴麻布制的礼帽，居丧时先散乱地系上麻带，这三种车服与远古的质朴是一致的。三年期的服丧，痛哭时放声直号而没有曲折的声调；《清庙》的颂歌，一人领唱而三个人随声咏叹；乐器只挂

broth is served first to honor the root of food and drink. At the Xiang sacrifice, the *zun* goblet holding the dark liquid is offered first, and then distilled and sweet spirits are served as well. At the sacrificial feast panicum and setaria millet are served first, and then rice and sorghum are offered as well. At the regular sacrifice, the host raises the grand broth to his lips, and then ample viands are offered. Each of these practices pays honor to the root but also employs familiar foods."Honoring the root" is called "good form";"employing familiar foods" is called "rational order." When the two of them are conjoined with perfected good form, everything is restored to the conditions of Primordial Unity; this is what should be called the "Grand Exaltation."

The *zun* goblet being used to offer up the dark liquid, the *zu* offering table being used to offer the raw fish, and the wooden *dou* vase being used to offer the grand broth first— all entail one and the same principle. [The impersonator] not consuming the goblet of wine offered by the chief steward; his not tasting the offerings on the *zu* table at the completion of the affair; and his not eating after thrice being served—all these practices involve one and the same principle. Before the purification ceremony in the great marriage rite, before the impersonator of the dead has entered in the great rite in the ancestral temple, and before the lesser dressing has begun in the first moments after death—these all are one and the same kind of moment. The plain silk covering of the Great Chariot, the hempen cap worn in the sacrifice at the Suburban Altar, and the hempen sash worn loose at the beginning of the mourning ceremony—all these are one and the same type of ritual usage. In mourning until the third year, the wailing is formless, and in the performances of the *Pure Temple Ode*, one singer intones and the other three hum in harmony, with only one bell hung and the addition of the leathern chaff-drum, the *ge* sounding box,

【原文】

之歌，一倡而三叹也，县一钟，尚拊之膈，朱弦而通越也，一也。

19.7 凡礼；始乎棁，成乎文，终乎悦校。故至备，情文俱尽；其次，情文代胜；其下，复情以归大一也。天地以合，日月以明；四时以序，星辰以行；江河以流，万物以昌；好恶以节，喜怒以当；以为下则顺，以为上则明；万物变而不乱，贰之则丧也。礼岂不至矣哉！立隆以为极，而天下莫之能损益也。本末相顺，终始相应；至文以有别，至察以有说。天下从之者治，不从者乱；从之者安，不从者

【今译】

一口钟，而崇尚使用拊搏与鞷，把琴弦染成红色而打通瑟底的孔。这三种做法是和远古的质朴一致的。

19.7 大凡礼，总是从简略开始，到有了礼节仪式就形成了，最后又达到使人称心如意的程度。所以最完备的礼，所要表达的感情和礼节仪式都发挥得淋漓尽致；比它次一等的，是所要表达的感情和礼节仪式互有参差；那最下等的，就是使所要表达的感情回到原始状态，从而趋向于远古的质朴。但无论如何，天地因为礼的作用而风调雨顺，日月因为礼的作用而光辉明亮；四季因为礼的作用而井然有序，星辰因为礼的作用而正常运行；江河因为礼的作用而奔流入海，万物因为礼的作用而繁荣昌盛；爱憎因为礼的作用而有所节制，喜怒因为礼的作用而恰如其分；用它来治理臣民就可使臣民服从依顺，用它来规范君主就可使君主通达英明；万事万物千变万化而不混乱，但如果背离了礼就会丧失一切。礼难道不是登峰造极了吗？圣人确立了发展到高度成熟的礼制而把它作为最高的准则，因而天下没有谁再能增减改变它。这种礼制的根本原则和具体细节之间互不抵触，人生终结的仪式与人生开始的仪式互相应合。它极其完美而有明确的等级区别，极其明察而有详尽的理论说明。天下遵循礼的国家治理得好，不

and the zither with red, dressed strings and penetrating sound holes—these are all one and the same.

19. 7

All rites begin with coarseness, are brought to fulfillment with form, and end with pleasure and beauty. Rites reach their highest perfection when both emotion and form are fully realized. In rites of the next order, emotions and form in turn prevail. In the lowest order of rites, all reverts to emotion through returning to the conditions of Primordial Unity.

Through rites, Heaven and Earth are conjoined,
the sun and moon shine brightly,
the four seasons observe their natural precedence,
the stars and planets move in ranks,
the rivers and streams flow,
and the myriad things prosper.
Through them, love and hate are tempered,
and joy and anger made to fit the occasion.

They are used to make inferiors obedient and to make superiors enlightened. Through a myriad transformations nothing becomes disorderly; but if one is divided in his loyalty to them, he will be brought to ruin. Surely it is true that the rites are indeed perfection!

Establish them and exalt them, make of them the ridgepole, and nothing in the world can add to or subtract from them. Root and branch accord with one another; end and beginning are fitting and proper, one to the other. As a consequence of their perfected form there are the various distinctions made by ritual principles, and as a consequence of their perfect discernment there are explanations provided for everything. When

【原文】

危；从之者存，不从者亡。小人不能测也。

19.8 礼之理诚深矣，“坚白”、“同异”之察入焉而溺；其理诚大矣，擅作典制、辟陋之说入焉而丧；其理诚高矣，暴慢恣睢轻俗以为高之属入焉而队。故绳墨诚陈矣，则不可欺以曲直；衡诚县矣，则不可欺以轻重；规矩诚设矣，则不可欺以方圆；君子审于礼，则不可欺以诈伪。故绳者，直之至；衡者，平之至；规矩者，方圆之至；礼者，人道之极也。然而不法礼，不足礼，谓之无方之民；法礼，足

【今译】

遵循礼的国家混乱；遵循礼的国家安定，不遵循礼的国家危险；遵循礼的国家存在，不遵循礼的国家灭亡。礼的这些作用小人是不能估量到的。

19.8 礼的道理真深啊，那些“坚白”、“同异”等所谓明察的辨析一进入礼的道理之中就被淹没了；礼的道理真大啊，那些擅自编造典章制度、邪僻浅陋的学说一进入礼的道理之中就没命了；礼的道理真高啊，那些把粗暴傲慢恣肆放荡轻视习俗作为高尚的人一进入礼的道理之中就垮台了。所以木工的墨线真正拉出来了，就不可能再用曲直来搞欺骗；秤真正挂起来了，就不可能再用轻重来搞欺骗；圆规角尺真正设置了，就不可能再用方圆来搞欺骗；君子对礼了解得明白清楚，就不可能再用诡诈来欺骗他。所以墨线这种东西，是直的极点；秤这种东西，是平的极点，圆规角尺这种东西，是方与圆的极点；礼这种东西，是社会道德规范的极点。既然这样，那么不遵循礼，不充

the world observes their precepts, there is order; when it does not, there is anarchy. When it observes them, there is safety; when it does not, there is danger. When it observes them, there is survival; when it does not, there is annihilation. But petty men are unable to fathom this.

19. 8

The rational order of ritual is so genuinely profound that when the kind of discernment which distinguishes "hard and white" and "identity and difference" enters the domain of ritual, it is soon out of its depth. Their rational order is so genuinely great that when people who create statutes and regulations on their own authority and advance despised and backward theories enter the domain of ritual, they are brought to ruin. Their principle of rational order is so genuinely lofty that when those cruel, negligent, wanton, overbearing men who deprecate custom, considering themselves superior to others, enter the realm of ritual, they meet their downfall.

Thus, if the blackened marking line is set true, then it is impossible to be deceived about what is straight and what crooked. If the balance is hung true, then it is impossible to be fooled about lightness or heaviness. If the compass and square are adjusted true, then it is impossible to be deceived about square and round. So too, if the gentleman is thoroughly acquainted with ritual principles, then he cannot be fooled by fraud and pretense. Thus, just as the marking line is the perfection of straightness; the balance the perfection of equalness; and the compass and square the perfection of square and roundness,so too, ritual principles are the ridgepole of the Way of Man. This being so, those who do not model themselves after ritual and are not satisfied with ritual principles are called

【原文】

礼，谓之有方之士。礼之中焉能思索，谓之能虑；礼之中焉能勿易，谓之能固。能虑，能固，加好者焉，斯圣人矣。故天者，高之极也；地者，下之极也；无穷者，广之极也；圣人者，道之极也。故学者，固学为圣人也，非特学为无方之民也。

19.9 礼者，以财物为用，以贵贱为文，以多少为异，以隆杀为要。文理繁，情用省，是礼之隆也。文理省，情用繁，是礼之杀也。文理情用相为内外表里，并行而杂，是礼之中流也。故君子上致其隆，下尽其杀，而中处其中。步骤、驰骋、厉骛不外是矣，是君子之

【今译】

分地掌握礼，就叫做没有原则的人；遵循礼，充分地掌握礼，就叫做有原则的贤士。在遵循礼掌握礼的过程中能够思考探索，叫做善于谋虑；在遵循礼掌握礼的过程中能不变，叫做能够坚定。善于谋虑，能够坚定，再加上爱好礼，就是圣人了。所以天，是高的极点；地，是低的极点；没有尽头，是广阔的极点；圣人，是道德的极点。所以学习的人，本来就该学做圣人，而不是学做不走正道的人。

19.9 礼，把钱财物品作为工具，把尊贵与卑贱的区别作为礼仪制度，把享受的多少作为尊卑贵贱的差别，把隆重和简省作为要领。礼节仪式繁多，但所要表达的感情、所要起到的作用却简约，这是隆重的礼。礼节仪式简约，但所要表达的感情、所要起到的作用却繁多，这是简省的礼。礼节仪式和它所要表达的感情、所要起到的作用之间相互构成内外表里的关系，两者并驾齐驱而交错配合，这是适中的礼。所以知礼的君子对隆重的礼仪就极尽它的隆重，对简省的礼仪就极尽它的简省，而对适中的礼仪也就作适中的处置。慢走快跑、驱

people who lack any method or standard. Those who model themselves after ritual and find satisfaction in ritual principles are said to be scholars who have method and standards. Those who keep to the mean provided by ritual and are able to ponder and meditate on it are said to be able to think. Those who keep to the mean provided by ritual and are able not to alter it are said to be steadfast. One who, being able to think and to stay steadfast, adds to them a fondness for ritual—this is to be a sage. Thus, just as Heaven is the limit of highness, Earth the limit of depth, and the boundless the limit of extension, so the sage is the ridgepole of the Way. Hence, the true student assuredly studies how to become a sage and does not devote his attention to studying merely to become one of the people who lacks standards.

19. 9

Rites employ valuables and ordinary objects to make offerings, use distinctions between noble and base to create forms, vary the quantity according to differences of station, and elaborate or simplify to render each its due. When form and principle are emphasized and emotions and offerings are treated perfunctorily, there is the greatest elaboration of ritual. When emotion and offerings are emphasized and form and principle are treated perfunctorily, there is greatest simplification of ritual. When form and principle, and emotion and offerings, are treated as inside to outside, external manifestation to inner content, so that both are translated into action and commingled, there is the mean course of ritual.

Thus, the gentleman could make the elaborate forms of ritual more florid or make its simplified forms leaner, but he dwells in the mean of its mean course. Whether he walks or runs, dashes after or hurries about,

【原文】

坛宇宫廷也。人有是，士君子也；外是，民也。于是其中焉，方皇周挟，曲得其次序，是圣人也。故厚者，礼之积也；大者，礼之广也；高者，礼之隆也；明者，礼之尽也。《诗》曰：“礼仪卒度，笑语卒获。”此之谓也。

19.10 礼者，谨于治生死者也。生，人之始也；死，人之终也。终始俱善，人道毕矣。故君子敬始而慎终。终始如一，是君子之道、礼义之文也。夫厚其生而薄其死，是敬其有知而慢其无知也，是奸人之道而倍叛之心也。君子以倍叛之心接臧、穀，犹且羞之，而况以事其所隆亲乎！故死之为道也，一而不可得再复也，臣之所以致重其

【今译】

马驰骋、剧烈奔跑都不越出这个规矩，这就是君子的活动范围。人如果把活动限定在这个范围之中，就是士君子；如果越出了这个规矩，就是普通的人；如果在这个规矩中间，来回周旋，处处符合它的次序，这就是圣人了。所以圣人的厚道，是靠了礼的积蓄；圣人的大度，是靠了礼的深广；圣人的崇高，是靠了礼的高大；圣人的明察，是靠了礼的透彻。《诗》云：“礼仪全都合法度，说笑就都合时务。”说的就是这种情况啊。

19.10 礼，是严谨地处理生与死的。生，是人生的开始；死，是人生的终结。这终结和开始都处理得好，那么为人之道也就完备了。所以君子严肃地对待人生的开始而慎重地对待人生的终结。对待这终结与开始就像对待同一件事一样，这是君子的原则，是礼义的具体规定。看重人活着的时候而看轻人的死亡，这是敬重活人的有知觉而怠慢死人的没有知觉，这是邪恶之人的原则，是背叛的心理。君子拿背叛别人的心肠去对待奴仆、儿童，尚且感到羞耻，更何况是用这种心肠来事奉自己所尊重的君主和亲爱的父母呢！再说死亡有一条规律，就是每人只死一次而不可能再重复一次，所以臣子要表达对

moves with urgency or runs quickly hither and thither, he does not depart from ritual, for it is "the outer boundary of his proper dwelling." Men who possess it are scholars and gentlemen; those who remain outside it are petty men. A person who lives within its mean, so that "wherever he goes in making his circuit" each small matter is precisely as it ought to be, is a sage. Thus,his generosity is the accumulation of ritual; his greatness, the breadth of ritual; his loftiness, the exaltation of ritual; and his brilliance, the mastery of ritual. An *Ode* says:

Every rite and ceremony according to rule,
every smile and word as it should be.

This expresses my meaning.

19. 10

Ritual is sedulous in giving order to matters of birth and death, for birth is the beginning of man and death his end. When both the beginning and end are good, the Way of Man is complete. Thus, the gentleman takes strict reverent care with beginnings and is conscientious about the end, so that end and beginning are as one. Such is the Way of the gentleman and the cultivated form of ritual and morality. To be generous on occasions of birth and niggardly at death is to be respectful of those having awareness, but disrespectful of those lacking awareness. This is to follow the way of degenerates and to have a heart that rebels against nature. A gentleman, moreover, would be ashamed to deal with even a Cang or Huo with a rebellious heart, how much more then would he be ashamed so to serve those whom he exalts and loves!

Because there is only one opportunity to treat the dead in the proper way, and it can never be repeated, the minister's demonstration of high-

【原文】

君，子之所以致重其亲，于是尽矣。故事生不忠厚，不敬文，谓之野；送死不忠厚，不敬文，谓之瘠。君子贱野而羞瘠。故天子棺椁十重，诸侯五重，大夫三重，士再重；然后皆有衣衾多少厚薄之数，皆有翣蒌文章之等；以敬饰之，使生死始终若一，一足以为人愿，是先王之道、忠臣孝子之极也。天子之丧动四海，属诸侯。诸侯之丧动通国，属大夫。大夫之丧动一国，属修士。修士之丧动一乡，属朋友。庶人之丧，合族党，动州里。刑余罪人之丧，不得合族党，独属妻子，棺椁三寸，衣衾三领，不得饰棺，不得昼行，以昏殣，凡缘而往

【今译】

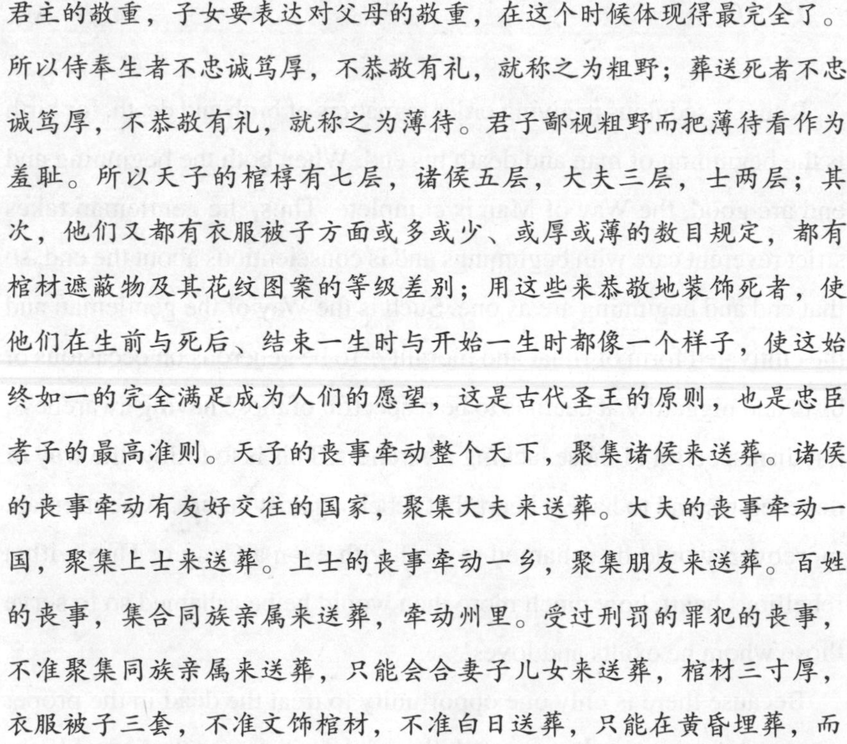

君主的敬重，子女要表达对父母的敬重，在这个时候体现得最完全了。所以侍奉生者不忠诚笃厚，不恭敬有礼，就称之为粗野；葬送死者不忠诚笃厚，不恭敬有礼，就称之为薄待。君子鄙视粗野而把薄待看作为羞耻。所以天子的棺椁有七层，诸侯五层，大夫三层，士两层；其次，他们又都有衣服被子方面或多或少、或厚或薄的数目规定，都有棺材遮蔽物及其花纹图案的等级差别；用这些来恭敬地装饰死者，使他们在生前与死后、结束一生时与开始一生时都像一个样子，使这始终如一的完全满足成为人们的愿望，这是古代圣王的原则，也是忠臣孝子的最高准则。天子的丧事牵动整个天下，聚集诸侯来送葬。诸侯的丧事牵动有友好交往的国家，聚集大夫来送葬。大夫的丧事牵动一国，聚集上士来送葬。上士的丧事牵动一乡，聚集朋友来送葬。百姓的丧事，集合同族亲属来送葬，牵动州里。受过刑罚的罪犯的丧事，不准聚集同族亲属来送葬，只能会合妻子儿女来送葬，棺材三寸厚，衣服被子三套，不准文饰棺材，不准白日送葬，只能在黄昏埋葬，而

est respect for his ruler and the son's expression of the greatest honor for his parents must be fully conveyed on this last occasion. Hence, not to serve the living with honest generosity and with respectful forms should be called boorishness; failing to bury the dead with an honest generosity and respectful forms should be called miserliness. The gentleman despises boorishness and is ashamed of miserliness.

Accordingly, the inner and outer coffins of the Son of Heaven consisted of seven layers, those of the feudal lords of five layers, those of the grand officers of three layers, and those of knights of a double layer. Beyond this for each there was a correct number for the quantity and quality of clothing and offerings of food and a specific type of ornament and design appropriate to their rank, such as the flabellum for the coffin, proper respect being shown by the specific decorations. In this way, birth and death, end and beginning, are treated the same, and men's yearnings are satisfied. Such was the Way of the Ancient Kings, and the highest expression of the loyalty of the minister and the piety of the filial son.

The funeral of the Son of Heaven affects all within the four seas and brings together the feudal lords. The funeral of a feudal lord affects the states with which he maintains relations and brings together his grand officers. The funeral of a grand officer affects a single country and brings together the senior knights. The funeral of a senior knight affects a single prefecture and brings together his friends. The funeral of an ordinary man unites his kin and neighbors and affects his district and community.

The funeral of a castrated criminal does not involve uniting his family and neighbors, but brings together only his wife and children. His inner and outer coffins are but three inches thick, with only three thicknesses of grave cloth covering his corpse and with no decorations permitted on the inner coffin. His procession is not permitted to proceed by day, but

【原文】

埋之，反，无哭泣之节，无衰麻之服，无亲疏月数之等，各反其平，各复其始，已葬埋，若无丧者而止，夫是之谓至辱。

19.11 礼者，谨于吉凶不相厌者也。纩听息之时，则夫忠臣孝子亦知其闵已，然而殡敛之具未有求也；垂涕恐惧，然而幸生之心未已，持生之事未辍也；卒矣，然后作具之。故虽备家，必逾日然后能殡，三日而成服。然后告远者出矣，备物者作矣。故殡，久不过七十

【今译】

且妻子儿女只能穿着平常的服装去埋掉他，回来后，没有哭泣的礼节，没有披麻戴孝的丧服，没有因为亲戚的亲疏关系而形成的服丧日期的等级差别，各人都回到自己平常的情况，各人都恢复到自己当初的样子，已经把他埋葬之后，就像没有死过人一样而什么也不做，这叫做最大的耻辱。

19.11 礼，严谨地对待吉凶两类事，不使它们相互混淆。把新棉絮放在临终者鼻前而倾听其气息的时候，就是那些忠臣孝子也知道他垂危了，但是停柩入殓的用具却还来不及顾及；虽然这时他们挂着眼泪惊恐害怕，但是希望他能侥幸活下去的心思还没有止息，维持他生命的事情也没有中止；直到他死了，才开始准备治丧的物品。所以，即使是治丧物品齐备的人家，也必须过了一天才能入棺停柩，到第三天才穿上丧服守丧。然后去远方报丧的人才出发了，准备治丧物品的人才开始操办了。所以停放灵柩的时间，长不超过七十天，快也不少

they must bury him under the cover of darkness. They wear everyday clothing when they follow along going to bury the corpse. When they return from the burial, there is no term of weeping and wailing, no sack-cloth mourning clothes, no gradations of proper lengths of mourning for near and distant relatives. Each returns to the ordinary course of his life and resumes his business as before. As soon as his body is interred in the earth, everything ends as though there had never been a funeral. Truly this is the ultimate disgrace.

19. 11

Ritual is sedulous in matters of auspicious and inauspicious signs to keep them from affecting each other. When they hold the silk floss before his nose and await the sign of his breathing, although at the time the loyal minister and the filial son know already that he is critically ill, nonetheless they do not as yet have the search begun for all the materials needed for dressing and encoffining the corpse. Tears may fall, and they may be filled with fear and anxiety; nonetheless, by some good fortune the life in his heart might not have ceased and his hold on the functions of life not yet ended. Only after it is certain that he is dead do they start preparations for the funeral.

Thus, even in a well-provided household it is certain to be only after a day has passed that they are able to place the body in the coffin and only on the third day do they wear mourning clothes. Only after all this is the death announcement sent out to those who are distant. Only then do those in charge of preparing the burial goods begin their tasks. Hence, the period when the body lies in state is not allowed to last more than seventy days, nor are things rushed so that it lasts less than fifty days.

【原文】

日，速不损五十日。是何也？曰：远者可以至矣，百求可以得矣，百事可以成矣。其忠至矣，其节大矣，其文备矣，然后月朝卜日，月夕卜宅，然后葬也。当是时也，其义止，谁得行之？其义行，谁得止之？故三月之葬，其貌以生设饰死者也，殆非直留死者以安生也，是致隆思慕之义也。

19.12 丧礼之凡：变而饰，动而远，久而平。故死之为道也，不饰则恶，恶则不哀；尔则玩，玩则厌，厌则忘，忘则不敬。一朝而丧其严亲，而所以送葬之者不哀不敬，则嫌于禽兽矣。君子耻之。故变

【今译】

于五十天。这是为什么呢？是因为：远方来奔丧的亲友可以赶到了，各种需求可以获得了，各种事情可以办成了。人们的忠诚尽到了，对长辈的礼节盛大了，仪式也齐备了，然后才在月底占卜确定埋葬的地点，在月初占卜确定埋葬的日期，然后才去埋葬。在这个时候，那道义上禁止的事，谁能去做它？那道义上推行的事，谁能禁止它？所以停柩三个月的葬礼，它表面上是用生者的设施来装饰死者，但实际上恐怕不是只保留一下死者来安慰生者，这是在表达尊重怀念的意思啊。

19.12 丧礼的一般原则是：人死后要装饰，举行丧礼仪式要使死者逐步远去，时间长了便恢复到平常的状态。那死亡有一种规律，即：如果对死者不装饰，就丑恶难看；丑恶难看，人们就不会哀痛了；如果死者近了，人们就会漫不经心；漫不经心，就会厌弃；厌弃了，就会怠慢；怠慢了，就会不恭敬。有朝一日死了自己尊敬的父母亲，但用来为他们送葬的行为却是不哀痛、不恭敬，那就近于禽兽了。君

Why is this? I say because those who are distant must be allowed time to arrive, the various articles required for the funeral must be obtained, and all the necessary arrangements must be completed. When this amount of time has passed, their loyalty is most evident; it is when the critical points of ritual are of greatest significance, and it is when the forms to be followed are most perfect. Afterward, at the beginning of the month, the day for the burial is divined, and at the end of the month the place of burial is divined. Only then is the body interred. On such an occasion, who could do more than what duty prescribes, and who would fail to do what the rules require? Hence, interment in the third month gives the appearance of using the accoutrements of life to adorn the dead and is not, as it seems, detaining the dead to give comfort to the living. It is rather the expression of the most exalted thoughts of longing and remembrance.

19. 12

The general principles of mourning are that with each change the corpse is adorned, with each move it is taken farther away, and with the passage of time the ordinary course of life is resumed. Hence, the way of the dead is that if the corpse is not adorned, it becomes hideous, and if it is hideous, no grief is felt. If it is kept close at hand, one begins to scorn it; when having it close at hand makes it the object of scorn, one begins to weary of it; when one wearies of it, one becomes unmindful of one's duty to it; and if one becomes unmindful of one's duties, then one no longer shows proper respect. If one morning one should have to bury one's revered parent, and if in attending to the ceremonies of the funeral one shows neither grief nor respect, then one has conducted oneself as a

【原文】

而饰，所以灭恶也；动而远，所以遂敬也；久而平，所以优生也。

19.13 礼者，断长续短，损有余，益不足，达爱敬之文而滋成行义之美者也。故文饰、粗恶，声乐、哭泣，恬愉、忧戚，是反也；然而礼兼而用之，时举而代御。故文饰、声乐、恬愉，所以持平奉吉也；粗衰、哭泣、忧戚，所以持险奉凶也。故其立文饰也，不至于窕冶；其立粗衰也，不至于瘠弃；其立声乐、恬愉也，不至于流淫惰慢；其立哭泣、哀戚也，不至于隘慑伤生。是礼之中流也。

19.14 故情貌之变，足以别吉凶、明贵贱亲疏之节，期止矣；外

【今译】

子以此为耻辱。人死后进行装饰，是用来消除丑恶难看的；举行丧礼仪式时使死者远去，是用来成全恭敬的；时间长了就恢复到平常状态，是用来协调生者的。

19.13 礼，是截长补短，减损有余，增加不足，使爱怜恭敬的仪式能完全实施，从而养成美好的德行道义的。所以仪文修饰和粗略简陋，音乐和哭泣，安适愉快和忧愁悲伤，这些都是相反的，但是礼对它们一并加以应用，按时拿出来交替使用。仪文修饰、音乐、安适愉快，是用来对待平安和吉祥的；粗略简陋、哭泣、忧愁悲伤，是用来对待凶恶和不幸的。所以礼在确立仪文修饰的规范时，不会弄到妖艳的地步；它在确立粗略简陋的规范时，不会弄到毁伤形体的地步；它在确立音乐、安适愉快的规范时，不会弄到放荡懈怠的地步；它在确立哭泣、哀痛的规范时，不会弄到过度悲戚、伤害身体的地步。这就是礼的中庸之道。

19.14 所以神情容貌的变化，能够用来区别吉利与不幸，表明贵

beast would. The gentleman would be ashamed of such behavior. Therefore, with each change he adorns the corpse, whereby he disguises its hideousness. With each move he takes it farther away, whereby he ensures continued respect. With the passage of time he resumes the ordinary course of life, whereby he cares for the needs of the living.

19. 13

Rites trim what is too long, stretch out what is too short, eliminate excess, remedy deficiency, and extend cultivated forms that express love and respect so that they increase and complete the beauty of conduct according to one's duty. Thus,elegant adornment and gross ugliness, the sounds of music and the sobs of crying, contented happiness and grief-stricken distress are all opposites, yet rites use them all, substituting and changing them as the occasion requires. Elegant adornment, music, and happiness are what sustain tranquillity and serve auspicious occasions. Gross ugliness, weeping, and sorrow are what sustain anxiety and serve inauspicious occasions. Hence, their utilization of elegant adornment does not go so far as to be sensuous or seductive, nor gross ugliness so far as to produce emaciation or self-neglect. Their use of music and happiness does not go so far as to be wayward and abandoned or indolent and rude, nor do weeping and sorrow go so far as to produce despondency or injury to life. Such is the middle course of ritual.

19. 14

Thus, the changes of emotion and of manner should be sufficient to distinguish the auspicious from the inauspicious and to make clear that

【原文】

是，奸也；虽难，君子贱之。故量食而食之，量要而带之。相高以毁瘠，是奸人之道也，非礼义之文也，非孝子之情也，将以有为者也。故说豫娩泽，忧戚萃恶，是吉凶忧愉之情发于颜色者也。歌谣謷笑，哭泣谛号，是吉凶忧愉之情发于声音者也。刍豢、稻粱、酒醴、餰鬻，鱼肉，菽藿、酒浆，是吉凶忧愉之情发于食饮者也。卑绕、黼黻、文织，资粗、衰绖、菲繐、菅屦，是吉凶忧愉之情发于衣服者也。疏房、檖䫉、越席、床笫、几筵，属茨、倚庐、席薪、枕块，是吉凶忧愉之情发于居处者也。两情者，人生固有端焉。若夫断之继

【今译】

贱亲疏之间的礼节等级，就作罢了；超出了这个程度，就是奸邪的行为；即使是难以做到的，君子也鄙视它。所以要根据食量吃东西，根据腰身扎带子。拿哀伤得毁坏自己的身体而消瘦不堪来向别人标榜自己的高尚，这是奸邪之人的行径，不是礼义的规定，也不是孝子的真情，而是要用它来有所作为的。高兴欢乐时和颜悦色容光焕发，忧愁悲伤时面色憔悴愁眉苦脸，这是碰到吉利与不幸时忧愁愉快的心情在脸色上的表现。歌唱嬉笑，哭泣啼号，这是碰到吉利与不幸时忧愁愉快的心情在声音上的表现。牛羊猪狗等肉食、稻米谷子等细粮、甜酒、鱼肉、稀饭、豆叶、汤水，这是碰到吉利与不幸时忧愁愉快的心情在饮食上的表现。礼服礼帽、礼服上的花纹、有彩色花纹的丝织品、丧服粗布衣、麻条麻带、薄麻衣、用茅草编成的鞋，这是碰到吉利与不幸时忧愁愉快的心情在衣服上的表现。窗户通明的房间、深邃的朝堂、柔软的蒲席、床上的竹铺、短桌与竹席、编结茅草而成的屋顶、靠在墙边上的简陋房屋、居丧所铺的柴草、所枕的土块，这是碰到吉利与不幸时忧愁愉快的心情在居住上的表现。忧愁愉快这两种心情，在人的生性中本来就存在着根源，至于使这两种心情断绝或

the rank is high or low and that the relation is near or distant, but with this they stop. Any practice that exceeds these goals is evil, and although such practices may be difficult to accomplish, the gentleman disdains them. Hence, to eat only a measured quantity of food, to measure the waist when tying the sash round it, and to try to surpass each other in appearing distraught and emaciated is the way of evil men. It is not the cultivated form of ritual and duty, nor is it the emotion proper to the filial son; rather, it is done for the sake of effect. Thus a happy and joyous look with a winsome smile or a grief-stricken, distressed look with a care-worn, distorted countenance appear naturally on the face as the expressions of sorrow or happiness and as the reactions to auspicious and inauspicious events. Singing and laughing or weeping and crying out appear naturally in the voice as expressions of sorrow or happiness and as reactions to auspicious and inauspicious events. Grain- and grass-fed animals, rice and millet, distilled and sweet spirits, meat and fish or alternatively thick and thin congee, beans and young bean leaves, water and rice water appear in one's food and drink as expressions of sorrow or happiness and as reactions to auspicious and inauspicious events. Skirts with ornamented bottom borders and ceremonial caps, elaborate embroideries, designs woven of colored silk, or coarse hempen garments, sackcloth clothes, hempen headbands, straw sandals, loosely woven materials, and rush-rope sandals appear in one's dress as expressions of sorrow or happiness and as reactions to auspicious and inauspicious events. Spacious rooms, secluded pavilions, plaited grass mats or thatched huts, lean-to sheds, and brushwood mats with a clod of earth as a pillow appear in one's dwellings as expressions of sorrow or happiness and as reactions to auspicious and inauspicious events. Both emotions inherently have their beginnings in man's inborn nature. If these emotions are trimmed or

【原文】

之，博之浅之，益之损之，类之尽之，盛之美之，使本末终始莫不顺比，足以为万世则，则是礼也。非顺孰修为之君子，莫之能知也。

19.15 故曰：性者，本始材朴也；伪者，文理隆盛也。无性，则伪之无所加；无伪，则性不能自美。性伪合，然后成圣人之名，一天下之功于是就也。故曰：天地合而万物生，阴阳接而变化起，性伪合而天下治。天能生物，不能辨物也；地能载人，不能治人也；宇中万物生人之属，待圣人然后分也。《诗》曰："怀柔百神，及河乔岳。"此之谓也。

【今译】

持续，使它们较多地被人了解或较少地被人了解，使它们增强或减损，使它们既合乎法度又能充分地表达出来，使它们既旺盛又美好，使根本原则和具体细节、人生终结的仪式和人生开始的仪式没有不和顺的，完全可以用来作为千秋万代的法则，这就是礼啦。如果不是顺从礼、精通礼、学习礼、实行礼的君子，是不能够懂得这些道理的。

19.15 所以说：先天的本性，就像是原始的未加工过的木材；后天的人为加工，则表现在礼节仪式的隆重盛大。没有本性，那么人为加工就没有地方施加；没有人为加工，那么本性也不能自行完美。本性和人为的加工相结合，然后才能成就圣人的名声，统一天下的功业也因此而能完成了。所以说：上天和大地相配合，万物就产生了；阴气和阳气相接触，变化就出现了；本性和人为的加工改造相结合，天下就治理好了。上天能产生万物，但不能治理万物；大地能负载人民，但不能治理人民；宇宙间的各种东西和各类人，得依靠圣人才能安排好。《诗》云："招徕安抚众神仙，来到黄河高泰山。"说的就是这

stretched, broadened or narrowed, diminished or increased, if they are put into their proper category and fully conveyed, if they are brought to completion and made refined, if caused in root and branch, end and beginning, to have nothing lacking obedience and if joined in a pure, unmixed, and perfect whole that can serve ten thousand generations, then they have become as rituals. None but the gentleman who has become obedient and has thoroughly cultivated himself through conscious effort is able to know how to do this.

19. 15

Therefore I say: Inborn nature is the root and beginning, the raw material and original constitution. Conscious activity is the form and principle of order, the development and completion. If there were no inborn nature, there would be nothing for conscious exertion to improve; if there were no conscious exertion, then inborn nature could not refine itself. Only after inborn nature and conscious exertion have been conjoined is the concept of the sage perfected, and the merit of uniting the world brought to fulfillment. Hence, it has been said that when Heaven and Earth conjoin, the myriad things are begot; when the Yin and Yang principles combine, transformations and transmutations are produced; when inborn nature and conscious activity are joined, the world is made orderly. Heaven is able to beget the myriad things, but it cannot differentiate them. Earth can support man, but it cannot govern him. The myriad things under the canopy of heaven and all those who belong among living people depend upon the appearance of the sage, for only then is each assigned its proper station. An *Ode* says:

He attracts and pacifies the hundred spirits,

【原文】

19.16 丧礼者，以生者饰死者也，大象其生以送其死也。故如死如生，如亡如存，终始一也。始卒，沐浴、鬠体、饭唅，象生执也。不沐则濡栉，三律而止；不浴，则濡巾三式而止。充耳而设瑱，饭以生稻，唅以槁骨，反生术矣。设亵衣，袭三称，缙绅而无钩带矣，设掩面儇目，鬠而不冠笄矣。书其名，置于其重，则名不见而柩独明矣。荐器，则冠有鍪而毋縰，瓮、庑虚而不实，有簟席而无床笫，木器不成斫，陶器不成物，薄器不成内，笙、竽具而不和，琴、瑟张而不均，舆藏而马反，告不用也。具生器以适墓，象徙道也。略而不

【今译】

种情况啊。

19.16 丧葬的礼仪，就是按照活人的情形来装饰死人，大致地摹拟他的生前来送他的终。所以侍奉逝世如同侍奉出生，侍奉死人如同侍奉活人，对待人生的终结与对待人生的开始一个样。刚死的时候，给死者洗头洗澡，束头发剪指甲，把含物放入口中，这是摹拟他生前的操作。如果不洗头，就用沾湿的梳篦梳理三下就可以了；如果不洗澡，就用沾湿的毛巾擦三遍就可以了。在死者的耳朵里塞上玉石，把生米喂入口中，把贝塞在嘴里，这就和出生时的办法相反了。给死者穿好内衣，再穿上三套外衣，束上腰带但不用带钩，裹上遮脸的白绢和遮眼的黑色丝巾，束起头发而不戴帽子，不插簪子。把死者的名字写在狭长的明旌上，然后把它覆在死者的临时神主牌上，那么他的名字就看不见而只有灵柩十分明显了。送给死者的随葬器物，戴在头上的有头盔似的帽子而没有包发的丝巾，瓮、甏空着不放东西，有竹席而没有床上的竹铺，木器不作加工，陶器不制成成品，竹子芦苇做成的器物不中用，笙、竽具备而不调和，琴、瑟绷上弦而不加调节，装运棺材的车子随同埋葬而马却牵回去，这些都

even those of the River and High Mountain.

19. 16

In the funeral rites, one uses objects of the living to adorn the dead and sends them to their grave in a fashion that resembles the way they lived. Thus one treats the dead like the living and one treats their absence just as one treated them when they were still present, so that end and beginning are as one. When a person has just died, his hair is washed, his body is bathed, his hair tied in a knot, his nails are trimmed, and food is put in his mouth, imitating what one did for him when he was still alivc. (If thc hair is not washed, then it is combed through exactly three times; if the body is not bathed, then it is wiped exactly three times with a wet towel.) But filling the ears by putting in plugs, providing food by using raw rice, and closing the mouth with a white cowry shell are practices contrary to what is done for the living.

Arrange the underclothing, add three layers of outer robes, and insert the broad sash, but do not fasten the sash hook. Arrange the face covering, bind the eyes, and comb the hair, but do not put on a cap or hairpin. Write out the name of the deceased and place it directly on the tablet, then the name is not seen, but the name is clear only on the coffin. The ceremonial offerings include a cap with bands but no strings, earthen water and wine jugs that are empty and never filled, and there are bamboo mats but neither beds nor couches. The carvings on the wooden vessels are left incomplete. Earthenwares are left as unfinished objects. Thin wares are too incomplete to be used. The reed pipes and reed organs are whole but are not tuned. The zithers and lutes are strung but not adjusted. The carriage is buried, but the horses are returned. All these

【原文】

尽，貌而不功，趋舆而藏之，金革辔靷而不入，明不用也；象徙道，又明不用也。是皆所以重哀也。故生器文而不功，明器貌而不用。凡礼，事生，饰欢也；送死，饰哀也；祭祀，饰敬也；师旅，饰威也。是百王之所同，古今之所一也，未有知其所由来者也。故圹垄，其貌象室屋也；棺椁，其貌象版、盖、斯象、拂也；无帾、丝歶、缕翣，其貌以象菲、帷、帱、尉也；抗折，其貌以象槾、茨、番、阏也。故丧礼者，无它焉，明死生之义，送以哀敬而终周藏也。故葬埋，敬藏

【今译】

表示随葬的东西是不用的。准备好了生前的用具而送到墓中，这是模拟搬家的办法。随葬的器物简略而不完备，只具外貌而不精致，赶着丧车去把它埋葬掉，但拉车的马及其设备却不埋进去，这些都是为了表明随葬的东西是不用的；模拟搬家的办法，也是表明那些随葬的东西不用了。这些都是为了加重哀悼之情的。所以，生前的用具只起礼仪的作用而不再用它，随葬的器物只具外貌而不精致。凡是礼仪，侍奉出生，是为了润饰欢乐之情；葬送死者，是为了更好地表现哀悼之情；祭祀，是为了修饰恭敬之情；军队，是为了装饰威武之势。这是各代帝王都相同，古今都一致的，但是没有人知道它是从什么时代传下来的。所以，墓穴和坟冢的形状像房屋；内棺外椁的形状像车旁板、车顶盖、车前皮盖、车后革 帘构成的车厢；尸体与棺材上的被子、丝织麻织的遮蔽品、棺材的遮蔽物的形状是模仿门帘和各种帷帐的；承负坟冢、覆盖墓穴的葬具抗折的形状是模仿墙壁、屋顶、篱笆和门户的。所以，丧葬的礼仪，并没有其它的涵义，而是为了彰明生死的意义，以悲哀恭敬的心情去葬送死者而最

practices are to indicate that these articles are not intended to be used. The articles of life are taken to the tomb to give the impression that only the abode has changed. A selection from his belongings is made, but the whole of them is not entombed; so the form is there, but no substance. A carriage is taken to the tomb and buried, but its metal and leather fittings, reins and harnesses, are not included, to make clear that it is not intended for use. Both giving the impression that only the abode has changed and making clear that funeral objects will never be used are means used to emphasize the feelings of grief at death. Thus, the articles of life have the proper form, but not the function; the hallowed articles have the appearance but not the use.

As a general principle, ritual in treating birth provides ornamentation for expressions of joy, and in sending off the dead it provides ornamentation for expressions of grief. In presenting sacrificial offerings rituals embellish feelings of reverence, and in marshaling troops they embellish feelings of awe-inspiring majesty. In this, the Hundred Kings have agreed, and antiquity and today are one and the same, although we have no knowledge of how this camc to be.

From of old the grave chamber and the tumulus raised above it have resembled the form of a house. The inner and outer coffins have resembled the form of the side, top, front, and back boards of a carriage. The baldachin over the coffin with its decorations of spouts and fish and the flabellum have resembled the form of rush-grass screens, curtains, and the netted coveings and hangings of a room. The wooden lining and protective framework of the tomb have resembled the form of rafters and beams of the roof and its obstructing fence. Thus, the purpose of the mourning rites is nothing other than to make clear the duties of the living to the dead, to send the dead off with grief and reverence, and to conclude by completing the

【原文】

其形也；祭祀，敬事其神也；其铭、诔、系世，敬传其名也。事生，饰始也；送死，饰终也。终始具而孝子之事毕，圣人之道备矣。

19.17 刻死而附生谓之墨，刻生而附死谓之惑，杀生而送死谓之贼。大象其生以送其死，使死生终始莫不称宜而好善，是礼义之法式也，儒者是矣。

19.18 三年之丧，何也？

曰：称情而立文，因以饰群，别亲疏、贵贱之节而不可益损也。故曰：无适不易之术也。创巨者，其日久；痛甚者，其愈迟。三年之

【今译】

终把他周到地掩藏好。所以，埋葬是为了恭敬地掩藏死者的躯体；祭祀，是为了恭敬地侍奉死者的灵魂；那些铭文、诔辞、传记家谱，是为了恭敬地传颂死者的名声。事奉出生的礼仪，是装饰人生的开始；葬送死者的礼仪，是装饰人生的终结。这终结与开始的礼仪全部做到了，那么孝子的事情也就完成了，圣人的道德也就具备了。

19.17 削减死者的用度来增加生者的用度叫做刻薄，削减生者的用度来增加死者的用度叫做迷惑，杀掉生者来殉葬叫做残害。大致地摹拟他的生前来送他的终，使逝世和在世、人生终结和人生开始时的仪式无不得当合宜而尽善尽美，这就是礼义的法度标准了，儒者就是这样的啊。

19.18 三年的服丧，是为了什么呢？

回答说：这是根据人的感情来确立礼仪制度，借以整治亲族，区别亲近的人与疏远的人之间、高贵者与卑贱者之间的不同礼节，而不能再增减的了。所以说：这是无论到什么地方也不可改变的措施。创伤大的，它的愈合时间就长；疼痛厉害的，它的痊愈就慢。三年的服

burial. Hence, at the interment into the grave one reverently buries the bodily form, at the offering of sacrifices one reverently serves the spirit, and with the inscription, eulogy, and the genealogical record one reverently transmits his name to posterity. In treating birth, rites ornament the beginning; in sending off the dead, they ornament the end. When both end and beginning have been fully attended to, then the service proper for a filial son is finished and the Way of the Sage is fulfilled.

19. 17

To deprive the dead in order to add to what the living have is termed "having blackly impure principles"; to deprive the living to supplement offerings for the dead is termed "delusion"; and to execute the living so that they can escort the dead is termed "predation." To send off the dead in a fashion that generally imitates the way they lived; to cause nothing in death or in birth, in end or in beginning, to be unseemly or inappropriate; and in everything to be fond of the good—such is the model and paradigm of ritual and duty. The true Ru are thus.

19. 18

Why does mourning extend into the third year? I say that the practice was established to be equal to the emotions involved. Use of these forms ornaments social relations. They provide distinctions between the obligations due near and far relations and the eminent and humble. They admit neither of diminution nor of addition. Thus it is said that they are methods that are matchless and unchanging.

The greater the wound, the longer it remains; the more pain it gives,

【原文】

丧，称情而立文，所以为至痛极也。齐衰、苴杖、居庐、食粥、席薪、枕块，所以为至痛饰也。三年之丧，二十五月而毕，哀痛未尽，思慕未忘，然而礼以是断之者，岂不以送死有已，复生有节也哉？凡生乎天地之间者，有血气之属必有知，有知之属莫不爱其类。今夫大鸟兽则失亡其群匹，越月逾时，则必反铅；过故乡，则必徘徊焉，鸣号焉，踯躅焉，踟蹰焉，然后能去之也。小者是燕爵犹有啁噍之顷焉，然后能去之。故有血气之属莫知于人，故人之于其亲也，至死无穷。将由夫愚陋淫邪之人与？则彼朝死而夕忘之，然而纵之，则是曾鸟兽之不若也，彼安能相与群居而无乱乎？将由夫修饰之君子与？则

【今译】

丧，是根据人的感情来确立的礼仪制度，是用来给极其悲痛的感情所确立的最高期限。穿着丧服，撑着孝棍，住在简陋的房屋中，吃稀粥，把柴草当作垫席，把土块当作枕头，是用来给极其悲痛的心情所作的外表装饰。三年的服丧，二十五个月就完毕了，但哀痛之情并没有了结，思念之心并没有忘怀，然而礼制却规定在这个时候终止服丧，这难道不是因为送别死者要有个终结，恢复正常的生活要有所节制吗？凡是生长在天地之间的，有血气的种属一定有智能，而有智能的种属没有不爱自己同类的。现在那些大的飞禽走兽如果失去了它的群体或配偶，那么过了一个月或超过了一定的时间，就一定会返回合群；经过原来住过的地方，就一定会在那里徘徊周旋，在那里啼鸣吼叫，在那里驻足踏步，在那里来回走动，然后才能离开那里。小的嘛就是燕子麻雀之类也还要在那里叽叽喳喳个一会儿，然后才能离开那里。有血气的种属没有比人更聪明的了，所以人对于自己父母的感情，到死也没有穷尽。要依从那些愚蠢浅陋放荡邪恶的人么？那么他们的父母亲早晨死了，到晚上就忘了。像这种情况如果还放任他们，那么他们就连鸟兽也不如了，他们又怎么能互相在一起合群居住而没

the more slowly it heals. The practice of mourning into the third year deals with occasions when the extreme pain of grief has reached its pinnacle, so the mourning practices were established to equal the emotions expressed. The unhemmed garment of the mourner, his clothes of sackcloth, and his bamboo staff, the lean-to hut where he lives, the gruel he eats, his brushwood mat, and his clod of earth for a pillow are all emblems of his extreme grief. That the mourning rite is finished in the twenty-fifth month means that even though the grief and pain have not ended and although thoughts of the dead and longing for him have not been forgotten, this ritual practice cuts off these things, for otherwise would not sending off the dead have no conclusion, and must there not be a definite interval for the return to daily life?

As a general principle, all creatures that live between Heaven and Earth and have blood and breath are certain to possess awareness. Having awareness, each of them loves its own kind. Consider the case of large birds and animals: if one loses its mate or is separated from its group, then even after a month or season has passed, it is sure to circle when it passes its old home. It looks about, round and round, crying and calling, sometimes moving, sometimes stopping, gazing about uncertainly and hesitantly, before it can leave the place. Even small birds like swallows and sparrows chatter and cry for a few moments before they can leave. Hence, since no creature with blood and breath has more awareness than man, the feeling of a man for his parents is not exhausted even till death.

Will we follow after those stupid provincials and depraved men who by evening have forgotten a parent who died that morning? And if we indulge in such behavior are we not lower even than these birds and beasts? How could we even dwell together in the same community with

【原文】

三年之丧，二十五月而毕，若驷之过隙，然而遂之，则是无穷也。故先王圣人安为之立中制节，一使足以成文理，则舍之矣。

19.19 然则何以分之?

曰：至亲以期断。

是何也?

曰：天地则已易矣，四时则已遍矣，其在宇中者莫不更始矣，故先王案以此象之也。

然则三年何也?

曰：加隆焉，案使倍之，故再期也。

由九月以下，何也?

曰：案使不及也。故三年以为隆，缌、小功以为杀，期、九月以为间。上取象于天，下取象于地，中取则于人，人所以群居和一之理

【今译】

有动乱呢?要依从那些注重道德修养的君子么?那么三年的服丧，二十五个月就完毕了，他们会觉得那时间快得就像驾车的四匹马经过一个墙缝一样；像这种情况如果还是成全他们，那么他们就会无限期地服丧。所以先王圣人就给人们确立了适中的标准，制定了这服丧三年的礼节，一律使人们能够完成礼仪，然后就除去丧服。

19.19 既然这样，怎么来区分亲疏的丧期呢?

回答说：对于最亲近的父母在一周年时终止服丧。

这是为什么呢?

回答说：因为经过一周年，天地都已经变换了，四季也已经循环了一遍，那些在宇宙中的动植物没有不重新开始其生长的了，所以古代的圣王就用这一周年的丧礼来象征它。

既然这样，那么三年的丧期又是为了什么呢?

回答说：是为了表示加倍的隆重，所以给丧期加倍，再加两年。

服丧在九个月以下的，又是为什么呢?

回答说：那是为了使它不及为父母的服丧隆重。把服丧三年作为隆重的礼，把服丧三个月、五个月的缌麻、小功作为简省的礼，把服丧一周年、九个月作为它们中间的礼。这礼的制定，上取法于天，下取法于地，中取法于人，人们所以能合群居住而和谐一致的道理也就被全

such men and not have disorder! Or will we follow after those "cultivated and ornamented" gentlemen? For them the twenty-five months of the three-year mourning period pass as quickly as a running horse glimpsed through the crack in a wall, and if we follow their example, mourning will have no limit at all. Therefore the Ancient Kings and Sages acted to establish some mean, and to regulate it with a definite interval. As soon as enough time has been allowed to perfect cultivated form and to fulfill the dictates of reason, then mourning was to be put aside.

This being so, how then is it to be apportioned? I say that for one's closest kin, the completion of a year's time concludes it. Why is this so? I say: Heaven and Earth have completed their changes, the four seasons have come full circle, and everything under the canopy of heaven has begun anew. Thus, the Ancient Kings based themselves on this and used it for their pattern.

19. 19

This being so, why is there the practice of mourning into the third year? I say it is because they wanted to increase and exalt it, so they caused the time to be doubled and thus a second full year's time.

For others the time is nine months or less, why is this? I say it is to prevent such mourning periods from equaling the longer periods. Hence, the three-year period is considered the culmination of mourning and the three- and five-month periods its diminution, with the full-year and the nine-month periods falling in between. The highest take their pattern from Heaven, the lowest take theirs from Earth, and the middle take theirs from Man. The ordering principle that allows different people to live together in a community in harmony and unity is therein fully realized. Thus

【原文】

尽矣。故三年之丧，人道之至文者也。夫是之谓至隆。是百王之所同，古今之所一也。

19.20 君之丧所以取三年，何也？

曰：君者，治辨之主也，文理之原也，情貌之尽也，相率而致隆之，不亦可乎？《诗》曰："恺悌君子，民之父母。"彼君子者，固有为民父母之说焉。父能生之，不能养之；母能食之，不能教诲之；君者，已能食之矣，又善教诲之者也，三年毕矣哉？乳母，饮食之者也，而三月；慈母，衣被之者也，而九月；君，曲备之者也，三年毕乎哉？得之则治，失之则乱，文之至也。得之则安，失之则危，情之至也。两至者俱积焉，以三年事之犹未足也，直无由进之耳！故社，

【今译】

盘体现出来了。所以三年的服丧，是为人之道最高的礼仪。这叫做最隆重的礼仪。这是各代帝王都相同，古今都一致的。

19.20 君主的丧礼期限之所以要选取三年，为什么呢？

回答说：君主，是治理社会的主宰，是礼仪制度的本源，是忠诚的内情和恭敬的外貌所要侍奉的尽头，人们互相遵循而极其尊崇他，不也是可以的吗？《诗》云："和乐平易的君子，就是人民的父母。"那些君子本来就有是民众父母的说法。父亲能生下自己，但不能喂养自己；母亲能喂养自己，又不能教诲自己；君主是既能养育自己，又善于教诲自己的人，为君主服丧三年就完毕了吗？奶妈，是喂养自己的人，因而为她服丧三个月；抚育自己的庶母，是为自己料理衣着被服的人，因而为她服丧九个月；君主，是各方面都照顾自己的人，为他服丧三年就完毕了吗？做到了这一点，国家就能治理好；做不到这一点，国家就会混乱；它是礼仪制度中最重要的礼节啊。做到了这一点，国家就安定；做不到这一点，国家就危险；它是忠诚之情的最高体现啊。这最重要的礼节与最高的情感体现都积聚在君主的丧礼上

mourning into the third year is the perfection of good form in the Way of Man. Truly this is to be called its perfect culmination. In this, the Hundred Kings have agreed, and antiquity and today are one and the same.

19. 20

Why was the practice of mourning into the third year chosen for one's lord? I say that the lord is the ruler of order and management, the source of good form and rational order, and the ideal of emotion and appearance. Is it not indeed proper that all men should join together in exalting him above all others? An *Ode* says:

> This amiable and fraternal gentleman
> is the father and mother of his people.

Here the term "gentleman" assuredly has as its meaning his acting as the father and mother to his people. The father can beget the child, but he cannot suckle it. The mother can suckle the child but is unable to instruct and correct it. The lord not only is able to feed his people but is adept at teaching and correcting them. Yet when mourning for him reaches the third year, it is finished! A wet nurse who provides food and drink for the child is mourned three months; a nanny who dresses the child is mourned nine months; yet the lord who takes cares of every detail of all his subjects' welfare is mourned for but into the third year and it is finished!

When one finds such a lord, there is order, and where he is lost, there is disorder—for he is the highest expression of proper form. When one finds him, there is peace, and where he is lost, there is disorder—for he is the highest expression of proper feeling. Since he combines the highest expression of both these, mourning only into the third year would seem to

【原文】

祭社也；稷，祭稷也；郊者，并百王于上天而祭祀之也。

19.21 三月之殡，何也？

曰：大之也，重之也。所致隆也，所致亲也，将举错之，迁徙之，离宫室而归丘陵也，先王恐其不文也，是以繇其期，足之日也。故天子七月，诸侯五月，大夫三月，皆使其须足以容事，事足以容成，成足以容文，文足以容备，曲容备物之谓道矣。

19.22 祭者，志意思慕之情也。愅诡唈僾而不能无时至焉。故人

【今译】

了，所以用三年时间来侍奉君主的神灵仍然是不够的，只是无法再将这丧期增加罢了！所以社祭，只祭土地神；稷祭，只祭谷神；郊祭，就把各代帝王和上天合并在一起而祭祀他们。

19.21 三个月的停柩，为什么呢？

回答说：这是要扩大丧礼的规模，加重丧礼的分量。对自己极尊重的人、极亲近的人，将要安排他，迁移他，使他离开宫室而埋葬到陵墓中去，古代的圣王怕这些事情不合乎礼仪，因此延长停柩的日期，使办丧事的人有足够的时间。所以天子停柩七个月，诸侯五个月，大夫三个月，这都是为了使逗留时间足够用来操办各种事情，这些事情足够用来保证丧事的成功，这成功足够用来保证礼仪的实施，这实施足够用来保证丧葬物品的完备，各个方面都能确保丧葬物品的完备就可以叫做正确的原则了。

19.22 祭祀，是为了表达心意和思慕之情的。人们感动郁闷了就

honor him inadequately, yet there is simply no way to extend it. Hence, though in the sacrifice at the Altar of Soil only the spirit of the soil receives offerings, and though in the sacrifice at the Altar of Grain only the spirit of the grain receives offerings, in the sacrifice at the Suburban Altar, the Hundred Kings are combined with High Heaven in common sacrifice.

19. 21

Why does the body of the ruler lie in state for three months? I say it is to stress the importance and gravity of the occasion, because he is the one we most exalt and for whom we have the greatest affection. The Ancient Kings feared that in taking up and moving the dead, in escorting him from his house and in putting him into the burial mound, the forms proper to what is to be exalted to the utmost and what is to be cherished to the highest degree might not be observed. For this reason they extended the period to allow sufficient time for the preparations. Thus, for the Son of Heaven the period is seven months, for the feudal lords five months, and for grand officers three months. All this was done to ensure that the allotted time would be sufficient to permit all the necessary undertakings, that the tasks undertaken be completed, that in completing them proper forms be observed, and that these forms would be executed perfectly. When the preparations involved permit the perfection of things, it is said to be the right way [to bury the dead].

19. 22

Sacrifice originates in the emotions stirred by remembrance and re-

【原文】

之欢欣和合之时，则夫忠臣孝子亦悖诡而有所至矣。彼其所至者，甚大动也，案屈然已，则其于志意之情者惆然不嗛，其于礼节者阙然不具。故先王案为之立文，尊尊亲亲之义至矣。故曰：祭者，志意思慕之情也。忠信爱敬之至矣，礼节文貌之盛矣，苟非圣人，莫之能知也。圣人明知之，士君子安行之，官人以为守，百姓以成俗。其在君子，以为人道也；其在百姓，以为鬼事也。故钟、鼓、管、磬、琴、瑟、竽、笙，《韶》、《夏》、《护》、《武》、《汋》、《桓》、《箾》、简、

【今译】

不能没有机会来表达。人们欢欣鼓舞和睦相处的时候，那些忠臣孝子也会感动，而思念君主、双亲不得同享欢乐的心情也要有所表达了。他们所要表达的这种心情，是一种非常大的激动，如果空空地没有祭祀的礼仪，那么他们的心意在感情方面就会感到惆怅而不满足，他们在礼节方面就会感到欠缺而不完备。所以古代的圣王为他们制定了礼仪制度，这样，尊崇君主、亲爱父母的道义就能表达了。所以说：祭祀，是为了表达心意和思慕之情的。它是忠信敬爱的最高表现，是礼节仪式的极点了，如果不是圣人，是不能懂得这一点的。圣人明白地理解祭祀的意义，有道德的士君子安心地进行祭祀，官吏把它当作为自己的职守，百姓使它成为自己的习俗。它在君子那里，被当作治理社会的一种道德规范；它在百姓那里，被当作为侍奉鬼神的事。钟、鼓、管、磬、琴、瑟、竽、笙等乐器被使用，《韶》、《夏》、《护》、《武》、《汋》、《桓》、《箾》、《象》等乐曲被演奏，这些是君子

collection of the dead and by thinking of and longing for the departed. There inevitably are occasions in everyone's life when he is seized by an unexpected change of mood, when feelings of disquietude and melancholy cause him to sigh involuntarily or to feel that his breath is short from deep emotion. Thus, even in the midst of enjoying himself with congenial company, the loyal minister and the filial son are sometimes overcome with such changes of mood. When they do come, they are profoundly moving. If they are repressed, the emotions stirred by remembrance of the dead will be frustrated and remain unexpressed, and the rituals in dealing with such matters will seem lacking and incomplete. Thus, the Ancient Kings acted to establish proper forms wherein men could express the full measure of their obligation to pay honor to those deserving honor and to show affection to those whom they cherished.

Hence, I say that sacrifice originates in the emotions stirred by remembrance and recollection of the dead and by thinking of and longing for the departed, expresses the highest loyalty, faithfulness, love, and reverence, and is the fulfillment of ritual observances and formal bearing. If it were not for the sages, no one would be capable of understanding the meaning of sacrifice. The sage clearly understands ritual, the scholar and gentleman find comfort in carrying it out, officials of government have as their task preserving it, and the Hundred Clans incorporate it into their customs. For the gentleman, ritual observances are considered to be part of the Way of Man. Among the Hundred Clans, they are thought to be a matter of serving the ghosts of the departed.

Hence, bells and drums, flutes and chime-stones, lutes and zithers, reed pipes and reed organs, musical performances such as the *Succession*, the *Elegant*, the *Guarding*, the *Martial*, the *Libation*, the *Militant*, the *Panpipe*, and the *Imitation*—these the gentleman considers the proper

【原文】

《象》，是君子之所以为悼诡其所喜乐之文也。齐衰、苴杖、居庐、食粥、席薪、枕块，是君子之所以为悼诡其所哀痛之文也。师旅有制，刑法有等，莫不称罪，是君子之所以为悼诡其所敦恶之文也。卜筮视日，斋戒修涂，几筵、馈荐，告祝，如或飨之。物取而皆祭之，如或尝之。毋利举爵，主人有尊，如或觞之。宾出，主人拜送，反，易服，即位而哭，如或去之。哀夫！敬夫！事死如事生，事亡如事存，状乎无形影，然而成文。

【今译】

被他所喜悦的事情感动了从而用来表达这种感情的礼仪形式。穿丧服，拄孝棍，住陋屋，吃稀粥，以柴草为垫席，把土块当枕头，这是君子被他所哀痛的事情感动了，从而用来表达这种感情的礼仪制度。军队有一定的制度，刑法有轻重的等级，没有什么刑罚不与罪行相当，这些是君子被他所憎恶的事情感动了从而用来表达这种感情的礼法制度。占卜算卦，观察日期时辰是否吉利，整洁身心，修饰清理祠庙，摆好祭祀的席位，献上牺牲黍稷等祭品，受祭者吩咐男巫，好像真的有神来享用过祭品。事先积聚的祭品都献给代表死者受祭的人，受祭者一一尝用，好像真的有神尝过它们。不让助食的人举杯向受祭者敬酒，主人亲自劝受祭者饮酒，受祭者便饮用，好像真的有神拿酒杯喝了酒。祭祀结束后宾客退出，主人拜揖送行，然后返回，换掉祭服而穿上丧服，来到坐位上痛哭，好像真的有神离开了他。悲哀啊！恭敬啊！侍奉死者如同侍奉生者一样，侍奉已不存在的人如同侍奉还活着的人一样，所祭祀者虽无形无影，但是它可以成为人类社会中的一种礼仪制度。

forms expressive of sudden feelings of pleasure and joy. The unhemmed garment of the mourner, his clothes of sackcloth and his bamboo staff, the lean-to hut where he lives, the gruel he eats, his brushwood mat, and his clod of earth for a pillow—these the gentleman considers the proper forms expressive of his changed feelings of grief and pain. The marshaling of troops has proper regulations and the punishments prescribed in law have gradations of severity so that none go unpunished in a manner befitting their offense— these the gentleman considers the proper form expressive of unexpected feelings of loathing and hatred.

One divines with the tortoise shell and milfoil, determines auspicious days, purifies oneself and fasts, repairs and sweeps the temple, lays out the low tables and bamboo mats, presents the ceremonial offerings, and informs the invocator as though someone were really going to enjoy the sacrifice. One takes up the offerings and presents each of them as though someone were really going to taste them. The chief waiter does not lift up the wine cup, but the chief sacrificer himself has that honor, as though someone were really going to drink from it. When the guests leave, the chief sacrificer bows and escorts them out, returns and changes his clothing, resumes his place, and weeps as though someone had really departed with the guests. How full of grief, how reverent this is! One serves the dead as one serves the living, those who have perished as those who survive, just as though one were giving visible shape to what is without shape or shadow, and in so doing one perfects proper form!

乐论第二十

【原文】

20.1 夫乐者，乐也，人情之所必不免也。故人不能无乐；乐则必发于声音，形于动静；而人之道——声音、动静、性术之变，尽是矣。故人不能不乐，乐则不能无形，形而不为道，则不能无乱。先王恶其乱也，故制《雅》、《颂》之声以道之，使其声足以乐而不流，使其文足以辨而不諰，使其曲直、繁省、廉肉、节奏，足以感动人之善心，使夫邪污之气无由得接焉。是先王立乐之方也。而墨子非之，奈何？

【今译】

20.1 音乐，就是欢乐的意思，它是人的情感绝对不能缺少的东西。人不可能没有欢乐；欢乐了就一定会在歌唱吟咏的声音中表现出来，在手舞足蹈的举止中体现出来；可见人的所作所为——包括声音、举止、性情及其表现方式的变化，就全都体现在这音乐之中了。所以，人不可能不快乐，快乐了就不可能不表现出来，但这种表现如果不进行引导，就不可能没有祸乱。古代的圣王憎恶那祸乱，所以创作了《雅》、《颂》的音乐来引导他们，使那歌声足够用来表达快乐而不淫荡，使那歌词足够用来阐明正确的道理而不流于花巧，使那音律的宛转或舒扬、繁复或简单、清脆利落或圆润丰满、节奏停顿或推进加快，都足够用来感动人的行善之心，使那些邪恶肮脏的风气没有途径能和民众接触。这就是古代圣王设置音乐的原则啊。但是墨子却反对音乐，又能怎么样呢？

Book 20

Discourse on Music

20. 1

Music is joy. Being an essential part of man's emotional nature, the expression of joy is, by necessity, inescapable. This is why men cannot do without music. Where there is joy, it will issue forth in the sounds of the voice and be manifest in the movement of the body. And it is the Way of Man that singing and movement, which are excitations of man's emotional states according to the rules of inborn nature, are fully expressed in music. Hence, since it is impossible for men not to be joyful, where there is joy, it is impossible that it should not be given perceptible form. But if its form is not properly conducted, then it is impossible that disorder should not arise.

The Ancient Kings hated such disorder. Thus they instituted as regulations the sounds of the *Odes* and the *Hymns* to offer guidance. This would cause the sounds to be sufficient to give expression to the joy, but not to lead to dissipation. It would cause the patterns to be sufficient to mark the separations, but not so as to seem forced. It would cause the intricacy or directness of melody, the elaboration or simplification of instrumentation, the purity or richness of sound, and the rhythm and meter of the music to be sufficient to stir and move the good in men's hearts and to keep evil and base *qi* sentiments from finding a foothold there. Such was the plan of the Ancient Kings in establishing their music. Yet Mozi condemns it. How can this be endured!

【原文】

20.2 故乐在宗庙之中，君臣上下同听之，则莫不和敬；闺门之内，父子兄弟同听之，则莫不和亲；乡里族长之中，长少同听之，则莫不和顺。故乐者，审一以定和者也，比物以饰节者也，合奏以成文者也；足以率一道，足以治万变。是先王立乐之术也。而墨子非之，奈何?

20.3 故听其《雅》、《颂》之声，而志意得广焉；执其干戚，习其俯仰屈伸，而容貌得庄焉；行其缀兆，要其节奏，而行列得正焉，进退得齐焉。故乐者，出所以征诛也，入所以揖让也。征诛揖让，其

【今译】

20.2 所以音乐在祖庙之中，君臣上下一起听了它，就再也没有人不和谐恭敬的了；在家门之内，父子兄弟一起听了它，就再也没有人不和睦相亲的了；在乡村里弄之中，年长的和年少的一起听了它，就再也没有人不和协顺从的了。音乐，是审定一个主音来确定其他和音的，是配上各种乐器来调整节奏的，是一起演奏来组成众音和谐的乐曲的；它足能用来率领统一的原则，足能用来整治各种变化。这就是古代圣王设置音乐的方法啊。可是墨子却反对音乐，又能怎么样呢?

20.3 所以，人们听那《雅》、《颂》的音乐，志向心胸就能宽广了；拿起那盾牌、斧头等舞具，练习那低头抬头弯曲伸展等舞蹈动作，容貌就能庄重了；行动在那舞蹈的行列位置上，迎合那舞曲的节奏，队列就能不偏不斜了，进退就能整齐一致了。所以音乐，对外可用来

20. 2

Hence, when music is performed within the ancestral temple, lord and subject, high and low, listen to the music together and are united in feelings of reverence. When music is played in the private quarters of the home, father and son, elder and younger brother, listen to it together and are united in feelings of close kinship. When it is played in village meetings or clan halls, old and young listen to the music together and are joined in obedience. Hence, for musical performances the pitch of the prime note is set in order to determine the proper pitch of the other notes. The temperament of the other instruments is adjusted to match in order to prepare the modal key. The entrances of the instruments are made in unison to complete the musical form. It is sufficient to bring conformity with the single Way and to bring order to the myriad transformations. Such was the method of the Ancient Kings in establishing their music. Yet Mozi condemns it. How can this be endured!

20. 3

Hence, when we listen to the sounds of the *Odes* and *Hymns*, our aspirations and sense of purpose gain breadth from the experience. When we observe the way the shields and battle-axes are brandished and the repetitive episodes of the dancers gazing down and lifting their faces up, bending and straightening their bodies, our demeanor and bearing acquire dignity from it. When we observe their ranks move within the borders of fixed areas and their coordination with the rhythm and meter of the music, the arrangement of our own ranks is corrected and our advances and withdrawals are made uniform. Thus, in musical performances, the ranks

【原文】

义一也。出所以征诛，则莫不听从；入所以揖让，则莫不从服。故乐者，天下之大齐也，中和之纪也，人情之所必不免也。是先王立乐之术也。而墨子非之，奈何？

20.4 且乐者，先王之所以饰喜也；军旅鈇钺者，先王之所以饰怒也。先王喜怒皆得其齐焉。是故喜而天下和之，怒而暴乱畏之。先王之道，礼乐正其盛者也，而墨子非之。故曰：墨子之于道也，犹瞽之于白黑也，犹聋之于清浊也，犹欲之楚而北求之也。

【今译】

征伐，对内可用来行礼让。对于征伐与礼让，音乐的作用是一样的。对外用音乐作为征伐的工具，那就没有人不听从；对内用音乐作为礼让的手段，那就没有人不服从。所以音乐是齐一天下的工具，是中正和平的要领，是人的情感绝对不能脱离的东西。这就是古代圣王设置音乐的策略。可是墨子却反对音乐，又能怎么样呢？

20.4 况且音乐，是古代的圣王用来表现喜悦的；军队和刑具，是古代的圣王用来表现愤怒的。古代圣王的喜悦和愤怒都能通过音乐与军队刑具而表达得恰如其分。所以，圣王喜悦了，天下人就附和他；圣人愤怒了，凶暴作乱的人就害怕他。古代圣王的政治原则中，礼制和音乐正是其中的大事，但墨子却反对它们。所以说：墨子对于正确的政治原则，就好像是瞎子对于白色和黑色不能分辨一样，就好像是聋子对于音质的清浊不能区别一样，就好像是想到南方的楚国却到北方去寻找它一样。

moving forward is the way to suggest punitive expeditions and punishing offenders and their stepping back the way to suggest saluting and yielding.

The intent of punitive expeditions and punishing offenders is one and the same as saluting and yielding in musical performances. When the ranks move forward as the way to punish offenders, then none will fail to listen and follow. When the ranks step back as the way to salute and yield, none will fail to follow and submit. Thus musical performances are the greatest creator of uniformity in the world, the guiding line of the mean and of harmony, and a necessary and inescapable expression of man's emotional nature. Such was the method of the Ancient Kings in establishing their music. Yet Mozi condemns it. How can this be endured!

20. 4

Further, musical performances were what the Ancient Kings used to exhibit their delight. Armies and troops, battle-axes and halberds, were what they used to exhibit their anger. Both the delight and anger of the Ancient Kings obtained equal and uniform expression in this way. For this reason, when they showed delight, the whole world joined with them, and when they showed anger the violent and rebellious were filled with fear. It is precisely in their ritual and music that the Way of the Ancient Kings has its highest expression. Yet Mozi condemns it. Thus, I say that Mozi's understanding of the Way is like that of a blind man trying to distinguish white from black, or of a deaf man bass and treble notes, or like someone who tries to reach Chu [in the south] by traveling to the north.

【原文】

20.5 夫声乐之入人也深，其化人也速，故先王谨为之文。乐中平，则民和而不流；乐肃庄，则民齐而不乱。民和齐，则兵劲城固，敌国不敢婴也。如是，则百姓莫不安其处，乐其乡，以至足其上矣。然后名声于是白，光辉于是大，四海之民，莫不愿得以为师。是王者之始也。乐姚冶以险，则民流僈鄙贱矣。流僈则乱，鄙贱则争。乱争，则兵弱城犯，敌国危之。如是，则百姓不安其处，不乐其乡，不足其上矣。故礼乐废而邪音起者，危削侮辱之本也。故先王贵礼乐而

【今译】

20.5 那音乐渗入人心是很深的，它感化人心是很快的，所以古代的圣王谨慎地给它文饰。音乐中正平和，那么民众就和睦协调而不淫荡；音乐严肃庄重，那么民众就同心同德而不混乱。民众和睦协调，同心同德，那么兵力就强劲，城防就牢固，敌国就不敢来侵犯了。像这样，那么老百姓就无不满足于自己的住处，喜欢自己的家乡，以使自己的君主获得满足。然后，君主的名声就会因此而显著，光辉因此而增强，天下的民众，就没有谁不希望得到他让他做自己的君长。这是称王天下的开端啊。音乐妖冶轻浮而邪恶，那么民众就淫荡轻慢卑鄙下贱了。民众淫荡轻慢，就会混乱；卑鄙下贱，就会争夺。混乱又争夺，那就会兵力衰弱，城池被侵犯，敌国就会来危害了。像这样，那么老百姓就不会安居在自己的住处，就不会喜欢自己的家乡，也不会使自己的君主满足了。所以，礼制雅乐被废弃而靡靡之音兴起来，这是国家危险削弱、遭受侮辱的根源。所以古代的圣王

20. 5

The influence of music and sound on man is very profound, and the transformations they produce in him can be very rapid. Thus, the Ancient Kings were assiduous in creating proper forms. If music accords exactly with the mean and is evenly balanced, the people will be harmonious and not given to dissipation. If it is solemn and dignified, then the people will behave in a uniform manner and will not be inclined to disorder. Where the people are harmonious and behave in a uniform manner, the army is powerful and the cities securely defended so that enemy states will not dare try to surround and attack them. When this situation prevails, the Hundred Clans feel secure in their homes, and all take pleasure in their native villages and are entirely satisfied with their superiors. Only then do the name and fame of a state become plainly evident to all, its glory and brilliance become magnificently great, and all the people within the Four Seas long to obtain its ruler as their leader. Such is the beginning of true kingship.

If music spoils and seduces toward wickedness, then the people will become dissipated and indolent and will be mean-spirited and base. Where they are dissipated and indolent, there is disorder; where they are mean-spirited and base, there is conflict. Where there is disorder and conflict, the army is weak and the city walls are broken through, so that enemy states can threaten the existence of the state. When this situation prevails, the Hundred Clans feel insecure even in their own homes, are discontent with their native villages, and are dissatisfied with their superiors. Thus, casting aside ritual and music and allowing evil songs to develop is the root of danger and territorial encroachment for the country and of insult and dishonor for the ruler. Thus, the Ancient Kings esteemed ritual

【原文】

贱邪音。其在序官也，曰："修宪命，审诛赏，禁淫声，以时顺修，使夷俗邪音不敢乱雅，太师之事也。"

20.6 墨子曰："乐者，圣王之所非也，而儒者为之，过也。"君子以为不然。乐者，圣人之所乐也，而可以善民心，其感人深，其移风易俗易，故先王导之以礼乐而民和睦。

20.7 夫民有好恶之情而无喜怒之应，则乱。先王恶其乱也，故修其行，正其乐，而天下顺焉。故齐衰之服，哭泣之声，使人之心悲；带甲婴軸，歌于行伍，使人之心伤；姚冶之容，郑、卫之音，使

【今译】

看重礼制雅乐而鄙视靡靡之音。他在论列官职时，说："遵循法令，审查诗歌乐章，禁止淫荡的音乐，根据时势去整治，使蛮夷的落后风俗和邪恶的音乐不敢扰乱正声雅乐，这是太师的职事。"

20.6 墨子说："音乐，是圣明的帝王所反对的，而儒者却讲求它，那是错误的。"君子认为并不是这样。音乐是圣人所喜欢的，而且可以用来改善民众的思想，它感人至深，它改变风俗也容易，所以古代的圣王用礼制音乐来引导人民而人民就和睦了。

20.7 民众有了爱憎的感情而没有表达喜悦愤怒的方式来和它相应，就会混乱。古代的圣王憎恶这种混乱，所以修养自己的德行，端正国内的音乐，因而天下人就顺从他了。那披麻戴孝的丧服，哭泣的声音，会使人的内心悲痛；穿上铠甲，系上头盔，在部队中歌唱，会使人的内心忧伤；妖艳的容貌，郑国、卫国的靡靡之音，会使人的内

and music and despised evil songs. This is to be found in the "Precedence of Officials," where it says that the official duties of the Grand Master [of Music] encompass preparing model pieces and instructions, examining odes and note pitches, proscribing lewd tones, and following the appropriate season in his preparations so as to keep barbarian customs and unorthodox music from presuming to bring confusion to "elegant standard."

20. 6

Mozi says:"Music was something the sage kings condemned; so the Ru err in making music."

The gentleman considers that this is not true. Music was enjoyed by the sage kings; it can make the hearts of the people good; it deeply stirs men; and it alters their manners and changes their customs. Thus, the Ancient Kings guided the people with ritual and music, and the people became harmonious and friendly.

20. 7

If the people have the emotions of love and hate but have no means of responding with joy and anger, then there will be disorder. The Ancient Kings hated such disorder; thus, they reformed their own conduct and made their music correct so the whole world became obedient. Hence, garments for fasting and mourning and the sounds of lamentation and weeping cause the heart to be sad; donning armor and strapping on helmets with songs sung by marching columns cause the hearts of men to be roused. Seductive looks and the songs of Zheng and Wei cause the hearts

【原文】

人之心淫；绅端章甫，舞《韶》歌《武》，使人之心庄。故君子耳不听淫声，目不视女色，口不出恶言。此三者，君子慎之。

20.8 凡奸声感人而逆气应之，逆气成象而乱生焉；正声感人而顺气应之，顺气成象而治生焉。唱和有应，善恶相象，故君子慎其所去就也。

20.9 君子以钟鼓道志，以琴瑟乐心。动以干戚，饰以羽旄，从以磬管。故其清明象天，其广大象地，其俯仰周旋有似于四时。故乐行而志清，礼修而行成。耳目聪明，血气和平，移风易俗，天下皆

【今译】

心淫荡；系着宽大的腰带，穿着礼服，戴着礼帽，随着《韶》、《武》的乐曲载歌载舞，会使人的内心严肃。所以君子耳朵不聆听淫荡的音乐，眼睛不注视女子的美貌，嘴巴不说出邪恶的语言。这三件事，君子是慎重地对待的。

20.8 大凡淫邪的音乐感染人以后就有歪风邪气来应和它，歪风邪气形成了气候，那么混乱的局面就产生了。正派的音乐感动人以后就有和顺的风气来应和它，和顺的风气成了社会现象，那么秩序井然的局面就产生了。有唱必有和，善良的或邪恶的风气也随之而形成，所以君子对自己抛弃什么音乐，接受什么音乐是很慎重的。

20.9 君子用钟、鼓来引导人们的志向，用琴、瑟来使人们心情快乐。拿着盾牌、斧头等舞具来跳舞，用野鸡毛和牦牛尾等舞具做装饰，用石磬、箫管来伴奏。所以那乐声的清朗像天空，广大像大地，那舞姿的俯仰旋转又和四季的变化相似。所以音乐推行后人们的志向就会高洁，礼制遵循后人们的德行就能养成。要使人们耳聪目明，感

of men to be dissipated. The broad sash, straight gown, and Zhangfu cap with the *Succession* dance and the *Martial* music cause the hearts of men to be filled with dignity. Thus, the gentleman will not let his ear hear lewd sounds, or his eye gaze on the female body, or his mouth utter evil words. About these three matters, the gentleman is careful.

20. 8

As a general rule, when lewd music rouses, it is a rebellious spirit [*qi*] that is the response, and where that spirit achieves full representation, disorder is born. When correct music stirs men, it is an obedient spirit that is the response, which, when completely represented, gives birth to order. Just as the harmony of the singers is in response to the melody of the singing master, good and evil are fulfilled in their respective forms. Thus, the gentleman is careful in what he chooses and rejects.

20. 9

The gentleman uses the bell and drum to guide the inner mind and the *se* and *qin* zithers to gladden the heart. He is excited by the shields and battle-axes, is refined by the feathers and yak tails, and is made obedient by the chime stones and flutes. Thus, the music's purity and clarity [of melody] are in the image of Heaven; its breadth and greatness [of its rhythmic beat] are in the image of Earth; the dancers' poses and positions, their revolutions and movements, generally resemble the four seasons.

Hence, when music is performed, the inner mind becomes pure; and when ritual is cultivated, conduct is perfected. The ears become acute

【原文】

宁，莫善于乐。故曰：乐者，乐也。君子乐得其道，小人乐得其欲。以道制欲，则乐而不乱；以欲忘道，则惑而不乐。故乐者，所以道乐也。金石丝竹，所以道德也。乐行而民向方矣。故乐者，治人之盛者也，而墨子非之。

20.10 且乐也者，和之不可变者也；礼也者，理之不可易者也。乐合同，礼别异。礼乐之统，管乎人心矣。穷本极变，乐之情也；著诚去伪，礼之经也。墨子非之，几遇刑也。明王已没，莫之正也。愚者学之，危其身也。君子明乐，乃其德也。乱世恶善，不此听也。於

【今译】

情温和平静，改变风俗，天下都安宁，没有什么比音乐更好的了。所以说：音乐，就是欢乐的意思。君子把从音乐中获得道义作为欢乐，小人把从音乐中满足欲望当作欢乐。用道义来控制欲望，那就能欢乐而不淫乱；为满足欲望而忘记了道义，那就会迷惑而不快乐。所以音乐是用来引导人们娱乐的。金石丝竹之类的乐器是用来引导人们修养道德的。音乐推行后民众就向往道义了。所以音乐是治理人民的重大工具，但墨子却反对它。

20.10 况且音乐，是协调人情时不可变更的手段；礼制，是治理社会时不可更换的原则。音乐使人们同心同德，礼制使人们区别出等级的差异。所以礼制音乐的纲领，可以总管人们的思想了。深入地触动，极大地改变人的心性，是音乐的本质；彰明真诚，去掉虚伪，是礼制的永恒原则。墨子反对它们，近乎犯罪。圣明的帝王已经死去，没有人来加以纠正。愚蠢的人学习他，会危害自己的生命。君子彰明音乐，这才是仁德。混乱的社会厌恶善行，不听这提倡音乐的

and the eye clear-sighted; the blood humour becomes harmonious and in equilibrium, manners are altered and customs changed. The entire world is made tranquil, and enjoys together beauty and goodness. Therefore it is said:"music is joy." The gentleman enjoys obtaining proper instruction; the petty man enjoys obtaining what he desires. When music is used to guide and regulate the desires, there is enjoyment but no disorder; when it is used for the desires with no thought of guidance, there is delusion but no enjoyment. Therefore, musical performances are the means of guiding enjoyment.The instruments of metal, stone, silk, and bamboo are the means to guide the music, for whenever music is performed, the people sit in the direction to face it. Thus, music is the most perfect method of bringing order to men. Yet Mozi condemns it!

20. 10

Further music embodies harmonies that can never be altered, just as ritual embodies principles of natural order that can never be changed. Music joins together what is common to all; ritual separates what is different. The guiding principles of ritual and music act as the pitch pipe that disciplines the human heart.

It is the essential nature of music to seek to exhaust the root of things and to carry change to its highest degree. It is the continuous theme of ritual to illuminate what is genuine and to eliminate what is artificial.

One would have expected that Mozi, who condemns music, would have met with some kind of punishment. But all the enlightened kings had already died, and there was no one to put things aright. Stupid fools study him and thereby endanger their own existence. But the gentleman makes clear and brilliant his music and therewith his inner power. A chaotic age

【原文】

乎哀哉！不得成也。弟子勉学，无所营也。

20.11 声乐之象：鼓大丽，钟统实，磬廉制，竽、笙、箫、和、筦、籥发猛，埙、篪翁博，瑟易良，琴妇好，歌清尽，舞意天道兼。鼓，其乐之君邪？故鼓似天，钟似地，磬似水，竽、笙、箫、和、筦、籥似星辰日月，鞉、柷、拊、鞷、椌、楬似万物。曷以知舞之意？曰：目不自见，耳不自闻也，然而治俯仰诎信进退迟速莫不廉制，尽筋骨之力以要钟鼓俯会之节而靡有悖逆者，众积意谔谔乎。

【今译】

话。唉呀可悲啊！音乐因此而不能见成效。学生们努力学习吧，不要因为墨子的反对而有所迷惑啊。

20.11 音乐的象征：鼓声洪大高亢，钟声洪亮浑厚，磬声清越明朗，竽、笙、箫、和、管、籥等管乐器的声音昂扬激越，埙、篪的声音浩瀚磅礴，瑟的声音平易温良，琴的声音柔婉优美，歌声清朗而曲尽其情，舞蹈的意象则包容了自然界的一切现象。鼓，大概是音乐的主宰吧？所以鼓声像天，钟声像地，磬声像水，竽、笙、箫、和、管、籥等管乐器的声音像日月星辰，鞉、柷、拊、鞷、椌、楬的声音像万物。凭什么来了解舞蹈的意象呢？回答说：跳舞的人眼睛不能看见自己的形体，耳朵不能听到自己的声音，但是处理低头、抬头、弯曲、伸直、前进、后退、缓慢、快速的动作时无不干净利落明白清楚，尽身体的力量去迎合钟、鼓的节奏，而无所违背，众人集中注意力真认真啊！

despises goodness and will not listen to such teachings. Alas, is it not a cause for sadness, for they will never attain any success? Students exert yourselves in your studies lest you be bedazzled!

20. 11

The Symbolism of Music

The drum represents vastness and grandeur; the bell, fullness and wholeness; the chime stone, restrained control; the reed pipes and *sheng* reed organ, solemn harmony; the tubc flute and flageolet, spirited outburst; the ocarina and bamboo flute, rising mists; the *qin* zither, easy kindness; the *se* zither, tender grace; the singers, pure fulfillment; and the spirit of the dance is conjoined with the Way of Heaven.

Is not the drum the lord of the music! Thus, the drum resembles Heaven; the bell resembles Earth; the chime stones, water; the reed pipes, *sheng* reed organs, tube flute, and flageolet, the heavenly bodies—the stars, comets, moon, and sun; and the pellet drum and tambour, the leathern chaff drum and the *ge* sounding box, and the *qiang* tambourine and *qia* sounding box, the myriad things.

How can we know the idea of the dance? I say the eyes do not see it and the ears do not hear it. Rather, it happens only when the order of every episode of gazing down and lifting up the face, of bending and straightening, of advancing and retreating, and of retardation and acceleration is excuted with proper, restrained control; when the strength of bone and flesh has been so thoroughly trained that every movement is in such agreement with the rhythm of the drums, bells, and ensemble that there is never an awkward or wayward motion; and when these, through constant practice, are combined into an ideal that is realized again and again.

【原文】

20.12 吾观于乡而知王道之易易也。主人亲速宾及介，而众宾皆从之；至于门外，主人拜宾及介，而众宾皆入；贵贱之义别矣。三揖至于阶，三让以宾升，拜至，献酬，辞让之节繁；及介省矣；至于众宾，升受，坐祭，立饮，不酢而降；隆杀之义辨矣。工人，升歌三终，主人献之；笙入，三终，主人献之；间歌三终，合乐三终，工告乐备，遂出。二人扬觯，乃立司正。焉知其能和乐而不流也。宾酬

【今译】

20.12 我看到了乡中请人喝酒的礼仪就知道先王的政治原则实施起来是容易又容易的了。主人亲自去邀请贤德的贵宾和德行稍次的陪客，而一般客人就都跟着他们来了；来到门外，主人向贵宾和陪客拱手鞠躬，而一般客人就都进门了；对高贵者和卑贱者的不同礼仪就这样分别开来了。主人拱手作揖三次才与贵宾来到厅堂的台阶下，再谦让三次而使贵宾登上厅堂，再拜谢贵宾的到来，主人献酒酬宾，推辞谦让的礼节十分繁多；至于陪客，那礼节就减少了；至于一般客人，登堂受酒，坐着酹酒祭神，站着饮酒，不用酒回敬主人就退下堂去了；隆重与简省的礼仪就这样分别开来了。乐工进来，登上厅堂，把《鹿鸣》、《四牡》、《皇皇者华》三首歌各唱一遍，主人敬酒；吹笙的人进来，把《南陔》、《白华》、《华黍》三支乐曲各吹奏一遍，主人敬酒；乐工与吹笙的间隔着轮流歌唱演奏各三曲，再合着歌唱演奏各三曲，乐工报告乐曲已经完备，就出去了。主人的两个侍从举起酒杯帮

20. 12

When I observe the village wine ceremony, I realize how easy and gentle is the Way of the King. The host goes in person to greet the chief guest and his attendant; all the other guests follow afterward. When they reach the outer gate of the host's house, the host bows in welcome to the chief guest and his attendant; all the other guests simply enter of themselves. In this way the obligations due the noble are kept separate from those due the more humble. With the exchange of three bows between host and guest, they reach the steps, and after the guest has thrice deferred, the host takes the guest up to his place. Bowing deeply, he presents the wine cup in pledge. There follow many episodes of deferring and polite refusals between host and chief guest, but they are more sparing with his attendant. The other guests ascend the stairs to receive the cup, kneel to make an offering of some of the wine, stand up to drink it, and without presenting the pledge cup to the host in response, they descend the stairs. In this way the obligations due those who are exalted are kept distinct from those due persons of lesser station.

The performers enter, ascend the stairs, and sing three pieces, at the conclusion of which the host presents them the wine cup. The *sheng* reed organ players enter and perform their three pieces, at the end of which the host offers the wine cup to them as well. The singers and *sheng* reed organ players then play three pieces in which they perform antiphonally. When these have been completed, they perform in ensemble three additional pieces. At the end of these, the performers announce that the musical entertainment is over and proceed to leave.

【原文】

主人，主人酬介，介酬众宾，少长以齿，终于沃洗者。焉知其能弟长而无遗也。降，脱屦升坐，修爵无数。饮酒之节，朝不废朝，莫不废夕。宾出，主人拜送，节文终遂。焉知其能安燕而不乱也。贵贱明，隆杀辨，和乐而不流，弟长而无遗，安燕而不乱，此五行者，足以正身安国矣。彼国安而天下安。故曰：吾观于乡而知王道之易易也。

【今译】

助敬酒，于是又设置了监督行礼的专职人员。从这些礼仪之中可以知道他们能够和睦安乐而不淫荡。贵宾向主人敬酒表示答谢，主人向陪客敬酒表示答谢，陪客向一般客人敬酒表示答谢，宾主按年龄长少排列次序依次酬谢，最后轮到向主人手下盥洗酒杯的人酬谢。从这些礼仪之中可以知道他们能够尊敬年长的而不遗漏一个人。退下堂去，脱去鞋子，再登堂就坐，依次不断地敬酒。请人喝酒的限度是，在早晨饮酒不耽误早上的工作，在傍晚喝酒不耽误晚上的事情。贵宾出门，主人拱手鞠躬送行，礼节仪式就完成了。从这些礼仪中可以知道他们能够逸乐而不乖乱。高贵者和卑贱者被区别清楚，隆重的礼仪和简省的礼仪被分别开来，和睦安乐而不淫荡，尊重年轻的尊敬年长的而不遗漏一个人，逸乐而不乖乱，这五种行为，足够用来端正身心安定国家了。那国家安定了，那么整个天下也就安定了。所以说：我看到了乡中请人喝酒的礼仪就知道先王的政治原则实施起来是极其容易的。

Two men are designated by the host to raise the horn tankard in a toast to the guest of honor, and at the same time another man is made master of ceremonies. From this we know that it is possible to be congenial and to enjoy oneself without dissipation. The chief guest pledges the wine cup to the host; the host pledges it to his attendant; and the attendant pledges it to the other guests. Young and old take a drink from it in order of age. At the conclusion the tankard is rinsed and washed. In this way we know that it is possible for junior and senior to drink together without anyone being left out.

At the end of the formal ceremonies, descending the stairs, they remove their sandals; ascending again, they resume their places. Now they may "cultivate" the wine cup without limit on the number of drinks. But there should be moderation in the drinking of the wine, for the duties of the morning at court may not be neglected nor may those of the evening. When the main guest departs, the host bows deeply and escorts him out; thus the regulations and forms are concluded. From this we can see that it is possible to be content and at ease yet in no way become disorderly.

Being clear about the distinction between noble and base; keeping distinct those to be exalted and those to be diminished; being congenial and enjoying oneself without dissipation; observing the distinctions between junior and senior without leaving anyone out; and being content and at ease yet in no way becoming disorderly—these five patterns of conduct are sufficient to rectify the individual and to make the country tranquil. When the country has been made tranquil, the empire can be made tranquil. Thus, I say that when I observe the village wine ceremony, I realize how easy and gentle is the Way of the King.

【原文】

20.13乱世之征：其服组，其容妇，其俗淫，其志利，其行杂，其声乐险，其文章匿而采，其养生无度，其送死瘠墨，贱礼义而贵勇力，贫则为盗，富则为贼。治世反是也。

【今译】

20.13混乱的社会的迹象：那里的服装华丽，男人的容貌打扮得像妇女一样妖媚，那里的风俗淫荡，人们的志向是惟利是图，人们的行为驳杂不纯，那里的音乐邪恶怪僻，那里的文章内容邪恶而辞藻华美，那里的人将养身体没有限度，葬送死人俭省刻薄，轻视礼制与道义而崇尚勇敢与武力，贫穷的就盗窃，富裕的就贼害他人。治理得好的社会则与此相反。

20. 13

The Evidence of a Chaotic Age

Men wear brightly colored clothing; their demeanor is softly feminine; their manners are lascivious; their minds are bent on profit; their conduct lacks consistency; their music is wicked; and their patterns and decorations are gravely in error and gaudy. They nurture the needs of the living without measure, but they send off their dead in a niggardly manner and with blackly impure principles. They despise ritual and moral principles, and prize instead valor and feats of strength. When they are poor, they become robbers;when they are rich, they become predators. An orderly age is the opposite of this.

解蔽第二十一

【原文】

21.1 凡人之患，蔽于一曲而暗于大理。治则复经，两疑则惑矣。天下无二道，圣人无两心。今诸侯异政，百家异说，则必或是或非，或治或乱。乱国之君，乱家之人，此其诚心莫不求正而以自为也，妒缪于道而人诱其所迨也。私其所积，唯恐闻其恶也。倚其所私以观异术，唯恐闻其美也。是以与治虽走而是已不辍也。岂不蔽于一曲而失正求也哉?心不使焉，则白黑在前而目不见，雷鼓在侧而耳不闻，况

【今译】

21.1 大凡人的毛病，是被事物的某一个局部所蒙蔽而不明白全局性的大道理。整治思想就能回到正道上来，在偏见与大道理两者之间拿不定主意就会疑惑。天下不会有两种对立的正确原则，圣人不会有两种对立的思想。现在诸侯各国的政治措施不同，各个学派的学说不同，那么必定是有的对，有的错；有的能导致安定，有的会造成混乱。搞乱国家的君主，搞乱学派的学者，这些人的真心没有不想找一条正道来为自己服务，只是由于他们对正确的原则既嫉妒又带有偏见，因而别人就能根据他们的爱好去引诱他们。他们偏爱自己平时积累的学识，只怕听到对自己学识的非议。他们凭自己所偏爱的学识去观察与自己不同的学说，只怕听到对异己学说的赞美。因此，他们与正确的治理原则背道而驰了却还自以为是，不能勒马。这难道不是被事物的一个局部所蒙蔽而失去了对正道的追求吗?如果心思不用在正道上，那么白的黑的就是摆在面前而眼睛也会看不见，雷鼓就在身旁

Book 21

Dispelling Blindness

21. 1

It is the common flaw of men to be blinded by some small point of the truth and to shut their minds to the Great Ordering Principle. If cured of this flaw, they can return to the classical standard, but if they remain with double principles, they will stay suspicious and deluded. The world does not have two Ways, and the sage is not of two minds.

Now, since the feudal lords employ different principles of government and the Hundred Schools offer different explanations, of necessity some will be right and others wrong, some will produce order and others disorder. The lords of disorderly states and men from disorderly schools all seek in their genuine minds after what is right and from their point of view believe that this is what they have done, but having misconstrued the proper Way, others entice them with what pleases them. Partial to their own accumulated experience, they fear only that they will hear of some fault in it. Since they are totally dependent on their partialities, when they see methods other than their own, they fear only that they will hear something good about them. This is why they abandon and run away from anything that would cure the faults in their knowledge. Still they do not cease to regard themselves as being in the right. How indeed could they not be obsessed with a small point of the truth and miss the very thing they sought! When the mind is not employed, then although black and white are in front of a person's own eyes, he will not see them, or although the thunder drums are sounding on either side of him, his ears

【原文】

于使者乎！德道之人，乱国之君非之上，乱家之人非之下，岂不哀哉？

21.2 故为蔽？欲为蔽，恶为蔽；始为蔽，终为蔽；远为蔽，近为蔽；博为蔽，浅为蔽；古为蔽，今为蔽。凡万物异，则莫不相为蔽，此心术之公患也。

21.3 昔人君之蔽者，夏桀、殷纣是也。桀蔽于末喜、斯观而不知关龙逢，以惑其心而乱其行；纣蔽于妲己、飞廉而不知微子启，以惑其心而乱其行。故群臣去忠而事私，百姓怨非而不用，贤良退处而隐逃，此其所以丧九牧之地而虚宗庙之国也。桀死于亭山，纣县于赤

【今译】

敲击而耳朵也会听不进，何况对那些被他们视为异端的用心于正道的人，就更看不见，听不进了。掌握了正确的政治原则的人，搞乱国家的君主在上面非难他，搞乱学派的学者在下面非难他，这难道不是很可悲的吗？

21.2 什么东西会造成蒙蔽？爱好会造成蒙蔽，憎恶也会造成蒙蔽；只看到开始会造成蒙蔽，只看到终了也会造成蒙蔽；只看到远处会造成蒙蔽，只看到近处也会造成蒙蔽；知识广博会造成蒙蔽，知识浅陋也会造成蒙蔽；只了解古代会造成蒙蔽，只知道现在也会造成蒙蔽。大凡事物有不同的对立面的，无不会交互造成蒙蔽，这是思想方法上一个普遍的祸害啊。

21.3 从前君主中有被蒙蔽的，夏桀、商纣就是。夏桀被妹喜、斯观所蒙蔽而不赏识关龙逢，因而使自己思想惑乱而行为荒唐；商纣被妲己、飞廉所蒙蔽而不赏识微子启，因而使自己思想惑乱而行为荒唐。所以，群臣都抛弃了对他们的忠心而去谋求私利，百姓都怨恨责怪他们而不为他们效劳，贤能优秀的人才都辞官在家而隐居避世，这就是他们丧失九州的土地而使建有宗庙的国都成为废墟的原因。夏桀死在鬲山，商纣的头被悬挂在红色的旗帜飘带上，他们自己不能预先

will not hear them. How much more then is this true of a person whose mind is obsessed like theirs! The man who has attained the Way is condemned by lords of disorderly states on the one hand and by men of the Hundred Schools on the other. Are they not to be pitied indeed!

21. 2

What makes for blindness? One can be blinded by desire or aversion, by the beginnings of things or their end, by what is remote or what is near, by broadness or shallowness, by antiquity or modernity. Since each of the myriad things evokes a different reaction, there is none that could not obsess the mind. This is the universal flaw of the operation of the mind.

21. 3

In the past, Jie of the Xia dynasty and Zhou Xin of the Yin dynasty were lords of men who were blinded. Jie was beclouded by Mo Xi and Si Guan and so was insensible to the merits of Guan Longfeng . Thereby his mind became deluded and his conduct disorderly. Zhou Xin was beclouded by Daji and Feilian and so was insensible to the merits of Viscount Qi of Wei. Thereby his mind became deluded and his conduct disorderly. Thus, the whole of their ministers forsook the loyalty due their lord and served their own selfish ends; the Hundred Clans were enraged at their wrongdoing and could not be employed; and the worthy and good withdrew from court and fled into seclusion. This is the reason they lost the territory of the Nine Shepherds and made a ruin of the country of their ancestral temples. Jie died on Mount Li, and Zhou Xin's head was hung from the red pennon. They were not themselves prescient of their bad end,

【原文】

旆，身不先知，人又莫之谏，此蔽塞之祸也。

成汤鉴于夏桀，故主其心而慎治之，是以能长用伊尹而身不失道，此其所以代夏王而受九有也。文王鉴于殷纣，故主其心而慎治之，是以能长用吕望而身不失道，此其所以代殷王而受九牧也。远方莫不致其珍，故目视备色，耳听备声，口食备味，形居备宫，名受备号，生则天下歌，死则四海哭，夫是之谓至盛。《诗》曰："凤凰秋秋，其翼若干，其声若箫。有凤有凰，乐帝之心。"此不蔽之福也。

21.4 昔人臣之蔽者，唐鞅、奚齐是也。唐鞅蔽于欲权而逐载子，

【今译】

知道自己的过错，而别人又没有谁劝阻他们，这就是蒙蔽的祸害啊。

商汤以夏桀为前车之鉴，所以拿定主意而谨慎地治理国家，因此能够长期地任用伊尹而本身又不背离正确的治国原则，这就是他取代夏桀而得到九州的原因。周文王吸取了商纣王的教训，所以拿定主意而谨慎地治理国家，因此能够长期地任用吕望而本身又不背离正确的治国原则，这就是他取代商纣王而得到九州的原因。远方的国家无不送上自己的珍贵物品，所以他们的眼睛能观赏所有的美色，耳朵能听到各种各样的美妙音乐，嘴巴能吃上所有的山珍海味，身居各种豪华的宫殿，名字上被加上各种美好的称号；活着的时候天下人都歌功颂德，死了以后天下人都痛哭流涕，这叫做极其昌盛伟大。《诗》云："凤凰翩翩起舞飞翔，它的翅膀像盾牌一样，它的鸣声像洞箫悠扬。又有凤来又有凰，使王心中喜洋洋。"这就是不被蒙蔽的幸福啊。

21.4 从前臣子中有被蒙蔽的，唐鞅、奚齐就是。唐鞅蒙蔽于追

and no one was able to remonstrate with them. Such is the misfortune of blindness and being closed to the truth.

Tang the Successful looked in the mirror for a Jie of Xia, thus controlling his mind and attentively putting it in order. In this way he was able to long employ Yi Yin and in his own person did not miss the Way. This is why he succeeded the Xia King and received the Nine Possessions. King Wen looked in the mirror for a Zhou Xin of Yin and thus controlled his mind and attentively put it in order. In this way he was able to long employ Lü Wang and in his own person did not miss the Way. This is why he succeeded the Yin king and received the territory of the Nine Shepherds. From the most distant regions, none failed to send [Kings Tang and Wen] the rarest goods. Thus, their eyes beheld every kind of color, their ears listened to every kind of sound, their mouths tasted every conceivable flavor, their bodies rested in the most perfect of palaces, and their names received every title of honor. When they lived, all under heaven sang; when they died, all within the four seas wailed. Truly this may be called "perfect prosperity." An *Ode* says:

> The male and female phoenix posture and dance,
> their wings spread out like shields,
> their calls sounding forth like panpipes.
> When there is a female and a male phoenix,
> the heart of the Di Ancestor is gladdened.

Such are the blessings of not being obsessed.

21. 4

Formerly, Tang Yang and Xiqi were ministers who were beclouded. Tang Yang was blinded by his desire for power, and so he expelled Mas-

【原文】

奚齐蔽于欲国而罪申生。唐鞅戮于宋，奚齐戮于晋。逐贤相而罪孝兄，身为刑戮，然而不知，此蔽塞之祸也。故以贪鄙背叛争权而不危辱灭亡者，自古及今，未尝有之也。

鲍叔、宁戚、隰朋仁知且不蔽，故能持管仲而名利福禄与管仲齐。召公、吕望仁知且不蔽，故能持周公而名利福禄与周公齐。传曰："知贤之谓明，辅贤之谓能。勉之强之，其福必长。"此之谓也。此不蔽之福也。

21.5 昔宾孟之蔽者，乱家是也。墨子蔽于用而不知文，宋子蔽于欲而不知得，慎子蔽于法而不知贤，申子蔽于势而不知知，惠子蔽

【今译】

求权势而驱逐了戴驩，奚齐蒙蔽于争夺政权而加罪于申生。结果唐鞅在宋国被杀，奚齐在晋国被杀。唐鞅驱逐有德才的国相而奚齐加罪于孝顺的兄长，结果自己被杀了，然而仍不明白为什么，这就是蒙蔽的祸害啊。所以，因为贪婪鄙陋而违背正道争权夺利却又不遭到危险屈辱灭亡的，从古到今，还不曾有过。

鲍叔、宁戚、隰朋仁德明智而且不被蒙蔽，所以能够扶助管仲，而他们享有的名声财利幸福俸禄也和管仲相等。召公、吕望仁德明智而且不被蒙蔽，所以能够扶助周公，而他们享有的名声财利幸福俸禄也和周公相等。古书上说："能识别贤人叫做明智，能辅助贤人叫做贤能。努力识别贤人，尽力辅助贤人，他的幸福一定长久。"说的就是这个。这就是不被蒙蔽的幸福啊。

21.5 从前游士中有被蒙蔽的，搞乱学派的学者就是。墨子蒙蔽于只重实用而不知文饰，宋子蒙蔽于只见人有寡欲的一面而不知人有贪得的一面，慎子蒙蔽于只求法治而不知任用贤人，申子蒙蔽于只知权势的作用而不知才智的作用，惠子蒙蔽于只务名辩而不知实际，庄

ter Dai. Xiqi was obsessed with desire for the state, and so he incriminated Shensheng. Tang Yang was executed in Song, and Xiqi in Jin. One expelled a worthy prime minister and the other incriminated a filial elder brother. Both brought the punishment of execution on themselves, yet both remained insensible. Such is the misfortune of blindness and being closed to the truth. Thus, from antiquity to the present, there have never been any who, having been covetous, fomented rebellion, or wrangled for power, did not meet with mortal danger, disgrace, or ultimate destruction.

Bao Shu, Ning Qi, and Xi Peng were humane, wise, and also free from obsession, which is why they were able to support Guan Zhong and to obtain fame, benefits, blessings, and emoluments equal to those of Guan Zhong. The Duke of Shao and Lü Wang were humane, wise, and also not beclouded, which is why they were able to support the Duke of Zhou and to obtain fame, benefits, blessings, and emoluments equal to those of the duke. A tradition says:

> Intelligence means recognizing the worthy. Ability means assisting the worthy. Encourage and strengthen them and one's blessings are certain to be long lasting.

This expresses my meaning. Such are the blessings of not being obsessed.

21. 5

In the past, there was the blindness of senior retainers, of which the disordered schools are examples. Mo Di was blinded by utility and was insensible to the value of good form. Song Xing was blinded by desire and was insensible to satisfaction. Shen Dao was blinded by law and was insensible to worth. Shen Buhai was blinded by technique and was insensible to knowledge. Hui Shi was blinded by propositions and was insen-

【原文】

于辞而不知实，庄子蔽于天而不知人。故由用谓之道，尽利矣；由俗谓之道，尽嗛矣；由法谓之道，尽数矣；由势谓之道，尽便矣；由辞谓之道，尽论矣；由天谓之道，尽因矣。此数具者，皆道之一隅也。夫道者，体常而尽变，一隅不足以举之。曲知之人，观于道之一隅而未之能识也，故以为足而饰之，内以自乱，外以惑人，上以蔽下，下以蔽上，此蔽塞之祸也。

孔子仁知且不蔽，故学乱术足以为先王者也。一家得周道，举而用之，不蔽于成积也。故德与周公齐，名与三王并，此不蔽之福也。

【今译】

子蒙蔽于只知自然的作用而不知人的力量。所以，从实用的角度来谈道，就全谈功利了；从欲望的角度来谈道，就全谈满足了；从法治的角度来谈道，就全谈法律条文了；从权势的角度来谈道，就全谈权势的便利了；从名辩的角度来谈道，就全谈些不切实际的理论了；从自然的角度来谈道，就全谈些因循依顺了。这几种说法，都是道的一个方面。道，本体经久不变而又能穷尽所有的变化，一个角度是不能够用来概括它的。一知半解的人，只看到道的一个方面而没有能够真正认识它，所以把这一个方面当作为完整的道而研究它，于是内扰乱了自己学派的思想，外迷惑了别人，上被臣民所蒙蔽，下被君主所蒙蔽，这就是蒙蔽的祸害啊。

孔子仁德明智而且不被蒙蔽，所以多方学习，集其大成而足以用来辅助古代圣王的政治原则。只有孔子这一派掌握了周备全面的道，推崇并运用它，而不被成见旧习所蒙蔽。所以他的德行与周公相等

sible to realities. Zhuang Zhou was blinded by Nature and was insensible to men.

Thus in a doctrine called the Way grounded on "utility," everyone will be consumed with seeking profit. In a doctrine called the Way grounded in "desire," everyone will concentrate on seeking satisfaction. In one that grounds everything in "law," every decision becomes wholly a matter of calculation. In one that grounds everything in "technique," every action becomes wholly a matter of adaptation. In one that grounds philosophy in "propositions," thinking becomes entirely a matter of assessing things through logical argumentation. And in a doctrine called the Way grounded in "Nature," everything becomes wholly a matter of "relying on things as they occur in nature."

Each of these methods encompasses but a single corner of the Way. But the Way itself is constant in its form yet completely changeable. One corner is an insufficient basis for drawing conclusions about it. Men with knowledge of some small point gaze upon their single corner of the Way and are never able to recognize that it is only a small corner. Thus, they consider it sufficient and proceed to embroider upon it. Within they bring disorder upon themselves; without they cause others to be deluded. Those in high position cause their subordinates to be beclouded; those in subordinate positions cause their superiors to be blinded. Such are the misfortunes of blindness and being closed to the truth.

Confucius was humane, wise, and also free from obsession. This is why his study of methods that could produce order deserves to be considered equal to that of the Ancient Kings. One school achieved the universal Way, drew conclusions based upon it, and employed it, but did not become obsessed with what it had perfected and accumulated. Thus, the

【原文】

21.6圣人知心术之患，见蔽塞之祸，故无欲、无恶，无始、无终，无近、无远，无博、无浅，无古、无今，兼陈万物而中县衡焉。是故众异不得相蔽以乱其伦也。

21.7何谓衡?曰：道。故心不可以不知道。

心不知道，则不可道而可非道。人孰欲得恣而守其所不可，以禁其所可?以其不可道之心取人，则必合于不道人，而不知合于道人。以其不可道之心与不道人论道人，乱之本也。夫何以知?

【今译】

同，名声和三代开国之王相并列，这就是不被蒙蔽的幸福啊。

21.6圣人知道思想方法上的毛病，看到被蒙蔽的祸害，所以既不任凭爱好，又不任凭憎恶，既不是只看到开始，又不是只看到终了，既不是只看到近处，又不是只看到远处，既不只务广博，又不安于浅陋，既不是只了解古代，又不是只知道现在，而是同时摆出各种事物并在其中根据一定的标准进行权衡。所以众多的差异与对立面就不能互相掩盖以致搞乱了条理。

21.7什么是权衡事物的标准呢?回答说：就是道。所以心里不可以不了解道。

如果心里不了解道，就会否定道而认可违背道的东西。人有谁想要得到自在却遵奉自己否定的东西而用它来制止自己所赞成的东西呢?用他那种否定道的思想去选取人，就一定会和不奉行道的人情投意合，而不会和奉行道的人志同道合。带着他那种否定道的思想和不奉行道的人去议论奉行道的人，这就是社会混乱的祸根。像这样，那

moral authority of Confucius was equal to that of the Duke of Zhou and his reputation was on an equal footing with that of the Three Kings. Such are the blessings of not being obsessed.

21. 6

The sage knows the flaws of the mind's operation and perceives the misfortunes of blindness and being closed to the truth. This is why he is without desires and aversions, without beginnings and ends of things, without the remote or near, without broadness or shallowness, without antiquity or modernity. He lays out all the myriad things and causes himself to exactly match how each settles on the suspended balance. This is why for the sage, the multitude of different reactions to things cannot produce obsession by one thing's beclouding another and so disturbing their proper position.

21. 7

What is the balance? I say that it is the Way. This is why it is inadmissible for the mind not to know the Way. If the mind does not know the Way, then it may disallow the Way and allow what is contrary to the Way. What man freely able to obtain what he desires would hold on to what he rejects in order to exclude what he allows? If one uses a mind that rejects the Way to select men, then certainly one will congregate with others who are not of the Way and not join with men of the Way. To use a mind that rejects the Way to assess men of the Way with men who are not of the Way is the root of disorder. The root of disorder is to assess men of the Way with a mind that rejects the Way and that uses as its basis men

【原文】

曰：心知道，然后可道。可道，然后能守道以禁非道。以其可道之心取人，则合于道人而不合于不道之人矣。以其可道之心与道人论非道，治之要也。何患不知？

故治之要在于知道。

21.8 人何以知道？曰：心。

心何以知？曰：虚一而静。心未尝不臧也，然而有所谓虚；心未尝不满也，然而有所谓一；心未尝不动也，然而有所谓静。人生而有知，知而有志；志也者，臧也；然而有所谓虚，不以所已臧害所将受，谓之虚。心生而有知，知而有异；异也者，同时兼知之；同时兼知之，两也。然而有所谓一，不以夫一害此一谓之一。心卧则梦，偷

【今译】

还凭什么去了解奉行道的人呢？

再说：心里了解了道，然后就会赞成道。赞成道，然后就能遵奉道来制止违背道的东西。用他那种赞成道的思想去选取人，就会和奉行道的人情投意合，而不会和不奉行道的人同流合污了。带着他那种赞成道的思想和奉行道的人去议论违背道的人，这是社会得到治理的关键。像这样，又何必担忧不能了解奉行道的人呢？

所以，把社会治理好的关键在于了解道。

21.8 人靠什么来了解道呢？回答说：靠心。

心靠什么来了解道呢？回答说：靠虚心、专心和静心。心从来没有不储藏信息的时候，但却有所谓虚；心从来没有不彼此兼顾的时候，但却有所谓专；心从来没有不活动的时候，但却有所谓静。人生下来就有智能，有了智能就有记忆，记忆嘛，也就是储藏信息。但是有所谓虚，不让已经储藏在心中的见识去妨害将要接受的知识就叫做虚心。心生来就有智能，有了智能就能区别不同的事物；区别不同的事物，也就是同时了解了它们；同时了解它们，也就是彼此兼顾。但是有所谓专，不让那一种事物来妨害对这一种事物的认识就叫做专

who are not of the Way. How could this be knowledge?

The mind knows the Way. Only when the mind knows the Way can it approve the Way. And only after it approves the Way can it abide by the Way and exclude what is contrary to it. If one uses a mind that approves the Way to select men, then one will congregate with men of the Way and not join with men who are not of the Way. The crucial factor necessary to put things in order is to use a mind that approves the Way in conjunction with men of the Way whenever assessing what is contrary to the Way. How, then, could one suffer the calamities that come from being insensible? Therefore the critical factor necessary to put things in order consists in understanding the Way.

21. 8

What do men use to know the Way? I say that it is the mind. How does the mind know? I say by its emptiness, unity, and stillness. The mind never stops storing; nonetheless it possesses what is called emptiness. The mind never lacks duality; nonetheless it possesses what is called unity. The mind never stops moving; nonetheless it possesses what is called stillness. Men from birth have awareness. Having awareness, there is memory. Memories are what is stored, yet the mind has the property called emptiness. Not allowing what has previously been stored to interfere with what is being received in the mind is called emptiness. The mind from birth has awareness. Having awareness, there is perception of difference. Perception of difference consists in awareness of two aspects of things at the same time. Awareness of two aspects of things all at the same time entails duality; nonetheless the mind has the quality called unity. Not allowing the one thing to interfere with the other is called

【原文】

则自行，使之则谋，故心未尝不动也；然而有所谓静，不以梦剧乱知谓之静。未得道而求道者，谓之虚一而静，作之则。将须道者，之虚则人；将事道者，之壹则尽；将思道者，静则察。知道察，知道行，体道者也。虚一而静，谓之大清明。万物莫形而不见，莫见而不论，莫论而失位。坐于室而见四海，处于今而论久远，疏观万物而知其情，参稽治乱而通其度，经纬天地而材官万物，制割大理而宇宙里矣。恢恢广广，孰知其极？睪睪广广，孰知其德？涫涫纷纷，孰知其

【今译】

心。心，睡着了就会做梦，懈怠的时候就会擅自驰骋想象，使用它的时候就会思考谋划，所以心从来没有不活动的时候；但是有所谓静，不让梦幻和烦杂的胡思乱想扰乱了智慧就叫做静心。对于还没有掌握道而追求道的人，要告诉他们虚心、专心和静心的道理，以作为他们的行动准则。想要求得道的人，达到了虚心的地步就能够得到道；想要奉行道的人，达到了专心的地步就能够穷尽道的全部；想要探索道的人，达到了静心的地步就能够明察道。了解道十分明察，知道了道能实行，这就是实践道的人。达到了虚心、专心与静心的境界，这叫做最大的清澈澄明。他对万事万物，没有什么露出了形迹而看不见的，没有什么看见了而不能评判的，没有什么评判了而不到位的。他坐在屋里而能看见整个天下，处在现代而能评判远古，通观万物而能看清它们的真相，检验考核社会的治乱而能通晓它的法度，治理天地而能控制利用万物，掌握了全局性的大道理而整个宇宙就都了如指掌了。宽阔广大啊，谁能知道他智慧的尽头？浩瀚广大啊，谁能知道他德行的深厚？千变万化、纷繁复杂，谁能知道他思想的轮廓？光辉与

unity. When the mind is asleep, it dreams. When it relaxes, it moves of its own accord. When it is employed in a task, it plans. Thus the mind never stops moving; nonetheless it possesses the quality called stillness. Not allowing dreams and fantasies to bring disorder to awareness is called stillness.

One who has not yet attained the Way but is seeking it should be told of emptiness, unity, and stillness and should make of them his example. If you intend to seek the Way, become empty and you can enter into it. If you intend to serve the Way, attain oneness and you can exhaust it. If you intend to ponder the Way, attain stillness and you can discern it. A person who knows the Way and discerns it and puts it into practice embodies the Way. Emptiness, unity, and stillness are called the Great Pure Understanding.

Each of the myriad things has a form that is perceptible. Each being perceived can be assigned its proper place. Each having been assigned its proper place will not lose its proper position. Although a person sits in his own house, yet he can perceive all within the four seas. Although he lives in the present, he can put in its proper place what is remote in space and distant in time. By penetrating into and inspecting the myriad things, he knows their essential qualities. By examining and testing order and disorder, he is fully conversant with their inner laws. By laying out the warp and woof of Heaven and Earth, he tailors the functions of the myriad things. By regulating and distinguishing according to the Great Ordering Principle, he encompasses everything in space and time.

Extensive and complete, broad and wide—who knows his limits? Bright and luminous, brilliant and shining—who knows his inner power? Rolling and bubbling, multitudinous and multifarious—who can know his external form? Brightness comparable to the sun and moon; greatness filling the

【原文】

形?明参日月，大满八极，夫是之谓大人。夫恶有蔽矣哉?

21.9心者，形之君也，而神明之主也，出令而无所受令；自禁也，自使也；自夺也，自取也；自行也，自止也。故口可劫而使墨云，形可劫而使诎申，心不可劫而使易意，是之则受，非之则辞。故曰：心容，其择也无禁，必自见；其物也杂博，其情之至也不贰。《诗》云:“采采卷耳，不盈顷筐。嗟我怀人，寘彼周行。”顷筐易满也，卷耳易得也，然而不可以贰周行。故曰：心枝则无知，倾则不精，贰则疑惑。以赞稽之，万物可兼知也。身尽其故，则美。类不可

【今译】

太阳月亮相当，博大充塞了八方极远的地方，这样的人就叫做伟大的人。这种人哪里还会有被蒙蔽的呢?

21.9心是身体的主宰，是精神的主管，它发号施令而不从什么地方接受命令；它自己限制自己，自己驱使自己；它自己决定抛弃什么，自己决定接受什么；它自己行动，自己停止。所以，嘴巴可以强迫它沉默或说话，身体可以强迫它弯曲或伸直，心不可以强迫它改变意志，它认为什么对就接受，认为什么错就拒绝。所以说：心采纳外界事物的时候，它的选择是不受什么限制的，而一定根据自己的见解；它认识的事物虽然繁杂而广泛，但它的精诚到来时是不会三心二意的。《诗》云:“采呀采呀采卷耳，老装不满斜口筐。唉我怀念心上人，把筐放在大路上。”斜口筐是容易装满的，卷耳是容易采到的，但是不可以三心二意地呆在大路上。所以说：思想分散就不会有知识，思想偏斜就不会精当，思想不专一就会疑惑。如果拿专心一致的态度来辅助考察，那么万事万物就可以全部被了解了。亲自透彻地了

Eight Poles—such a person is truly what is meant by "Great Man." How indeed could he have obsessions!

21. 9

The mind is the lord of the body and master of the spiritual intelligence. It issues commands but does not receive commands. On its own authority it forbids or orders, renounces or selects, initiates or stops. Thus, the mouth can be forced to be silent or to speak. The body can be forced to crouch down or stretch out. But the mind cannot be forced to change its ideas. If the mind thinks something right, it will accept it; but if it thinks something wrong, then it will reject it. Therefore, it is said that the state of the mind is such that of necessity it perceives on its own. No prohibitions can be placed on what it selects. Its objects are diverse and extensive. When it has perfect concentration, it is not divided in purpose. An *Ode* says:

> I pick and pick the curly ear,
> But it will not fill my slanting basket.
> I sigh for my beloved man;
> he is placed in the ranks of Zhou.

A slanting basket is easy to fill. Curly ear is easy to obtain. Nonetheless, she could not fill the basket because she was divided in purpose over the ranks of Zhou. Therefore it is said:

> If the mind goes astray, it will lack knowledge. If it is deflected, it will not have unity of purpose. If it is divided in purpose, it will be filled with doubts and delusions.

By being one with the Way, and through using it to test things, the myriad things can be known in their entirety. If the body is wholly one

【原文】

两也，故知者择一而一焉。

21.10 农精于田而不可以为田师，贾精于市而不可以为市师，工精于器而不可以为器师。有人也，不能此三技而可使治三官。曰：精于道者也，精于物者也。精于物者以物物，精于道者兼物物。故君子一于道而以赞稽物。一于道则正，以赞稽物则察；以正志行察论，则万物官矣。

21.11 昔者舜之治天下也，不以事诏而万物成。处一之危，其荣

【今译】

解万事万物的所以然，那就完美了。认识事物的准则不可能有对立的两种，所以明智的人选择一种而专心于它。

21.10 农民精于种田，却不能以此做管理农业的官吏；商人精于买卖，却不能以此做管理市场的官吏；工人精于制造器物，却不能以此做管理器具制造的官吏。有些人，不会这三种技术，却可以让他们来管理这三种职业。所以说：有精于道的人，有精于具体事物的人。精于具体事物的人只能支配这种具体事物，精于道的人则能够全面地支配各种事物。所以君子专心于道而用它来帮助自己考察万物。专心于道就能正确无误，用它来帮助自己考察万物就能看得非常清楚；用正确的思想去处理非常清楚的调查结论，那么万物就能被利用了。

21.11 从前舜治理天下，不用事事告诫而各种事情都办成了。固守专心于道的原则而达到了戒惧的境界，他的光荣就会充满身旁；培

with the Way, the person is refined. Logical categories cannot have dual principles. Thus, the wise select oneness and unify everything in terms of it.

21. 10

The farmer concentrates on his fields, yet it would be inadmissible to consider him for the position of director of the fields. The merchant concentrates on the marketplace, but it would be inadmissible to consider him for director of the marketplace. The artisan concentrates on his wares, but it would be inadmissible to consider him for director of wares. There are men incapable of these three skills who could be commissioned to put in order any of these three offices. I say that they are men who concentrate on the Way and [not] merely on things. One who concentrates on things will treat each thing as a particular thing. One who concentrates on the Way will treat things in all their combinations as things. Thus, the gentleman is one with the Way and uses it to further his testing of things. If he is at one with the Way, then he will be right; and if he uses it to further his testing of things, then he will be discerning. If using the right frame of mind and proceeding with discernment he deploys things in their proper positions, the myriad things will perform their natural functions.

21. 11

In the past, when Shun put the world in order, he did not issue instructions about each task, yet the myriad things were brought to completion. Abide in unity, being anxiously on guard about it, and its flowering will fill

【原文】

满侧；养一之微，荣矣而未知。故《道经》曰：“人心之危，道心之微。”危微之几，惟明君子而后能知之。故人心譬如盘水，正错而勿动，则湛浊在下，而清明在上，则足以见须眉而察理矣。微风过之，湛浊动乎下，清明乱于上，则不可以得大形之正也。心亦如是矣。故导之以理，养之以清，物莫之倾，则足以定是非、决嫌疑矣。小物引之，则其正外易，其心内倾，则不足以决庶理矣。故好书者众矣，而仓颉独传者，一也；好稼者众矣，而后稷独传者，一也；好乐者众矣。而夔独传者，一也；好义者众矣，而舜独传者，一也。倕作弓，

【今译】

养专心于道的品德达到了精妙的境界，那就会在不知不觉中得到光荣。所以《道经》说：“一般人的思想只能达到戒惧的境界，得道之人的思想才能达到精妙的境界。”这戒惧与精妙的苗头，只有明智的君子才能了解它。人的思想就像盘中的水，端正地放着而不去搅动，那么沉淀的污浊的渣滓就在下面，而清澈的透明的水就在上面，那就能够用来照见胡须眉毛并看清楚皮肤的纹理了。但如果微风在它上面吹过，沉淀的污浊的渣滓就会在下面泛起，清澈的透明的水就会在上面被搅乱，那就不能靠它获得人体的正确映象了。人的思想也像这样啊。如果用正确的道理来引导它，用高洁的品德来培养它，外物就不能使它倾斜不正，那就能够用来判定是非、决断嫌疑了。如果有点小事牵制了他，那么他那端正的神态就在外表上发生了变化，他的思想就在胸中发生了倾斜，那就不能够用来决断各种事理了。古代喜欢写字的人很多，但只有仓颉一个人的名声流传了下来，这是因为他用心专一啊；喜欢种庄稼的人很多，但只有后稷一个人的名声流传了下来，这是因为他用心专一啊；爱好音乐的人很多，但只有夔一个人的名声流传了下来，这是因为他用心专一啊；爱好道义的人很多，但只有舜一个人的名声流传了下来，这是因为他用心专一啊。倕制造了弓，浮

every side. Nurture unity, being attentive to its subtlest manifestations, and its flowering will never be recognized. Thus, the *Classic of the Way* says:

> The mind of man is anxiously on guard; the mind of the Way is attentive to these subtle manifestations.

Only the gentleman who has already become bright and clear is able to know the first hints of being anxiously on guard or of attentiveness to subtle manifestations.

Hence, the human mind may be compared to a pan of water. If you place the pan upright and do not stir the water up, the mud will sink to the bottom, and the water on top will be clear and pure enough to see your beard and eyebrows and to examine the lines on your face. But if a slight wind passes over its surface, the submerged mud will be stirred up from the bottom, and the clarity and purity of the water at the top will be disturbed so that it is impossible to obtain the correct impression of even the general outline of the face.

Now, the mind is just the same. Thus, if you lead it with rational principles, nurture it with purity, and not allow mere things to "tilt" it, then it will be adequate to determine right and wrong and to resolve any doubtful points. But if small things pull at it so that its right relation with the external world is altered and the mind's inner workings are "tilted," then it will be inadequate to decide even gross patterns.

Thus, those who have been fond of writing have been many, yet that Cang Jie alone has been remembered is due to his unity of purpose. Those who have been fond of husbandry have been many, yet that Houji alone has been remembered is due to his unity of purpose. Those who have been fond of music have been many, yet that Kui alone has been remembered is due to his unity of purpose. Those who have been fond of

【原文】

浮游作矢，而羿精于射；奚仲作车，乘杜作乘马，而造父精于御。自古及今，未尝有两而能精者也。曾子曰："是其庭可以搏鼠，恶能与我歌矣？"

21.12 空石之中有人焉，其名曰觙。其为人也，善射以好思。耳目之欲接，则败其思；蚊虻之声闻，则挫其精。是以辟耳目之欲，而远蚊虻之声，闲居静思，则通。思仁若是，可谓微乎？孟子恶败而出妻，可谓能自强矣。有子恶卧而焠掌，可谓能自忍矣，未及好也。辟耳目之欲，可谓能自强矣，未及思也。蚊虻之声闻则挫其精，可谓危

【今译】

游创造了箭，而羿善于射箭；奚仲制造了车，乘杜发明了用四匹马拉车，而造父精通驾车。从古到今，还从来没有过一心两用而能专精的人。曾子说："唱歌的时候看着那打节拍的小棍而心想可以用它来打老鼠，又怎么能和我一起唱歌呢？"

21.12 空石的城邑内有一个人，他的名字叫觙。他生性善于猜测而喜欢思考。但耳朵、眼睛所向往的音乐、美色一旦和他接触，就会破坏他的思考；蚊子虻蝇的声音一传到他耳朵里，就会妨害他聚精会神。因此他避开耳朵、眼睛所向往的音乐、美色，并远离蚊子、虻蝇的声音，独自居住静静地思考，于是他的思路就畅通了。如果思考仁德也像这样，可以说达到精妙的境界了吗？孟子怕败坏了自己的仁德而把妻子休出家门，这可以说是能够自己勉力向上了，但还没有能达到思考仁德的地步。有子怕打瞌睡而用火烧灼自己的手掌，这可以说是能够自我克制的了，但还没有能达到爱好仁德的地步。觙避开耳朵、眼睛所向往的音乐、美色，并远离蚊子、虻蝇的声音，可以说是

morality have been many, yet that Shun alone has been remembered is due to his unity of purpose.

Chui invented the bow and Fuyou made the arrow, but it was Yi who concentrated on archery. Xizhong invented the chariot and Chengdu discovered how to harness horses to it, yet it was Zaofu who concentrated on charioteering. From antiquity until the present day there has never been anyone that was of two minds who was able to concentrate on a single purpose. Master Zeng said:"If a man is looking at his courtyard to see whether he can catch a rat, how can he be able to sing with me?"

21. 12

There was a man who lived in a stone cave whose name was Ji . He was the kind of man who was expert at guessing riddles, which he was fond of pondering. But if the desires of his eye and ear were stimulated, then his thoughts would be shattered. If he heard the sounds of mosquitoes or gnats, it would destroy his concentration. For this reason, he avoided the desires of the eye and ear and went far away from the sounds of mosquitoes and gnats. So he lived apart and pondered in quietude until he completely understood. If he had pondered the principle of humanity like this, could he be said to have attained subtly?

Mencius hated the impropriety of his wife's breaking convention and so he turned her out. This could be said to show he had personal strength of will but that he never reached real thought. Master You hated falling asleep so he burned the palm of his hand. This could be said to show that he was able to exercise self-endurance, but that he never reached real devotion to thought. To avoid the desires of the eyes and ears and (···) [go far away from] the sounds of mosquitoes and

【原文】

矣，未可谓微也。夫微者，至人也。至人也，何强？何忍？何危？故浊明外景，清明内景。圣人纵其欲，兼其情，而制焉者理矣。夫何强？何忍？何危？故仁者之行道也，无为也；圣人之行道也，无强也。仁者之思也，恭；圣人之思也，乐。此治心之道也。

21.13 凡观物有疑，中心不定，则外物不清；吾虑不清，则未可定然否也。冥冥而行者，见寝石以为伏虎也，见植林以为后人也，冥冥蔽其明也。醉者越百步之沟，以为跬步之浍也；俯而出城门，以为小之闺也；酒乱其神也。厌目而视者，视一以为两；掩耳而听者，听

【今译】

达到戒惧的境界了，但还不可以说是达到了精妙的境界。那达到了精妙境界的人，就是思想修养达到了最高境界的人。既然是思想修养达到了最高境界的人，还要什么勉力？还要什么克制？还要什么戒惧？所以混沌地明白道的人只能在外表露出光彩，清楚地明白道的人才能在心灵深处闪发出光芒。圣人即使放纵自己的欲望，尽量满足自己的情感，但他管理的事情仍然能治理好。那还要什么勉力？还要什么克制？还要什么戒惧？所以仁者奉行道，是无所作为的；圣人奉行道，是没有什么勉强的。仁者的思索恭敬慎重；圣人的思索轻松愉快。这就是修养思想的方法。

21.13 大凡观察事物有疑惑，内心不平静，那么外界的事物就看不清；自己的思想混乱不清，那就不能判断是非。在昏暗中走路的人，看见横卧的石头就以为是趴着的老虎，看见矗立的树林就以为是跟随着的人，这是昏暗蒙蔽了他的视力。喝醉酒的人过百步宽的水道，以为是过一二步宽的小沟；低着头走出城门，以为是走出狭小的宫中小门；这是酒扰乱了他的心神。按捺眼睛去看的人，看一件东西

gnats could be called anxiously keeping oneself on guard, but could never be called subtle.

True subtlety is the quality of the Perfect Man. What need has the Perfect Man for strength of will, for endurance, or for anxiously keeping himself on guard? Thus,a muddied brightness casts an external shadow, and a pure brightness shows a reflection from within.

The sage follows his desires and fulfills his emotions, but having regulated them, he accords with rational principles of order. Truly what need has he for strength of will, for endurance, or for keeping guard against unsteadiness? Thus, the man of humane principles in practicing the Way requires no assertion in his actions. The sage's practice of the will requires no strength of will. The thought of the man of humane principles is reverent; that of the sage is joyous. This is the Way of putting the mind in order.

21. 13

As a general rule, when examining things about which there are doubts, if the mind is not inwardly settled, then external things will not be clear. If my reflections are not clear, then I will never be able to settle what is so of a thing and what is not so of it.

Someone walking along a road in the dark may see a fallen stone and think it a tiger crouching in ambush, or he may see an upright tree and think it a standing man. The darkness has beclouded the clarity of his vision. A drunk may jump across a ditch a hundred paces wide, thinking it a drain half a pace wide, or may stoop down to go out the city gate, thinking it a small doorway. The drink has disordered his spirit. Pressing against the eye while looking at an object will make it appear double;

【原文】

漠漠而以为哅哅；势乱其官也。故从山上望牛者若羊，而求羊者不下牵也，远蔽其大也。从山下望木者，十仞之木若箸，而求箸者不上折也，高蔽其长也。水动而景摇，人不以定美恶，水势玄也。瞽者仰视而不见星，人不以定有无，用精惑也。有人焉，以此时定物，则世之愚者也。彼愚者之定物，以疑决疑，决必不当。夫苟不当，安能无过乎？

21.14 夏首之南有人焉，曰涓蜀梁，其为人也，愚而善畏。明月而宵行，俯见其影，以为伏鬼也；仰视其发，以为立魅也；背而走，比至其家，失气而死。岂不哀哉？凡人之有鬼也，必以其感忽之间、

【今译】

会以为是两件；捂住耳朵去听的人，听那默默无声会以为是嗡嗡作响；这是因为外力扰乱了他的官能。从山上远望山下的牛就好像是羊，但求取羊的人是不会下山去牵的，这是距离掩盖了牛的高大。从山下远望山上的树木，七丈高的树木像根筷子，但求取筷子的人是不会上山去折的，这是高远掩盖了树木的长度。水晃动而影子也晃动，人们不会以此来判定容貌的美丑，这是水形使人眼花了。瞎子抬头观望而看不见星星，人们不会以此来判定星星的有无，这是眼睛看不清东西。如果有人在这种时候断定事物，那就是世界上的蠢人。那些蠢人断定事物，是用疑惑不清的心去判断疑惑不清的事物，判断一定不得当。判断如果不得当，又怎么能没有错误呢？

21.14 夏首的南边有一个人，名叫涓蜀梁，他生性愚蠢而容易害怕。在月光明亮的夜晚行走，低头看见自己的身影，就以为是趴在地上的鬼；抬头看见自己的头发，就以为是站着的妖怪；于是转身就跑，等跑到自己的家中，就断气死了。这难道不可悲吗？大凡人认为有鬼，一定是在他精神恍惚的当口、疑惑迷乱的时候来判定它的。这

covering the ears when listening will make silence seem like a clamor. The force applied to the sense organs has disordered them. Hence, looking down at oxen from the top of a mount will make them appear the size of a sheep, but someone looking for sheep will not go down to lead them away. The distance has obscured their true size. If from the foot of a mountain you look up at the trees, trees ten cubits high look like chopsticks, but someone looking for chopsticks would not climb up to break them off. The height has obscured their true length. When water is moving and reflections waver, men do not use it to determine their beauty or ugliness. The circumstances of the water make for deception. A blind man [tilting his head back] and looking up will not see the stars; so men do not have him determine whether there are stars or not. The essential vigor of his eyes is impaired. If there were anyone who would use occasions such as these to determine the nature of things, then he would be the biggest fool in the world. Such a fool's determination of things uses what is doubtful to judge doubtful points. The judging would of necessity be invalid. And if indeed his judging is invalid, how can he not err?

21. 14

South of the mouth of the Xia river there was a man named Juan Shuliang. He was a foolish man who was prone to fright. One evening when the moon was bright, he was out walking when he looked down and saw his own shadow, which he took to be a crouching ghost. Raising his head, he caught sight of his own hair and took it to be an ogre standing over him. He turned his back on the shadow and raced away. Just when he reached his house, he lost his *qi* vital breath and died. Alas, what a shame!

As a general rule, when men think there are ghosts, the confirmation

【原文】

疑玄之时正之。此人之所以无有而有无之时也，而己以正事。故伤于湿而击鼓——鼓痹，则必有敝鼓丧豚之费矣，而未有俞疾之福也。故虽不在夏首之南，则无以异矣。

21.15 凡以知，人之性也；可以知，物之理也。以可以知人之性，求可以知物之理，而无所疑止之，则没世穷年不能遍也。其所以贯理焉虽亿万，已不足以浃万物之变，与愚者若一。学，老身长子，而与愚者若一，犹不知错，夫是之谓妄人。故学也者，固学止之也。恶乎止之?曰：止诸至足。曷谓至足?曰：圣也。圣也者，尽伦者也；王也者，尽制者也；两尽者，足以为天下极矣。故学者，以圣王

【今译】

正是人们把有当作没有，把没有当作有的时候，但他们自己却在这个时候去判定事情。有人得了风湿病却想敲鼓来驱除疾病，并烹猪求神，那就一定会有打破鼓、丧失猪的破费了，而不会有治愈疾病的幸福。所以这种人即使不住在夏首的南边，却也与涓蜀梁没有什么区别的了。

21.15 一般地说，能够认识事物，是人的本性；事物可以被认识，是事物的规律。凭借可以认识事物的人的本性，去探求可以被认识的事物的规律，如果对此没有一定的限制，那么过完了一辈子，享尽了天年也不能遍及可以认识的事物。人们学习贯通事理的方法即使有成亿上万条，但如果最终不能够用它们来通晓万事万物的变化，那就和蠢人相同了。像这样来学习，自己老了，子女长大了，仍和蠢人相同，却还不知道放弃这种无益的做法，这就叫做无知妄人。学习嘛，本来就要有个学习的范围。把自己的学习范围限制在哪里呢?回答说：把它限制在最圆满的境界。什么叫做最圆满的境界?回答说：就是通晓圣王之道。圣人嘛，就是完全精通事理的人；王者嘛，就是彻底精通制度的人；这两个方面都精通的人，就完全可以成为天下最

of it is certain to be an occasion when they are startled or confused. These are occasions when these men take what does not exist for what does and what does exist for what does not, and they settle the matter on the basis of their own experience. Hence, if a person affected by the dampness contracts rheumatism, and being afflicted by rheumatism, he beats a drum and boils a piglet, the only certain result is that he has worn out a drum and has squandered a pig, but he will never have the blessing of being cured of his illness. Thus, although he does not live to the south of the mouth of the Xia, there is no difference between him and the man who did.

21. 15

As a general principle, the faculty of knowing belongs to the inborn nature of man. That things are knowable is a part of the natural principle of order of things. Men use their innate faculty of knowing to seek the natural principles of order, which allow things to be known. But if no boundary to the search is fixed, then even to the end of your life you will be incapable of knowing everything. Although you may make countless attempts to master the natural principles of order, in the end your effort will be insufficient to encompass the complete cycle of the transformation of the myriad things, and you and the fool will be as one. Although you study until old age and your children have grown up, you and the fool will still be as one, for even then you do not know when to give up. Truly this is to be what is called a reckless fool.

Thus, true learning inherently has a terminus to study. Where is its terminus? I say that it is at complete sufficiency. Who has such sufficiency? I say it is the sage [king]. Sageliness consists in a comprehensive grasp of the natural relationships between men. True kingship consists in

【原文】

为师，案以圣王之制为法，法其法以求其统类，以务象效其人。向是而务，士也；类是而几；君子也；知之，圣人也。故有知非以虑是，则谓之惧；有勇非以持是，则谓之贼；察孰非以分是，则谓之篡；多能非以修荡是，则谓之知；辩利非以言是，则谓之詍。传曰："天下有二：非察是，是察非。"谓合王制与不合王制也。天下有不以是为隆正也，然而犹有能分是非、治曲直者邪？若夫非分是非、非治曲直、非辨治乱、非治人道，虽能之，无益于人，不能，无损于人；案直将治怪说，玩奇辞，以相挠滑也；案强钳而利口，厚颜而忍诟，无正而

【今译】

高的师表了。所以学习嘛，要把圣王当作老师，要把圣王的制度当作自己的法度，效法圣王的法度而探求他们的纲领，并努力效法他们的为人。向往这种圣王之道而努力追求的，就是士人；效法这种圣王之道而接近它的，就是君子；通晓这种圣王之道的，就是圣人。所以，有了智慧却不是用来考虑这圣王之道，那就叫做畏怯；有了勇力却不是用来维护这圣王之道，那就叫做贼害；观察问题仔细周详却不是用来分析这圣王之道，那就叫做篡逆；很有才能却不是用来学习研究并发扬光大这圣王之道，那就叫做巧诈；能说会道口齿伶俐却不是用来宣传这圣王之道，那就叫做废话。古书上说："天下有两个方面：一是根据错误的来考察正确的，一是根据正确的来考察错误的。"这所谓的正确与错误，是指符合圣王的法度和不符合圣王的法度。天下如果不把这圣王的法度作为最高标准，那还有能分辨是非、整治曲直的东西吗？至于那种不分辨是非、不整治曲直、不辨别治乱、不整治人类社会道德规范的学说，即使精通它，对人也没有什么裨益，即使不能掌握它，对人也没有什么损害，这不过是要钻研奇谈怪论，玩弄怪僻的词句，用来互相扰乱罢了；他们强行钳制别人而能说会道，厚着脸

a comprehensive grasp of the regulations for government. A comprehensive grasp of both is sufficient to become the ridgepole for the world. Hence, the student should take the sage king as his teacher and the regulations of the sage king as the model. By patterning himself after their example, he seeks out their guiding principles and general categories and devotes his attention to making himself into the image and imitation of these men. To strive for this goal to be a scholar-knight. To come close to realizing this ideal is to be a gentleman. To know it is to be a sage.

Hence, knowledge not used to reflect on the Sage kings' regulations is called "thievery." Bravery not used to support them is called "predation." Skill in investigation not used to analyze them to apportion social duties with them is called "presumption." An abundance of abilities not used to cultivate and enlarge his regulations is called "cleverness." Eloquence in discriminations not used to discuss them is called "loquaciousness." A tradition says:

> The world has two principles for judging: through the wrong to discern the right and through the right to discern the wrong.

In this "right" refers to what is consistent with the regulations of the king and "wrong" to what is not. In the world some do not consider these regulations to the exalted norm of what is correct. This being so, although they have ability, could they properly separate the right from the wrong or determine what is straight and what crooked? If they cannot separate things as right and wrong, cannot determine what is straight and what crooked, cannot engage in disputations on the causes of order and chaos, and cannot make orderly the Way of men, their having ability is without value to mankind and their not having ability is of no harm. Directly one will see them treating abstruse theories and playing with shocking propositions in order to dismay and confound each other. Violently aggressive

【原文】

恣睢，妄辨而几利，不好辞让，不敬礼节，而好相推挤，此乱世奸人之说也。则天下之治说者，方多然矣。传曰："析辞而为察，言物而为辨，君子贱之。博闻强志，不合王制，君子贱之。"此之谓也。

21.16 为之无益于成也，求之无益于得也，忧戚之无益于几也，则广焉能弃之矣，不以自妨也，不少顷干之胸中。不慕往，不闵来，无邑怜之心，当时则动，物至而应，事起而辨，治乱可否，昭然明矣！

21.17 周而成，泄而败，明君无之有也。宣而成，隐而败，暗君

【今译】

皮而忍受着辱骂，不守正道而恣肆放荡，胡乱诡辩而惟利是图，不喜欢谦让，不尊重礼节，而喜欢互相排挤，这是混乱的社会中奸诈之人的学说啊。可是，现在天下研究思想学说的人，却大多是这样。古书上说："分析言辞而自以为明察，空谈名物而自以为善于辨别，君子鄙视这种人，见识广而记忆力强，但不符合圣王的法度，君子鄙视这种人。"说的就是这种情况啊。

21.16 如果做了而无益于成功，追求了而无益于取得，担忧了而无益于实现愿望，那就统统可以抛弃，不让那些事妨碍自己，不让它们有片刻的时间在心中干扰自己。不羡慕过去，不担忧未来，没有忧愁怜悯的心情，适合时势就行动，外物来了就接应，事情发生了就处理，这样，是治还是乱，是合适还是不合适，就明明白白地都清楚了。

21.17 牢守秘密而成功，泄露秘密而失败，英明的君主没有这种

yet glib, brazenly impudent yet impervious to shame, without personal rectitude and so unrestrained and overbearing, proposing absurd arguments with an eye only for profit, not fond of showing appropriate deference, not taking care to observe the main points of ritual courtesy, but fond of pushing and shoving for advantage over each other—such are the theories of the evil men of a disordered age. And yet, of those who treat theories in today's world, are not most like this? A tradition says:

> To analyze propositions without discernment and to discuss things without using discriminations—the gentleman despises that. To be broadly learned and strong of memory and not to conform to the regulations of the king—the gentleman despises that.

This is my meaning.

21. 16

If actions do not contribute to success, if the search does not lead to attainment, and if distress and anxiety do not contribute to resolving the crisis, then you should cast them completely aside. Do not allow them to thwart you; do not allow them to stir in your breast for even a moment. Do not think longingly over what has gone by; do not worry over what is to come; do not let your heart be regretful or grieving. If it is the proper time, act. Respond to things as they arrive. Discriminate matters as they occur. Then matters of order and disorder and what is allowable and what is not will be clearly evident.

21. 17

There has never been an enlightened lord who was secretive yet suc-

【原文】

无之有也。故君人者周，则谗言至矣，直言反矣，小人迩而君子远矣。《诗》云："墨以为明，狐狸而苍。"此言上幽而下险也。君人者宣，则直言至矣，而谗言反矣，君子迩而小人远矣。《诗》曰："明明在下，赫赫在上。"此言上明而下化也。

【今译】

事。袒露真情而成功，隐瞒真相而失败，昏暗的君主没有这种事。统治人民的君主如果讲求隐蔽周密，那么毁谤的话就来了，正直的话就缩回去了，小人接近而君子远离了。《诗》云："你把黑暗当光明，他说狐狸呈深蓝。"这是说君主昏庸愚昧，那么臣民就会险恶。统治人民的君主如果开诚布公，那么正直的话就来了，而毁谤的话就缩回去了，君子接近而小人远离了。《诗》云："皎洁明亮在下方，光辉灿烂在上方。"这是说君主光明正大，那么臣民就会被感化。

cessful or frank yet a failure. Nor has there been a case of a benighted ruler who was open yet successful or mysterious yet a failure. Hence, if one who is a lord of men is secretive, then only words of slander will reach him, and honest advice will be turned back. Petty men will approach, and gentlemen will keep their distance. An *Ode* says:

Black darkness is thought bright light;
The yellow foxes dance about.

These words refer to how dark secretiveness of the superior results in a threat represented by his inferiors. If a lord of men is open, honest advice will come forward and slanderous words will be turned back. Gentlemen will approach, and petty men will keep at a distance. An *Ode* says:

Bright and clear are those below;
Glorious and brilliant the one above.

These words say that when the superior is enlightened, his subjects are transformed.

正名第二十二

【原文】

22.1 后王之成名：刑名从商，爵名从周，文名从《礼》，散名之加于万物者则从诸夏之成俗曲期。远方异俗之乡，则因之而为通。

散名之在人者：生之所以然者谓之性。性之和所生、精合感应、不事而自然谓之性。性之好、恶、喜、怒、哀、乐谓之情。情然而心为之择谓之虑。心虑而能为之动谓之伪。虑积焉，能习焉，而后成谓之伪。正利而为谓之事。正义而为谓之行。所以知之在人者谓之知。知

【今译】

22.1 现代圣王确定名称：刑法的名称依从商朝的，爵位的名称依从周朝的，礼仪制度的名称依从《礼经》，赋予万物的各种具体名称则依从中原地区华夏各诸侯国已经形成的习俗与各方面的共同约定。远方不同习俗的地区，就依靠这些名称来进行交流。

在人事方面的各种具体名称：人生下来之所以这样叫做天性。天性的和气所产生的、精神接触外物感受的反应、不经人为努力而自然形成的东西叫做本性。本性中的爱好、厌恶、喜悦、愤怒、悲哀、快乐叫做感情。感情是这样，而心灵对它进行选择，叫做思虑。心灵思虑后，官能为之而行动，叫做人为。思虑不断积累，官能反复练习，而后形成一种常规，也叫做人为。为了功利去做叫做事业。为了道义去做叫做德行。在人身上所具有的用来认识事物的能力叫做知觉。知

Book 22

On the Correct Use of Names

22. 1

The established names of the Later Kings: They followed the Shang dynsaty in the terminology of criminal law, the Zhou dynasty in the names of titles of rank and dignity, and the *Rituals* in the names of forms of culture. In applying various names to the myriad things, they followed the established custom and general definitions of the central Xia states. For villages of distant regions that practice divergent customs, they relied on the standard terminology [of the Xia states] and enabled these villages to be put into communication.

The various names for what is within man:What characterizes a man from birth is called his "nature." What is produced out of the harmony of inborn nature, out of the sensibilities of the organ tallying as the senses respond to stimuli, and what from birth is effortless and spontaneous are called "nature." The feelings of liking and disliking, of delight and anger, and of sorrow and joy that are inborn in our nature are called "emotions." The emotions being so paired, the mind's choosing between them is called "thinking." The mind's thinking something and the natural abilities' acting on it is called "conscious exertion." When thoughts are accumulated and one's natural abilities have been practiced so that something is completed, it is called "conscious exertion." Acting on considerations of legitimate profit is called "business"; acting on considerations of a correct sense of moral principles is called "[virtuous] conduct." The means of knowing which is within

【原文】

有所合谓之智。智所以能之在人者谓之能。能有所合谓之能。性伤谓之病。节遇谓之命。

是散名之在人者也，是后王之成名也。

22.2 故王者之制名，名定而实辨，道行而志通，则慎率民而一焉。故析辞擅作名以乱正名，使民疑惑，人多辨讼，则谓之大奸，其罪犹为符节、度量之罪也。故其民莫敢托为奇辞以乱正名，故其民悫。悫则易使，易使则公。其民莫敢托为奇辞以乱正名，故一于道法而谨于循令矣。如是，则其迹长矣。迹长功成，治之极也。是谨于守名约之功也。

【今译】

觉和所认识的事物有所符合叫做智慧。在人身上所具有的用来处置事物的能力叫做本能。本能和处置的事物相适合叫做才能。天性受到伤害叫做疾病。制约人生的遭遇叫做命运。

这些就是在人事方面的各种具体名称，这些就是现代圣王确定的名称。

22.2 王者制定事物的名称，名称一旦确定，那么实际事物就能分辨了；制定名称的原则一旦实行，那么思想就能沟通了；于是就慎重地率领民众统一到这些名称上来。所以，支解词句、擅自创造名称来扰乱正确的名称，使民众疑惑不定，使人们增加争辩，那就要称之为罪大恶极的坏人，他的罪和伪造信符与度量衡的罪一样。所以圣王统治下的民众没有谁敢依靠制造怪僻的词句来扰乱正确的名称，因此他的民众就很朴实。朴实就容易使唤，容易使唤就能成就功业。他的民众没有谁敢依靠制造怪僻的词句来扰乱正确的名称，所以就专心于遵行法度而谨慎地遵守政令了。像这样，那么他的统治就长久了。统治长久而功业建成，是政治的最高境界啊。这是严谨地坚持用名称来约束民众的功效啊。

man is called "awareness." Awareness tallying with the facts is called "knowledge." The means of being able that is within man is called "ability." Ability corresponding with the requirements of a situation is called "being capable." Injury to original nature is called "illness." Opportunities encountered unexpectedly are called "fate." Such are the various names for what is within man. They are the established names of the Later Kings.

22. 2

Accordingly, the way a True King institutes names [is as follows]. Because fixed names keep objects distinguished and because when his Way is practiced his goals are universally understood, he takes pains to produce uniformity [in regard to names and his Way] among the people. Because hair-splitting with propositions and creating names on one's own authority brings confusion to the correct use of names and causes the people to be suspicious, multiplying argument and litigation among them, the True King labels these "Great Evils, " to be punished as severely as the crimes of forging credentials or tampering with weights and measures. Hence, none of his people dare avail themselves of odd propositions in order to create confusion in the correct use of names. Thus they are guileless. Being guileless, they are easy to control. Being easy to control, there is meritorious accomplishment. Since none dare avail themselves of odd propositions to bring confusion to the correct use of names, his people are thus united in adhering to his laws and meticulously follow their orders. When such a situation prevails, his legacy will long endure. To have one's legacy long endure and one's meritorious accomplishments brought to completion is the epitome of good government. These are the results of being assiduous in seeing that agreed upon names are observed.

【原文】

22.3 今圣王没，名守慢，奇辞起，名实乱，是非之形不明，则虽守法之吏、诵数之儒，亦皆乱也。若有王者起，必将有循于旧名，有作于新名。然则所为有名，与所缘以同异，与制名之枢要，不可不察也。

22.4 异形离心交喻，异物名实玄纽，贵贱不明，同异不别。如是，则志必有不喻之患，而事必有困废之祸。故知者为之分别制名以指实，上以明贵贱，下以辨同异。贵贱明，同异别，如是，则志无不

【今译】

22.3 现在圣明的帝王去世了，名称的管理松懈了，怪僻的词句产生了，名称和实际事物的对应关系很混乱，正确和错误的轮廓不清楚，那么即使是掌管法度的官吏、讲述礼制的儒生，也都昏乱不清。如果再有王者出现，一定会对旧的名称有所沿用，并创制一些新的名称。这样的话，那么对于为什么要有名称、使事物的名称有同有异的根据、以及制定名称的关键等问题，就不能不搞清楚了。

22.4 不同的人如果用不同的意念来互相晓喻，不同的事物如果让名称和实际内容混乱地缠结在一起，那么社会地位的高贵和卑贱就不能彰明，事物的相同和相异就不能分别。像这样，那么意思就一定会有不能被了解的忧患，而事情就一定会有陷入困境而被废弃的灾祸。所以明智的圣王给万事万物分别制定名称来指明实际事物，上用来彰明高贵和卑贱，下用来分辨相同和相异。高贵和卑贱彰明了，相

22. 3

Now, since the sage kings are no more, the preservation of names is neglected, strange propositions have sprung up, names and their realities have become confused, and the boundary between right and wrong has become unclear. Even both the officials charged with preserving the codes of law and the Ru who recite their texts and enumerate their topics are also confused. Should a True King appear, he would certainly retain some old names but he would also have to invent new names. That being so, it is indispensable that he investigate (1) the purpose for having names together with (2) what is the basis for distinguishing the similar from the different and (3) the crucial considerations for instituting names.

22. 4

[Since there are no sage kings,] in regard to different bodies, alienated minds influence the factors that are relative in the terms we use to illustrate our meaning; and in regard to different things, the connection between the name and the object is obscure, what is noble and base is unclear, and things that are alike and things that are different are not distinguished. Given this situation, intentions are certain to be frustrated through a failure to explain fully, and the execution of a person's duties is certain to suffer from being hampered and obstructed. This is why wise men made "distinctions"and "separations."They instituted names to refer to objects, making distinctions in order to make clear what is noble and what base and separations in order to discriminate between

【原文】

喻之患，事无困废之祸。此所为有名也。

22.5 然则何缘而以同异？曰：缘天官。凡同类同情者，其天官之意物也同，故比方之疑似而通，是所以共其约名以相期也。形体、色、理，以目异；声音、清浊、调竽、奇声，以耳异；甘、苦、咸、淡、辛、酸、奇味，以口异；香、臭、芬、郁、腥、臊、洒、酸、奇臭，以鼻异；疾、养、沧、热、滑、铍、轻、重，以形体异；说、故、喜、怒、哀、乐、爱、恶、欲，以心异。心有征知，征知。

【今译】

同和相异区别了，像这样，那么意思就不会有不能被了解的忧患，事情就不会有陷入困境而被废弃的灾祸。这就是为什么要有名称的原因。

22.5 那么，根据什么而要使事物的名称有同有异呢？回答说：根据天生的感官。凡是同一个民族、具有相同情感的人，他们的天生感官对事物的体会是相同的，所以对事物的描摹只要模拟得大体相似就能使别人通晓了，这就是人们能共同使用那些概括的名称来互相交际的原因。形体、颜色、纹理，因为眼睛的感觉而显得不同；单声与和音、清音与浊音、协调乐器的竽声、奇异的声音，因为耳朵的感觉而显得不同；甜、苦、咸、淡、辣、酸以及奇异的味道，因为嘴巴的感觉而显得不同；香、臭、花的香气、鸟的腐臭、猪腥气、狗臊气、马膻气、牛膻气以及奇异的气味，因为鼻子的感觉而显得不同；痛、痒、冷、热、滑爽、滞涩、轻、重，因为身体的感觉而显得不同；愉快、烦闷、欣喜、愤怒、悲哀、快乐、爱好、厌恶以及各种欲望，因为心灵的感觉而显得不同。心灵能够验

things that are the same and those that are different. When the noble and base are clear and the same and different are kept apart, conveying intentions is no longer frustrated through a failure to explain, and carrying out duties no longer suffers from being hampered and obstructed. This is the purpose of having names.

22. 5

This being so, what is the basis of deeming something the same or different? I say that it is based on the sense organs given us by nature. As a general rule, whenever things belong to the same category of being or have the same essential characteristics, the representation of them presented by the senses is the same. Thus, when put side by side and compared, they resemble each other and are fully interchangeable. That is why they are given a general conventional name and used to define each other.

Forms, colors, and designs are differentiated by the eye. Pitch and timbre, bass and treble, modal keys and rhythm, and odd noises are differentiated by the ear. Sweet and bitter, salty and bland, pungent and sour, and distinctive tastes are differentiated by the mouth. Fragrances and stenches, perfumes and rotten odors, putrid and rancid smells, foul and sour odors, and distincive strange smells are differentiated by the nose. Pain and itching, cold and heat, smoothness and roughness, and lightness and heaviness are differentiated by the body. (Speech and phenomena,) pleasure and anger, sorrow and joy, love and hate, and desire are differentiated by the mind.

[The basis upon which we judge that things are the same of different is] the awareness that the mind has of the defining characteristics that

【原文】

则缘耳而知声可也，缘目而知形可也，然而征知必将待天官之当簿其类然后可也。五官簿之而不知，心征之而无说，则人莫不然谓之不知。此所缘而以同异也。

22.6 然后随而命之：同则同之，异则异之；单足以喻则单；单不足以喻则兼；单与兼无所相避则共，虽共，不为害矣。知异实者之异名也，故使异实者莫不异名也，不可乱也，犹使异实者莫不同名也。故万物虽众，有时而欲遍举之，故谓之“物”。“物”也者，大共名也。推而共之，共则有共，至于无共然后止。有时而欲遍举之，故

【今译】

知外界事物。既然心灵能够验知外界事物，那么就可以依靠耳朵来了解声音了，就可以依靠眼睛来了解形状了，但是心灵之验知外物，却又一定要等到感官接触事物的性状之后才行。如果五官接触了外界事物而不能认知，心灵验知外物而不能说出来，那么，说他无知，人们是不会不同意的。这些就是事物的名称之所以有同有异的根据。

22.6 这些道理明确后，就依照它来给事物命名：相同的事物就给它们相同的名称，不同的事物就给它们不同的名称；单音节的名称足以使人明白的就用单音节的名称；单音节的名称不能用来使人明白的就用多音节的名称；单音节的名称和多音节的名称如果没有互相回避的必要就共同使用一个名称，虽然共同使用一个名称，也不会造成什么害处。知道实质不同的事物要用不同的名称，所以使实质不同的事物无不具有不同的名称，这是不可错乱的，就像使实质相同的事物无不具有相同的名称一样。万物虽然众多，有时候却要把它们全面地举出来，所以把它们叫做“物”。“物”这个名称，是个最大的共用名称。依此推求而给事物制定共用的名称，那么共用的名称之中又有

distingusih things. Only when it rests on the evidence provided by the ear is it possible for this awareness of the defining characteristics to know sound, and only when it rests on the evidence provided by the eye is it possible to know shape. This being so, the mind's awareness of defining characteristics necessarily requires that the sense organ be impressed by the type of thing to which that sense organ [is sensitive]. If the five senses come into contact with a thing and you do not become aware of it, or if the mind notes its defining characteristics and you can offer no explanation, then everyone will agree that there is "no knowing."

22. 6

When all these have been done, we name things accordingly. If things are the same, then we should give them the same name; if they are different, we should give them different names. When a single name is sufficient to convey our meaning, a single name is used; when it is not, we use a compound name. If the single name and the compound name do not conflict, then a general name is used. Although it is the general name, it will not create inconsistencies. The idea that to avoid confusion one should give each different reality a different name, because one understands the fact that different realities have different names, is no better than assigning all the different objects the same name. Thus, although the myriad things are of multitudinous types, there are occasions when we want to refer to them collectively by name. One thus calls them "things." "Thing" is the name of greatest generality. By extending the process, one makes terms more general names, and from these generalized names one further generalizes until one reaches the point where

【原文】

谓之“鸟”、“兽”。“鸟”、“兽”也者，大别名也。推而别之，别则有别，至于无别然后止。名无固宜，约之以命，约定俗成谓之宜，异于约则谓之不宜。名无固实，约之以命实，约定俗成谓之实名。名有固善，径易而不拂，谓之善名。物有同状而异所者，有异状而同所者，可别也。状同而为异所者，虽可合，谓之二实。状变而实无别而为异者，谓之化；有化而无别，谓之一实。此事之所以稽实定数也。此制名之枢要也。

后王之成名，不可不察也。

【今译】

共用的名称，直到不再有共用的名称，然后才终止。有时候想要把它们部分地举出来，所以把它们叫做“鸟”、“兽”。“鸟”、“兽”这种名称，是一种最大的区别性名称。依此推求而给事物制定区别性的名称，那么区别性的名称之中又有区别性的名称，直到不再有区别性的名称，然后才终止。名称并没有本来就合宜的，而是人们相约命名的，约定俗成了就可以说它是合宜的，和约定的名称不同就叫做不合宜。名称并没有固有的表示对象，而是人们相约给实际事物命名的，约定俗成了就把它称为某一实际事物的名称。名称有本来就起得好的，直接平易而不违背事理，就叫做好的名称。事物有形状相同而实体不同的，有形状不同而实体相同的，这是可以区别的。形状相同却是不同的实体的，虽然可以合用一个名称，也应该说它们是两个实物。形状变了，但实质并没有区别而成为异物的，叫做变化；有了变化而实质没有区别的，应该说它是一个实物。这是对事物考察实质确定数目的方法。这些就是制定名称的关键。

现代圣王确定名称，是不能不弄清楚的。

there are no further generalizations to be drawn, and only then does one stop. There are other occasions when one wants to refer to things in part, so one refers to them as "birds" or "animals." "Bird" and "animal" are the names of the largest divisions of things. By extending the process, one draws distinctions within these groups, and within these distinctions one draws further distinctions until there are no further distinctions to be made, and only then does one stop.

Names have no intrinsic appropriateness. They are bound to something by agreement in order to name it. The agreement becomes fixed, the custom is established, and it is called "appropriate." If a name differs from the agreed name, it is then called "inappropriate."

Names have no intrinsic object. They are bound to some reality by agreement in order to name that object. The object becomes fixed, the custom is established, and it is called the name of that object.

Names do have intrinsic good qualities. When a name is direct, easy, and not at odds with the thing, it is called a "good name."

Things that have the same appearance but different locations and things that have different appearances but the same location should be kept distinct. Where the appearance is the same, but they are deemed to have different locations, even though they may properly be conjoined, they are called two objects. Where the appearance undergoes metamorphosis, but there is no distinction in the reality, yet they are deemed different, it is called "transformation." Where there is transformation but no distinction, it is called one object. By this procedure, one examines objects and determines their number. These are the crucial considerations in instituting names. The established names of the Later Kings cannot but be investigated.

【原文】

22.7“见侮不辱”，“圣人不爱己”，“杀盗非杀人也”，此惑于用名以乱名者也。验之所以为有名而观其孰行，则能禁之矣。“山渊平”，“情欲寡”，“刍豢不加甘，大钟不加乐”，此惑于用实以乱名者也。验之所缘无以同异而观其孰调，则能禁之矣。“非而谒楹”，“有牛马非马也”，此惑于用名以乱实者也。验之名约，以其所受悖其所辞，则能禁之矣。凡邪说辟言之离正道而擅作者，无不类于三惑者矣。故明君知其分而不与辨也。

22.8 夫民易一以道而不可与共故，故明君临之以势，道之以道，

【今译】

22.7“被侮辱而不以为耻辱”，“圣人不爱惜自己”，“杀死盗贼不是杀人”，这些是在使用名称方面迷惑了以致搞乱了名称的说法。用为什么要有名称的道理去检验它们，并观察它们有哪一种能行得通，那就能禁止这些说法了。“高山和深渊一样平”，“人的本性是欲望很少”，“牛羊猪狗等肉食并不比一般食物更加香甜，大钟的声音并不比一般的声音更加悦耳”，这些是在措置事实方面迷惑了以至搞乱了名称的说法。用为什么要使事物的名称有同有异的根据去检验它们，并观察它们有哪一种能协调，那就能禁止这些说法了。“飞箭经过柱子可以说明停止”，“有牛马，但它不是马”，这是在使用名称方面迷惑了以至搞乱了事实的说法。用名称约定的原则去检验它们，用这些人所能接受的观点去反驳他们所拒绝的观点，那就能禁止这些说法了。凡是背离了正确的原则而擅自炮制的邪说谬论，无不与这三种惑乱的说法类似。英明的君主知道它们与正确学说的区别而不和他们争辩。

22.8 民众容易用正道来统一却不可以和他们共同知道那缘由，

22.7

"To suffer insult is no disgrace," "the sage does not love himself," "to kill a robber is not to kill a man"—these are examples of errors in the use of names that disorder names. If we test such examples against the purpose of having names and observe which alternative works, then we will be able to exclude such statements.

"Mountain and marshes are level," "the essential desires are few," "grain- and grass-fed animals add nothing to the taste; the great bell adds nothing to the music"—these are examples of errors in the use of objects that disorder names. When we test these statements with the senses—which are the basis for distinguishing the similar from the different—and observe which alternative accords with them, then we will be able to exclude such statements.

"The flying arrow does not pass the pillar," "a white horse is not a horse"—these are examples of errors in the use of names that disorder objects. If we test such cases against the agreed use of names and if we use "what one accepts" to show that "what one rejects" is fallacious, then we can exclude such statements.

As a general principle, all unorthodox explanations and perverse sayings, having been detached from the correct Way and created on individual authority, belong to one of these three categories of error. Thus, because he understands the proper divisions, an enlightened lord does not engage in dialectics.

22. 8

The people are easy to unify by using the Way, but you cannot share

【原文】

申之以命，章之以论，禁之以刑。故其民之化道也如神，辨势恶用矣哉?今圣王没，天下乱，奸言起，君子无势以临之，无刑以禁之，故辨说也。实不喻然后命，命不喻然后期，期不喻然后说，说不喻然后辨。故期、命、辨、说也者，用之大文也，而王业之始也。名闻而实喻，名之用也。累而成文，名之丽也。用、丽俱得，谓之知名。名也者，所以期累实也。辞也者，兼异实之名以论一意也。辨说也者，不异实名以喻动静之道也。期命也者，辨说之用也。辨说也者，心之象道也。心也者，道之工宰也。道也者，治之经理也。心合于道，说合

【今译】

所以英明的君主用权势来统治他们，用正道来引导他们，用命令来告诫他们，用理论来晓喻他们，用刑法来禁止他们。所以他统治下的民众融化于正道就像被神仙支配了一样，哪里还用得着辩说那所以然呢?现在圣明的帝王死了，天下混乱，奸诈邪恶的言论产生了，君子没有权势去统治他们，没有刑法去禁止他们，所以要辩论解说。实际事物不能让人明白就给它们命名，命名了还不能使人了解就会合众人来约定，约定了还不能使人明白就解说，解说了还不能使人明白就辩论。所以，约定、命名、辩论、解说，是名称使用方面最重要的修饰，也是帝王大业的起点。名称一被听到，它所表示的实际事物就能被了解，这是名称的使用。积累名称而形成文章，这是名称的配合。名称的使用、配合都符合要求，就叫做精通名称。名称，是用来互相约定从而联系实际事物的。言语，是并用不同事物的名称来阐述一个意思的。辩论与解说，是不使名实相乱来阐明是非的道理。约定与命名，是供辩论与解说时使用的。辩论与解说，是心灵对道的认识的一种表象。心灵，是道的主宰。道，是政治的永恒法则。心意符合于

with them the generalized reasons. Thus, the enlightened lord presides over them with the authority inherent in his position, leads them with the Way, reinforces it among them with decrees, illustrates it to them with his proclamations, and forbids them with punishments. Thus, his people's conversion to the Way is as if by magic. What need, indeed, would he have for dialectics and explanations!

Now the sages are no more, the world is in chaos, and pernicious doctrines have arisen. Because gentlemen lack positions of authority with which to control them and lack the requisite punishments to restrain them, people engage in dialectics and explanations.

It is when the object is not fully understood that it is "named."It is when the name still does not fully convey the meaning that it is defined. It is when the definition is not completely clear that it is explained. It is when the explanation is not fully understood that we employ dialectics. Thus, defining and naming, dialectics and explanations, being the primary forms for practical activities, were the first principles of the royal enterprise. The "use"of a particular name consists in the object being clearly understood when the name is heard. The "linkage"of names [into syntactical units] consists in compositions being formed by stringing words together. When both the use and the links between names are grasped, we are said to know the name.

Names are used to define different realities. Propositions connect the names of different realities in order to express a single idea. Dialectics and explanations, by not allowing objects to become differentiated from their names, are used to illustrate the Way of action and repose. Defining and naming are the function of dialectics and explanation. Dialectics and explanation are the mind's representation of the Way. The mind is the artisan and manager of the Way. The Way is the classical standard and

【原文】

于心，辞合于说；正名而期，质请而喻；辨异而不过，推类而不悖；听则合文，辨则尽故。以正道而辨奸，犹引绳以持曲直，是故邪说不能乱，百家无所窜。有兼听之明，而无奋矜之容；有兼覆之厚，而无伐德之色。说行，则天下正；说不行，则白道而冥穷。是圣人之辨说也。《诗》曰："颙颙卬卬，如珪如璋，令闻令望。岂弟君子，四方为纲。"此之谓也。

22.9 辞让之节得矣，长少之理顺矣；忌讳不称，祆辞不出；以

【今译】

道，解说符合于心意，言语符合于解说；使名称正确无误并互相约定，使名称的内涵质朴直观而使人明白；辨别不同的事物而不失误，推论类似的事物而不违背情理；这样，听取意见时就能合于礼法，辩论起来就能彻底揭示其所以然。用正确的原则来辨别奸邪，就像拉出墨线来判别曲直一样，所以奸邪的学说就不能混淆视听，各家的谬论也无处躲藏。有同时听取各方意见的明智，而没有趾高气扬、骄傲自大的容貌；有兼容并包的宽宏大量，而没有自夸美德的神色。自己的学说得到实行，那么天下就能治理好；自己的学说不能实行，那就彰明正道而让自己默默无闻。这就是圣人的辩论与解说。《诗》云："体貌温顺志高昂，品德如珪又如璋，美妙声誉好名望。和乐平易的君子，天下拿他作榜样。"说的就是这种情况啊。

22.9 谦让的礼节做到了，长幼的伦理顺序了；忌讳的话不称说，

rational principle of order.

When the mind conforms to the Way, explanations conform to the mind, propositions conform to explanations, and when names are used correctly and according to definition, the real and true qualities of things are clearly conveyed. Divisions and differences should be made but not so as to introduce errors. Inferences should be made from the characteristics of the category of a thing, but not to the point of introducing fallacies. Then when we listen, it will conform to good form, and when we engage in dialectics, we will fully express all that inheres in things. Using the correct Way to analyze pernicious doctrines is akin to stretching the marking line to test the crooked and straight. For this reason, unorthodox explanations cannot cause disorder, and the Hundred Schools will have no place to hide.

He has an understanding that has heard everything, but lacks any air of bluster or pride. He has a generosity that extends to everyone, but avoids any look of self-congratulation for his acts of kindness. If his explanations are put into practice, then the world will be made aright. If they are not carried out, then he makes plain the Way but lives in obscurity and poverty. Such are the dialectics and explanations of the sage. An *Ode* says:

> With majestic dignity, splendidly,
> Like a *gui* scepter, like a *zhang* mace.
> Excellent of fame, excellent of aspect.
> Oh joyous and happy gentleman,
> Guiding rule for the Four Quarters.

This expresses my meaning.

22. 9

Due measure in polite refusals and courtesy has been attained.The

【原文】

仁心说，以学心听，以公心辨；不动乎众人之非誉，不治观者之耳目，不赂贵者之权势，不利传辟者之辞；故能处道而不贰，吐而不夺，利而不流，贵公正而贱鄙争。是士君子之辨说也。《诗》曰："长夜漫兮，永思骞兮。大古之不慢兮，礼义之不愆兮，何恤人之言兮？"此之谓也。

22.10 君子之言，涉然而精，俛然而类，差差然而齐。彼正其名，当其辞，以务白其志义者也。彼名辞也者，志义之使也，足以相

【今译】

奇谈怪论不出口；用仁慈的心去解说道理，用求学的心去听取意见，用公正的心去辩论是非；不因为众人的非议和赞誉而动摇，不修饰辩辞去遮掩旁人的耳目，不赠送财物去买通高贵者的权势，不喜欢传播邪说者的言辞；所以能坚持正道而不三心二意，大胆发言而不会被人强行改变观点，言语流利而不放荡胡说，崇尚公正而鄙视庸俗粗野的争论。这是士君子的辩论与解说。《诗》云："长长的黑夜漫无边，我常思索我的缺点。远古的原则我不怠慢，礼义上的错误我不犯，何必担忧别人说长道短？"说的就是这种情况啊。

22.10 君子的言论，深入而又精微，贴近人情世故而有法度，具体说法参差错落而大旨始终一致。他使名称正确无误，辞句恰当确切，以此来努力阐明他的思想学说。那些名称、辞句，是思想、学说

pattern for orderly relations between old and young is obediently observed. Forbidden subjects and tabooed names are not mentioned. Magical incantations do not issue from his lips. He explains with a humane compassion, listens with a studious attitude, and engages in disputation with an impartial mind. He is unmoved by the praise or blame of the multitude. He is not seductive to the eyes and ears of those who observe him. He does not use gifts to seek the power and influence of those in high position. He takes no pleasure in the proposals of flatterers and favorites. Thus, he can abide in the Way and not be of two minds. He may bend, but he does not compromise his position. He may be fluent, but he is not inconstant. He prizes the impartial and upright and despises the vulgar and quarrelsome. Such are the disputations and explanations of the scholar and gentleman. An *Ode* says:

> This long night drags on,
> I constantly ponder over my faults.
> If I do not neglect high antiquity,
> if I do not err in ritual and morality,
> why be distressed over what men say?

This expresses my meaning.

22. 10

The discourses of the gentleman are wide-ranging in subject yet contain the essence of the matter, are simply presented yet are precisely applicable to the subject, and are diverse in content yet have unity. Those men use their names correctly and make their propositions fit with the facts in order to ensure that their meaning and intention are made plainly evident. Their kind of words and propositions acts as messengers of in-

【原文】

通则舍之矣，苟之，奸也。故名足以指实，辞足以见极，则舍之矣。外是者谓之讱，是君子之所弃，而愚者拾以为己宝。故愚者之言，芴然而粗，啧然而不类，谘谘然而沸。彼诱其名，眩其辞，而无深于其志义者也。故穷藉而无极，甚劳而无功，贪而无名。故知者之言也，虑之易知也，行之易安也，持之易立也，成则必得其所好而不遇其所恶焉。而愚者反是。《诗》曰："为鬼为蜮，则不可得；有靦面目，视人罔极？作此好歌，以极反侧。"此之谓也。

【今译】

的使者，能够用来互相沟通就可以撇下不管了；但如果不严肃地使用它们，就是一种邪恶。所以名称能够用来表示实际事物，辞句能够用来表达主旨，就可以撇下不管了。背离这种标准的叫做语言迟钝，这是君子所抛弃的，但愚蠢的人却拣来当作自己的宝贝。所以蠢人的言论，模糊而粗疏，吵吵嚷嚷而不合法度，啰唆而嘈杂。他们使名称富有诱惑力，辞句显得眼花缭乱，而在思想学说方面却毫无深意。所以他们尽量搬弄词句却没有个主旨，非常劳累却没有功效，贪于立名却没有声誉。所以，智者的言论，思索它容易理解，实行它容易安定，坚持它容易站得住，成功了一定能得到自己所喜欢的东西而不会得到自己所厌恶的东西。可是愚蠢的人却与此相反。《诗》云："你若是鬼是短狐，那就无法看清楚；你的面目这样丑，给人看就看不透？作此好歌唱一唱，用来揭穿你的反复无常。"说的就是这种人啊。

tention and meaning. If these are judged sufficient to communicate with others, they explicate the matter no further. To make the words and propositions more involved has pernicious results. Therefore, if a name is sufficient to point to its object and if a proposition is sufficient to make manifest the core of the matter, then explicate the matter no further. What goes beyond this is called "belaboring the point."

The gentleman discards such laboriousness over speech, but the fool snatches it up, considering it to be his own treasure. Thus, the fool's speech is hastily formulated and crude, given to contention but not proper to the category of its subject, and endlessly babbles on and on and gushes forth. Those men use their words to seduce and make their propositions deceptive, but there is no depth to their meanings and intentions. Thus, they investigate and borrow, but there is no core meaning; they work quite hard, but are without accomplishment; and although they covet one, they acquire no reputation.

Thus, the speech of the wise, when reflected on, is easy to understand, when acted on, readily produces security, and, when upheld, is easy to establish. When the intentions conveyed in their words are fully carried out, they necessarily obtain what is desired and will not chance to encounter what is disliked. Fools are the opposite of this. An *Ode* says:

If you were a specter or a water-imp,
I could not apprehend your true features;
But since you have a face with the normal countenance and eyes,
Your true features will be seen in the end.
I am writing this good song
to show the full extent of your inconstancy.

This expresses my meaning.

【原文】

22.11 凡语治而待去欲者，无以道欲而困于有欲者也。凡语治而待寡欲者，无以节欲而困于多欲者也。有欲无欲，异类也，生死也，非治乱也。欲之多寡，异类也，情之数也，非治乱也。欲不待可得，而求者从所可。欲不待可得，所受乎天也；求者从所可，受乎心也。所受乎天之一欲，制于所受乎心之多，固难类所受乎天也。人之所欲，生甚矣；人之所恶，死甚矣。然而人有从生成死者，非不欲生而欲死也，不可以生而可以死也。故欲过之而动不及，心止之也。心之

【今译】

22.11 凡是谈论治国之道而依靠去掉人们的欲望的，是没有办法来引导人们的欲望而被人们已有的欲望难住了的人。凡是谈论治国之道而依靠减少人们的欲望的，是没有办法来节制人们的欲望而被人们过多的欲望难住了的人。有欲望与没有欲望，是不同类的，是生与死的区别，但不是国家安定与动乱的原因。欲望的多与少，是不同类的，是人情的必然现象，也不是国家安定与动乱的原因。人的欲望并不等到其所欲之物可能得到才产生，但追求满足欲望的人却总是认为可能得到而争取。欲望并不等到其所欲之物可能得到才产生，这是来自天赋的；追求满足欲望的人却总是认为可能得到而争取，这是出于内心的。来自天赋的单纯的欲望，被那些出于内心的众多的思考所制约，结果当然很难再类似于来自天赋的本性了。人们想要得到的，莫过于生存；人们所厌恶的，莫过于死亡。但是人却有舍生就死的，这不是不想活而想死，而是因为在那种情势下不可以活而只可以死。所以，有时欲望超过了某种程度而行动却没有达到那种程度，这是因为

22. 11

As a general rule, those who contend "order requires that we first rid ourselves of desires"are those who lack the means to guide their desires and so are embarrassed by their having desires.

As a general rule, those who contend "order requires that first we reduce the number of our desires"are those who lack the means to moderate their desires and so are embarrassed that their desires are numerous.

"Having desires"and "lacking desires"belong to different categories, those of life and death, not those of order and disorder. The quantity of our desires, few or many, belongs to a different category, that of the calculation of our essential nature, not that of order and disorder. Desire does not depend on the object of desire first being obtainable, but what is sought after follows after what is possible. That the occurrence of desire does not depend on its object's first being obtainable is a quality we receive from nature. That what we seek to satisfy our desires by following after what is possible is what we receive from the mind. It is natural to our inborn nature to have desires, and the mind acts to control and moderate them. The simple desires we receive from nature are controlled by the complex devises exercised by the mind until it becomes inherently difficult to properly categorize what one has received from nature.

What men desire most is life, and what they hate most is death. Be that as it may, men sometimes follow the pursuit of life and end up with death. It is not that they do not really desire life and rather desire death; it is that it proved impossible to continue living and it was possible to die. Thus, when desires run to excess, actions do not reach that point be-

【原文】

所可中理，则欲虽多，奚伤于治?欲不及而动过之，心使之也。心之所可失理，则欲虽寡，奚止于乱?故治乱在于心之所可，亡于情之所欲。不求之其所在而求之其所亡，虽曰:"我得之"，失之矣。

22.12 性者，天之就也；情者，性之质也；欲者，情之应也。以所欲为可得而求之，情之所必不免也；以为可而道之，知所必出也。故虽为守门，欲不可去，性之具也。虽为天子，欲不可尽。欲虽不可尽，可以近尽也；欲虽不可去，求可节也。所欲虽不可尽，求者犹近尽；欲虽不可去，所求不得，虑者欲节求也。道者，进则近尽，退则

【今译】

内心限制了行动。内心所认可的如果符合道理，那么欲望即使很多，又哪会妨害国家的安定呢?有时欲望没有达到某种程度而行动却超过了那种程度，这是因为内心驱使了行动。内心所认可的如果违背道理，那么欲望即使很少，又哪能阻止国家的动乱呢?所以国家的安定与动乱取决于内心所认可的是否合乎道理，而不在于人情的欲望是多是少。不从根源所在的地方去寻找原因，却从没有关系的地方去找原因，虽然自称“我找到了原因”，其实却是把它丢了。

22.12 本性，是天然造就的；情感，是本性的实际内容；欲望，是情感对外界事物的反应。认为想要的东西可以得到从而去追求它，这是情感必不能免的现象；认为可行而去实行它，这是智慧必定会作出的打算。所以即使是卑贱的看门人，欲望也不可能去掉，因为这是本性所具有的。即使是高贵的天子，欲望也不可能全部满足。欲望虽然不可能全部满足，却可以接近于全部满足；欲望虽然不可能去掉，但对满足欲望的追求却是可以节制的。欲望虽然不可能全部满足，追求的人还是能接近于全部满足的；欲望虽然不可能去掉，但追求的东

cause the mind stops them. If what the mind permits coincides with reason, then although the desires be numerous, how could there be harm to order! Although the desires are not strong enough to motivate a person, his actions may exceed his desires because the mind has ordered them to do so. If what the mind permits conflicts with what is reasonable, then although the desires be few, how could it stop at disorder! Thus, order and disorder lie in what the mind permits and not with the desires that belong to our essential natures. Although you may claim to have succeeded in finding the cause of order and disorder, if you do not seek it where it lies but instead seek it where it does not lie, then you will miss the truth.

22. 12

"Inborn nature"is the consequence of Heaven."Emotions"are the substance of that nature."Desires"<are the resources of nature>. ["Seeking"what is desired] is the response of the emotions. When what is desired is judged to be obtainable, it will be pursued. That is a necessary and inescapable part of our essential nature. Judging it possible and leading the way to it is where the intelligence must come into play.

Thus, even though one were a mere gatekeeper, one could not get rid of his desires (…), and even though one were the Son of Heaven, one could not satisfy them all. Although one's desires cannot be completely fulfilled, one can approach complete satisfaction, and although one cannot get rid of the desires, the pursuit of their satisfaction can be moderated. What is desired, though not completely satisfiable, can if pursued be made nearly complete. Although one cannot rid himself of desire and since what one seeks is unattainable, one who ponders the matter will desire to moderate his pursuit.

【原文】

节求，天下莫之若也。

22.13 凡人莫不从其所可而去其所不可。知道之莫之若也而不从道者，无之有也。假之有人而欲南无多，而恶北无寡。岂为夫南者之不可尽也，离南行而北走也哉?今人所欲无多，所恶无寡。岂为夫所欲之不可尽也，离得欲之道而取所恶也哉?故可道而从之，奚以损之而乱?不可道而离之，奚以益之而治?故知者论道而已矣，小家珍说之所愿皆衰矣。

22.14 凡人之取也，所欲未尝粹而来也；其去也，所恶未尝粹而

【今译】

西不能得到，用心思考的人就会打算节制自己的追求。正道是这样的：进则可以接近于完全满足自己的欲望，退则可以节制自己的追求，天下没有什么能及得上它。

22.13 凡是人无不依从自己所赞同的而背弃自己所不赞同的。知道没有什么及得上正道却又不依从正道的，是没有这种人的。假如有人想到南方去，不管路有多远；而厌恶到北方去，不管有多近。他难道会因为那往南去的路走不到头就离开了向南的道路而向北奔跑吗?现在人们想要得到的，就无所谓多；所厌恶的，就无所谓少。他们难道会因为那想要得到的东西不可能全部得到就离开了那实现欲望的道路而去求取厌恶的东西吗?所以，人们赞同正道而依从它，还能用什么来损害它而使国家动乱呢?人们不赞同正道而背离它，还能用什么来增益它而使国家安定呢?所以明智的人只讲究正道就是了，那些渺小的学派及其奇谈怪论所追求的一套就都会衰微了。

22.14 大凡人们求取的时候，想要的东西从来没有能完全彻底地

The true Way is such that when advance is possible, complete satisfaction of the desires is attainable, and when retreat is necessary, it is possible to moderate their pursuit. In all the world, there is nothing to compare with it!

22. 13

As a general rule, all men follow what they regard as allowable and reject what they regard as not allowable. There is no instance of someone understanding that there is nothing to compare with the Way and yet not following the Way.

Consider the case of the man who liked traveling south, thinking it never too much, and hated traveling north, thinking it never little enough. Surely he would not abandon his southern journey and turn back northward just because he could not cover all the south! Just so, of what men desire, they never think it too much, and of what they hate, they never think it little enough. Surely they would not abandon the way of obtaining what they desire and choose instead what they hate just because they could not satisfy all they desire!

Thus, when they affirm the Way and follow it, how could increasing the desires produce disorder, and when they do not approve of the Way but abandon it, how could decreasing them produce order. Therefore, the wise judge on the basis of the Way and nothing else. All that the exotic theories of the trivial schools long for will fade away.

22. 14

As a general rule, when men choose, what they get is never only

【原文】

往也。故人无动而不可以不与权俱。衡不正，则重县于仰，而人以为轻；轻县于俛，而人以为重；此人所以惑于轻重也。权不正，则祸托于欲，而人以为福；福托于恶，而人以为祸；此亦人所以惑于祸福也。道者，古今之正权也；离道而内自择，则不知祸福之所托。

22.15 易者，以一易一，人曰无得亦无丧也；以一易两，人曰无丧而有得也；以两易一，人曰无得而有丧也。计者取所多，谋者从所可。以两易一，人莫之为，明其数也。从道而出，犹以一易两也，奚丧?离道而内自择，是犹以两易一也，奚得?其累百年之欲，易一时之嫌，然且为之，不明其数也。

【今译】

得到；人们舍弃的时候，所厌恶的东西从来没有能完全彻底地去掉。所以人们无论什么行动，都不能不用正确的准则来衡量。秤如果不准，那么重的东西挂上去反而会翘起来，而人们就会把它当作是轻的；轻的东西挂上去反而会低下去，而人们就会把它当作是重的；这就是人们对轻重发生迷惑的原因。衡量行为的准则如果不正确，那么灾祸就会寄寓在人们所追求的事物中，而人们还把它当作幸福；幸福就会依附于人们所厌恶的事物中，而人们还把它当作灾祸；这也就是人们对祸福发生迷惑的原因。道，是从古到今都正确的衡量标准；离开了道而由内心擅自抉择，那就会不知道祸福所依存的地方。

22.15 交易，拿一件换一件，人们就说没有收获也没有损失；拿一件换两件，人们就说没有损失而有收获；拿两件换一件，人们就说没有收获而有损失。善于计算的人择取多的东西，善于谋划的人追求合宜的东西。拿两件换一件，人没有一个肯干这种事，因为大家都明了它们的数目。依从道去行动，就好比拿一件去换两件，有什么损失?离开了道而由内心擅自抉择，这就好比拿两件去换一件，有什么收获?那种积累了长时间的欲望，只能换取暂时的满足，然而还是去做，实在是不明了它们的数量关系了。

what they wanted; when they reject, what they lose is never only what they disliked. Thus, a man should weigh and balance both before he acts. If the steelyard is not correctly calibrated, a heavier object may rise up so men will think it light and a lighter object may sink down so men will think it heavy. This is why men become deluded about light and heavy. If the balance is not correctly adjusted, then any misfortune inherent in what we desire may be deemed good fortune and any good fortune inherent in what we dislike may be deemed misfortune. This is the reason men become deluded about fortune and misfortune. The Way, from antiquity to the present, has been the right balance. If one abandons the Way and rather selects on the basis of personal considerations, then he will not know where misfortune and fortune lie.

22. 15

Of a trader who exchanges one for one, people say that there was no gain and no loss. Of exchanging one for two, people say there was no loss but rather gain. Of exchanging two for one, people say there was no gain but rather loss. One who calculates chooses what is most numerous; one who plans follows what is possible. No man acts so as to exchange two for one, because he understands how to count.

To proceed by following the Way is like exchanging one for two. How could there be loss! But to abandon the Way and select on the basis of personal considerations is like exchanging two for one. How could there be gain! Anyone who would exchange the desires accumulated over a hundred years for the gratification of the moment, and there are indeed such actions, does not understand how to count.

【原文】

22.16 有尝试深观其隐而难其察者。志轻理而不重物者，无之有也；外重物而不内忧者，无之有也。行离理而不外危者，无之有也；外危而不内恐者，无之有也。心忧恐，则口衔刍豢而不知其味，耳听钟鼓而不知其声，目视黼黻而不知其状，轻暖平簟而体不知其安。故向万物之美而不能嗛也，假而得问而嗛之，则不能离也。故向万物之美而盛忧，兼万物之利而盛害。如此者，其求物也，养生也？粥寿也?故欲养其欲而纵其情，欲养其性而危其形，欲养其乐而攻其心，欲养其名而乱其行。如此者，虽封侯称君，其与夫盗无以异；乘轩戴

【今译】

22.16 我又试探着深入地观察那些隐蔽而又难以看清楚的情况。心里轻视道义而又不看重物质利益的，没有这种人；外看重物质利益而内心不忧虑的，没有这种人。行为违背道义而在外又不危险的，没有这种人；外表危险而内心不恐惧的，没有这种人。心里忧虑恐惧，那么嘴里衔着牛羊猪狗等肉食也感觉不到美味，耳朵听着钟鼓奏出的音乐也感觉不到悦耳，眼睛看着锦绣的花纹也察觉不到形状，穿着轻软暖和的衣服坐在竹席上身体也感觉不到舒适。所以享受到了万物中美好的东西也仍然不能满足，即使得到短暂时间的满足，那还是不能脱离忧虑恐惧。所以享受到了万物中美好的东西却仍然非常忧虑，占有了万物的利益却仍然十分有害。像这样的人，他追求物质利益，是在保养生命呢?还是在延长寿命?想要满足自己的欲望却放纵自己的情欲，想要保养自己的性命却危害自己的身体，想要培养自己的乐趣却伤害自己的心灵，想要提高自己的名声却胡作非为。像这样的人，即使被封为诸侯而称为国君，他们和那些盗贼也没有什么不同；即使

22. 16

Let us try to examine more profoundly a principle that is hidden and difficult to investigate. Everybody who in his inner mind minimizes the importance of rational principles attaches great importance to things in the external world. Everybody who outwardly attaches great importance to things is inwardly anxious. Everybody who abandons rational principles in his conduct faces danger from without. Everybody who faces danger from without is inwardly filled with fear.

If the mind is anxious or filled with fear, then although the mouth is filled with fine meats, it will not be aware of their taste. Although the ear hears bells and drums, it will not be aware of their sound. Although the eye beholds fine embroidered patterns, it will not be aware of their appearance. And, although the body is clothed in warm, light garments and rests on a fine bamboo mat, it will not be aware of their comfort. Thus, were such a man to have all the beautiful things of the world for his enjoyment, he would be unable to find satisfaction in them. And, even supposing he were to feel a moment of satisfaction, he would be unable to leave his anxiety and fear behind. Thus, even with all the beautiful things of the world to enjoy, he is filled with anxiety. Combining together all the benefits of the myriad things, he is consumed by suffering. Thus fare those who seek after mere things. Do they nurture life? Or have they traded away their longevity?

Thus, wanting to nurture their desires, they indulge the emotions. Wanting to nurture their inborn nature, they endanger the body. Wanting to nurture their pleasures, they attack the mind. And, wanting to nurture their reputation, they bring disorder to their conduct. Such men, although they be an enfeoffed marquis or styled a lord, are no different from a

【原文】

绝，其与无足无以异。夫是之谓以己为物役矣!

22.17 心平愉，则色不及佣而可以养目，声不及佣而可以养耳，蔬食菜羹而可以养口。粗布之衣、粗𬘓之履而可以养体，局室、芦帘、葭稾蓐、尚机筵而可以养形。故无万物之美而可以养乐，无势列之位而可以养名。如是而加天下焉，其为天下多，其和乐少矣，夫是之谓重己役物。

22.18 无稽之言，不见之行，不闻之谋，君子慎之。

【今译】

坐着高级的马车，戴着大官的礼帽，他们和没有脚的人也没有什么不同。这就叫做使自己被物质利益所奴役了。

22.17 心境平静愉快，那么颜色就是不如一般的，也可以用来调养眼睛；声音就是不如一般的，也可以用来调养耳朵；粗饭、菜羹，也可以用来调养口胃；粗布做的衣服、粗麻绳编制的鞋子，也可以用来保养身躯；狭窄的房间、芦苇做的帘子、芦苇稻草做的草垫子、破旧的几桌竹席，也可以用来保养体态容貌。所以，虽然没有享受到万物中美好的东西而仍然可以用来培养乐趣，没有权势封爵的地位而仍然可以用来提高名望。像这样而把统治天下的权力交给他，他就会为天下操劳得多，为自己的享乐考虑得少了，这就叫做看重自己而役使外物。

22.18 没有根据的言论，没有见过的行为，没有听说过的计谋，君子对它们是谨慎对待的。

common thief, and although they ride in an officer's carriage and wear ceremonial cap, are no different from a pauper. This is just what is called making one's self the servant of things.

22. 17

If the mind is serene and happy, then colors that are less than ordinary can nurture the eye. Sounds that are less than average can nurture the ear. A diet of vegetables and a broth of greens can nurture the mouth. Robes of coarse cloth and shoes of rough hemp can nurture the body. And a cramped room, reed blinds, a bed of dried straw, plus a stool and mat can nurture the bodily frame. Thus, even without enjoyment of all the beautiful things of the world, he can nurture his happiness. With no position of authority and rank, he can nurture his reputation. In the case of such men, were they given the whole world, although it might mean much to the world, it would mean little to their peace and happiness. This indeed may be called "stressing oneself and making a servant of things."

22. 18

Theories that have not been tested, actions that have not been observed, and plans that have not been heard about—of these the gentleman is cautious.

性恶第二十三

【原文】

23.1 人之性恶，其善者伪也。

23.2 今人之性，生而有好利焉，顺是，故争夺生而辞让亡焉；生而有疾恶焉，顺是，故残贼生而忠信亡焉；生而有耳目之欲，有好声色焉，顺是，故淫乱生而礼义文理亡焉。然则从人之性，顺人之情，必出于争夺，合于犯分乱理，而归于暴。故必将有师法之化、礼

【今译】

23.1 人的本性是邪恶的，他们那些善良的行为是人为的。

23.2 人的本性，一生下来就有喜欢财利之心，依顺这种人性，所以争抢掠夺就产生而推辞谦让就消失了；一生下来就有妒忌憎恨的心理，依顺这种人性，所以残杀陷害就产生而忠诚守信就消失了；一生下来就有耳朵、眼睛的贪欲，有喜欢音乐、美色的本能，依顺这种人性，所以淫荡混乱就产生而礼义法度就消失了。这样看来，放纵人的本性，依顺人的情欲，就一定会出现争抢掠夺，一定会和违犯等级名分、扰乱礼义法度的行为合流，而最终趋向于暴乱。所以一定要有了师长和法度的教化、礼义的引导，然后人们才会从推辞谦让出发，

Book 23

Man's Nature Is Evil

23. 1

Human nature is evil; any good in humans is acquired by conscious exertion.

23. 2

Now, the nature of man is such that he is born with a love of profit. Following this nature will cause its aggressiveness and greedy tendencies to grow and courtesy and deference to disappear. Humans are born with feelings of envy and hatred. Indulging these feelings causes violence and crime to develop and loyalty and trustworthiness to perish. Man is born possessing the desires of the ears and eyes (which are fond of sounds and colors). Indulging these desires causes dissolute and wanton behavior to result and ritual and moral principles, precepts of good form, and the natural order of reason to perish.

This being the case, when each person follows his inborn nature and indulges his natural inclinations, aggressiveness and greed are certain to develop. This is accompanied by violation of social class distinctions and throws the natural order into anarchy, resulting in a cruel tyranny. Thus, it is necessary that man's nature undergo the transforming influence of a teacher and the model and that he be guided by ritual and moral principles. Only after this has been accomplished do courtesy and deference develop. Unite these qualities with precepts of good form and reason,

【原文】

义之道，然后出于辞让，合于文理，而归于治。用此观之，然则人之性恶明矣，其善者伪也。

23.3 故枸木必将待檃栝烝矫然后直，钝金必将待砻厉然后利。今人之性恶，必将待师法然后正，得礼义然后治。今人无师法，则偏险而不正；无礼义，则悖乱而不治。古者圣王以人之性恶，以为偏险而不正，悖乱而不治，是以为之起礼义，制法度，以矫饰人之情性而正之，以扰化人之情性而导之也。使皆出于治、合于道者也。今之人，化师法、积文学、道礼义者为君子，纵性情、安恣睢而违礼义者

【今译】

遵守礼法，而最终趋向于安定太平。由此看来，人的本性是邪恶的就很明显了，他们那些善良的行为则是人为的。

23.3 所以弯曲的木料一定要依靠整形器进行熏蒸、矫正，然后才能挺直；不锋利的金属器具一定要依靠磨砺，然后才能锋利。人的本性邪恶，一定要依靠师长和法度的教化才能端正，要得到礼义的引导才能治理好。人们没有师长和法度，就会偏邪险恶而不端正；没有礼义，就会叛逆作乱而不守秩序。古代圣明的君王认为人的本性是邪恶的，认为人们是偏邪险恶而不端正、叛逆作乱而不守秩序的，因此给他们建立了礼义，制定了法度，用来矫正、整顿人们的性情而端正他们，用来驯服感化人们的性情而引导他们。使他们都能从遵守秩序出发，合乎正确的道德原则。现在的人，能够被师长和法度所感化，积累文献经典方面的知识，遵行礼义的，就是君子；纵情任性，习惯于

and the result is an age of orderly government. If we consider the implications of these facts, it is plain that human nature is evil and that any good in humans is acquired by conscious exertion.

23. 3

Thus, a warped piece of wood must first await application of the press-frame, steam to soften it, and force to bend its shape before it can be made straight. A dull piece of metal must first be whetted on the grindstone before it can be made sharp.

Now, since human nature is evil, it must await the instructions of a teacher and the model before it can be put aright, and it must obtain ritual principles and a sense of moral right before it can become orderly. Nowadays, since men lack both teacher and model, they are prejudiced, wicked, and not upright. Since they lack ritual principles and precepts of moral duty, they are perverse, rebellious, and disorderly.

In antiquity the sage kings took man's nature to be evil, to be inclined to prejudice and prone to error, to be perverse and rebellious, and not to be upright or orderly. For this reason they invented ritual principles and precepts of moral duty. They instituted the regulations that are contained in laws and standards. Through these actions they intended to "straighten out"and develop man's essential nature and to set his inborn nature aright. They sought to tame and transform his essential nature and to guide his inborn nature with the Way. They caused both his essential and inborn natures to develop with good order and be consistent with the true Way.

Those men of today who are transformed by their teacher and the model, who accumulate good form and learning, and who are guided by the Way of ritual principles and moral duty become gentlemen. But those

【原文】

为小人。用此观之，然则人之性恶明矣，其善者伪也。

23.4 孟子曰："人之学者，其性善。"

曰：是不然。是不及知人之性，而不察乎人之性、伪之分者也。凡性者，天之就也，不可学，不可事。礼义者，圣人之所生也，人之所学而能、所事而成者也。不可学、不可事而在人者，谓之性；可学而能、可事而成之在人者，谓之伪，是性、伪之分也。今人之性，目可以见，耳可以听。夫可以见之明不离目，可以听之聪不离耳。目明而耳聪，不可学，明矣。

【今译】

恣肆放荡而违反礼义的，就是小人。由此看来，那么人的本性是邪恶的就很明显了，他们那些善良的行为则是人为的。

23.4 孟子说："人们要学习的，是那本性的善良。"

我说：这是不对的。这是还没有能够了解人的本性，而且也不明白人的先天本性和后天人为之间的区别的一种说法。大凡本性，是天然造就的，是不可能学到的，是不可能人为造作的。礼义，才是圣人创建的，是人们学了才会、努力从事才能做到的。人身上不可能学到，不可能人为造做的东西，叫做本性；人身上可以学会，可以通过努力从事而做到的，叫做人为，这就是先天本性和后天人为的区别。那人的本性，眼睛可以用来看，耳朵可以用来听。那可以用来看东西的视力离不开眼睛，可以用来听声音的听力离不开耳朵。眼睛的视力和耳朵的听力不可能学到是很清楚的了。

who indulge their inborn and essential natures, who are content with unrestrained passion and an overbearing manner, and whose conduct contravenes ritual principles and moral duty remain petty men. If we consider the implications of these facts, it is plain that human nature is evil and that any good in humans is acquired by conscious exertion.

23. 4

Mencius contended that "since man can learn, his nature is good."

I say that this is not so. It shows that Mencius did not reach any real understanding of what man's inborn nature is and that he did not investigate the division between those things that are inborn in man and those that are acquired. As a general rule, "inborn nature" embraces what is spontaneous from Nature, what cannot be learned, and what requires no application to master. Ritual principles and moral duty are creations of the sages. They are things that people must study to be able to follow them and to which they must apply themselves before they can fulfill their precepts. What cannot be gained by learning and cannot be mastered by application yet is found in man is properly termed "inborn nature." What must be learned before a man can do it and what he must apply himself to before he can master it yet is found in man is properly called "acquired nature." This is precisely the distinction between "inborn" and "acquired" natures.

Now, it belongs to the inborn nature of man that the eye is able to see and the ear to hear. The ability to see clearly cannot be separated from the eye, nor the ability to hear acutely from the ear. It is quite impossible to learn to be clear-sighted or keen of hearing.

【原文】

23.5 孟子曰:“今人之性善，将皆失丧其性，故也。”

曰：若是则过矣。今人之性，生而离其朴，离其资，必失而丧之，用此观之，然则人之性恶明矣。

所谓性善者，不离其朴而美之，不离其资而利之也。使夫资朴之于美，心意之于善若夫可以见之明不离目，可以听之聪不离耳。故曰目明而耳聪也。

23.6 今人之性，饥而欲饱，寒而欲暖，劳而欲休，此人之情性也。今人饥，见长而不敢先食者，将有所让也；劳而不敢求息者，将有所代也。夫子之让乎父，弟之让乎兄；子之代乎父，弟之代乎兄；

【今译】

23.5 孟子说：“人的本性是善良的，他们的作恶一定都是丧失了他们的本性的缘故啊。”

我说：像这样来解释就错了。孟子所谓本性善良，是指不离开他的素质而觉得他很美，不离开他的资质而觉得他很好。那天生的资质和美的关系、心意和善良的关系就像那可以看东西的视力离不开眼睛、可以听声音的听力离不开耳朵一样罢了。所以说资质的美和心意的善良就像眼睛的视力和耳朵的听力一样。如果人的本性生来就脱离他的素质，脱离他的资质，一定会丧失它的美和善良，由此看来，那么人的本性是邪恶的就很明显了。

23.6 人的本性，饿了想吃饱，冷了想穿暖，累了想休息，这些就是人的情欲和本性。人饿了，看见父亲兄长而不敢先吃，这是因为要有所谦让；累了，看见父亲兄长而不敢要求休息，这是因为要有所代劳。儿子对父亲谦让，弟弟对哥哥谦让；儿子代替父亲操劳，弟弟

23. 5

Mencius said:

Now, the nature of man is good, so the cause [of evil] is that all men lose or destroy their original nature.

I say that portraying man's inborn nature like this transgresses the truth. Now, it is man's nature that as soon as he is born, he begins to depart from his original simplicity and his childhood naiveté so that of necessity they are lost or destroyed. (If we consider the implications of these facts, it is plain that man's nature is evil.)

Those who say man's inborn nature is good admire what does not depart from his original simplicity and think beneficial what is not separated from his childhood naiveté. They treat these admirable qualities and the good that is in man's heart and thoughts as thought they were inseparably linked to his inborn nature, just as seeing clearly is to the eye and hearing acutely is to the ear. Thus, inborn nature they say is "like the clear sight of the eye and the acute hearing of the ear."

23. 6

Now, it is the inborn nature of man that when hungry he desires something to eat, that when cold he wants warm clothing, and that when weary he desires rest—such are essential qualities inherent in his nature. But when in fact a man is hungry, if he sees one of his elders, he will not eat before his elder does; rather, he will defer to him. When he is weary from work, he does not presume to ask to be given rest time, for he realizes that he should relieve others. A son's deference to his father and a younger brother's deference to his elder brother; a son's relieving his

【原文】

此二行者，皆反于性而悖于情也，然则孝子之道、礼义之文理也。故顺情性则不辞让矣，辞让则悖于情性矣。用此观之，然则人之性恶明矣，其善者伪也。

23.7 问者曰："人之性恶，则礼义恶生?"

应之曰：凡礼义者，是生于圣人之伪，非故生于人之性也。故陶人埏埴而为器，然则器生于工人之伪，非故生于人之性也。故工人斫木而成器，然则器生于工人之伪，非故生于人之性也。圣人积思虑，习伪故，以生礼义而起法度，然则礼义法度者，是生于圣人之伪，非故生于人之性也。若夫目好色，耳好声，口好味，心好利，骨体肤理

【今译】

代替哥哥操劳；这两种德行，都是违反本性而背离情欲的，但却是孝子的原则、礼义的制度。所以依顺情欲本性就不会推辞谦让了，推辞谦让就违背情欲本性了。由此看来，那么人的本性邪恶就很明显了，他们那些善良的行为则是人为的。

23.7 有人问；"人的本性是邪恶的，那么礼义是从哪里产生出来的呢?"

我回答他说：所有的礼义，都产生于圣人的人为努力，而不是原先产生于人的本性。制作陶器的人搅拌揉打粘土而制成陶器，那么陶器产生于陶器工人的人为努力，而不是原先产生于人的本性。木工砍削木材而制成木器，那么木器产生于工人的人为努力，而不是原先产生于人的本性。圣人深思熟虑，熟悉人为的事情，从而使礼义产生了，使法度建立起来了，那么礼义法度便是产生于圣人的人为努力，而不是原先产生于人的本性。至于那眼睛爱看美色，耳朵爱听音乐，

father of work and a younger brother's relieving his elder brother—these two modes of conduct are both contrary to inborn nature and contradict his true feelings. Nonetheless, it is the Way of the filial son and the proper form and natural order contained in ritual principles and moral duty. Thus, to follow inborn nature and true feelings is not to show courtesy or defer to others. To show courtesy and to defer to others contradicts the true feelings inherent in his inborn nature. If we consider the implications of these facts, it is plain that human nature is evil and that any good in humans is acquired by conscious exertion.

23. 7

Someone may ask:"If man's nature is evil, how then are ritual principles and moral duty created?"The reply is that as a general rule ritual principles and moral duty are born of the acquired nature of the sage and are not the product of anything inherent in man's inborn nature. Thus, when the potter shapes the clay to create the vessel, this is the creation of the acquired nature of the potter and not the product of anything inherent in his inborn nature. When an artisan carves a vessel out of a piece of wood, it is the creation of his acquired nature and not the product of his inborn nature. The sage accumulates his thoughts and ideas. He masters through practice the skills of his acquired nature and the principles involved therein in order to produce ritual principles and moral duty and to develop laws and standards. This being the case, ritual principles and moral duty, laws and standards, are the creation of the acquired nature of the sage and not the product of anything inherent in his inborn nature.

With regard to such phenomena as the eye's love of colors, the ear's

【原文】

好愉佚，是皆生于人之情性者也，感而自然，不待事而后生之者也。夫感而不能然，必且待事而后然者，谓之生于伪。是性伪之所生，其不同之征也。故圣人化性而起伪，伪起而生礼义，礼义生而制法度。然则礼义法度者，是圣人之所生也。故圣人之所以同于众、其不异于众者，性也；所以异而过众者，伪也。夫好利而欲得者，此人之情性也。假之人有弟兄资财而分者，且顺情性，好利而欲得，若是则兄弟相拂夺矣；且化礼义之文理，若是则让乎国人矣。故顺情性，则弟兄

【今译】

嘴巴爱吃美味，内心爱好财利，身体喜欢舒适安逸，这些才都是产生于人的本性的东西，是一有感觉就自然形成、不依赖于人为的努力就会产生出来的东西。那些并不由感觉形成、一定要依靠努力从事然后才能形成的东西，便叫做产生于人为。这便是先天本性和后天人为所产生的东西及其不同的特征。圣人改变了邪恶的本性而作出了人为的努力，人为的努力作出后就产生了礼义，礼义产生后就制定了法度。那么礼义法度这些东西，便是圣人所创制的了。圣人和众人相同而跟众人没有什么不同的地方，是先天的本性；圣人和众人不同而又超过众人的地方，是后天的人为努力。那爱好财利而希望得到，这是人的本性。假如有人弟兄之间要分财产而依顺爱好财利而希望得到的本性，那么兄弟之间也会反目为仇，互相争夺了；如果受到礼义规范的教化，那就会把财利推让给普通人了。所以依顺本性，那就兄弟相

fondness of sounds, the mouth's love of tastes, the mind's love of profit, and the fondness of the bones, flesh, and skin-lines for pleasant sensations and relaxation—all these are products of man's essential and inborn nature. When there is stimulation, they respond spontaneously. They do not require that a person first apply himself before they are produced. But what cannot be produced by such stimulation but rather must await application before it can be produced is called the result of acquired nature. These are the distinguishing characteristics that show that what is produced by man's acquired nature is not the same as what is produced by the characteristics inherent in man's inborn nature.

Thus, the sage by transforming his original nature develops his acquired nature. From this developed acquired nature, he creates ritual principles and moral duty. Having produced them, he institutes the regulations of laws and standards. This being so, ritual principles, moral duty, laws, and standards are all products of the sage. Thus, where the sage is identical to the common mass of men and does not exceed their characteristics, it is his inborn nature. Where he differs from them and exceeds them, it is his acquired nature.

A love of profit and the desire to obtain it belong to man's essential and inborn nature. Now, suppose that younger and elder brothers have valuable goods that are supposed to be apportioned among them, and further suppose that they follow the true feelings of their inborn nature—namely, a love of profit and the desire to obtain it—then younger and elder brothers will fall into fighting among themselves and robbing each other. Further, where they have been transformed by the proper forms and the natural order contained in ritual principles and precepts of moral duty, they will yield their claim to others of their own country. Thus, following one's essential and inborn nature will lead to strife even among brothers,

【原文】

争矣；化礼义，则让乎国人矣。

23.8 凡人之欲为善者，为性恶也。夫薄愿厚，恶愿美，狭愿广，贫愿富，贱愿贵，苟无之中者，必求于外。故富而不愿财，贵而不愿势，苟有之中者，必不及于外。用此观之，人之欲为善者，为性恶也。今人之性，固无礼义，故强学而求有之也；性不知礼义，故思虑而求知之也。然则性而已，则人无礼义，不知礼义。人无礼义则乱，不知礼义则悖。然则性而已，则悖乱在已。用此观之，人之性恶明矣，其善者伪也。

【今译】

争；受到礼义教化，那就会连普通人都会相让。

23.8 一般地说，人们想行善，正是因为其本性邪恶的缘故。那微薄的希望丰厚，丑陋的希望美丽，狭窄的希望宽广，贫穷的希望富裕，卑贱的希望高贵，如果本身没有它，就一定要向外去追求。所以富裕了就不羡慕钱财，显贵了就不羡慕权势，如果本身有了它，就一定不会向外去追求了。由此看来，人们想行善，实是因为其本性邪恶的缘故。人的本性，本来是没有什么礼义观念的，所以才努力学习而力求掌握它；本性是不懂礼义的，所以才开动脑筋而力求了解它。那么如果只有本性，人就不会有礼义，就不会懂得礼义。人没有礼义就会混乱无序，不懂礼义就会悖逆不道。那么如果人只有本性，在他身上就只有逆乱了。由此看来，人的本性是邪恶的就很明显了，他们那些善良的行为则是人为的。

but when it has been transformed by ritual and morality, brothers will yield their claim to others of their own country.

23. 8

As a general rule, the fact that men desire to do good is the product of the fact that their nature is evil. Those with very little think longingly about having much, the ugly about being beautiful, those in cramped quarters about spacious surroundings, the poor about wealth, the base about eminence—indeed whatever a man lacks within himself he is sure to desire from without. Thus, those who are already rich do not wish for valuables nor do the eminent wish for high position, for indeed whatever a person has within he does not seek from without. If we consider the implications of these facts, it is plain that man's desiring to good is the product of the fact that his nature is evil.

Now, man assuredly does not possess ritual principles and precepts of morality as part of his inborn nature; therefore he must study very hard when seeking them. Inborn nature is unaware of them; therefore in his thoughts and ideas he has to seek to understand ritual principles and precepts of morality. This being the case, if we consider man as he is at birth and nothing else, then he lacks ritual and moral principles and is unaware of them. A man who lacks them will be rebellious, and one who does not understand them will be perverse. This being the case, if we consider man as he is at birth and nothing else, then it is perversity and rebelliousness that characterize him. If we consider the implications of these facts, it is plain that human nature is evil and that any good in humans is acquired by conscious exertion.

【原文】

23.9 孟子曰："人之性善。"

曰：是不然。凡古今天下之所谓善者，正理平治也；所谓恶者，偏险悖乱也。是善恶之分也已。今诚以人之性固正理平治邪，则有恶用圣王?恶用礼义矣哉?虽有圣王礼义，将曷加于正理平治也哉?今不然，人之性恶。故古者圣人以人之性恶，以为偏险而不正、悖乱而不治，故为之立君上之势以临之，明礼义以化之，起法正以治之，重刑罚以禁之，使天下皆出于治，合于善也。是圣王之治而礼义之化也。今当试去君上之势，无礼义之化，去法正之治，无刑罚之禁，倚

【今译】

23.9 孟子说："人的本性是善良的。"

我说：这不对。凡是从古到今、普天之下所谓的善良，是指端正顺理安定有秩序；所谓的邪恶，是指偏邪险恶悖逆作乱。这就是善良和邪恶的区别。果真认为人的本性本来就是端正顺理安定守秩序的吧，那么又哪里用得着圣明的帝王，哪里用得着礼义了呢?即使有了圣明的帝王和礼义，在那端正顺理安定守秩序的本性上又能增加些什么呢?其实并不是这样，人的本性是邪恶的。古代的圣人认为人的本性是邪恶的，认为人们是偏邪险恶而不端正、悖逆作乱而不守秩序的，所以给他们确立了君主的权势去统治他们，彰明了礼义去教化他们，建立起法治去管理他们，加重刑罚去限制他们，使天下人都从遵守秩序出发，符合于善良的标准。这就是圣明帝王的治理和礼义的教化。如果抛掉君主的权势，没有礼义的教化，废弃法治的管理，没有

23. 9

Mencius claims that man's nature is good.

I say that this is not so. As a rule, from antiquity to the present day, what the world has called good is what is correct, in accord with natural principles, peaceful, and well-ordered. What has been called evil is what is wrong through partiality, what wickedly contravenes natural principles, what is perverse, and what is rebellious. This is precisely the division between the good and the evil. Now, can one truly take man's inborn nature to have as its essential characteristics correctness, accord with natural principles, peacefulness, and order? Were that the case, what use would there be for sage kings, and what need for ritual and moral principles! And even supposing that there were sage kings and ritual and moral principles, what indeed could they add to correctness, natural principles, peace, and order!

Now, of course this is not so. The nature of man is evil. Thus, in antiquity the sages considered his nature evil, to be inclined to prejudice and wickedness, and not toward uprightness, to be perverse and rebellious, and not to be orderly. Thus, they established the authority of lords and superiors to supervise men, elucidated ritual and moral principles to transform them, set up laws and standards to bring them to order, and piled on penal laws and punishments to restrain them. They caused the entire world to develop with good order and to be consistent with the good. Such was the government of the sage kings and the transforming influence of ritual and moral principles.

Now, let us try to imagine a situation where we do away with the authority of lords and superiors, do without the transforming influence of ritual and morality, discard the order provided by the laws and rectitude,

【原文】

而观天下民人之相与也；若是，则夫强者害弱而夺之，众者暴寡而哗之，天下之悖乱而相亡不待顷矣。用此观之，然则人之性恶明矣，其善者伪也。

23.10 故善言古者，必有节于今；善言天者，必有征于人。凡论者，贵其有辨合，有符验。故坐而言之，起而可设，张而可施行。今孟子曰“人之性善”，无辨合符验，坐而言之，起而不可设，张而不

【今译】

刑罚的制约，站在一边观看天下民众的相互交往；那么，那些强大的就会侵害弱小的而掠夺他们，人多的就会欺凌人少的而压制他们，天下人悖逆作乱而各国互相灭亡的局面不等片刻就会出现了。由此看来，那么人的本性是邪恶的就很明显了，他们那些善良的行为则是人为的。

23.10 善于谈论古代的人，一定对现代有验证；善于谈论天的人，一定对人事有应验。凡是议论，可贵的在于像契券般可核对，像信符般可检验。所以坐着谈论它，站起来就可以部署安排，推广出去就可以实行。现在孟子说“人的本性善良”，没有与它相契合的证据及可以验证的凭据，坐着谈论它，站起来不能部署安排，推广出去不

do without the restraints of penal laws and punishments—were this to occur, let us consider how the people of the world would deal with each other. In such a situation the strong would inflict harm on the weak and rob them; the many would tyrannize the few and wrest their possessions from them; and the perversity and rebelliousness of the whole world would quickly ensure their mutual destruction. If we consider the implications of these facts, it is plain that human nature is evil and that any good in humans is acquired by conscious exertion.

23. 10

Accordingly, those who are expert at theorizing about antiquity will certainly show how their ideas tally with the situation of the present. Those expert at theorizing about Nature will certainly support their notions with evidence from the human condition. As a general principle, what is to be prized in the presentation of a thesis is that there is consistency in the structure of the discrimination advanced to support it and that there is evidentiary support for the thesis which shows that the facts accord with the reality like the two halves of a tally. Thus, they will sit on their mats to propound their theories, will rise up to show that they apply comprehensively, and will stand up straight to show that it is possible for the ideas they have propounded to be put into practice.

Now, Mencius says that man's nature is good. But there is a lack of consistency in the structure of the discrimination advanced to support it and there is a failure to provide evidentiary support for the thesis that shows that the facts accord with the reality like the two halves of a tally. Yet, having sat on his mat propounding this theory, would not his error be vividly shown were he to rise up to try showing that it applies comprehen-

【原文】

可施行，岂不过甚矣哉？故性善，则去圣王息礼义矣；性恶，则与圣王贵礼义矣。故檃栝之生为枸木也；绳墨之起为不直也；立君上，明礼义，为性恶也。用此观之，然则人之性恶明矣，其善者伪也。

23.11 直木不待檃栝而直者，其性直也。枸木必将待檃栝烝矫然后直者，以其性不直也。今人之性恶，必将待圣王之治、礼义之化，然后皆出于治、合于善也。用此观之，然则人之性恶明矣，其善者伪也。

23.12 问者曰："礼义积伪者，是人之性，故圣人能生之也。"

【今译】

能实行，这难道不是错得很厉害了吗？认为人的本性善良，那就会摒除圣明的帝王，取消礼义了；认为人的本性邪恶，那就会拥护圣明的帝王，推崇礼义了。整形器的产生，是因为有弯曲的材料；墨线墨斗的出现，是因为有不直的东西；置立君主，彰明礼义，是因为人的本性邪恶。由此看来，那么人的本性是邪恶的就很明显了，他们那些善良的行为则是人为的。

23.11 笔直的木材不依靠整形器就笔直，因为它的本性就是笔直的。弯曲的木材一定要依靠整形器进行熏蒸矫正然后才能挺直，因为它的本性不直。人的本性邪恶，一定要依靠圣明帝王的治理，礼义的教化，然后才能都从遵守秩序出发，合乎善良的标准。由此看来，那么人的本性是邪恶的就很明显了，他们那些善良的行为则是人为的。

23.12 有人问："积累人为因素而制定成礼义，这也是人的本性，

sively or that it can be established in practice!

Hence, if the nature of man were good, then one could dispense with sage kings and put aside ritual and moral principles. But since the nature of man is evil, we must adhere to the sage kings and esteem ritual and moral principles.

Thus, the genesis of the press-frame is to be found in warped wood, and the advent of the blackened marking line is to be found in things that are not straight. So too the need to establish lords and superiors and to elucidate ritual and moral principles is to be found in man's nature being evil. If we consider the implications of these facts, it is plain that human nature is evil and that any good in humans is acquired by conscious exertion.

23. 11

A straight board does not first need the press-frame to be straight; it is straight by nature. But a warped board must first await application of the press-frame, steam to soften it, and force to bend it into shape before it can be made straight; this is because by nature it is not straight. Now, since the nature of man is evil, it must await the government of the sage kings and the transformation effected by ritual and morality before everything develops with good order and is consistent with the good. If we consider the implications of these facts, it is plain that human nature is evil and that any good in humans is acquired by conscious exertion.

23. 12

An inquirer says: Ritual principles, morality, accumulated effort, and

【原文】

应之曰：是不然。夫陶人埏埴而生瓦，然则瓦埴岂陶人之性也哉?工人斫木而生器，然则器木岂工人之性也哉?夫圣人之于礼义也，辟亦陶埏而生之也。然则礼义积伪者，岂人之本性也哉?凡人之性者，尧、舜之与桀、跖，其性一也；君子之与小人，其性一也。今将以礼义积伪为人之性邪，然则有曷贵尧、禹，曷贵君子矣哉?凡所贵尧、禹、君子者，能化性，能起伪，伪起而生礼义；然则圣人之于礼义积伪也，亦犹陶埏而生之也。用此观之，然则礼义积伪者，岂人之性也哉?所贱于桀、跖、小人者，从其性，顺其情，安恣睢，以出乎贪利争夺。故人之性恶明矣，其善者伪也。

【今译】

所以圣人才能创造出礼义来啊。”

回答他说：这不对。制作陶器的人搅拌揉打粘土而生产出瓦器，那么把粘土制成瓦器难道就是陶器工人的本性么?木工砍削木材而造出器具，那么把木材制成器具难道就是木工的本性么?圣人对于礼义，打个比方来说，也就像陶器工人搅拌揉打粘土而生产出瓦器一样，那么积累人为因素而制定成礼义，难道就是人的本性了么?凡是人的本性，圣明的尧、舜和残暴的桀、跖，他们的本性是一样的；有道德的君子和无行的小人，他们的本性是一样的。如果要把积累人为因素而制定成礼义当作是人的本性吧，那么又为什么要推崇尧、禹，为什么要推崇君子呢?一般说来，人们所以要推崇尧、禹、君子，是因为他们能改变自己的本性，能作出人为的努力，人为的努力作出后就产生了礼义；既然这样，圣人对于积累人为因素而制定成礼义，也就像陶器工人搅拌揉打粘土而生产出瓦器一样。由此看来，那么积累人为因素而制定成礼义，哪里是人的本性呢?人们所以要鄙视桀、跖、小人，是因为他们放纵自己的本性，顺从自己的情欲，习惯于恣肆放荡，以致做出贪图财利争抢掠夺的暴行来。所以人的本性邪恶是很明显的了，他们那些善良的行为则是人为的。

acquired abilities are part of man's nature, which is why the sages were able to produce them. The reply is that this is not so. The potter molds clay to make an earthenware dish, but how could the dish be regarded as part of the potter's inborn nature? The artisan carves wood to make a vessel, but how could the wooden vessel be regarded as part of the artisan's inborn nature? The sage's relation to ritual principles is just like that of the potter molding his clay. This being so, how could ritual principles, morality, accumulated effort, and acquried abilities be part of man's original nature?

As a general rule, the nature men share is one and the same whether they be a Yao and Shun or a Jie and Robber Zhi. The gentleman and the petty man share one and the same nature. Now, how could one take ritual, morality, accumulated effort, and acquired abilities to be part of man's inborn nature! Were this so, why would we esteem a Yao or Yu or prize the gentleman?

As a general rule, what should be prized about Yao, Yu, and the gentleman is that they were able to transform their inborn natures and were able to develop acquired abilities, which in turn produced ritual and moral principles. This being the case, the sage's relation to ritual and moral principles, accumulated effort, and acquired abilities is quite like that of the potter to his pots. (…) How indeed could ritual and moral principles, accumulated effort, and acquired nature be part of man's inborn nature! What is despised about Jie, Robber Zhi, and the petty man is that they follow their inborn nature, indulge their essential nature, and are content with unrestrained passion and an overbearing manner, which results in grasping avarice, fighting, and rapine. Therefore, <if we consider the implications of these facts, > it is plain that human nature is evil and that any good in humans is acquired by conscious exertion.

【原文】

23.13 天非私曾、骞、孝己而外众人也，然而曾、骞、孝己独厚于孝之实而全于孝之名者，何也?以綦于礼义故也。天非私齐、鲁之民而外秦人也，然而于父子之义、夫妇之别，不如齐、鲁之孝具敬父者，何也?以秦人之从情性，安恣睢，慢于礼义故也，岂其性异矣哉?

23.14 "'涂之人可以为禹。'曷谓也?"

曰：凡禹之所以为禹者，以其为仁义法正也。然则仁义法正有可知可能之理，然而涂之人也，皆有可以知仁义法正之质，皆有可以能仁义法正之具；然则其可以为禹明矣。今以仁义法正为固无可知可能

【今译】

23.13 上天并不是偏袒曾参、闵子骞、孝己而抛弃众人，但是惟独曾参、闵子骞、孝己丰富了孝道的实际内容而成全了孝子的名声，为什么呢?因为他们竭力奉行礼义的缘故啊。上天并不是偏袒齐国、鲁国的人民而抛弃秦国人，但是在父子之间的礼义、夫妻之间的分别上，秦国人不及齐国、鲁国的孝顺恭敬、严肃有礼，为什么呢?因为秦国人纵情任性，习惯于恣肆放荡而怠慢礼义的缘故啊，哪里是他们的本性不同呢?

23.14 "路上的普通人可以成为禹。这话怎么解释呢?"

回答说：一般说来，禹之所以成为禹，是因为他能实行仁义法度。既然这样，仁义法度就具有可以了解和可以做到的性质，而路上的普通人，也都具有可以了解仁义法度的资质，都具有可以做到仁义法度的才具；既然这样，他们可以成为禹也就很明显了。如果认为仁义法度本来就没有可以了解、可以做到的性质，那么，即使是禹也不

23. 13

Heaven did not bestow any special favor on Zeng Shen, Min Ziqian or Filial Yi that it withheld from the common mass of men. That being the case, how is it that they alone brought to fruition such a rich manifestation of filial deeds and established such a reputation for perfect filial piety? It is because of the extraordinary degree to which they embodied the precepts of ritual and morality.

Heaven has not bestowed special favors on the people of Lu and Qi that it withheld from those of Qin. This being the case, in regard to the duties between father and son and the separation of function between husband and wife, how is it that [the people of Qin] are not the equal of those of Lu and Qi both in their filial piety and respect and in their reverence for proper forms? It is because the people of Qin follow their inborn and essential nature, are content with unrestrained passion and an overbearing manner, and are remiss in regard to ritual and morality. How could their inborn natures be different!

23. 14

A man in the street can become a Yu. What does this saying mean? I say that in general what made Yu a Yu was his use of humaneness, morality, the model of law, and rectitude. Since this is so, then in each of these four there are rational principles that we can know and which we are capable of putting into practice. That being so, it is clear that the man in the street can become a Yu, since it is possible for every man to understand the substance of humaneness, morality, the model of law,

【原文】

之理邪，然则唯禹不知仁义法正，不能仁义法正也。将使涂之人固无可以知仁义法正之质，而固无可以能仁义法正之具邪，然则涂之人也，且内不可以知父子之义，外不可以知君臣之正。不然。今涂之人者，皆内可以知父子之义，外可以知君臣之正，然则其可以知之质，可以能之具，其在涂之人明矣。今使涂之人者，以其可以知之质，可以能之具，本夫仁义之可知之理、可能之具，然则其可以为禹明矣。今使涂之人伏术为学，专心一志，思索孰察，加日县久，积善而不息，则通于神明，参于天地矣。故圣人者，人之所积而致也。

【今译】

能了解仁义法度，不能实行仁义法度了。假如路上的人本来就没有可以了解仁义法度的资质，本来就没有可以做到仁义法度的才具吧，那么，路上的人将内不可能懂得父子之间的礼义，外不可能懂得君臣之间的准则了。实际上不是这样。现在路上的人都是内能懂得父子之间的礼义，外能懂得君臣之间的准则，那么，那些可以了解仁义法度的资质，可以做到仁义法度的才具，存在于路上的人身上也就很明显的了。现在如果使路上的人用他们可以了解仁义的资质，可以做到仁义的才具，去掌握那具有可以了解和可以做到的性质的仁义，那么，他们可以成为禹也就很明显的了。现在如果使路上的人信服道术进行学习，专心致志，思考探索仔细审察，日复一日持之以恒，积累善行而永不停息，那就能通于神明，与天地相并列了。所以圣人，是一般的人积累善行而达到的。

and rectitude and the ability to master their instruments.

Now, let us suppose that the rational principles contained in humanity, in morality, in the model of law, and in rectitude definitely neither could be known nor were capable of being put into practice. In that case, then even a Yu could not know them and would be incapable of putting them into practice. Now if the man in the street definitely had not the substance that makes it possible to know them nor the resources to become capable of them, then he also could not know the duties between father and son in terms of his own household and in terms of the outside he could not know the proper conduct between lord and subject.

Now, of course, this is not the case, for the man in the street understands both the moral obligations between father and son and the standards of rectitude between lord and minister. This being so, he has the substance that makes it possible to know them and the resources to become capable of them. Thus, it is clear that both belong to the nature of the man in the street. So if he could be induced to make use of the substance that makes it possible for him to know and the resources that enable him to become capable to build a foundation for the principles of natural order in humanity, morality, the model of law, and rectitude, then it is obvious that he could become a Yu.

Now, if the man in the street were induced to cleave to these methods, engage in study, focus his mind on a single aim, unify his intentions, ponder these principles, accomplish them each day over a long period of time, and to accumulate what is good without slacking off, then he could penetrate as far as spiritual intelligence and could form a Triad with Heaven and Earth. Thus the sage is a man who has reached this high state through accumulated effort.

【原文】

23.15曰:"圣可积而致，然而皆不可积，何也?"

曰：可以而不可使也。故小人可以为君子而不肯为君子，君子可以为小人而不肯为小人。小人君子者，未尝不可以相为也，然而不相为者，可以而不可使也。故涂之人可以为禹，则然；涂之人能为禹，未必然也。虽不能为禹，无害可以为禹。足可以遍行天下，然而未尝有能遍行天下者也。夫工匠农贾，未尝不可以相为事也，然而未尝能相为事也。用此观之，然则可以为，未必能也；虽不能，无害可以为。然则能不能之与可不可，其不同远矣，其不可以相为明矣。

【今译】

23.15有人说:"圣人可以通过积累善行而达到，但是一般人都不能积累善行，为什么呢?"

回答说：可以做到，却不可强使他们做到。小人可以成为君子而不肯做君子，君子可以成为小人而不肯做小人。小人和君子，未尝不可以互相对调着做，但是他们没有互相对调着做，是因为可以做到却不可强使他们做到啊。所以，路上的普通人可以成为禹，那是对的；路上的人都能成为禹，就不一定对了。虽然没有能成为禹，但并不妨害可以成为禹。脚可以走遍天下，但是还没有能走遍天下的人。工匠、农夫、商人，未尝不可以互相调换着做事，但是没有能互相调换着做事。由此看来，可以做到，不一定就能做到；即使不能做到，也不妨害可以做到。那么，能够不能够与可以不可以，它们的差别是很大的了，他们不可以互相对调也是很清楚的了。

23. 15

Someone asks:"How is it possible for the sage to reach this high state through his accumulated effort, but the rest of mankind cannot?"

I say that although it is possible for them to do so, they cannot be induced to do so. Thus, although the petty man is capable of becoming a gentleman, he is unwilling to do so, although the gentleman could become a petty man, he is unwilling to do so. It has never been impossible for the petty man and the gentleman to become other. The fact they have never done so, although it is possible for them to do so, is because they cannot be induced to do so. Thus, although it is true that it is possible for the man in the street to become a Yu, that the man in the street has the real capacity to become a Yu is not necessarily so. Even though one is unable to become a Yu, this does not contradict the possibility of his becoming a Yu.

It is possible for a man to travel by foot across the width of the whole world, yet there has never been a case where anyone was able to travel across the world by foot. So, too, although it has never been impossible for the artisan, carpenter, farmer, or trader to practice each other's business, they have never been able to do so. If we consider the implications of these facts, we see that something's being possible does not guarantee having the ability to do it. Even though one is unable to do something, this does not contradict the possibility of doing it. This being the case, that something is possible or impossible is entirely dissimilar from having or not having the ability to do it. It is evident that it has never been impossible for the one to become the other.

【原文】

23.16 尧问于舜曰:“人情如何?”

舜对曰:“人情甚不美,又何问焉?妻子具而孝衰于亲,嗜欲得而信衰于友,爵禄盈而忠衰于君。人之情乎!人之情乎!甚不美,又何问焉?唯贤者为不然。”

23.17 有圣人之知者,有士君子之知者,有小人之知者,有役夫之知者。多言则文而类,终日议其所以,言之千举万变,其统类一也,是圣人之知也。少言则径而省,论而法,若佚之以绳,是士君子之知也。其言也谄,其行也悖,其举事多悔,是小人之知也。齐给便

【今译】

23.16 尧问舜说:“人之常情怎么样?”

舜回答说:“人之常情很不好,又何必问呢?有了妻子儿女,对父母的孝敬就减弱了;嗜好欲望满足了,对朋友的守信就减弱了;爵位俸禄满意了,对君主的忠诚就减弱了。人之常情啊!人之常情啊!很不好,又何必问呢?只有贤德的人不是这样。”

23.17 有圣人的智慧,有士君子的智慧,有小人的智慧,有奴仆的智慧。话说得多,但合乎礼义法度,整天谈论他的理由,说起话来旁征博引,千变万化,它的纲纪法度则始终一致,这是圣人的智慧。话说得少,但直截了当而简洁精练,头头是道而有法度,就像用墨线扶持着一样,这是士君子的智慧。他的话奉承讨好,行为却与说的相反,他做事经常后悔,这是小人的智慧。说话快速敏捷但没有法度,

23. 16

Yao asked Shun:"What are the true feelings of mankind like?"

Shun replied: "Man's true feelings are very unlovely things. But why need you ask about them? When a man has both wife and child, the filial obligations that he observes toward his parents decrease. When he has satisfied his desires and obtained the things he enjoys, his good faith toward his friends withers away. When he has fully satisfied his desire for high office and good salary, his loyalty to his lord diminishes. Oh man's true feelings! Man's true feelings—how very unlovely they are! Why need you ask about them!"

It is only in the case of the worthy that this becomes not so.

23. 17

There is the understanding of the sage, that of the scholar and gentleman, that of the petty man, and that of the menial servant.

Speaking frequently with words that are well-composed and precisely to the category of his topic; being able to discourse for a whole day on the reasons for something; discussing it in terms of a thousand references and a myriad transformations; and unifying the guiding principles and proper categories—such is the understanding of the sage.

Speaking but seldom and then briefly and succinctly; putting things into their proper grades and positions in accord with the model of law as though they had been put into an even row with the marking-line—such is the understanding of the scholar and gentleman.

Speaking only to flatter;acting in a rebellious manner;recommending undertakings that frequently occasion regret—such is the understanding

【原文】

敏而无类，杂能旁魄而无用，析速粹孰而不急，不恤是非，不论曲直，以期胜人为意，是役夫之知也。

23.18 有上勇者，有中勇者，有下勇者。天下有中，敢直其身；先王有道，敢行其意；上不循于乱世之君，下不俗于乱世之民；仁之所在无贫穷，仁之所亡无富贵；天下知之，则欲与天下同苦乐之；天下不知之，则傀然独立天地之间而不畏：是上勇也。礼恭而意俭，大齐信焉而轻货财；贤者敢推而尚之，不肖者敢援而废之：是中勇也。

【今译】

技能驳杂，广博而无用，分析问题迅速，遣词造句熟练但无关紧要，不顾是非，不讲曲直，把希望胜过别人作为心愿，这是奴仆的智慧。

23.18 有上等的勇敢，有中等的勇敢，有下等的勇敢。天下有了中正之道，敢于挺身捍卫；古代的圣王有正道传下来，敢于贯彻执行他们的原则精神；上不依顺动乱时代的君主，下不混同于动乱时代的人民；在仁德存在的地方不顾贫苦穷厄，在仁德丧失的地方不愿富裕高贵；天下人都知道他，就要与天下人同甘共苦；天下人不知道他，就岿然屹立于天地之间而无所畏惧：这是上等的勇敢。礼貌恭敬而心意谦让，重视中正诚信而看轻钱财，对于贤能的人敢于推荐而使他处于高位，对于不贤的人敢于把他拉下来罢免掉：这是中等的勇敢。看

of the petty man.

Quick, fluent, facile, and glib, yet not to the proper category of thc subject; versatile, capable, encyclopedic, and comprehensive, yet quite useless; decisive, clever, exact, and proficient, but concerning matters of no urgency; caring nothing for considerations of right and wrong; not putting things into their proper position concerning what is straight and what crooked; aiming at triumphing over the common ideas of men—such is the understanding of menials.

23. 18

There is valor of the highest order, valor of the middle order, and valor of an inferior order.

When the Mean prevails in the world, to be daring in holding oneself straight and erect; when the Way of the Ancient Kings prevails, to be bold in carrying its ideals into practice; in a high position not to go along with lords of an age given to anarchy; in a humble position not to acquire the customs of the people of chaotic times; to consider that there is neither poverty nor misery where humane principles are to be found and that there is neither wealth nor eminence where they are absent; when the world recognizes your merits to desire to share in the world's joys;and when the world does not recognize your merits to stand grandly alone in the world yet not be over-awed—such is valor of the highest type.

Respectful in ritual conduct and modest in one's ideas;attaching primary importance to purity of self and personal integrity but considering material wealth trivial; to presume to push forward the worthy and get them elevated and to hold back the undeserving and get them dismissed—such is valor of the middle order.

【原文】

轻身而重货，恬祸而广解苟免；不恤是非、然不然之情，以期胜人为意：是下勇也。

23.19 繁弱、钜黍，古之良弓也，然而不得排檠，则不能自正。桓公之葱，太公之阙，文王之录，庄君之曶，阖闾之干将、莫邪、钜阙、辟闾，此皆古之良剑也，然而不加砥砺则不能利，不得人力则不能断。骅骝、骐骥、纤离、绿耳，此皆古之良马也，然而必前有衔辔之制，后有鞭策之威，加之以造父之驭，然后一日而致千里也。夫人虽有性质美而心辩知，必将求贤师而事之，择良友而友之。得贤师而事之，则所闻者尧、舜、禹、汤之道也；得良友而友之，则所见者忠信敬让之行也；身日进于仁义而不自知也者，靡使然也。今与不善人

【今译】

轻自己的生命而看重钱财，不在乎闯祸而又多方解脱苟且逃避罪责；不顾是非、正误的实际情况，把希望胜过别人作为自己的心愿：这是下等的勇敢。

23.19 繁弱、钜黍，是古代的良弓，但是得不到矫正器的矫正，就不会自行平正。齐桓公的葱，齐太公的阙，周文王的录，楚庄王的曶，吴王阖闾的干将、莫邪、钜阙、辟闾，这些都是古代的好剑，但是不加以磨砺就不会锋利，不凭借人力就不能斩断东西。骅骝、骐骥、纤骊、绿耳，这些都是古代的良马，但是必须前有马嚼子、马缰绳的控制，后有鞭子的威胁，再给它们加上造父的驾驭，然后才能一天跑得到上千里。人即使有了资质的美好，而且脑子善于辨别理解，也一定要寻找贤能的老师去事奉他，选择德才优良的朋友和他们交往。得到了贤能的老师去事奉他，那么所听到的就是尧、舜、禹、汤的正道；得到了德才优良的朋友而和他们交往，那么所看到的就是忠诚守信、恭敬谦让的行为；自己一天天地进入到仁义的境界之中而自己

To think unimportant one's own character but to place great store on material wealth; to remain complacent in face of calamity and remain negligent and inattentive; to…in an attempt to avoid blame; to disregard matters of right and wrong and the essential characteristics of what is so and what not; and to aim at triumphing over the common ideas of men—such is inferior valor.

23. 19

Fanruo and Jushu were the best bows of antiquity, yet had they not been pressed into shape in the bow-frame, they would have been incapable of shaping themselves. The Zong of Duke Huan, the Que of the Grand Duke, the Lu of King Wen, the Hu of Lord Zhuang, and the Ganjiang, Moye, Juque, and Bilü of King Helü were the best swords of antiquity, yet had one not added grinding on the whetstone, it would have been impossible to sharpen them, and were there no strong man to wield them, then they would be incapable of cutting anything. Hualiu, Qiji, Xianli, and Lü'er were the best horses of antiquity, yet it was necessary first to train them with the bit and bridle, then intimidate them with whip and cane, and finally add to those the skillful driving of a Zaofu before they could travel a thousand *li* in a single day.

Although a man may have fine talents and a mind with a discriminating intelligence, he must seek out a worthy teacher to serve and select good men as the friends with whom to associate. If he obtains a worthy teacher, then what he hears will be the Way of Yao, Shun, Yu, and Tang. If he obtains good men as his friends, then what he sees will be conduct marked by loyalty, trust, respect, and politeness. Each day he will advance in humaneness and morality without his being conscious of it be-

【原文】

处，则所闻者欺诬、诈伪也，所见者污漫、淫邪、贪利之行也，身且加于刑戮而不自知者，靡使然也。传曰："不知其子视其友，不知其君视其左右。"靡而已矣！靡而已矣！

【今译】

也没有察觉到，这是外界接触使他这样的啊。如果和德行不好的人相处，那么所听到的就是欺骗造谣、诡诈说谎，所看到的就是污秽卑鄙、淫乱邪恶、贪图财利的行为，自己将受到刑罚杀戮还没有自我意识到，这也是外界接触使他这样的啊。古书上说："不了解自己的儿子就看看他的朋友怎么样，不了解自己的君主就看看他身边的人怎么样。"这就是潜移默化的影响啊！这就是潜移默化的影响啊！

cause his environment has caused it. But if he lives among men who are not good, then what he hears will be deception, calumny, treachery, and hypocrisy and what he sees will be conduct that is base and reckless, wanton and wicked, and greedy for profits so that although he is unaware of it, he will further increase the risk of punishment and disgrace because his environment has caused it. A tradition says:

> If you do not know your son, look at his friends; if you do not know your lord look to his attendants.

It is the environment that is critical! It is the environment that is critical!

君子第二十四

【原文】

24.1“天子无妻”，告人无匹也。“四海之内无客礼”，告无适也。“足能行，待相者然后进；口能言，待官人然后诏；不视而见，不听而聪，不言而信，不虑而知，不动而功”，告至备也。天子也者，势至重，形至佚，心至愈，志无所诎，形无所劳，尊无上矣。《诗》曰:“普天之下，莫非王土；率土之滨，莫非王臣。”此之谓也。

24.2 圣王在上，分义行乎下，则士大夫无流淫之行，百吏官人

【今译】

24.1“天子没有妻子”，是说别人没有和他地位相等的。“天子在四海之内没有人用对待客人的礼节接待他”，是说没有人做他的主人。“天子脚能走路，但一定要依靠礼宾官才向前走；嘴能说话，但一定要依靠传旨的官吏才下命令；天子不用亲自去看就能看得见，不用亲自去听就能听清楚，不用亲自去说就能取信于民，不用亲自思考就能理解，不用亲自动手就能有功效”，这是说天子的下属官员极其完备。天子权势极其重大，身体极其安逸，心境极其愉快，志向没有什么受挫折的，身体没有什么可劳累的，尊贵的地位是无以复加的了。《诗》云：“凡在苍天覆盖下，无处不是天子的土地；从陆地到海滨，无人不是天子的臣民。”说的就是这个啊。

24.2 圣明的帝王在上，名分、道义推行到下面，那么士大夫就

Book 24

On the Gentleman

24. 1

That the Son of Heaven has no mate informs men that he is without peer. That within the four seas there are no ceremonies which treat him as a guest informs men that there is no one to match him. Although he is able to walk by foot, he awaits his assistants before he moves. Although he can speak with his mouth, he awaits his officers before he gives instructions. He does not look yet sees, does not listen yet hears, does not speak yet is trusted, does not ponder over things yet knows, does not move yet accomplishes. He has only to make announcements, and all is brought to perfect fulfillment. One who is a Son of Heaven has the position of greatest power and authority, a body that enjoys total leisure, and a heart that is perfectly contented. There is nothing to which his will must unwillingly submit, nothing that will bring weariness to his body, and nothing that is superior to his honored position. An *Ode* says:

> Under the vastness of Heaven,
> there is no land that is not the king's land.
> To the far shores of the earth,
> none are not royal servants.

This expresses my meaning.

24. 2

When a sage king occupies the highest position and the responsibili-

【原文】

无怠慢之事，众庶百姓无奸怪之俗，无盗贼之罪，莫敢犯上之禁。天下晓然皆知夫盗窃之不可以为富也，皆知夫贼害之不可以为寿也，皆知夫犯上之禁不可以为安也。由其道，则人得其所好焉；不由其道，则必遇其所恶焉。是故刑罚綦省而威行如流，世晓然皆知夫为奸则虽隐窜逃亡之由不足以免也，故莫不服罪而请。《书》曰："凡人自得罪。"此之谓也。

24.3 故刑当罪则威，不当罪则侮；爵当贤则贵，不当贤则贱。古者刑不过罪，爵不逾德，故杀其父而臣其子，杀其兄而臣其弟。刑

【今译】

不会有放肆淫荡的行为，群臣百官就不会有懈怠傲慢的事情，群众百姓就不会有邪恶怪僻的习俗，不会有偷窃劫杀的罪行，没有人敢触犯君主的禁令。天下的人明明白白地都知道盗窃是不可能发财致富的，都知道抢劫杀人是不可能获得长寿的，都知道触犯了君主的禁令是不可能得到安宁的。都知道遵循圣明帝王的正道，就每人都能得到他所喜欢的奖赏；如果不遵循圣明帝王的正道，那就一定会遭到他所厌恶的刑罚。所以刑罚极少用而威力却像流水一样扩展出去，社会上都明明白白地知道为非作歹后即使躲藏逃亡也还是不能够免受惩罚，所以无不伏法认罪而主动请求惩处。《尚书》说："所有的人都自愿得到惩处。"说的就是这种情况。

24.3 所以刑罚与罪行相当就有威力，和罪行不相当就会受到轻忽；官爵和德才相当就会受人尊重，和德才不相当就会被人看不起。古代刑罚不超过犯人的罪行，官爵不超过官员的德行，所以杀了父亲

ties and duties proper to each social class are observed by his subjects, then knights and grand officers do not engage in wayward and abandoned conduct. Minor officers and bureaucrats are not indolent or negligent in the execution of their duties. The mass of commoners, the Hundred Clans, have no lewd or exotic customs and do not commit the offenses of theft or banditry. None presumes to transgress the prohibitions of his superiors. The whole world will then clearly perceive that it is impossible for theft and robbery to lead to riches, for predation and doing harm to others to lead to old age, or for transgressions of the prohibitions of superiors to lead to a secure existence. If they follow his Way, they will obtain what they are fond of; but if they do not, they are certain to meet with what they hate. For this reason, penal sanctions and punishments were extremely rare, for the majesty of his conduct will overawe the people like flooding waters. Everyone in his age then clearly perceives that although one might try to hide in some secret place or flee and disappear, it would be to no avail, for the consequences of acting in an evil way could not be evaded. Thus, none will fail to submit freely to his proper punishment. A *Document* says:

The people voluntarily acknowledged their offenses.

This expresses my meaning.

24. 3

Thus, if the punishment fits the crime, there is awe-inspiring majesty. If it does not, there is ridicule of authority. If rank fits the worth of the individual holding it, there is esteem; where it does not, there is contempt. In antiquity, penal sanctions did not exceed what was fitting to the crime, and rank did not go beyond the moral worth of the person. Thus,

【原文】

罚不怒罪，爵赏不逾德，分然各以其诚通。是以为善者劝，为不善者沮；刑罚綦省而威行如流，政令致明而化易如神。传曰："一人有庆，兆民赖之。"此之谓也。

24.4 乱世则不然。刑罚怒罪，爵赏逾德，以族论罪，以世举贤。故一人有罪而三族皆夷，德虽如舜，不免刑均，是以族论罪也。先祖当贤，后子孙必显，行虽如桀、纣，列从必尊，此以世举贤也。以族

【今译】

而让儿子做臣子，杀了哥哥而让弟弟做臣子。刑律的处罚不超过犯人的罪行，官爵的奖赏不超过官员的德行，分明地各自按照实际情况来贯彻执行。因此做好事的人受到鼓励，干坏事的人得到阻止；刑罚极少用而威力像流水一样扩展出去，政策法令极明确而教化像神灵一样蔓延四方。古书上说："天子一个人有了美好的德行，亿万人民就能靠他的福。"说的就是这种情况。

24.4 混乱的时代就不是这样。刑律的处罚超过了犯人的罪行，官爵的奖赏超过了官员的德行，按照亲属关系来判罪，根据世系来举用贤人。一个人有了罪而父、母、妻三族都被诛灭，德行即使像舜一样，也不免受到同样的刑罚，这是按照亲属关系来判罪。祖先曾经贤能，后代的子孙就一定显贵，行为即使像夏桀、商纣王一样，位次也

although the father had been executed, his son could be employed in the government; although the elder brother had been killed, the younger could be employed. Penal sanctions and punishments did not transgress what was proper to the offense, rank and reward did not go beyond the moral worth of the person. Each was allotted what was his due according in every case to his true circumstances. In this way, those who acted on behalf of good would be encouraged, and those who acted in the interests of what was not good would be stymied. When penal sanctions and punishments are exceedingly rare, the majesty of his conduct will overawe the people like flooding waters;when the rules and ordinance of government have been made perfectly clear, the transformations and reforms are like those of a spirit.A tradition says:

> The Single Man shall enjoy happiness; the countless people will receive the advantage of it.

This expresses my meaning.

24. 4

In a chaotic age this is not so. Penal sanctions and punishments exceed the offense; rank and reward exceed moral worth. The family is used in judging the offense; the genealogy is used in recommending the worthy. Thus, when a single man is adjudged guilty, three full generations are destroyed. Even though [a member of the family] has the moral worth of a Shun, he would, all the same, not evade the penal sanctions, for this is the result of using the family to judge the offense. Where the founding patriarch of a family was worthy, his descendants in later generations are certain to be given special distinction. Even if [a member of the family] conducts himself like a Jie or Zhou Xin, his position and status

【原文】

论罪，以世举贤，虽欲无乱，得乎哉？《诗》曰：“百川沸腾，山冢崒崩，高岸为谷，深谷为陵，哀今之人，胡憯莫惩？”此之谓也。

24.5 论法圣王，则知所贵矣；以义制事，则知所利矣。论知所贵，则知所养矣；事知所利，则动知所出矣。二者，是非之本，得失之原也。故成王之于周公也，无所往而不听，知所贵也。桓公之于管

【今译】

一定尊贵，这是根据世系来举用贤人。按照亲属关系来判罪，根据世系举用贤人，即使想没有祸乱，办得到吗？《诗》云：“很多河流在沸腾，山峰碎裂往下崩，高高的山崖成深谷，深深的峡谷成山陵。可哀当今的执政者，为什么竟然不警醒？”说的就是这种情况啊。

24.5 议论效法圣明的帝王，就知道什么人是应该尊重的了；根据道义来处理事情，就知道什么办法是有利的了。议论时知道所要尊重的人，那就会懂得所要修养的品德了；做事时知道有利的办法，那么行动时就会懂得从什么地方开始了。这两个方面，是正确与错误的根本原因，是成功与失败的根源。周成王对于周公，没有什么方面不听从，这是懂得了所要尊重的人。齐桓公对于管仲，凡是国家大事没

are sure to be honorable, for this is the result of using the genealogy to recommend the worthy. By using the family when judging the offense and the genealogy when recommending the worthy, however much one might hope to avoid anarchy, how could one help but have it! An *Ode* says:

The hundred streams bubble up and flow;
the mountain tops break and collapse.
High banks become valleys;
deep valleys become hills.
Alas for the men of today!
Why has nobody corrected these things?

This expresses my meaning.

24. 5

If things are assigned to their proper position on the basis of the model of the sage kings, one will know what is valuable; if a sense of moral rightness is used to regulate undertakings, one will know what is beneficial. If things are assigned their proper position through knowing what is valuable, one will know what nurtures; if tasks are undertaken with knowledge of what is beneficial, one will know the result. These two things [, knowing what is valuable and what is beneficial,] are the root sources of what is right and what wrong. They are the wellspring of what succeeds and what fails.

Thus, the relation between King Cheng and the Duke of Zhou was that he heeded the duke's advice on everything that transpired, for he realized what was valuable. The relation of Duke Huan to Guan Zhong was that in the business of state he used Guan for everything that devel-

【原文】

仲也，国事无所往而不用，知所利也。吴有伍子胥而不能用，国至于亡，倍道失贤也。故尊圣者王，贵贤者霸，敬贤者存，慢贤者亡，古今一也。故尚贤使能，等贵贱，分亲疏，序长幼，此先王之道也。故尚贤使能，则主尊下安；贵贱有等，则令行而不流；亲疏有分，则施行而不悖；长幼有序，则事业捷成而有所休。故仁者，仁此者也；义者，分此者也；节者，死生此者也；忠者，惇慎此者也；兼此而能之，备矣；备而不矜，一自善也，谓之圣。不矜矣，夫故天下不与争能而致善用其功。有而不有也，夫故为天下贵矣。《诗》曰："淑人君

【今译】

有什么方面不听从，这是懂得了有利的办法。吴国有了伍子胥而不能听从他，国家落到灭亡的地步，是因为违背了正道失掉了贤人啊。所以使圣人尊贵的君主能称王天下，使贤人尊贵的君主能称霸诸侯，尊敬贤人的君主可以存在下去，怠慢贤人的君主就会灭亡，从古到今都是一样的。崇尚贤士，使用能人，使高贵的和卑贱的有等级的区别，区分亲近的和疏远的，按照次序来安排年长的和年幼的，这就是古代圣王的正道。崇尚贤士，使用能人，那么君主就会尊贵而臣民就会安宁；高贵的和卑贱的有了等级差别，那么命令就能实行而不会滞留；亲近的和疏远的有了分别，那么恩惠就能正确赐予而不会违背情理；年长的和年幼的有了次序，那么事业就能迅速成功而有了休息的时间。讲究仁德的人，就是喜欢这正道的人；讲究道义的人，就是把这正道当作职分的人；讲究节操的人，就是为这正道而献身的人；讲究忠诚的人，就是忠厚真诚地奉行这正道的人；囊括了这仁德、道义、节操、忠诚而全能做到，德行就完备了；德行完备而不向人夸耀，一切都是为了改善自己的德行，就叫做圣人。不向人夸耀了，所以天下的人就不会和他争能，因而他就能极好地利用人们的力量。有了德才而不自以为有德才，所以就被天下人尊重了。《诗》云："善人君子忠

oped, for he knew what was beneficial. The kingdom of Wu had Wu Zixu but was incapable of using him, so ultimately the country was destroyed, for it turned against the Way and lost this worthy man. Thus, those who honored sages became kings; those who valued the worthy became lords-protector; those who respected the worthy survived; and those that scorned them were destroyed. Antiquity and today are one and the same in regard to this. Thus, to elevate the worthy and employ the able; to place them in a ranked hierarchy, eminent to base; to distinguish between near and far relatives; and to assign precedence according to age from old to young—such was the Way of the Ancient Kings.

Hence, if he elevates the worthy and employs the able, then the ruler will be honored and his subjects contented. If there is a ranked hierarchy for the eminent and base, then the ordinances of government will be put into practice without delay. If there is proper division in the treatment of near and distant relatives, then the bounties he bestows will be accepted without rebellion. If there is set precedence between old and young, then undertakings and projects will be completed with time for leisure.

Hence, one who is humane will be humane in regard to these matters; one who is moral will apportion everything in terms of these; one who is moderate lives and dies in accordance with these; and one who is loyal will show staunch honesty and conscientiousness in regard to these. When all these are combined together and one has ability, one can perfect everything. To perfect everything yet not be boastful and to unite oneself with the good is to be called a sage. Not being boastful will cause the world not to contest one's abilities and enable one to attain the greatest skill in making use of the people's achievements. To have ability and not be boastful is the reason one becomes the most honored in the world. An *Ode* says:

【原文】

子，其仪不忒；其仪不忒，正是四国。”此之谓也。

【今译】

于仁，坚持道义不变更。他的道义不变更，四方国家他坐镇。”说的就是这种情况啊。

That good man is my gentleman:
his deportment has no flaw.
His deportment has no flaw:
he rectifies the Four Countries.

This expresses my meaning.

成相第二十五

【原文】

25.1 请成相，世之殃。

愚暗愚暗堕贤良。

人主无贤，如瞽无相，何伥伥!

25.2 请布基，慎圣人，

愚而自专事不治。

主忌苟胜，群臣莫谏，必逢灾。

25.3 论臣过，反其施，

尊主安国尚贤义。

【今译】

25.1 让我敲鼓说一场，先说世间的祸殃，

愚昧昏庸又糊涂，竟然陷害那忠良。

君主没有好国相，就像瞎子没人帮，无所适从多迷惘。

25.2 让我陈述那根本，请你把它仔细听，

愚昧独断又专行，国家大事办不成。

君主嫉妒又好胜，群臣没人敢谏诤，灾难一定会降临。

25.3 考察臣子的过错，要看他是怎么做，

是否尊君安祖国，崇尚贤人道义多。

Book 25

Working Songs

25. 1

Let me sing a working song!
The ruination of our generation:
stupid and benighted, stupid and benighted, bringing to naught the worthy and virtuous,
these rulers of men who have no worthies
are like the blind without their assistant.
How aimlessly they wonder about!

25. 2

Let me a foundation lay,
Listen carefully to my words!
Stupid yet willful, his affairs are not ordered.
Where the ruler allows suspicion to overcome him,
none of his assembled ministers remonstrate,
so disaster is certain to befall him.

25. 3

Assess the transgressions of ministers,
who violate their proper duties:
honoring ruler, safeguarding state, promoting the worthy and

【原文】

拒谏饰非，愚而上同，国必祸。

25.4 曷谓罢?国多私，

比周还主党与施。

远贤近谗，忠臣蔽塞，主势移。

25.5 曷谓贤?明君臣，

上能尊主爱下民。

主诚听之，天下为一，海内宾。

25.6 主之孽，谗人达，

【今译】

拒绝劝谏又文过，愚昧附和君主说，国家一定会遭祸。

25.4 什么叫做不贤能?国家内部多私门，

紧密勾结封闭君，同党布置一层层。

远离贤人近谗人，忠臣被隔不得近，君主权势被侵吞。

25.5 什么叫做有德行?君臣职分能分明，

对上能够尊重君，对下能够爱人民。

君主真能听从他，天下统一全平定，四海之内都归顺。

25.6 再说君主的祸灾，在于谗佞都显贵，

righteous.
By refusing to remonstrate, glossing over wrong,
"conforming to the opinions of one's superior" where stupidly he acts,
the state is sure to suffer calamity.

25. 4

What kind of man is called unfit?
In the state frequently pursuing private interests,
partisan and intimate thereby to delude their ruler and extend the associations of their clique,
they keep worthy men at a distance and cozy up to slanderers,
so loyal ministers are concealed and repressed,
and the authority of the ruler is usurped.

25. 5

What kind of man is called worthy?
Keeping clear the distinction between lord and minister,
above they are able to pay honor to the ruler and below to love the people.
When the ruler truly heeds their advice,
the whole world becomes as one,
and all within the seas do "guest service."

25. 6

The harbinger of tragedy for the lord:
slanderers advance to prominence;

【原文】

贤能遁逃国乃蹶。

愚以重愚，暗以重暗，成为桀。

25.7 世之灾，妒贤能，

飞廉知政任恶来。

卑其志意，大其园囿，高其台。

25.8 武王怒，师牧野，

纣卒易乡启乃下。

武王善之，封之于宋，立其祖。

25.9 世之衰，谗人归，

【今译】

贤能逃亡全躲开，国家因此而垮台。

愚昧之上加愚昧，已经昏庸又加倍，成为夏桀同一类。

25.7 再说商代的灾害，在于嫉妒好人才，

飞廉竟然能执政，还要任用那恶来。

使得纣王心狭隘，增大园林讲气派，高高筑起那露台。

25.8 武王因此而发怒，进军牧野攻打纣，

纣王士兵齐倒戈，微子投降做俘虏。

武王赞赏微子启，把他封在宋国住，建立庙宇供祭祖。

25.9 商代衰落将灭亡，谗佞归附商纣王，

worthy and able men flee and hide so the nation is therewith torn apart;
the stupid are used to give importance to the stupid,
the benighted importance to the benighted,
the end result being creation of another Jie.

25. 7

The sign of catastrophe for our generation:
the jealous envy of the worthy and able.
When Feilian was in charge of the government and gave office to Wulai,
they debased their lord's ambitions and ideas,
enlarging his parks and gardens,
raising high his pavilion towers.

25. 8

King Wu, filled with outrage,
led forth his army to the fields of Mu,
Zhou Xin's host changed allegiance and turned to King Wu, and Qi had to surrender.
King Wu, thinking him a good man,
enfeoffed him with Song,
there to be established as patriarch.

25. 9

In an age of decadence and decline,

【原文】

比干见刳箕子累。

武王诛之，吕尚招麾，殷民怀。

25.10 世之祸，恶贤士，

子胥见杀百里徙。

穆公任之，强配五伯，六卿施。

25.11 世之愚，恶大儒，

逆斥不通孔子拘。

展禽三绌，春申道缀，基毕输。

25.12 请牧基，贤者思，

【今译】

比干被剖挖心脏，箕子囚禁在牢房。

武王诛杀商纣王，吕尚指挥战旗扬，商朝民众全归往。

25.10 再说人间的祸殃，厌恶贤能的宰相，

子胥被杀而死亡，百里陪嫁到他邦。

穆公任用百里奚，匹敌五霸国家强，设置六卿威风扬。

25.11 再说人间的糊涂，憎恶伟大的名儒，

不被重用遭驱逐，孔子几次被围住。

展禽三番被废黜，春申德政被废除，儒术基业全倾覆。

25.12 请听治国的根本，在于思慕用贤臣，

slanderers revert to their worst form,
so Bigan's heart was cut out, and the Viscount of Ji was bound in prison.
But King Wu punished such men,
Lü Shang raised troops and led the battle,
so the people of Yin cherished him for it.

25. 10

It is the misfortune of our age
that worthy knights are despised.
Wu Zixu was killed and Baili Xi banished.
But Duke Mu employed Baili
and became the powerful equal of the Five Lords-Protector,
instituting the Six Ministries.

25. 11

The stupidity of this age
is its hatred of the great Ru.
They are opposed, rebuffed, and made unsuccessful, like Confucius being seized.
Zhan Qin was thrice degraded,
The Way of Chunshen was cut short,
and its realization brought down.

25. 12

Let us be as shepherds to its foundations;

【原文】

尧在万世如见之。

谗人罔极，险陂倾侧，此之疑。

25.13 基必施，辨贤罢，

文、武之道同伏戏。

由之者治，不由者乱，何疑为？

25.14 凡成相，辨法方，

至治之极复后王。

慎、墨、季、惠，百家之说，诚不详。

25.15 治复一，修之吉，

【今译】

唐尧距今虽万代，依然可见其德政。

谗人作恶无止境，险恶邪僻心不正，怀疑用贤的方针。

25.13 基本国策须实施，辨别贤才与无知，

文王、武王的政治，以及伏羲都如此。

遵循此道国家治，不遵循它混乱至，为何怀疑这种事？

25.14 总括敲鼓我所唱，就在辨明方法上，

国家大治的准则，在于效法后代王。

慎、墨、惠子与季梁，以及百家的主张，胡言乱语真不良。

25.15 治国之道归于一，遵行此道就大吉，

let those who are worthy ponder over it,
let Yao who belongs to ten thousand generations be visible in ours.
"The slanderers have no limit, "
presenting it as a threat, distorting and perverting,
they cast doubts upon this.

25. 13

The foundation must be established
to discriminate the worthy from the incompetent.
The Way of Kings Wen and Wu is the same as that of Fuxi.
Those who proceed along it achieve order;
those that do not produce anarchy.
How can doubts be cast upon this!

25. 14

Whenever one sings this working song,
one discriminates the model and its standards,
the ultimate perfection of government lies in a return to the Later Kings.
Shen [Dao] and Mo [Di], Ji [Liang], and Hui [Shi],
the persuasions of the Hundred Schools,
truly one should not know them in detail.

25. 15

Good government restores unity.
To cultivate it produces auspicious results.

【原文】

君子执之心如结。

众人贰之，谗夫弃之，形是诘。

25.16 水至平，端不倾，

心术如此像圣人。

而有势，直而用抴，必参天。

25.17 世无王，穷贤良，

暴人刍豢仁人糟糠。

礼乐灭息，圣人隐伏，墨术行。

25.18 治之经，礼与刑，

【今译】

君子坚守这原则，思想就像打了结。

众人三心又二意，谗人把它来抛弃，对此用刑查到底。

25.16 一杯水啊极其平，端起它来不斜倾，

心计若像这样正，就像伟大的圣人。

如果有权不忘本，严正律己宽容人，如用舟船接客乘，功高齐天一定成。

25.17 世间没有好帝王，走投无路那贤良，

残暴之人鲜肉尝，仁德之人吃糟糠。

礼崩乐坏都灭亡，圣人隐居又躲藏，墨家学说流行广。

25.18 治理国家的纲领，就是礼制与用刑，

The gentleman cleaves to it as though his mind were tied to it.
The mass of men are of two minds about it.
Slanderers try to get them to reject it,
punishments are what they inquire about.

25. 16

Water is perfectly level,
its correctness cannot be made to tilt to one side.
When the operations of the mind are like this, they resemble the sage.
Being [worthy]···yet possessing authority,
being straight yet useful as a bow-frame,
he is sure to form a Triad with Heaven.

25. 17

An age that lacks a True King
will impoverish worthy and virtuous men.
Violently cruel men will eat grass- and grain-fed animals, the humane only dregs and husks.
Ritual and music are destroyed, ceasing to be used.
Sages go into hiding and secret themselves,
so the methods of Mo Di are put into practice.

25. 18

The classical standards of order
are rituals associated with punishments.

【原文】

君子以修百姓宁。

明德慎罚，国家既治，四海平。

25.19 治之志，后势富，

君子诚之好以待。

处之敦固，有深藏之，能远思。

25.20 思乃精，志之荣，

好而一之神以成。

精神相反，一而不贰，为圣人。

25.21 治之道，美不老，

【今译】

君子用礼来修身，百姓怕刑而安宁。

彰明美德慎用刑，不但国家能太平，普天之下全平定。

25.19 治理国家的意念，权势财富放后边，

君子真心为国家，凭此善心等推荐。

对此忠厚意志坚，深深把它藏心田，能够考虑得长远。

25.20 思考如果能精心，思想开花定丰盛，

爱好它啊又专一，神而明之便养成。

精心神明紧相跟，专心一致不二分，就能成为大圣人。

25.21 治理国家的正道，完美经久不衰老，

Where the gentleman keeps them in repair, the Hundred Clans are tranquil.
He makes brilliant inner power and is cautious with punishments,
so the nation will become orderly
and [all within] the four seas peaceful.

25. 19

The purpose of good government
is to place power and wealth in the background.
The gentleman keeps authentic this purpose and cherishes making provisions for it.
He dwells in it, steadfastly and earnestly,
keeping it deeply within himself and storing it up.
so he is able to be far-reaching in his thoughts.

25. 20

His thoughts are therewith refined to the essence,
the flowering of his purpose.
Cherish it, unify it, so the spirit is made complete.
When essence and spirit revert to one another,
when they are as one and not a duality,
he becomes a sage.

25. 21

The Way to good government

【原文】

君子由之佼以好。

下以教诲子弟，上以事祖考。

25.22 成相竭，辞不蹶，

君子道之顺以达。

宗其贤良，辨其殃孽。

25.23 请成相，道圣王，

尧、舜尚贤身辞让。

许由、善卷，重义轻利，行显明。

25.24 尧让贤，以为民，

【今译】

君子遵循这正道，美好之上加美好。

对下用来教子弟，对上用来事祖考。

25.22 敲鼓说完这一场，我的话语还没光，

君子遵行我的话，顺利通达幸福长。

千万尊崇那贤良，仔细辨明那祸殃。

25.23 让我敲鼓说一场，说说圣明的帝王，

尧、舜崇尚贤德人，亲自来把帝位让。

许由、善卷志高尚，看重道义把利忘，德行显扬放光芒。

25.24 尧让帝位给贤人，全是为了老百姓，

is a thing of beauty that does not grow old.
The gentleman proceeding along it is made handsome through
cherishing it.
Below he instructs and corrects his children and younger brothers,
above he serves his grandfather and father.

25. 22

This working song has run its course,
its verses have not stumbled.
When the gentleman travels its route, he easily penetrates everywhere;
he lifts high the worthy and virtuous,
……………………………………………
discriminating signs of ruination and calamity.

25. 23

Let me sing a working song,
telling of the sage kings.
Yao and Shun elevated worthy men and personally resigned their
positions.
Xu You and Shan Juan
valued morality and deprecated gain:
their conduct was brilliantly displayed.

25. 24

Yao yielded his position to a worthy

【原文】

泛利兼爱德施均。

辨治上下，贵贱有等，明君臣。

25.25 尧授能，舜遇时，

尚贤推德天下治。

虽有贤圣，适不遇世，孰知之?

25.26 尧不德，舜不辞，

妻以二女任以事。

大人哉舜，南面而立，万物备。

【今译】

普遍造福爱众人，恩德布施全均匀。

上上下下都治理，贵贱有别等级分，职分分明君和臣。

25.25 尧把帝位传贤能，虞舜遇上好时辰，

推崇贤能与德行，天下治理得太平。

现在虽然有贤圣，恰恰不遇好时运，谁能知道他贤能?

25.26 尧不自夸有德行，舜不推辞来做君，

尧把二女嫁给舜，又将国事来委任。

伟大的人啊是虞舜!朝南而立在朝廷，万物齐备都丰盛。

and thereby became a subject.

Everywhere benefiting and universally loving, his moral worth
was made manifest equally to all.

He discriminated and put in order high and low,

provided gradations of rank for noble and base,

and clarified the distinction between lord and minister.

25. 25

Yao resigned in favor of an able man;

Shun happened to meet with opportunity.

He elevated the worthy and promoted those with moral worth so
the world was well ordered.

But though a man be a worthy or even a sage,

if he does not meet with an opportune age,

who will know of him?

25. 26

Yao claimed no moral worth,

Shun did not decline.

Yao gave his two daughters as wives, entrusted him with the
government.

What a great man was Shun indeed!

Facing south, he took his position,

and the myriad things were provided for.

【原文】

25.27 舜授禹，以天下，

尚得推贤不失序，

外不避仇，内不阿亲，贤者予。

25.28 禹劳心力，尧有德，

干戈不用三苗服。

举舜甽亩，任之天下，身休息。

25.29 得后稷，五谷殖，

夔为乐正鸟兽服。

契为司徒，民知孝弟，尊有德。

【今译】

25.27 舜把帝位传给禹，将天下大权来相许，

崇尚德行把贤举，不丢规矩有次序，

外不避嫌把仇取，内不偏袒把儿去，贤能之人就给予。

25.28 大禹操心用武力，尧有德行不着急，

盾牌戈矛全不用，三苗心悦诚服帖。

提拔虞舜田亩里，给他天下使称帝，自己离位去休息。

25.29 得到后稷管农务，教导人民种五谷，

夔做乐正奏乐曲，鸟兽起舞全驯服。

契管教化做司徒，民知顺兄孝父母，有德之人受敬慕。

25. 27

Shun resigned in favor of Yu
his power over the world.
He elevated those of moral worth and promoted the worthy so
none lost the proper precedence.
Without, he did not avoid enemies,
within, he was not partial to intimates,
for it was worthy men with whom he associated.

25. 28

Yao possessed inner power,
toiling with his mind and body,
Though the shield and battle-axe were never used, the Three
Miao tribes submitted.
He raised Shun up from the ditches and fields,
entrusted to him rule of the world,
and gave himself leisure and rest.

25. 29

When Yao obtained the Sovereign of Millet,
the Five Foods thrived.
When Kui was made Corrector of Music, the birds and beasts
offered their submission.
When Xie became Director of the Multitude,
the people became aware of filial piety and fraternal submission,

【原文】

25.30 禹有功，抑下鸿，

辟除民害逐共工，

北决九河，通十二渚，疏三江。

25.31 禹傅土，平天下，

躬亲为民行劳苦，

得益、皋陶、横革、直成为辅。

25.32 契玄王，生昭明，

居于砥石迁于商。

十有四世，乃有天乙，是成汤。

【今译】

25.30 夏禹治水有大功，疏导排泄治大洪，

排除祸害为民众，驱逐流放那共工，

北方开掘那九河，全国河道都疏通，疏浚三江流向东。

25.31 夏禹领导治水土，安定天下重任负，

亲自为民来奔走，做事劳累又辛苦，

得到伯益、皋陶、横革、直成作辅助。

25.32 契因玄鸟称玄王，生下昭明好儿郎，

开始住在砥石冈，后来迁到封地商。

十又四代传下来，便有天乙做商王，天乙就是那成汤。

of giving honor to those who possessed inner power.

25. 30

Yu had the great accomplishment
of restraining and suppressing the flooding waters,
eliminating and removing their injury to the people, and he drove back Gonggong.
To the north he cut channels for the nine rivers,
brought into communication the twelve islets,
and opened the way for the three streams.

25. 31

Yu laid out the land,
and gave peace to the world.
He personally took part in the bitter toil of hard labor with the people.
He obtained Yi and Gaoyao,
Heng Ge and Zhi Cheng,
whom he made his assistants.

25. 32

Xie, the Dark King,
begot Zhao Ming,
who dwelt first in Dishi and moved then to Shang.
When fourteen generations had passed,
then there was Tianyi

【原文】

25.33 天乙汤，论举当，

身让卞随举牟光。

道古贤圣，基必张。

25.34 愿陈辞，

世乱恶善不此治。

隐讳疾贤良，由奸诈，鲜无灾。

25.35 患难哉! 阪为先，

圣知不用愚者谋。

前车已覆，后未知更，何觉时!

【今译】

25.33 商王天乙号称汤，选拔人才都恰当，

亲自让位给卞随，又把天下给牟光。

遵循效法古圣王，国家基业必扩张。

25.34 愿把说辞来张扬，

世道混乱恶善良，却不治理这状况。

隐讳过错恨贤良，任用奸诈作主张，那就很少没祸殃。

25.35 遭殃遭殃真遭殃! 歪门邪道是志向，

圣人智士不任用，却和蠢人去商量。

前边车子已倾覆，后车尚未知改向，何时觉悟不乱闯。

who was Tang the Successful.

25. 33

Tianyi, who was Tang,
made his assessments of grade and promotions match,
so he personally tried to resign his post in favor of
Bian Sui and Mou Guang.
....
Following in the path of ancient worthies and sages,
the foundation was sure to be enlarged.

25. 34

I want to advance a proposition:
....
An age that confuses good with evil will not make this orderly.
To conceal faults and dislike the worthy,
ever following after treacherous deceit,
is seldom without disastrous consequences.

25. 35

Distress and difficulties indeed!
Rebellion causes it!
When sagely wisdom is not used, the stupid will lay schemes.
The chariots in the van have already overturned,
but the rearguard still knows no need to alter course

【原文】

25.36 不觉悟，不知苦，

迷惑失指易上下。

忠不上达，蒙掩耳目，塞门户。

25.37 门户塞，大迷惑，

悖乱昏莫不终极。

是非反易，比周欺上，恶正直。

25.38 正直恶，心无度，

邪枉辟回失道途。

【今译】

25.36 君主实在不觉悟，不知如此会受苦，

迷惑糊涂不作主，上下颠倒成下属。

忠言不能告君主，君主耳目被蒙住，就像堵住了门户。

25.37 听言途径被堵住，就会迷乱极糊涂，

惑乱昏暗真愚昧，永远如此没限度。

是非颠倒正为误，互相勾结骗君主，正直之士被憎恶。

25.38 正直之士被憎恶，君主心中没法度，

邪曲不正又险恶，昏乱迷惑失正路。

—when will they be awakened?

25. 36

Unaware and not realizing,
they do not understand the bitter pain.
Led astray by delusions, losing their direction, interchanging up and down,
loyal subjects do not come in contact with their superior,
for he has covered his eyes, shut his ears,
and barred his doors and gates.

25. 37

When doors and gates are barred,
going astray through delusion is magnified.
Rebellion and anarchy will be the dark night that has no end, no limit.
Right and wrong will be reversed and interchanged.
Partisan cliques will cheat their superior
and hate the correct and upright.

25. 38

When the correct and upright are hated,
their hearts will know no measure.
The depraved and crooked, the perverse and corrupt, lose their way along the road.
Do not personally find fault with others

【原文】

己无尤人，我独自美，岂独无故？

25.39 不知戒，后必有，

恨后遂过不肯悔。

谗夫多进，反复言语，生诈态。

25.40 人之态，不如备，

争宠嫉贤利恶忌。

妒功毁贤，下敛党与，上蔽匿。

25.41 上壅蔽，失辅势，

任用谗夫不能制。

孰公长父之难，厉王流于彘。

【今译】

自己不要责怪人，惟我独好太自负，难道自己没错误？

25.39 不知警惕出事故，以后一定有错误，

凶悍固执难劝阻，一错到底不悔悟。

谗人进用又很多，颠三倒四来告诉，欺诈邪恶全干出。

25.40 对于臣子的邪僻，不知防备与警惕，

臣下争宠把贤嫉，彼此憎恨相猜忌。

妒忌功臣毁贤能，下聚党羽相勾结，上把君主来蒙蔽。

25.41 君主在上被蒙蔽，失去辅佐和权势，

任用进谗的小人，不能把他来控制。

虢公长父太放肆，因把灾难来招致，厉王流窜逃到彘。

considering that you yourself alone are fine
—how could you be without blame?

25.39

Where they know no need for precaution,
they are certain to repeat it,
maliciously obstinate in continuing to transgress, unwilling to repent.
Slanderers multiply and advance in office,
their words and arguments expressing contradiction and rebellion,
they give birth to deceptive appearances.

25. 40

Such appearances of men
—they do not know the need for preparation.
Quarreling over his favor, envying the worthy, keen in hatred and envy,
jealous of accomplishment, they revile the worthy.
Subordinates gather together in cliques,
their superior to blind by hiding the truth.

25. 41

When the superior is blinded and obstructed,
he loses his assistants and his authority.
He will employ and entrust responsibility to slanderers incapable of administration.
The difficulties caused by Zhangfu, Duke of Guo,

【原文】

25.42 周幽、厉，所以败，

不听规谏忠是害。

嗟我何人，独不遇时，当乱世。

25.43 欲衷对，言不从，

恐为子胥身离凶。

进谏不听，刭而独鹿，弃之江。

25.44 观往事，以自戒，

治乱是非亦可识。

托于成相，以喻意。

【今译】

25.42 周幽王与周厉王，所以失败有原因，

别人规劝全不听，专门残害那忠臣。

唉呀我算什么人，偏偏不遇好时辰，活在乱世无所成。

25.43 想向君主诉衷情，担心说话君不听，

恐怕成为伍子胥，自己反而遭厄运。

进言劝谏君不听，被赐属镂割脖颈，还被抛尸在江心。

25.44 回顾观察已往事，用来戒备把身治，

安定混乱是与非，从中也可有所知。

凭借敲鼓这曲子，用来表明我心志。

forced King Li to flee to Zhi.

25. 42

Of Kings Li and You of Zhou,
the reason they were violated
was that they would not hear admonition and remonstrance so
that loyal ministers were done harm.
Alas, why should I be the lone man
who never encountered any opportunity
in the chaotic age I live!

25. 43

Desiring to reply with inward good feelings
even when his words of advice are not heeded,
he fears he will endure the tragic personal difficulties of [Wu] Zixu
who went forward in remonstrance, but was not heeded,
so his throat was cut and he was put in a sack
to be cast away, thrown into the Yangtze.

25. 44

We observe past events
that we can take precautions against them.
Order, anarchy, right and wrong as well can be recognized in them.
………………………………
I have given this working song the task

【原文】

25.45 请成相，言治方，

君论有五约以明。

君谨守之，下皆平正，国乃昌。

25.46 臣下职，莫游食，

务本节用财无极。

事业听上，莫得相使，一民力。

25.47 守其职，足衣食，

厚薄有等明爵服。

【今译】

25.45 让我敲鼓说你听，说说治国的方针，

为君之道有五条，不但简要又分明。

君主严格遵守它，臣民安宁都端正，国家也就会昌盛。

25.46 臣民必须都尽职，不准游荡吃白食，

从事农耕省开支，财富无穷国库实。

做事听从君安排，不得擅自相指使，统一民力君控制。

25.47 臣民恪守其本职，就能丰衣又足食，

俸禄多少有等级，明确爵位与服饰。

of giving illustration to my thoughts.

25. 45

Let me sing a working song,
telling of the methods of government.
The issues fundamental to the lord number five, which are kept brief to make them clear.
When the lord assiduously safeguards them,
when his subjects are pacified and corrected,
his state will thereupon flourish.

25. 46

The responsibilities of ministers and subordinates:
None will roam about in search of emolument,
as they devote themselves to the fundamental occupations and moderate expenditures so that the revenues should be without limit.
They execute their tasks by listening to their superiors
and none try to order the others around,
so that the strength of the people is combined as one.

25. 47

By safeguarding their responsibilities,
each will have sufficient food and clothing.
The important and the trivial will have their appropriate grade made clear by rank and dress.

【原文】

利往仰上，莫得擅与，孰私得？

25.48 君法明，论有常，

表仪既设民知方。

进退有律，莫得贵贱，孰私王？

52.49 君法仪，禁不为，

莫不说教名不移。

修之者荣，离之者辱，孰它师？

25.50 刑称陈，守其银，

【今译】

财利只能靠君赐，臣下不得自布施，谁能私下得财资？

25.48 君主法度很严明，言论合法有定准，

规章制度已设立，人民了解方向明。

任免官吏有标准，贵贱不得任意定，谁会私下讨好君？

25.49 君主法度是标准，禁止之事不敢碰，

无不喜欢君教令，名号政权不变更。

遵循法度荣耀成，背离法度屈辱生，谁敢越轨去横行？

25.50 刑法得当陈列明，遵守规定界限清，

There is profit only from looking up to one's superiors,
and none will try to presume power over others.
So who could offer private favors?

25. 48

When the lord's laws are clear,
the assignment of proper grade follows constant principles,
since when the signposts of proper deportment have been set up,
the people will know the direction of right conduct.
Advancement and demotion will follow fixed standards,
for none but will succeed to their proper eminent or humble position.
So who would seek private access to the king?

25. 49

When the lord's laws serve as the standard of deportment,
what is forbidden is not done.
None will fail to enjoy his teachings and his names will not be altered.
Those who cultivate them are honored,
those who reject them are disgraced.
So who will have another teacher?

25. 50

When penal sanctions fit what has been set forth,
the people stay within their bounds.
Subordinate officials do not try to use them, considering their own

【原文】

下不得用轻私门。

罪祸有律，莫得轻重，威不分。

25.51 请牧祺，明有基，

主好论议必善谋。

五听循领，莫不理续，主执持。

25.52 听之经，明其请，

参伍明谨施赏刑。

显者必得，隐者复显，民反诚。

25.53 言有节，稽其实，

【今译】

臣下不得擅用刑，豪门权势自会轻。

惩处罪过有法令，不得加重或减轻，君权也就不被分。

25.51 请听治国的根本，要有福气在贤明，

君主爱听臣议论，谋划一定会精深。

五条原则都听信，遵循为君的纲领，无不研治相继承，君主掌权才牢稳。

25.52 处理政事的常规，在于明了那实情，

比较检验情况明，谨慎实施赏和刑。

明显之事必查清，隐蔽之事也显形，民众就会归真诚。

25.53 要人说话有分寸，就得考核那实情，

private interests unimportant.
When punishments and chastisements have fixed standards,
no one tries to make them lighter or more severe,
so that their majestic authority remains undivided.

25. 51

Let me tend the foundation
and make clear the good fortune it contains.
When the ruler is fond of discussions and deliberations, he is sure to be adept at laying plans.
When the Five Judicial Examinations are cultivated and regulated,
and none fail to apply reason to their duties,
the ruler's authority is maintained.

25. 52

The classical standards for judicial investigations
clarify the essential circumstances of the case.
Having thrice, even five times, clearly and assiduously examined it, rewards are granted and punishments applied.
When open cases are certain to be solved
and those in hiding certain of exposure,
the people will once again be truthful.

25. 53

When what is said has regulated bounds,

【原文】

信诞以分赏罚必。

下不欺上，皆以情言，明若日。

25.54 上通利，隐远至，

观法不法见不视。

耳目既显，吏敬法令，莫敢恣。

25.55 君教出，行有律，

吏谨将之无铍滑。

下不私请，各以宜，舍巧拙。

【今译】

真话假话已分清，赏罚一定要实行。

臣民不敢再欺君，说话都会吐真情，就像太阳一样明。

25.54 君主不被人蒙蔽，目光锐利又灵敏；

隐微之事显原形，远处情况会来临；

深入观察法外事，人所未见能看清。

君主耳目已聪明，官吏就会重法令，没人再敢任意行。

25.55 君主发布那教令，臣民行为有标准，

官吏谨慎来奉行，不敢邪僻乱法令。

臣不私下去求情，各人以道侍奉君，舍弃投机取巧心。

the true reality of things is examined.
What is trustworthy and what exaggerated will be distinguished,
rewards and punishments made certain.
When subordinates do not deceive their superiors
and both make use of the truth in speaking,
all will be clear as the light of day.

25. 54

When the superior facilitates communication,
the hidden and distant will be known to him.
He will see the effect of his laws where there is no law and be able to observe what is not seen.
When their eyes and ears have known its splendor,
the officials will respect the model and its ordinances,
so that none will dare indulge in unrestrained license.

25. 55

When the doctrine of the lord has been issued,
conduct is regulated by statutes.
Officials will assiduously follow it with no treachery.
Subordinates will not make private requests,
each using what is appropriate to his station,
so that artfulness and ineptitude are stopped.

【原文】

25.56 臣谨修，君制变，

公察善思论不乱，

以治天下，后世法之，成律贯。

【今译】

25.56 臣下谨慎守法严，君主控制变法权，

公正考察善思索，伦理关系不混乱，

用它来把天下治，后世效法作典范，成为常规代代传。

25. 56

When ministers assiduously keep them in repair,
and the lord issues regulations for their reform,
with impartial investigation and expert examination, his judicial examinations will not be brought into confusion.
Through the order thereby created throughout the world,
later generations make them their model,
so that perfected statutes will be handed down.

赋第二十六

【原文】

26.1 爰有大物，
非丝非帛，文理成章。
非日非月，为天下明。
生者以寿，死者以葬；
城郭以固，三军以强。
粹而王，驳而伯，无一焉而亡。
臣愚不识，敢请之王。
王曰：
此夫文而不采者与?
简然易知而致有理者与?
君子所敬而小人所不者与?
性不得则若禽兽，性得之则甚雅似者与?

【今译】

26.1 这里有个重要东西，
既不是丝也不是帛，但其文理斐然成章。
既非太阳也非月亮，但给天下带来明亮。
活人靠它享尽天年，死者靠它得以殡葬；
内城外城靠它巩固，全军实力靠它加强。
完全依它就能称王，错杂用它就能称霸，完全不用就会灭亡。
我很愚昧不知其详，大胆把它请教大王。
大王说：
这东西是有文饰而不彩色的吗?
是简单易懂而极有条理的吗?
是被君子所敬重而被小人所轻视的吗?
是本性没得到它熏陶就会像禽兽，本性得到它熏陶就很端正吗?

Book 26

Fu—Rhyme-Prose Poems

26. 1

On Ritual Principles

Here there is a great thing:
It is not fine silk thread or cords of silk,
—Yet its designs and patterns are perfect, elegant compositions.
It is not the sun, nor is it the moon,
Yet it makes the world bright.
The living use it to live to old age;
The dead to be buried.
Cities and states use it for their security;
The three armies use it for strength.
"Those who possess it in pure form are True Kings;
"Those who have it in mixed form are lords-protector;
"And those who lack any at all are annihilated."
Your servant stupidly does not recognize it
And presumes to ask Your Majesty about it.
The King replied:
Is it not something that has cultivated form, yet is not brightly colored?
Is it not suddenly and easily understood, yet especially possesses natural order?
Is it not what the gentleman reveres and the petty man does not?
Is it not something that if inborn nature does not acquire it, one is like a wild beast;

【原文】

匹夫隆之则为圣人，诸侯隆之则一四海者与？
致明而约，甚顺而体，
请归之礼。

——礼

26.2 皇天隆物，以施下民；
或厚或薄，常不齐均。
桀、纣以乱，汤、武以贤。
涽涽淑淑，皇皇穆穆。
周流四海，曾不崇日。
君子以修，跖以穿室。
大参乎天，精微而无形。

【今译】

是一般人尊崇它就能成为圣人，诸侯尊崇它就能使天下统一的吗？
极其明白而又简约，非常顺理而又得体，
请求把它归结为礼。

——礼

26.2 上天降下一种东西，用来施给天下人民；
有人丰厚有人微薄，常常不会整齐平均。
夏桀、商纣因此昏乱，成汤、武王因此贤能。
有的混沌有的清明，浩瀚无涯静穆无闻。
四海之内全部流遍，竟然不到整整一天。
君子靠它修身养心，盗跖靠它打洞进门。
它的高大和天相并，它的细微不显其形。

And if inborn nature does acquire it, it produces elegant forms?
Is it not something that, if one of the masses would exalt it, he would become a sage;
And if one of the feudal lords exalted it, he would unite all within the four seas?
It provides the clearest of expressions, yet it is concise;
It is the extreme of obedience to the natural course of things, yet must be embodied in conduct.
I suggest where all these qualities come together is ritual principles.

26. 2

On Wisdom

August Heaven sends down this thing
In order to inform the people below.
Substantial in some men, but scarcely present in others,
It is never uniformly or evenly distributed.
Jie and Zhou Xin used it to produce anarchy;
Tang and Wu to become worthies.
Dull and confused or pure and clear,
August and grand or delicate and subtle,
It can make the full circuit of the four seas
In less than a whole day.
The gentleman uses it for cultivation;
Robber Zhi to tunnel into a house.
It is great enough to form a Triad with Heaven
And yet so fine and minute that it can be without form.
Conduct and deportment are rectified with it;

【原文】

行义以正，事业以成。
可以禁暴足穷，百姓待之而后宁泰。
臣愚不识，愿问其名。
曰：
此夫安宽平而危险隘者邪？
修洁之为亲而杂污之为狄者邪？
甚深藏而外胜敌者邪？
法禹、舜而能弇迹者邪？
行为动静待之而后适者邪？
血气之精也，
志意之荣也。
百姓待之而后宁也，
天下待之而后平也。
明达纯粹而无疵也，
夫是之谓君子之知。

——知

【今译】

德行道义靠它端正，事情功业靠它办成。
可以用来禁止暴行，可以用来致富脱贫；
百姓群众依靠了它，然后才能太平安定。
我很愚昧不知其情，希望打听它的名称。
回答说：
这东西是把宽广和平坦看作为安全
而把崎岖不平和狭窄看作为危险的吗？
是亲近美好廉洁之德而疏远杂乱肮脏之行的吗？
是很深地藏在心中而对外能战胜敌人的吗？
是效法禹、舜而能沿着他们的足迹继续前进的吗？
是行为举止靠了它然后才能恰如其分的吗？
它是血气的精华，
是意识的精英。
百姓依靠了它然后才能安宁，
天下依靠了它然后才能太平。
它明智通达纯粹而没有缺点毛病，
这叫做君子的智慧聪明。

——智

Undertakings and tasks are completed with it.
It can restrain the violent and give sufficiency to the impoverished;
And only after the Hundred Clans have it
Are they quiet and peaceful.
Your servant stupidly does not recognize it
And wishes to ask its name.

He replied:

Is it not something that gives security like a broad expanse of level ground and avoids the dangers of narrow defiles?
Does it not lead to closeness for those who cultivate its pristine state, and is it not alien to those who introduce a heteronomy that makes it impure?
Is it not what is more profoundly stored up and yet externally what is able to triumph over every challenge?
Is it not modeled after the examples of Yu and Shun, and enables one to follow in their footsteps?
Is it not, in activity and repose, what one's conduct must depend on, so that actions are carried out properly?
It brings out the essential vigor of the blood humour
And effects the flowering of aspirations and ideals.
Only after the Hundred Clans obtain it
Do they become tranquil,
And only when the world obtains it
Does the empire become peaceful.
It is bright, comprehensive, uniform, unadulterated,
And without defect.
And this is what is called:
The knowledge of the gentleman.

【原文】

26.3 有物于此，
居则周静致下，
动则綦高以钜。
圆者中规，方者中矩。
大参天地，德厚尧、禹。
精，微乎毫毛；而大，盈乎大寓。
忽兮其极之远也，
攭兮其相逐而反也，
昂昂兮天下之咸蹇也。
德厚而不捐，五采备而成文。
往来惛惫，通于大神，
出入甚极，莫知其门。
天下失之则灭，得之则存。

【今译】

26.3 在这里有种东西，
停留时就周遍地静处在极低点，
活动时就极高而广大无边。
圆的合乎圆规画的圆，方的和角尺画的能相掩。
大得可和天地相并列，德行比尧、禹还敦厚慈善。
小的时候比毫毛还细微，而大的时候可充满寥廓的空间。
迅速啊它们到达了很远很远，
分开啊它们互相追逐而返回山边，
高升啊天下人就都会生活维艰。
它德行敦厚而不丢弃任何人，五种色彩齐备而成为花纹，
它来去昏暗，变化莫测就像天神，
它进出很急，没人知道它的进出之门。
天下人失去了它就会灭亡，得到了它就能生存。

26. 3

On Clouds

There are things like this:
As long as they linger, they are dense, reposeful, and cover the earth,
Yet as soon as they begin to move, they attain lofty heights and immensity.
They can be round enough to correspond to the compass
Or square enough to fit the T-square.
Their greatness forms a Triad with Heaven and Earth
And their Power thickened becomes a Yao or Yu.
Their ethereal substance is more subtle than the finest hair;
Yet they can be large enough to fill the vastness of space.
How swift their coming from afar and their going away into the distance!
How they swirl apart, pursue one another, yet come back together again!
How they gather in lofty heights, letting the whole world take from them!
Their Power is substantial so they reject nothing.
The Five Colors are fully represented in them;
Yet they are perfected in form.
Their passing to and fro is obscure and puzzling
As though they were in communication with a great spirit.
Their appearance and disappearance are very quick
And no one knows the gate whence they come or go.
When the world loses them, there is destruction;

【原文】

弟子不敏，此之愿陈。
君子设辞，请测意之。
曰：
此夫大而不塞者与？
充盈大宇而不窕，入郄穴而不逼者与？
行远疾速而不可托讯者与？
往来惛憊而不可为固塞者与？
暴至杀伤而不亿忌者与？
功被天下而不私置者与？
托地而游宇，友风而子雨。
冬日作寒，夏日作暑。
广大精神，请归之云。

——云

26.4 有物于此，

【今译】

学生我不聪明，愿意把它陈述给先生。
君子设置这些隐辞，请您猜猜它的名称。
回答说：
这东西是庞大而不会被堵塞的吗？
是充满寥廓的空间而不会有间隙，进入缝隙洞穴而不觉其狭窄吗？
是走得很远而且迅速但不可寄托重物的吗？
是来去昏暗而不可能被固定堵塞的吗？
是突然来杀伤万物而毫不迟疑毫无顾忌的吗？
是功德覆盖天下而不自以为有德的吗？
它依靠大地而在空间遨游，以风为朋友而以雨为子女。
夏季兴起热浪，冬季兴起寒流。
它广大而又神灵，请求把它归结为云。

——云

26.4 在这里有种东西，

Where it obtains them, there is survival.

The student, wanting in earnest intelligence,

Would like to have this riddle solved.

Could the gentleman offer some lyrics,

Would he please offer a guess to fathom the idea?

He replied:

Are they not so great as to be enclosed by nothing?

Do they not completely fill the vastness of space with no gap, and enter into minute vacant spaces so that nothing is crowded out?

Do they not travel from afar with urgency and haste and yet cannot deliver messages?

Does not their passing to and fro in an obscure and puzzling fashion make it impossible to stop them or make them stationary?

Do they not arrive violently, killing and injuring, yet give no cause for mistrust or fright?

Do not their accomplishments cover the backs of the world, yet there are no private arrangements?

Residing on earth yet roaming space,

Companions to the wind, they have rain as their child.

On winter days they create the cold

And on summer days the heat.

They are vast, great, ethereal, and magical.

All this winds up in one thing: clouds.

26. 4

Fu on Silkworms

Here is a thing:

【原文】

儳儳兮其状，屡化如神，
功被天下，为万世文。
礼乐以成，贵贱以分。
养老长幼，待之而后存。
名号不美，与暴为邻。
功立而身废，事成而家败。
弃其耆老，收其后世。
人属所利，飞鸟所害。
臣愚而不识，请占之五泰。
五泰占之曰：
此夫身女好而头马首者与？
屡化而不寿者与？
善壮而拙老者与？
有父母而无牝牡者与？
冬伏而夏游？
食桑而吐丝，前乱而后治。

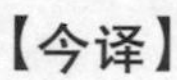

【今译】

赤裸裸啊它的形状，屡次变化奇妙如神，
它的功德覆盖天下，它为万代修饰人文。
礼乐制度靠它成就，高贵卑贱靠它区分。
奉养老人抚育小孩，依靠了它然后才成。
它的名称却不好听，竟和残暴互相邻近。
功业建立而自身被废，事业成功而家被破坏。
抛弃了它的老一辈，收留了它的后一代。
它被人类所利用，也被飞鸟所伤害。
我愚昧而不知道，请万事通把它猜一猜。
万事通推测它说：
这东西是身体像女人一样柔美而头像马头的吗？
是屡次蜕化而不得长寿的吗？
是善于度过壮年而不善于为年老图谋的吗？
是有父母而没有雌雄分别的吗？
是冬天隐藏而夏天出游的吗？
它吃桑叶而吐出细丝，起先纷乱而后来有条不紊。

How naked and bare its external form,
Yet it continually undergoes transformation like a spirit.
Its achievement covers the backs of the world,
For it has created decorations for a myriad generations.
Ritual ceremonies and musical performances are completed through it;
Noble and humble are assigned their proper lots with it.
It cares for the old and nurtures the young,
For with it alone one can survive.
Its name is not beautiful,
For it is a neighbor of cruelty.
When its work is done, its body is cast away;
When its undertaking is completed, its family is ruined.
It sacrifices its old and venerable
And brings an end to its descendants.
It benefits human beings,
But is harmed by flying birds.
Your servant, who does not recognize it,
Requests a divination answer from the Five Great Ones.
The Five Great Ones divined it and said:
Does not its body have a feminine charm and its head resemble that of a horse?
Does it not continually undergo transformation and never grow old?
Do not we think the product of its robust period excellent and that of its aged form worthless?
Does it not have a mother and father, but lack male and female forms?
It lies in hiding in winter, roams about in summer,
Eats the mulberry, spews out silk thread,
Begins in anarchy, and ends in order.

【原文】

夏生而恶暑，喜湿而恶雨。
蛹以为母，蛾以为父。
三俯三起，事乃大已。
夫是之谓蚕理。

——蚕

26.5 有物于此，
生于山阜，处于室堂。
无知无巧，善治衣裳。
不盗不窃，穿窬而行。
日夜合离，以成文章。
以能合从，又善连衡。
下覆百姓，上饰帝王。
功业甚博，不见贤良。
时用则存，不用则亡。

【今译】

生长在夏天而害怕酷暑，喜欢湿润却害怕雨淋。
把蛹当作为母亲，把蛾当作为父亲。
多次伏眠多次苏醒，事情才算最终完成。
这是关于蚕的道理。

——蚕

26.5 在这里有种东西，
产生于山冈，放置在内屋厅堂。
没有智慧没有技巧，却善于缝制衣裳。
既不偷盗也不行窃，却先打洞然后前往。
日夜使分离的相合，从而制成花纹式样。
既能够联合竖向，又善于连结横向。
下能够遮盖百姓，上能够装饰帝王。
功劳业绩非常巨大，却不炫耀自己贤良。
有时用它，就在身旁；不用它时，它就躲藏。

In summer it comes to life, but hates the hottest part.
It enjoys dampness, but hates the rain.
The pupa functions as its mother,
The moth as its father.
It three times becomes dormant and thrice rises up again,
And therewith its task is brought to its great conclusion.
This refers to the natural pattern of the silkworm.

26. 5

Fu on the Needle

Here is a thing:
Born in hills and mountains,
It dwells in palaces and pavilions.
Lacking knowledge and without skills,
It is accomplished at sewing every kind of clothing.
It does not rob nor does it steal,
Yet it moves by making tunnels and holes.
From dawn to dusk it joins together what is separate
In order to complete designs and patterns.
Using it one is capable of joining together the Vertical
And being expert in connecting the Horizontal.
Below it provides coverings for the Hundred Clans;
Above it provides adornment for Di Ancestors and kings.
Its achievements and works are very far-reaching,
But it does not make known its own worth and virtue.
If on suitable occasions you employ it, it will remain;
But if it is not used, it will disappear.

【原文】

臣愚不识，敢请之王。
王曰：
此夫始生巨其成功小者邪？
长其尾而锐其剽者邪？
头銛达而尾赵缭者邪？
一往一来，结尾以为事。
无羽无翼，反覆甚极。
尾生而事起，尾邅而事已。
簪以为父，管以为母。
既以缝表，又以连里。
夫是之谓箴理。

——箴

26.6 天下不治，请陈佹诗：
天地易位，四时易乡；
列星殒坠，旦暮晦盲；

【今译】

我很愚昧，不知其详，大胆把它请教大王。
大王说：
这东西是开始产生时很大而它制成后很小的吗？
是尾巴很长而末端很尖削的吗？
是头部锐利而畅通无阻、尾巴摇曳而缠绕的吗？
它一往一来地活动，把尾打结才开始。
没有羽毛也没有翅，反复来回很不迟。
尾巴一长工作就开始，尾巴打结工作才停止。
把大型簪针当父亲，而母亲就是那盛针的管子。
既用它来缝合外表，又用它来连结夹里。
这是关于针的道理。

——针

26.6 如今天下无秩序，请把怪诗叙一叙：
天地交换了位置，四季颠倒了方向；
天上恒星都坠落，早晚昏暗不明亮；

Your servant stupidly not recognizing it,
Presumes to inquire of Your Majesty about it.

The King replied:

Is it not something that originates from something colossal but as a finished product is small?
Is not its tail long and its tip sharply pointed?
Does not the sharp head penetrate and the tail shake and wind around?
Sometimes going, sometimes coming,
By stitching together with its tail it can execute its tasks.
Without feathers and lacking wings,
It turns back and repeats its movements with extreme speed.
When the tail comes to life the task commences,
When it turns round its task is finished.
The hairpin serves as its father;
The reed as its mother.
When it has been used to stitch up the outside,
it has also attached the inside.
This refers to the pattern of the needle.

26. 6

The World Is Not Well-ordered

The world is not well-ordered,
Let me set forth a poem of its strange happenings:
Heaven and Earth have exchanged position;
The four seasons have altered their proper sequence;
Stars fall from their celestial ranks;
Morning and evening, darkness envelops all.

【原文】

幽晦登昭，日月下藏。
公正无私，见谓从横；
志爱公利，重楼疏堂；
无私罪人，憼革贰兵；
道德纯备，谗口将将。
仁人绌约，敖暴擅强；
天下幽险，恐失世英。
螭龙为蝘蜓鸱枭为凤皇。
比干见刳，孔子拘匡。
昭昭乎其知之明也！
郁郁乎其遇时之不祥也！
拂乎其欲礼义之大行也！
暗乎天下之晦盲也！
皓天不复，忧无疆也。
千岁必反，古之常也。

【今译】

阴暗小人登显位，光明君子在下藏。
正直为公无私心，却被说成结私党；
心爱公利去做官，却被以为要楼房；
没有袒护有罪人，却被作敌来严防；
道德纯洁又完备，横遭毁谤瞎嚷嚷。
仁人被废遭穷困，骄横暴徒逞凶狂；
天下黑暗又凶险，时代精英恐丢光。
蛟龙被当作壁虎，鸱枭被看成凤凰。
王子比干被剖腹，孔子被困在陈匡。
明明白白啊他们的智慧是这样聪明亮堂。
忧忧郁郁啊他们碰上的时运是这样不祥。
违背时世啊他们想把礼义普遍推广。
黑沉沉啊天下是这样的昏暗不明亮！
光明之天不复返，忧思无边无限长。
千载定有反复时，古来常规是这样。

The dark and blind rise to shining glory;
The sun and moon descend into hiding.
The public-spirited, correct men who pursue no private interest,
Are said to advocate the Vertical and Horizontal.
Those whose inner minds love public benefit
Are said to advocate multistoried towers and spacious pavilions.
Those who pursue no personal interest by accusing others of crimes
Are said to promote the military in order to caution military preparedness.
Against those in whom the Way and its Power are richly perfected,
Tongues buzz in a chorus of slander.
Humane men are degraded and reduced to poverty,
While proud and violent men usurp and tyrannize at will.
The world has become dark and threatening,
And I fear that we have lost the heroic figures of our age.
Dragons have become chameleons and geckos;
Owls and horned owls have become phoenixes.
Bigan has his heart cut out;
Confucius is besieged in Kuang.
How illustrious, how brilliant was the clarity of their knowledge!
How utterly unpropitious that they should meet with no opportunity!
How elegant and refined was their desire to practice in a grand manner ritual and moral principles!
How benighted the world's dark blindness!
If Bright Heaven does not reverse it,
Our distress will be unending.
That before a thousand years have passed things undergo reversal
Has been the constant rule from antiquity.

【原文】

弟子勉学，天不忘也。

圣人共手，时几将矣。

26.7 “与愚以疑，愿闻反辞。”

其小歌曰：

念彼远方，何其塞矣。

仁人绌约，暴人衍矣。

忠臣危殆，谗人服矣。

琁、玉、瑶、珠，不知佩也。

杂布与锦，不知异也。

闾娵、子奢，莫之媒也。

嫫母、力父，是之喜也。

以盲为明，以聋为聪，

以危为安，以吉为凶。

【今译】

弟子努力去学习，上天不会把你忘。

圣人拱手来等待，即将重见好时光。

26.7 弟子说：“我因愚昧而疑惑，希望听您反复说。”

那短小的诗歌唱道：

想那遥远的地方，多么蔽塞有阻碍。

仁人被废遭穷困，暴徒得意多自在。

忠诚之臣遭危险，进谗之人受委派。

美玉琼瑶与宝珠，竟然不知去佩带。

将布与锦相混杂，竟然不知区别开。

美如闾娵与子都，没人给他们做媒。

丑如嫫母与力父，这种人却被人爱。

认为瞎子视力好，认为聋子听力好，

误把危险当安全，还把吉利当凶兆。

Students!devote yourselves to study,
For Heaven will not forget you.
The sage only folds his hands
Awaiting the approach of his opportunity.

26. 7

Short Song

Let us, the stupid, in our puzzlement,
Be willing to hear the reprise.
His short song said:
I recall that distant region:
How is it thus stymied?
Humane men are degraded and reduced to poverty,
Tyrannical men spread everywhere.
Loyal ministers live in constant danger,
While slanderers are given office.
Agates and jades, jasper and pearls,
He knows not how to wear them as girdle pendants.
Between coarse cloth and finest silks
He is unaware of any difference.
Not for a Lüqu or for a Zishe
Could he arrange a marriage,
For it is with the likes of Momu and Lifu
That he finds his pleasures.
The blind he considers clear-sighted,
The deaf keen of hearing.
He considers danger his security,

【原文】

呜呼上天！曷维其同？

【今译】

呜呼哀哉老天爷！怎能和他们同道？

Takes the auspicious for the unlucky.

Alas!Heaven on High,

when did I ever have anything in common with him?

大略第二十七

【原文】

27.1 大略：

27.2 君人者，隆礼尊贤而王，重法爱民而霸，好利多诈而危。

27.3 “欲近四旁，莫如中央。”故王者必居天下之中，礼也。

27.4 天子外屏，诸侯内屏，礼也。外屏，不欲见外也；内屏，不欲见内也。

【今译】

27.1 要略：

27.2 统治人民的君主，崇尚礼义尊重贤人就能称王天下，注重法治爱护人民就能称霸诸侯，贪图财利多搞欺诈就会危险。

27.3 “想要接近那四旁，那就不如在中央。”所以称王天下的君主一定住在天下的中心地区，这是一种礼制。

27.4 天子将照壁设在门外，诸侯将照壁设在门内，这是一种礼制。把照壁设在门外，是不想让里面看见外面；把照壁设在门内，是不想让外面看见里面。

Book 27

The Great Compendium

27. 1

The great compendium:

27. 2

A lord of men who exalts ritual principles and honors worthy men will become king;one who stresses the law and loves his people will become lord-protector;one who is fond of profit and much given to dissimulation will be imperiled.

27. 3

If one wants to be near the Four Sides, no location is better than the heartland. Thus, one who is king must dwell in the center of the world. This accords with ritual principles.

27. 4

The Son of Heaven has an external screen;the feudal lords an internal screen. This accords with ritual principles. One has an outside screen because he does not wish to see outside;one has an internal screen because he does not wish to be seen inside.

【原文】

27.5 诸侯召其臣，臣不俟驾，颠倒衣裳而走，礼也。《诗》曰：“颠之倒之，自公召之。”天子召诸侯，诸侯辇舆就马，礼也。《诗》曰：“我出我舆，于彼牧矣。自天子所，谓我来矣。”

27.6 天子山冕，诸侯玄冠，大夫裨冕，士韦弁，礼也。

27.7 天子御珽，诸侯御荼，大夫服笏，礼也。

【今译】

27.5 诸侯召见他的臣子时，臣子不等驾好车，没把衣裳穿整齐就跑，这是一种礼制。《诗》云：“颠倒歪斜穿衣裙，因人召我来自君。”天子召见诸侯的时候，诸侯让人拉着车子去靠近马，这是一种礼制。《诗》云：“我把我车往外拉，到那牧地把车驾。有人来自天子处，叫我快来就出发。”

27.6 天子穿画有山形图案的礼服，戴礼帽；诸侯穿黑色的礼服，戴礼帽；大夫穿裨衣，戴礼帽；士戴熟皮制的暗红色帽子；这是一种礼制。

27.7 天子使用上端呈椎形的大玉版，诸侯使用上端呈圆形的玉版，大夫使用斑竹制的手版，这是一种礼制。

27. 5

When a feudal lord summons his ministers, they do not wait for their horses to be harnessed to the carriage, but putting their clothes on upside down in the rush, they hurry out. This accords with ritual practice. An *Ode* says:

He turns them, puts them on upside down,
from the court they have summoned him.

When the Son of Heaven summons the feudal lords, they drag the carriages to the horses. This accords with ritual practice. An *Ode* says:

We bring out our carriages
to the pasture grounds.
From the place of the Son of Heaven
they tell us to come.

27. 6

The Son of Heaven wears a state ceremonial robe emblazoned with mountains;the feudal lords a deep-black hat; the grand officers a skirt with an ornamented border at the bottom;and the knights a leathern cap. This accords with ritual practice.

27. 7

The Son of Heaven carries in his girdle the *ting* jade baton;the feudal lords carry a *tu* jade baton;the grand officer carries a *hu* tablet. This accords with ritual practice.

【原文】

27.8 天子雕弓，诸侯彤弓，大夫黑弓，礼也。

27.9 诸侯相见，卿为介，以其教士毕行，使仁居守。

27.10 聘人以珪，问士以璧，召人以瑗，绝人以玦，反绝以环。

27.11 人主仁心设焉；知，其役也；礼，其尽也。故王者先仁而后礼，天施然也。

27.12《聘礼》志曰："币厚则伤德，财侈则殄礼。"礼云礼云，玉

【今译】

27.8 天子用雕有花纹的弓，诸侯用红色的弓，大夫用墨色的弓，这是一种礼制。

27.9 诸侯互相会见的时候，卿做介绍人，使自己那些受过礼仪教育的士人全部前往，让仁厚的人留守。

27.10 派使者到诸侯国去问候人用珪，去作国事访问用璧，召见人用瑗，与人断绝关系用玦，召回被断绝关系的人用环。

27.11 君主要存立仁爱之心；智慧，是仁爱之心役使的东西；礼制，是仁爱之心的完备体现。所以称王天下的人首先讲究仁德，然后才讲究礼节，自然的安排就是这样。

27.12《聘礼》记载说："礼物丰厚就会伤害德，财物奢侈就会吞

27. 8

The Son of Heaven has an engraved bow; the feudal lords a cinnabar-red bow; the grand officers a black bow. This accords with ritual practice.

27. 9

When the feudal lords see each other, their ministers act as envoys, their trained knights are used to complete the expedition, and officers noted for their humaneness are left at home to maintain the government.

27. 10

Ambassadors on goodwill missions use the *gui* baton. Knights on missions of inquiry use the *bi* disc. Officers who deliver summons use the *yuan* ring. Envoys who break off relations carry the *jue* jade crescent. For the restoration of broken relations, the *huan* jade circle is used.

27. 11

When a lord of men has established a humane heart within himself, knowledge becomes the servant of his humane heart and ritual its fulfillment. Thus, a True King gives first priority to humanity and next to ritual so that in the nature of things they are exhibited.

27. 12

The treatise *Rituals of Goodwill Missions* says:"If ceremonial of-

【原文】

帛云乎哉？《诗》曰："物其指矣，唯其偕矣。"不时宜，不敬交，不欢欣，虽指，非礼也。

27.13 水行者表深，使人无陷；治民者表乱，使人无失。礼者，其表也，先王以礼表天下之乱。今废礼者，是去表也，故民迷惑而陷祸患。此刑罚之所以繁也。

27.14 舜曰："维予从欲而治。"故礼之生，为贤人以下至庶民也，非为成圣也，然而亦所以成圣也。不学不成。尧学于君畴，舜学于务成昭，禹学于西王国。

【今译】

没礼。"礼呀礼呀，难道只是指玉帛这些礼品吗？《诗》云："各种食物味真美，因为它们合口味。"如果礼物送得不合时宜，送礼时不恭敬有礼貌，不喜悦快乐，那么即使礼物很美，也不合乎礼制。

27.13 在水中跋涉的人用标志来表明深度，使人不至于陷入深水淹死；治理民众的人用标准来表明祸乱，使人不至于失误。礼制，就是这种标准，古代的圣明帝王用礼制来彰明天下的祸乱。现在废除礼制，这是在丢掉标准啊，所以民众迷惑而陷于祸乱。这就是刑罚繁多的原因。

27.14 舜说："只有我能随心所欲地治理天下。"那礼制的制定，是为了贤人以及下面的群众的，并不是为了使人成为圣人，然而它也是使人成为圣人的一种工具。但是不向人学习是不能成为圣人的。尧曾向君畴学习，舜曾向务成昭学习，禹曾向西王国学习。

ferings are too rich, it damages moral authority. If displays of wealth are extravagant, ritual principles are destroyed." "Surely in saying 'ritual principles' one means more than offerings of jade and silk!" An *Ode* says:

These things are beautiful,
yet they are plentiful.

Things that are not timely or appropriate, not reverent or refined, not happy or joyful, although they are beautiful, are contrary to ritual principles.

27. 13

People who ford streams mark out the deep places to cause others not to sink into the waters. Those who govern men mark out the sources of disorder to cause the people not to fall into error. It is ritual principles that are the markers. The Former Kings employed ritual principles to indicate the causes of anarchy in the world. Today those who have cast ritual principles aside have pulled up the markers. Thus, the people are beguiled and deluded and so sink into misfortune and calamity. This is the reason that penal sanctions and punishments are so very numerous.

27. 14

Shun said:"It is only through following my desires that I have become orderly. "Thus, ritual was created on behalf of men from worthies down to the ordinary masses but not for perfected sages. Nonetheless, it is also the means by which to perfect sageness. Not to study is never to be perfected. Yao studied with Jun Chou, Shun with Wucheng Zhao, and Yu with Xiwang Guo.

【原文】

27.15 五十不成丧，七十唯衰存。

27.16 亲迎之礼：父南乡而立，子北面而跪，醮而命之："往迎尔相，成我宗事，隆率以敬先妣之嗣，若则有常。"子曰："诺，唯恐不能，不敢忘命。"

27.17 夫行也者，行礼之谓也。礼也者，贵者敬焉，老者孝焉，长者弟焉，幼者慈焉，贱者惠焉。

27.18 赐予其宫室，犹用庆赏于国家也；忿怒其臣妾，犹用刑罚

【今译】

27.15 五十岁的人不需要全部做到守丧的礼节，七十岁的人只要丧服在身就行了。

27.16 新郎亲自去迎接新娘的礼仪：父亲面向南站着，儿子面向北跪着，父亲一边斟酒祭神一边嘱咐儿子："去迎接你的贤内助，完成我家传宗接代以祭祀宗庙的大事，好好带领她去恭敬地做你亡母的继承人，你的行动则要有常规。"儿子说："是，我只怕没有能力做到，决不敢忘记您的嘱咐。"

17.17 所谓德行，就是指奉行礼义。所谓礼义，就是对地位高贵的人要尊敬，对年老的人要孝顺，对年长的人要敬从，对年幼的人要慈爱，对卑贱的人要给予恩惠。

27.18 在自己家庭内进行赏赐，应当像在国家中使用表彰赏赐一

27. 15

At age fifty, one does not complete the mourning observances. At seventy, only the sackcloth garment is retained.

27. 16

The Rites for Claiming the Bride. The father stands facing toward the south. His son faces north and kneels. The father offers the pledge cup to his son with the command: "Go now and claim your helpmate so that I may fulfill my responsibilities in our ancestral temple. Treat her generously and lead her with respect, for she is the successor to your mother. If you act in this fashion, then our family will be perpetuated." The son responds: "Yes, sir. Only I fear that I shall prove incapable, though how could I presume to forget your commands!"

27. 17

As to "putting it into practice," it is putting ritual into practice that is meant. Ritual principles include treating the eminent in a respectful manner; fulfilling one's filial duties to the old; behaving with fraternal courtesy toward one's elders; treating the young with affection;and being kind to the humble.

27. 18

Bestow rewards on your household just as you would provide recom-

【原文】

于万民也。

27.19 君子之于子，爱之而勿面，使之而勿貌，导之以道而勿强。

27.20 礼以顺人心为本，故亡于《礼经》而顺人心者，皆礼也。

27.21 礼之大凡：事生，饰欢也；送死，饰哀也；军旅，饰威也。

27.22 亲亲故故庸庸劳劳，仁之杀也。贵贵尊尊贤贤老老长长，

【今译】

样；对自己的奴婢发怒，应当像对民众使用刑罚一样。

27.19 君子对于子女，疼爱他们而不表现在脸上，使唤他们而不露神色，用正确的道理来引导他们而不强迫他们接受。

27.20 礼以顺应人心为根基，所以在《礼经》上没有但能顺应人心的，都是礼。

27.21 礼仪的大致情况是：用于侍奉生者的，是为了润饰喜悦之情；用于葬送死者的，是为了更好地表现悲哀之情；用于军队的，是为了装饰威武之势。

27.22 亲近父母亲，热情对待老朋友，奖赏有功劳的人，慰劳付

pense for deeds in behalf of the state. Display anger and wrath to servants and concubines just as you would enforce the penal sanctions and punishments on the myriad people.

27. 19

In his relations with his son, the gentleman loves him but does not show it in his face. He assigns his son tasks, but does not change expression over it. He guides him using the Way, but does not use physical compulsion.

27. 20

Ritual principles use obedience to the true mind of man as their foundation. Thus, were there no ritual principles in the *Classic of Ritual*, there would still be need for some kind of ritual in order to accord with the mind of man.

27. 21

The main general themes of ritual principles: to serve the living in a manner that provides ornamented expression to joy; to send off the dead in a manner that provides ornamented expression of grief; and in military formations to provide ornamented expression of awe-inspiring majesty.

27. 22

The graduated scale of humane conduct is to treat relatives in a man-

【原文】

义之伦也。行之得其节，礼之序也。仁，爱也，故亲。义，理也，故行。礼，节也，故成。仁有里，义有门。仁，非其里而虚之，非礼也。义，非其门而由之，非义也。推恩而不理，不成仁；遂理而不敢，不成义；审节而不知，不成礼；和而不发，不成乐。故曰：仁、义、礼、乐，其致一也。君子处仁以义，然后仁也；行义以礼，然后义也；制礼反本成末，然后礼也。三者皆通，然后道也。

【今译】

出劳力的人，这是仁方面的等级差别。尊崇身份贵重的人，尊敬官爵显赫的人，尊重有德才的人，敬爱年老的人，敬重年长的人，这是义方面的伦理。奉行这些仁义之道能恰如其分，就是礼的秩序。仁，就是爱人，所以能和人互相亲近。义，就是合乎道理，所以能够实行。礼，就是适度，所以能够成功。仁有安居之处，义有进出之门。仁，如果不是它应该安居的地方却去安顿在那里，就不是什么仁。义，如果不是它应该进出的门户而从那里进出，就不是什么义。施行恩惠而不合乎道理，就不成为仁；通达道理而不敢遵行，就不成为义；明白制度而不能使人们和睦协调，就不成为礼；和睦协调了而不抒发出来，就不成为乐。所以说：仁、义、礼、乐，它们要达到的目标是一致的。君子根据义来处置仁，然后才有了仁；根据礼来奉行义，然后才有了义；制定礼时回头抓住它的根本原则从而再完成它的细节，然后才有了礼。这三者都精通了，然后才是正道。

ner befitting their relation, old friends as is appropriate to their friendship, the meritorious in terms of their accomplishment, and laborers in terms of their toil. The gradations of position in moral conduct are to treat the noble as befits their eminent position, the honorable with due honor, the worthy as accords with their worth, the old as is appropriate to their age, and those senior to oneself as is suitable to their seniority.

In the order of precedence contained in ritual principles, each type of conduct receives its due measure. Humane behavior is the manifestation of love, and thus it is expressed in one's treatment of relatives. Morality is the manifestation of natural order and thus it is expressed in one's conduct. Ritual principles are the manifestation of measured moderation, and thus they are expressed in the perfection of things.

Humanity is like the village where one dwells;morality like the gate to one's dwelling. Where humane behavior is not the village where one dwells, there is no humanity. Where morality is not the gate through which one proceeds, there is no righteousness or justice. To extend kindnesses to others but not in accord with natural order is not to perfect humane conduct. To proceed in accord with natural order but not to show due measure is not to perfect moral conduct. To judge carefully due measure but not to be harmonious is not to perfect ritual principles. To be harmonious yet not to manifest it is not to perfect music. Thus it is said:"Humanity, morality, ritual, and music—their highest expression is one and the same."

Only after the gentleman has dwelt with humane principles through justice and morality is he truly humane;only after he conducts himself with justice and morality through ritual principles is he truly just and moral;and only where he regulates with ritual principles, returning to the root and perfecting the branch, is he truly in accord with ritual principles.

【原文】

27.23 货财曰赙，舆马曰赗，衣服曰襚，玩好曰赠，玉贝曰唅。赙、赗，所以佐生也；赠、襚，所以送死也。送死不及柩尸，吊生不及悲哀，非礼也。故吉行五十，奔丧百里，赗赠及事，礼之大也。

27.24 礼者，政之挽也。为政不以礼，政不行矣。

27.25 天子即位，上卿进曰："如之何忧之长也？能除患则为福，

【今译】

27.23 帮助别人办丧事而赠送的财物叫做赙，赠送的车马叫做赗，赠送的寿衣衾服叫做襚，赠送死者所玩赏嗜好的物品叫做赠，赠送的珠玉贝壳供死人含在口中的叫做唅。赙、赗，是用来帮助死者家属的；赠、襚，是用来葬送死者的。送别死者时不见到棺材里的尸体，哀悼死者而安慰其家属时不达到悲哀，是不合乎礼的。所以参加吉礼时一天走五十里，而奔丧时一天要跑一百里，帮助别人办丧事而赠送的东西一定要赶上丧事，这是礼节的大端啊。

27.24 礼，是政治的指导原则。治理政事不按照礼，政策就不能实行。

27.25 天子刚登上帝位时，上卿走上前说："忧虑这样深长，您怎么办呢？能够除去祸患就有幸福，不能除去祸患就会受害。"说完就

Only when these three have been made comprehensive has he reached the Way.

27. 23

Presents of money and valuables are called *fu* gifts. Presents of horses and carriages are called *feng* gifts. Presents of clothing and mourning garments are called *sui* gifts. Presents of valuable curiosities are called *zeng* gifts. Presents of jade and cowrie shells are called *han* gifts. *Fu* and *feng* gifts are used to assist the living; *zeng* and *sui* gifts are used to send off the dead. It is contrary to ritual principles that presents for sending off the dead should not arrive for the encoffining of the corpse and that visits of condolence should not be paid before grief and sadness have reached their peak. Thus, it is an important point of ritual that for auspicious occasions travel is up to fifty *li*, that one rushes up to a hundred *li* for funeral rites, and that *feng* and *zeng* gifts arrive in time to send off the dead.

27. 24

Ritual principles are the guiding ropes that pull the government. Where the exercise of government does not make use of ritual principles, the government will not succeed.

27. 25

When the Son of Heaven first takes his position, his senior minister advances, saying: "What is to be done about such prolonged sorrow!If we are able to deliver ourselves from the danger of calamity, then we

【原文】

不能除患则为贼。”授天子一策。中卿进曰:“配天而有下土者，先事虑事，先患虑患。先事虑事谓之接，接则事优成。先患虑患谓之豫，豫则祸不生。事至而后虑者谓之后，后则事不举。患至而后虑者谓之困，困则祸不可御。”授天子二策。下卿进曰：“敬戒无怠!庆者在堂，吊者在闾。祸与福邻，莫知其门。豫哉!豫哉!万民望之。”授天子三策。

27.26 禹见耕者耦，立而式；过十室之邑，必下。

【今译】

把第一篇册书交给天子。中卿走上前说:“和上天相配而拥有天下土地的人，在事情发生之前就要考虑到那事情，在祸患来到之前就要考虑到祸患。在事情发生之前就考虑到那事情，这叫做敏捷；能够敏捷，那么事情就会圆满成功。在祸患来到之前就考虑到祸患，这叫做预先准备；能够预先准备，那么祸患就不会发生。事情发生以后才加以考虑的叫做落后；落后了，那么事情就办不成。祸患来了以后才加以考虑的叫做困厄；困厄了，那么祸患就不能抵挡了。”说完就把第二篇册书交给天子。下卿走上前说：“慎重戒备而不要懈怠!庆贺的人还在大堂上，吊丧的人已到了大门口。灾祸和幸福紧靠着，没有人知道它们产生的地方。要预先准备啊!要预先准备啊!亿万人民都仰望着您。”说完就把第三篇册书交给天子。

27.26 禹看见耕地的人两人并肩耕作，就站起来扶着车厢前的横木；经过十来户人家的小镇，一定下车。

will create good fortune. If we are incapable of delivering ourselves, then we will create rapine." He delivers to the Son of Heaven the first tablet of investiture.

The middle-ranking minister advances and says:"He who acts as the assessor of Heaven yet lives here below on earth anticipates the affairs of government and plans for them and anticipates calamity and prepares for it. To anticipate the affairs of government is to be called adroit. If one is adroit, then the affairs of government are brought to an excellent conclusion. To anticipate calamity and plan for it is called foresight. If one has foresight, then misfortune will not be born. One who thinks of the affairs of government only after they have come to be is said to be 'after the fact.' If one is 'after the fact,' then the affairs of government will not be promoted. One who thinks of calamity only after it has happened is said to be beset with difficulties. If one is beset with difficulties, then misfortune cannot be withstood." He delivers to the Son of Heaven the second tablet.

The junior minister advances, saying: "Be respectful, be careful, and do not be remiss. Those who would congratulate you are in the audience hall;those who would offer condolences are at the street gate. Misfortune and fortune are neighbors, but no one knows which gate is which. Foresight! Foresight indeed! The myriad people hope for it." He delivers the third tablet to the Son of Heaven.

27. 26

When Yu saw farmers working as a team of plowmen, he would halt and salute them from the front bar of his chariot. When he passed by a hamlet of ten houses, he was certain to descend.

【原文】

27.27 杀大蚤，朝大晚，非礼也。治民不以礼，动斯陷矣。

27.28 平衡曰拜，下衡曰稽首，至地曰稽颡。

27.29 大夫之臣拜不稽首，非尊家臣也，所以辟君也。

27.30 一命齿于乡；再命齿于族；三命，族人虽七十，不敢先。

【今译】

27.27 猎取禽兽太早，上朝太晚，不合乎礼。治理民众不根据礼，一动就会失足。

27.28 弯腰后头与腰相平叫做拜，头比腰低叫做稽首，头着地叫做稽颡。

27.29 大夫的家臣对大夫只拜而不稽首，这不是为了提高家臣的地位，而是避免大夫和国君在礼节等级上的相同。

27.30 在乡内饮酒时，一级官员和乡里的人按照年龄大小来排列位次；二级官员和同宗族的人按年龄大小来排列位次；至于三级官员，那么同宗族的人即使七十岁了，也不敢排在他前面。

27. 27

To hunt excessively early in the morning and to stay in the audience hall too late are both contrary to ritual principles. To govern the people not using ritual principles is to take actions that will be entirely wasted.

27. 28

A bow that is level like a steelyard is called a *bai*. One that is low like a dipping steelyard is called a *qishou*. One that is low like the steelyard arm touching the ground is called a *qisang*.

27. 29

Servants of a grand officer do not perform the *qishou*, not from any honor paid the servant, but so that the grand officer might avoid transgressing on the homage due his own lord.

27. 30

Those who had received the first degree of rank took precedence according to age in village meetings. Those who had received the second took precedence according to age in meetings of their clan. Those who had received the third degree of rank would not presume in meetings of their clan to take precedence over any clansmen who was seventy years of age.

【原文】

27.31 上大夫，中大夫，下大夫。

27.32 吉事尚尊，丧事尚亲。

27.33 君臣不得不尊，父子不得不亲，兄弟不得不顺，夫妇不得不欢。少者以长，老者以养。故天地生之，圣人成之。

27.34 聘，问也。享，献也。私觌，私见也。

27.35 言语之美，穆穆皇皇。朝廷之美，济济铊铊。

【今译】

27.31 大夫分上大夫、中大夫、下大夫。

27.32 在吉庆的事中官位高的人位次在前，在丧事中与死者关系亲近的人位次在前。

27.33 君臣之间得不到君子的治理就不会有尊重，父子之间得不到君子的治理就不会亲近，兄弟之间得不到君子的治理就不会和顺，夫妻之间得不到君子的治理就不会欢乐。年幼的人靠了君子的治理而长大成人，年老的人靠了君子的治理而得到赡养，所以天地养育了人，圣人成就了人。

27.34 聘，就是问候。享，就是进献。私觌，就是私下会见。

27.35 形容说话的美好，就说“穆穆皇皇”。形容朝廷的美好，

27. 31

Senior Grand Officer, Middle Grand Officer, and Junior Grand Officer.

27. 32

In auspicious matters one elevates those who are honorable;in mourning rites one elevates those who are kin.

27. 33

Where ritual is not obtained, between lord and minister there is no honored position, between father and son is no affection; between elder and younger brother no submissiveness, and between husband and wife no rejoicing. Through it, the young grow to maturity, and the old acquire nourishment. Thus Heaven and Earth produce it and the sage perfects it.

27. 34

Missions of goodwill are to make inquiries. The entertainment at the drinking ceremony is to offer the wine cup in pledge. The private audience is for the personal interview.

27. 35

What is beautiful in statements and discourses is their majestic and august character; what is beautiful in court proceedings is the stately and

【原文】

27.36 为人臣下者，有谏而无讪，有亡而无疾，有怨而无怒。

27.37 君于大夫，三问其疾，三临其丧；于士，一问，一临。诸侯非问疾、吊丧，不之臣之家。

27.38 既葬，君若父之友食之，则食矣，不辟粱肉，有酒醴则辞。

27.39 寝不逾庙，燕衣不逾祭服，礼也。

【今译】

就说“济济跄跄”。

27.36 给人当臣子的，只能规劝而不能毁谤，只能出走而不能憎恨，只能埋怨而不能发怒。

27.37 君主对于大夫，在他生病时去慰问三次，在他死后去祭奠三次；对于士，慰问一次，祭奠一次。诸侯如果不是探望疾病、祭奠死者，不到臣子的家里。

27.38 父亲或母亲已经埋葬以后，君主或者父亲的朋友让自己吃饭，就可以吃了，不回避米饭肉食，但有酒就要谢辞。

27.39 寝殿的规模不能超过庙堂，参加敬老宴饮之礼所穿的衣服不能超过祭祀所穿的礼服，这是一种礼制。

balanced movements of the officers.

27. 36

Anyone who acts as a minister or subordinate should offer remonstrance but not engage in vilification, should absent himself but not fall into hatred inspired by jealousy, and should resent misdeeds but not display wrath.

27. 37

A lord thrice inquires about the illness of his grand officers and thrice attends his mourning observances. In the case of a knight he inquires once and attends once. A feudal lord, except to inquire about illness or offer condolences during the mourning, does not visit the family of his ministers.

27. 38

After the burial, if the ruler or a friend of his father feasted the mourner, he partook of the meal. He did not avoid the grain and meat dishes that were served, but if distilled spirits or sweet spirits were offered, these he declined.

27. 39

Private and state chambers should not surpass the ancestral temple;clothes for entertaining should not be superior to those used in sacrifice. This accords with ritual practice.

【原文】

27.40《易》之《咸》，见夫妇。夫妇之道，不可不正也，君臣、父子之本也。“咸”，感也，以高下下，以男下女，柔上而刚下。

27.41 聘士之义，亲迎之道，重始也。

27.42 礼者，人之所履也。失所履，必颠蹶陷溺。所失微而其为乱大者，礼也。

27.43 礼之于正国家也，如权衡之于轻重也，如绳墨之于曲直

【今译】

27.40《易经》中的《咸》卦，显示了夫妻之道。夫妻之道，是不能不端正的，它是君臣、父子关系的根本。“咸”，就是感应的意思，它的符号是把高的置于低的之下，把男的置于女的之下，是柔和在上面而刚劲在下面。

27.41 聘请贤士的仪式，新郎亲自去迎接新娘的办法，都是注重开端。

27.42 礼，是人的立身之处。失去了立身之处，就一定会跌倒沉沦。稍微失去一点而造成的祸乱很大的东西，就是礼。

27.43 礼对于整饬国家，就像秤对于轻重一样，就像墨线对于曲直一样。所以人没有礼就不能生活，事情没有礼就不能办成，国家没

27. 40

The hexagram *Xian*, "All, " of the *Changes* shows the relation of husband to wife. The Way of relations between husband and wife cannot be allowed to be incorrect, for it is the root source for the relations between lord and minister, father and son.

The hexagram *Xian* means "influence. " It uses the high to descend to the low, the male to descend to the female. It is weak and pliant above and strong and hard below.

27. 41

Both the sense for what is right manifested by a knight on a goodwill mission and the way of a bridegroom claiming his bride emphasize the beginning.

27. 42

Ritual principles provide the footing men tread on. When men lose this footing, they stumble and fall, sink and drown. When observance of small matters is neglected, the disorder that results is great. Such is ritual.

27. 43

The relationship of ritual principles to the correct governance of the nation is like that of the suspended balance and steelyard to the determination of weight or that of the darkened marking line to straightness.

【原文】

也。故人无礼不生，事无礼不成，国家无礼不宁。

27.44 和乐之声，步中《武》、《象》，趋中《韶》、《护》。

27.45 君听律习容而后出。

27.46 霜降逆女，冰泮杀止。

27.47 内，十日一御。

27.48 坐，视膝；立，视足；应对言语，视面。立视前六尺，而

【今译】

有礼就不得安宁。

27.44 车铃的声音，在车子慢行时合乎《武》、《象》的节奏，在车子奔驰时合乎《韶》、《护》的节奏。

27.45 君子要听听走路时佩玉的声音是否合律，并练习好举止仪表然后才出门。

27.46 从霜降开始娶妻，到第二年河里的冰融化时就停止婚娶。

27.47 对正妻，十天同房一次。

27.48 对方坐着，注视他的膝部；对方站着，注视他的脚；回答说话时，注视他的脸。对方站着时，在他前面六尺处注视他，而最

Thus, a man without ritual will not live, an undertaking without ritual will not succeed, and a nation without ritual will not be tranquil.

27. 44

There are the harmonious sounds of the tinkling bells on the horse's trappings;the chariot moves along in time with the *Martial* and *Imitation* music, and its horses gallop in time with the *Succession* and *Guarding* music.

27. 45

The gentleman, having listened to the pitch pipe and practiced his demeanor, goes out.

27. 46

When the hoarfrost descends, the bridegroom claims his woman;when the ice begins to melt, executions are halted.

27. 47

Once in every ten days the concubines visit.

27. 48

When seated, look at the knees;when standing, at the feet;and when replying or speaking, look into the face. When standing before your lord,

【原文】

大之，六六三十六，三丈六尺。

27.49 文貌情用相为内外表里，礼之中焉。

27.50 能思索谓之能虑。

27.51 礼者，本末相顺，终始相应。

27.52 礼者，以财物为用，以贵贱为文，以多少为异。

27.53 下臣事君以货，中臣事君以身，上臣事君以人。

【今译】

远，六六三十六，在三丈六尺之处注视他。

27.49 礼仪容貌和感情作用互相构成内外表里的关系，这是适中的礼。

24.50 善于思索叫做虑。

27.51 礼制，它的根本原则和具体细节互不抵触，人生终结的仪式与人生开始的仪式互相应合。

27.52 礼，把钱财物品作为工具，把尊贵与卑贱的区别作为礼仪制度，把享受的多少作为尊卑贵贱的差别。

27.53 下等的臣子用财物来侍奉君主，中等的臣子用生命来侍奉

look ahead six feet and multiply it by six. (Six sixes are thirty-six;three decades of feet and six feet.)

27. 49

When form and appearance, emotions and offerings, are treated as inside to outside, external manifestation to inner content, there is the mean course of ritual.

27. 50

Being able to ponder and meditate on this mean is called being able to think.

27. 51

In ritual principles, root and branch accord with one another; end and beginning are fitting and proper, one to the other.

27. 52

Rites employ valuables and objects to make offerings. They use distinctions between noble and base to create forms. They employ larger and smaller amounts to recognize differences of station.

27. 53

Junior ministers serve their lord with material objects;middle-rank min-

【原文】

27.54《易》曰:“复自道，何其咎？”

27.55《春秋》贤穆公，以为能变也。

27.56士有妒友，则贤交不亲；君有妒臣，则贤人不至。蔽公者谓之昧，隐良者谓之妒，奉妒昧者谓之交谲。交谲之人，妒昧之臣，国之秽孽也。

27.57口能言之，身能行之，国宝也。口不能言，身能行之，国

【今译】

君主，上等的臣子推荐人才来侍奉君主。

27.54《易经》说:“回到自己的道路，有什么过错？”

27.55《春秋》赞许秦穆公，认为他能够转变。

27.56士人有了妒忌的朋友，那么和贤人交往就不会亲密；君主有了妒忌的臣子，那么贤人就不会到来。埋没公正的人叫做欺昧，埋没贤良的人叫做妒忌，奉承妒忌欺昧的人叫做狡猾诡诈。狡猾诡诈的小人，妒忌欺昧的臣子，是国家的垃圾和妖孽。

27.57嘴里能够谈论礼义，自身能够奉行礼义，这种人是国家的

isters serve with their own person;and senior ministers serve with other men.

27. 54

The *Changes* says: “Returning and following his own Way. What might be his mistake?”

27. 55

The *Spring and Autumn Annals* treats Duke Mu as worthy because it considers him capable of reform.

27. 56

If a knight is jealous of his friends, worthy associates will not befriend him. If a lord is jealous of his ministers, worthy men will not come to him. One who beclouds the judgment of his duke is said to inspire blindness;one who keeps virtuous men hidden in obscurity is said to be inspired by jealousy. To promote persons inspired by jealousy who blind their superiors is said to be perversely and treacherously crafty. Men who are perversely and treacherously crafty and ministers who are inspired by jealousy and who blind their superiors are the “noxious weeds” and “concubine’s sons” of the state.

27. 57

A person who has a mouth capable of expressing ideas and has a

【原文】

器也。口能言之，身不能行，国用也。口言善，身行恶，国妖也。治国者敬其宝，爱其器，任其用，除其妖。

27.58 不富无以养民情，不教无以理民性。故家五亩宅，百亩田，务其业而勿夺其时，所以富之也。立太学，设庠序，修六礼，明十教，所以导之也。《诗》曰："饮之食之，教之诲之。"王事具矣。

27.59 武王始入殷，表商容之闾，释箕子之囚，哭比干之墓，天下乡善矣。

【今译】

珍宝。嘴里不能谈论礼义，自身能够奉行礼义，这种人是国家的器具。嘴里能够谈论礼义，自身不能奉行礼义，这种人是国家的工具。嘴里说得好，自身干坏事，这种人是国家的妖孽。治理国家的人敬重国家的珍宝，爱护国家的器具，使用国家的工具，铲除国家的妖孽。

27.58 不使民众富裕就无法调养民众的思想感情，不进行教育就无法整饬民众的本性。每家配置五亩宅基地，一百亩耕地，努力从事农业生产而不耽误他们的农时，这是使他们富裕起来的办法。建立国家的高等学府，设立地方学校，整饬六种礼仪，彰明七个方面的教育，这是用来引导他们的办法。《诗》云："给人喝啊给人吃，教育人啊指导人。"像这样，称王天下的政事就完备了。

27.59 周武王刚进入殷都的时候，在商容所住的里巷门口设立了标记以表彰他的功德，解除了箕子的囚禁，在比干的墓前痛哭哀悼，于是天下人就都趋向行善了。

body capable of acting on them is a treasure to the state. A person who is unable to express ideas but has a body that can act on them is a vessel for the state. A person who is capable of expressing ideas but has a body incapable of acting on them is an instrument for the state. But a person who speaks well with a body that behaves evilly is an ominous force against the state. Those who govern the state should revere its treasures, love its vessels, give responsibility to its instruments, but remove its ominous forces.

27. 58

A people that is not made prosperous will have no means of caring for the needs of their essential natures. A people that is not taught will have no means of introducing rational order into their inborn nature. Hence, the way to make families prosperous is to allot five *mou* "lots" for the abode and one hundred *mou* for the fields, to devote one's attention to their concerns, and not to rob them of the time required for their fields. The way to guide them is to establish colleges, set up academies and schools, cultivate the six types of ritual observances, and elucidate the seven teachings. An *Ode* says:

> Give them drink, give them food,
> teach them, instruct them.

The king's business includes all of these.

27. 59

When King Wu first entered Yin, he set up flags at the street of Shang Rong's village, freed the Viscount of Ji from prison, and wept at the grave of Bigan—the whole world turned toward the good.

【原文】

27.60 天下、国有俊士，世有贤人。迷者不问路，溺者不问遂，亡人好独。《诗》曰："我言维服，勿用为笑。先民有言：询于刍荛。"言博问也。

27.61 有法者以法行，无法者以类举。以其本知其末，以其左知其右。凡百事，异理而相守也。庆赏刑罚，通类而后应。政教习俗，相顺而后行。

27.62 八十者，一子不事；九十者，举家不事；废疾非人不养

【今译】

27.60 天下、一国都有才智出众的人，每个时代都有贤能的人。迷路的人不问道，溺水的人不问涉水的路，亡国的君主独断专行。《诗》云："我所说的是要事，不要以为开玩笑。古人曾经有句话：要向樵夫去请教。"这是说要广泛地询问各方面的人。

27.61 有法律依据的就按照法律来办理，没有法律条文可遵循的就按照类推的办法来办理。根据它的根本原则推知它的细节，根据它的一个方面推知它的另一个方面。大凡各种事情，道理虽然不同却互相制约着。对于表扬奖赏与用刑处罚，通达了类推的原理，然后才能有相应的处置。政治教化与风俗习惯相适应，然后才能实行。

27.62 八十岁的人，可以有一个儿子不服劳役；九十岁的人，全

27. 60

In every state of the world there are talented men, and in every generation worthy men. Those muddled by their own infatuations do not ask the route;those drowning in drink do not inquire how to proceed;and those who lose everything are fond of acting on their own. An *Ode* says:

My words are about our service,
do not make them a matter for laughter.
The ancient people had a saying:
"Consult the grass and firewood gatherers."

This means that one should inquire broadly about things.

27. 61

Where the model covers an affair, use it as the basis for action; where there is no provision in the model, use an analogical extension of the proper category as a basis for proceeding. Use the root of a thing to know its branches; use its left to know its right. As a rule, the hundred affairs, though different, have a rational order that they mutually observe.

In offering congratulations and making rewards, in applying penal sanctions and punishing, thoroughly understand the proper category before responding. Government, instruction, practice, and custom should be made to accord with each other and then put into practice.

27. 62

In a family with an octogenarian, one son does not do corvée labor.

【原文】

者，一人不事。父母之丧，三年不事；齐衰大功，三月不事。从诸侯不与新有昏，期不事。

27.63 子谓子家驹续然大夫，不如晏子；晏子，功用之臣也，不如子产；子产，惠人也，不如管仲；管仲之为人，力功不力义，力知不力仁，野人也，不可以为天子大夫。

27.64 孟子三见宣王不言事。门人曰："曷为三遇齐王而不言事？"孟子曰："我先攻其邪心。"

【今译】

家都可以不服劳役；残废有病、没有人照顾就不能活下去的，家里可以有一个人不服劳役。有父亲、母亲的丧事，可以三年不服劳役；齐衰和大功，可以三个月不服劳役。从其他诸侯国迁来以及新结婚的，可以一年不服劳役。

27.63 孔子说子家驹是增益君主明察的大夫，及不上晏子；晏子，是个有成效的臣子，及不上子产；子产，是个给人恩惠的人，及不上管仲；管仲的立身处事，致力于功效而不致力于道义，致力于智谋而不致力于仁爱，是个缺乏礼义修养的人，不可以做天子的大夫。

27.64 孟子三次见到齐宣王而不谈国事。他的学生说："为什么三次碰到齐王都不谈国事？"孟子说："我先要打击他的坏思想。"

In a family with a nonagenarian, the whole family is excused from it. For those who are cripples or ill and have no one to feed them, one man does not serve. During the mourning for father and mother, for three years the son does not serve. During the rites of purification and fasting and during the Greater Effort, for three months he does not serve. Anyone who, having followed his feudal lord to a new state, marries there does not serve for the full term of a year.

27. 63

The Master said of Zijia Ju that he was a rigidly correct grand officer, but was not the equal of Yan Ying;that Yan Ying was a minister who accomplished meritorious and useful services but was not the equal of Prince Chan [of Zheng];that Prince Chan was kind to his people but was not the equal of Guan Zhong;and that Guan Zhong was the kind of man who was strong on achievements but did not have a strong sense of right and who was strong in knowledge but not in humanity. He was a rustic boor who could not be considered a grand officer fit for the Son of Heaven.

27. 64

Mencius had three audiences with King Xuan [of Qi], but did not discuss affairs of state. A disciple asked why he had three times met with the king of Qi yet had not discussed affairs of state. Mencius replied: "I have first to overcome his errant heart."

【原文】

27.65 公行子之之燕，遇曾元于涂，曰："燕君何如？"曾元曰："志卑。志卑者轻物，轻物者不求助。苟不求助，何能举？氐、羌之虏也。不忧其系垒也，而忧其不焚也。利夫秋豪，害靡国家，然且为之，几为知计哉？"

27.66 今夫亡箴者，终日求之而不得；其得之，非目益明也，眸而见之也。心之于虑亦然。

27.67 义与利者，人之所两有也。虽尧、舜不能去民之欲利，然

【今译】

27.65 公行子之到燕国去，在路上碰到曾元，说："燕国国君怎么样？"曾元说："他的志向不远大。志向不远大的人看轻事业，看轻事业的人不找人帮助。如果不找人帮助，哪能攻克别国呢？他只能是氐族人、羌族人的俘虏。他不担忧自己被捆绑，却担忧自己死后不能按照氐族、羌族的习俗被火化。得到的利益就像那秋天新长出来的兽毛一样细微，而危害却有损于国家，这样的事他尚且要去做，哪能算是懂得谋划呢？"

27.66 现在那丢了针的人，整天找它都没找到；当他找到它时，并不是眼睛更加明亮了，而是睁大了眼睛才发现它的。心里考虑问题也是这样。

27.67 道义和私利，是人们兼有的东西。即使是尧、舜这样的贤君也不能除去民众追求私利的欲望，但是能够使他们对私利的追求敌

27. 65

When Gonghang Zizhi was en route to Yan, he chanced to encounter Zeng Yuan on the road and asked what the lord of Yan was like. Zeng Yuan replied: "He has a base mind. Those who have base minds make light of things. Those that make light of things do not seek assistance. If he does not seek assistance, how can he promote properly!"

Prisoners belonging to the Di and Qiang tribes are not distressed by being tied and bound, but are distressed that they will not be burned. This is to be eager for the fine autumn coat of animals at the cost of harm and despoliation of one's nation. If a person is going to behave in this fashion, how can he be thought to know how to calculate to real advantage!

27. 66

Consider the case of someone who has lost a needle and spends the whole day looking for it without success. When he does find it, it is not that his eyes have become sharper, but that he has bent down to look more carefully for it. So too it is with the mind pondering a matter.

27. 67

A sense of rightness and a sense for profits are two things humans possess. Although they were unable to get rid of the desire for profit in people, Yao and Shun nonetheless were able to cause them not to allow their desire for profit to triumph over their love of moral conduct. Al-

【原文】

而能使其欲利不克其好义也。虽桀、纣亦不能去民之好义，然而能使其好义不胜其欲利也。故义胜利者为治世，利克义者为乱世。上重义，则义克利；上重利，则利克义。故天子不言多少，诸侯不言利害，大夫不言得丧，士不通货财；有国之君不息牛羊，错质之臣不息鸡豚，冢卿不修币，大夫不为场圃；从士以上皆羞利而不与民争业，乐分施而耻积臧。然故民不困财，贫窭者有所窜其手。

27.68 文王诛四，武王诛二，周公卒业，至成、康则案无诛已。

【今译】

不过他们对道义的爱好。即使是夏桀、商纣这样的暴君也不能去掉民众对道义的爱好，但是能够使他们对道义的爱好敌不过他们对私利的追求。所以道义胜过私利的就是治理得好的社会，私利胜过道义的就是混乱的社会。君主看重道义，道义就会胜过私利；君主推崇私利，私利就会胜过道义。所以天子不谈论财物多少，诸侯不谈论有利还是有害，大夫不谈论得到还是失去，士不去贩运买卖货物；拥有国家的君主不养殖牛和羊，献身于君主的臣子不养殖鸡和小猪，上卿不放高利贷，大夫不筑场种菜；从士以上的官吏都以追求私利为羞耻而不和民众争抢职业，喜欢施舍而以囤积私藏为耻辱。所以民众不为钱财所困扰，贫穷的人也不会手足无措了。

27.68 周文王讨伐了四个国家，周武王诛杀了两个人，周公旦完成了称王天下的大业，到周成王、周康王的时候就没有杀伐了。

though even Jie and Zhou Xin were unable to get rid of people's love of moral conduct, they could nonetheless cause their desire for profit to conquer their love of moral conduct. Thus, one who causes morality to conquer profit makes his age well ordered, whereas one who causes profit to overcome morality creates a chaotic age.

When superiors stress the importance of morality, morality overcomes profit;when they stress profit, then profit overcomes morality. Thus, the Son of Heaven does not discuss quantities, feudal lords do not discuss benefit and harm, grand officers do not discuss success and failure, and knights do not discuss commerce and merchandise.

A lord who possesses a whole state does not raise cattle and sheep. A minister charged with arranging ceremonial gifts does not raise chickens and pigs. A great minister does not repair a broken fence. A grand officer does not take care of open spaces and gardens. When everyone, from knights to the highest officials, feels ashamed of being eager for profits, they will not compete with the people for goods. Rather, they will find enjoyment in their portions and grants, considering it disgraceful to engage in accumulating stores. This being the case will result in the people not being beset with difficulties over goods and in the poor and wretched having something to lay their hands on.

27. 68

King Wen used execution in only four instances, King Wu in two, and the Duke of Zhou completed their undertaking so that when Kings Cheng and Kang came to power, peace could be secured without the need for capital punishment.

【原文】

27.69 多积财而羞无有，重民任而诛不能，此邪行之所以起，刑罚之所以多也。

27.70 上好羞，则民暗饰矣，上好富，则民死利矣。二者，乱之衢也。民语曰："欲富乎？忍耻矣，倾绝矣，绝故旧矣，与义分背矣。"上好富，则人民之行如此，安得不乱？

27.71 汤旱而祷曰："政不节与？使民疾与？何以不雨至斯极也？宫室荣与？妇谒盛与？何以不雨至斯极也？苞苴行与？谗夫兴与？何

【今译】

27.69 赞许积聚钱财而把一无所有看作羞耻，加重人民的负担而惩处不堪负担的人，这是邪恶行为产生的根源，也是刑罚繁多的原因。

27.70 君主爱好义，那么民众就暗自整饬了。君主爱好富，那么民众就为利而死了。这两点，是治和乱的叉道。民间俗语说："想富吗？忍着耻辱吧，道德败坏吧，与故旧一刀两断吧，与道义背道而驰吧。"君主爱好富，那么人民的行为就这样，怎么能不乱？

27.71 商汤因为大旱而向神祷告说："是我的政策不适当吗？是我役使民众太苦了吗？为什么旱到这种极端的地步？是我的宫殿房舍太华丽了吗？是妻妾嫔妃说情请托太多了吗？为什么旱到这种极端的地

27. 69

Putting much emphasis on the accumulation of goods so that people consider it shameful to lack them and stressing the importance of the people's responsibilities so that people are executed for incompetence—these are the reasons that evil behavior arises and that punishments and penal sanctions are frequently applied.

27. 70

When superiors love moral conduct, then the people conduct themselves in a refined manner even in private. When superiors love wealth, then the people are willing to die for profits. These two are the crossroads to order and anarchy. A proverb among the people says: "Do you desire wealth? You will have to bear shame, throw out scruples, destroy yourself, cut yourself off from old friends and old ties, and turn your back on duty and station in life. " If superiors love wealth, then the conduct of their subjects will be like this. How could they but obtain chaos!

27. 71

On the occasion of the drought, Tang prayed: "Is my government not properly regulated? Does it cause the people grief? Why has the rain not come for so long a time? Are the palaces and chambers too glorious? Are the women of the harem too numerous? Why has the rain not come for so long a time? Are reed mats and sackcloth being offered in bribe? Do slanderers flourish? Why has the rain not come

【原文】

以不雨至斯极也？”

27.72 天之生民，非为君也；天之立君，以为民也。故古者，列地建国，非以贵诸侯而已；列官职，差爵禄，非以尊大夫而已。

27.73 主道，知人；臣道，知事。故舜之治天下，不以事诏而万物成。农精于田而不可以为田师，工贾亦然。

27.74 以贤易不肖，不待卜而后知吉。以治伐乱，不待战而后知克。

【今译】

步？是贿赂盛行吗？是毁谤的人发迹了吗？为什么旱到这种极端的地步？”

27.72 上天生育民众，并不是为了君主；上天设立君主，却是为了民众。所以在古代，分封土地建立诸侯国，并不只是用来尊重诸侯而已；安排各种官职，区别爵位俸禄的等级，并不只是用来尊重大夫而已。

27.73 为君之道，在于了解人；为臣之道，在于精通政事。从前舜治理天下，不用事事告诫而各种事情也就办成了。农夫对种地很精通却不能因此而去做管理农业的官吏，工匠和商人也是这样。

27.74 用贤能的人去替换没有德才的人，不等占卜就知道是吉利的。用安定的国家去攻打混乱的国家，不等交战就知道能攻克。

for so long a time?"

27. 72

Heaven did not create the people for the sake of the lord; Heaven established the lord for the sake of the people. Hence, in antiquity land was not granted in fiefs of ranked sizes just to give honored position to the feudal lords and for no other purpose. Offices and ranks were not arranged in hierarchical order and provided with suitable titles and emoluments just to give honored status to the grand officers and for no other purpose.

27. 73

The Way of a ruler lies in knowing men; that of a minister in knowing affairs of state. Hence when Shun governed the world, he did not have official tasks nor did he give issue proclamations, yet the myriad things were brought to completion.

The farmer has his single purpose in his fields, yet it would be inadmissible to deem him a director of the fields. Of the artisan and merchant the same is true.

27. 74

Using the worthy to reform the unworthy is to know what is auspicious without first having to await the outcome of the divination. Using what is ordered to overcome anarchy is to know victory without having first to engage in battle.

【原文】

27.75 齐人欲伐鲁，忌卞庄子，不敢过卞。晋人欲伐卫，畏子路，不敢过蒲。

27.76 不知而问尧、舜，无有而求天府。曰：先王之道，则尧、舜已；六贰之博，则天府已。

27.77 君子之学如蜕，幡然迁之。故其行效，其立效，其坐效，其置颜色出辞气效。无留善，无宿问。

27.78 善学者尽其理，善行者究其难。

【今译】

27.75 齐国人想攻打鲁国，顾忌卞庄子，不敢经过卞城。晋国人想攻打卫国，害怕子路，不敢经过蒲邑。

27.76 不懂政治就去询问尧、舜，没有财富就去寻求宝库。我说：古代圣王的政治原则，就是尧、舜；六经包含的丰富内容，就是宝库。

27.77 君子的学习就像蛇、蝉等脱壳一样，很快有所改变。所以他走路效仿，站立效仿，坐着效仿，他摆什么脸色，讲什么话，用什么口气都效仿。不把好事留下不做，不把要问的事拖过夜。

27.78 善于学习的人彻底搞通事物的道理，善于做事的人彻底克服工作中的困难。

27. 75

Some men of Qi wanted to attack Lu, but were so terrified of Viscount Zhuang of Bian that they dared not go past Bian. Some men of Jin wanted to attack Wei but were so overawed by Zilu that they did not presume to pass by Pu.

27. 76

Of "not knowing and asking Yao or Shun" and of "not having something and seeking it from the Treasury of Heaven," I say: The Way of the Ancient Kings already includes Yao and Shun, and the broad learning of the Six Arts already includes the Treasury of Heaven.

27. 77

The effect of learning on the gentleman is analogous to the changes of the butterfly in its chrysalis: having undergone change, he emerges altered. Thus, in his walking and in his sitting, in the expressions he composes on his face, and in the tones of the sentences he utters, its effects are seen. He seeks good without rest, and he never puts off questions to later.

27. 78

One who is adept at study exhausts principles of rational order. One who is adept at putting things into practice examines problems.

【原文】

27.79 君子立志如穷，虽天子、三公问正，以是非对。

27.80 君子隘穷而不失，劳倦而不苟，临患难而不忘细席之言。岁不寒，无以知松柏；事不难，无以知君子无日不在是。

27.81 雨小，汉故潜。夫尽小者大，积微者著，德至者色泽洽，行尽而声问远。小人不诚于内而求之于外。

【今译】

27.79 君子树立志向好像陷入困境一样不能变通，即使天子、三公询问政事，也根据是非来回答。

27.80 君子穷困而不丧失志气，劳累而不苟且偷安，面临祸患而不背弃平时坐席上说的话。岁月不寒冷，就无从知道松柏；事情不危难，就无从知道君子没有一天不在这样。

27.81 雨虽然小，汉水却照旧流入潜水。尽量收罗微小的就能变成巨大，不断积累隐微的就会变得显著，道德极高的人脸色态度就和润，品行完美的人名声就传得远。小人内心不真诚却到外界去追求声誉。

27. 79

The gentleman maintains his high ideals even in adversity, so that should the Son of Heaven or the Three Dukes ask him about governing, he could state what is right and what is wrong.

27. 80

Although a gentleman is in dire straits and bitter poverty, he does not lose his way. Although he is tired and exhausted, he does not behave indecorously. Although he observes the threat of calamity or great difficulties, he does not forget the smallest measure of the doctrine. Until winter comes, you do not know the character of the cypress and cedar; until affairs of government have encountered difficulties, you do not know the character of the gentleman. There is not a day that passes when he is not there.

27. 81

When rainfall is small, the Han River does not for that reason become [the size of its tributary] the Qian. What collects the small becomes the large. What accumulates the minute becomes visible. When inner power had been perfected in a person, it penetrates into and imbues his countenance. When his conduct fully realizes it, his reputation is known from afar. The petty man, not being authentic within, seeks this from without.

【原文】

27.82 言而不称师谓之畔，教而不称师谓之倍。倍畔之人，明君不内，朝士大夫遇诸涂不与言。

27.83 不足于行者，说过；不足于信者，诚言。故《春秋》善胥命，而《诗》非屡盟，其心一也。

27.84 善为《诗》者不说，善为《易》者不占，善为《礼》者不相，其心同也。

27.85 曾子曰："孝子言为可闻，行为可见。言为可闻，所以说远

【今译】

27.82 说话时不称道老师叫做反叛，教学时不称道老师叫做背离。背叛老师的人，英明的君主不接纳，朝廷内的士大夫在路上碰到他不和他说话。

27.83 在行动上不够的人，往往言过其实；在信用方面不够的人，往往夸夸其谈。《春秋》赞美互相之间口头约定，而《诗经》非议屡次订立盟约，他们的用心是一致的。

27.84 善于研治《诗》的人不作解说，善于研治《易》的人不占卦，善于研治《礼》的人不辅助行礼，他们的用心是相同的。

27.85 曾子说："孝子说的话是可以让人听的，做的事是可以让人看的。说的话可以让人听，是用来使远方的人高兴；做的事可以让人

27. 82

To discuss things in terms that do not agree with your teacher is called "rebellion." To teach in a fashion that does not correspond to what your teacher taught is called "subversion." An intelligent lord would not appoint such men to office, and the knights and grand officers of his court would not discuss things with such men should they be encountered on the road.

27. 83

Persuasions that recommend things that cannot be put into practice transgress the truth. Words that cannot be relied on only appear sincere. Hence, the *Annals* in considering "pledging each other" good and the *Odes* in condemning "frequent covenanting" are of one and the same mind.

27. 84

That one who is expert in the *Odes* does not engage in persuasions; that one who is expert in the *Changes* does not prognosticate;and that one who is expert in ritual principles does not act as master of ceremonies—all these involve the same frame of mind.

27. 85

Master Zeng said:"The filial son's speech brings approval wherever it is heard and his conduct aprroval wherever it is seen. Speech

【原文】

也；行为可见，所以说近也。近者说则亲，远者说则附。亲近而附远，孝子之道也。”

27.86 曾子行，晏子从于郊，曰：“婴闻之：‘君子赠人以言，庶人赠人以财。’婴贫无财，请假于君子，赠吾子以言：乘舆之轮，太山之木也，示诸檃栝，三月五月，为帱革敝，而不反其常。君子之檃栝，不可不谨也，慎之！兰茝、稿本，渐于蜜醴，一佩易之。正君渐于香酒，可谗而得也。君子之所渐，不可不慎也。”

27.87 人之于文学也，犹玉之于琢磨也。《诗》曰：“如切如磋，如

【今译】

看，是用来使近处的人高兴。近处的人高兴就会来亲近，远方的人高兴就会来归附。使近处的人来亲近而远方的人来归附，这是孝子遵行的原则。”

27.86 曾子要走了，晏子跟着送到郊外，说：“晏婴听说过这样的话：‘君子用言语赠送人，百姓用财物赠送人。’我晏婴贫穷没有财物，请让我冒充君子，拿话来赠送给您：马车的轮子，原是泰山上的木头，把它放置在整形器中，经过三五个月就做成了，那么就是裹住车毂的皮革坏了，也不会恢复到它原来的形状了。君子对于正身的工具，不能不谨慎地对待啊，要慎重地对待它！兰芷、稿本等香草，如果浸在蜂蜜和甜酒中，一经佩带就要更换它。正直的君主如果泡在香酒似的甜言蜜语中，也会被谗言俘虏。君子对于所渐染的环境，不能不谨慎地对待啊。”

27.87 人对于学习研究古代文献典籍，就像玉对于琢磨一样。

that brings approval wherever it is heard is the way to give pleasure to those who are distant;conduct that brings approval wherever it is seen is the way to give pleasure to those who are nearby. When those near at hand are pleased, they feel kinship with him. When those far away are pleased, they feel attached to him. To inspire feelings of kinship in those nearby and of attachment in those far away is the Way of the filial son."

27. 86

When Master Zeng was traveling, Master Yan followed him to the suburbs saying: "I have heard that gentlemen present others with words as gifts, whereas ordinary men present material objects as gifts. Since I am poor and have no goods, may I follow that practice of the gentleman and present you with some words. The wheel of a chariot was once a tree on Mount Tai. Placed in the press-frame for three to five months, wood can be used for the cover or hub of the wheel even until it wears out, yet it will never revert to its regular form. With the press-frame of the gentleman, one cannot but be careful. Be cautious with it! The dried roots of the orchid and valerian moistened with honey or sweet new wine will be exchanged as soon as they are worn hanging about the neck. A correct gentleman who has been moistened with fragrant spirits—might he not be slandered. What is used to 'moisten' the gentleman, one cannot but be cautious about!"

27. 87

Learning and culture are to men what polishing and grinding are to

【原文】

琢如磨。”谓学问也。和之璧，井里之厥也，玉人琢之，为天下宝。子赣、季路，故鄙人也，被文学，服礼义，为天下列士。

27.88 学问不厌，好士不倦，是天府也。

27.89 君子疑则不言，未问则不言。道远，日益矣。

27.90 多知而无亲、博学而无方、好多而无定者，君子不与。

【今译】

《诗》云：“就像治骨磨象牙，就像雕玉磨石器。”就是说的做学问啊。卞和的玉璧，原是乡里固定门闩的楔形石块，加工玉器的工匠雕琢了它，就成了天下的珍宝。子贡、子路，原是浅陋的人，受到了文献典籍的影响，遵从礼义，就成了天下屈指可数的名人。

27.88 学习请教不满足，爱好贤士不厌倦，这就是宝库。

27.89 君子疑惑的就不说，还没有请教过的就不说。道路长远，知识一天天增加。

27.90 知道得很多而没有什么特别的爱好、学习得很广而没有个主攻方向、喜欢学得很多而没有个确定目标的人，君子不和他结交。

jade. An *Ode* says:

Like bone cut, like horn polished,
like jade carved, like stone ground.

This refers to studying and questioning.

The *bi* disc made from the Bian He and the stone from Jingli, having been polished by men, became treasures to the whole world. Zigong and Jilu, who were originally men from a frontier district, clothed themselves in culture and learning and wrapped themselves in ritual and duty so that they became distinguished scholars of the world.

27. 88

Insatiable in study and inquiry, untiring in their love of scholars—such are the "Treasury of Heaven."

27. 89

If the gentleman has reservations, he does not discuss the matter. If he has not yet inquired about it, he does not discuss it. When the way is distant, each day he adds to his progress along it.

27. 90

The gentleman will not associate with those who possessing much knowledge have no close companions, those who though broadly learned have no methods, and those who being fond of many things have no fixed standards.

【原文】

27.91 少不讽诵，壮不论议，虽可，未成也。

27.92 君子一教，弟子一学，亟成。

27.93 君子进，则能益上之誉而损下之忧。不能而居之，诬也；无益而厚受之，窃也。

27.94 学者非必为仕，而仕者必如学。

27.95 子贡问于孔子曰："赐倦于学矣，愿息事君。"孔子曰：

【今译】

27.91 少年时不读书，壮年时不发表议论，即使资质还可以，也不能有所成就。

27.92 君子专心一意教授，学生专心一意学习，就能迅速取得成就。

27.93 君子入朝做官，就能增加君主的荣誉而减少民众的忧患。没有才能而呆在官位上，就是行骗；对君主民众毫无裨益而优厚地享受俸禄，就是盗窃。

27.94 学习的人不一定都去做官，而做官的人一定要去学习。

27.95 子贡问孔子说："我对学习感到厌倦了，希望休息一下去侍

27. 91

If you do not recite and chant when still small and discuss and deliberate when a youth, then although you may try, you will never master them.

27. 92

The gentleman who single-mindedly pursues his doctrines and the student who single-mindedly pursues his studies quickly perfect them.

27. 93

If the gentleman is advanced in office, then he will be able to increase the praises of his superiors and to lessen the sorrows of his inferiors. To be unable to fulfill the duties of an office and yet take a position is to be a sham; to be of no advantage and yet accept the generosity of one's ruler is to be a thief.

27. 94

Being learned does not guarantee holding office, but holding office does guarantee that one will rely on what one has learned.

27. 95

Zigong questioned Confucius, saying: "I am weary of study and would like to rest up from it in the service of a lord."

Confucius replied: "An *Ode* says:

【原文】

“《诗》云：‘温恭朝夕，执事有恪。’事君难，事君焉可息哉？”“然则赐愿息事亲。”孔子曰：“《诗》云：‘孝子不匮，永锡尔类。’事亲难，事亲焉可息哉？”“然则赐愿息于妻子，”孔子曰：“《诗》云：‘刑于寡妻，至于兄弟，以御于家邦。’妻子难，妻子焉可息哉？”“然则赐愿息于朋友。”孔子曰：“《诗》云：‘朋友攸摄，摄以威仪。’朋友难，朋友焉可息哉？”“然则赐愿息耕。”孔子曰：“《诗》云：‘昼尔于茅，宵尔索绹，亟其乘屋，其始播百谷。’耕难，耕焉可息哉？”“然则赐无

【今译】

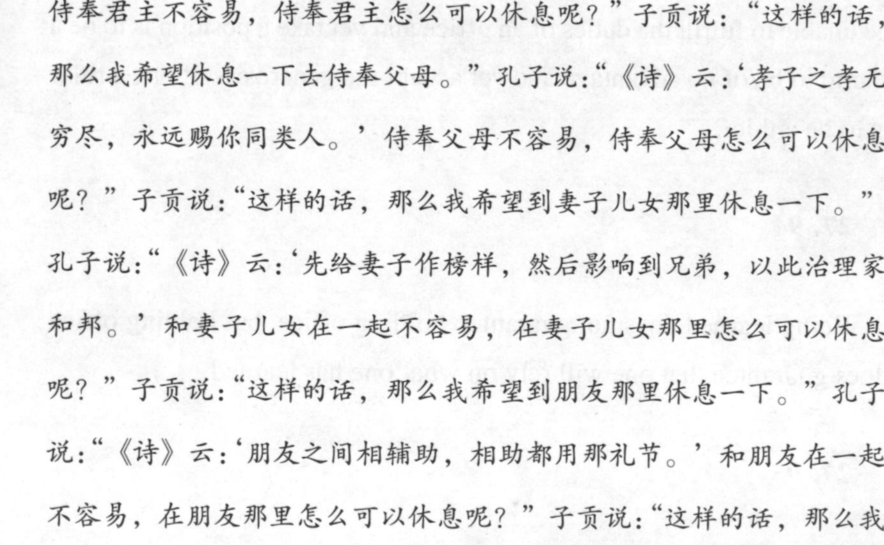

奉君主。”孔子说：“《诗》云：‘早晚温和又恭敬，做事认真又谨慎。’侍奉君主不容易，侍奉君主怎么可以休息呢？”子贡说：“这样的话，那么我希望休息一下去侍奉父母。”孔子说：“《诗》云：‘孝子之孝无穷尽，永远赐你同类人。’侍奉父母不容易，侍奉父母怎么可以休息呢？”子贡说：“这样的话，那么我希望到妻子儿女那里休息一下。”孔子说：“《诗》云：‘先给妻子作榜样，然后影响到兄弟，以此治理家和邦。’和妻子儿女在一起不容易，在妻子儿女那里怎么可以休息呢？”子贡说：“这样的话，那么我希望到朋友那里休息一下。”孔子说：“《诗》云：‘朋友之间相辅助，相助都用那礼节。’和朋友在一起不容易，在朋友那里怎么可以休息呢？”子贡说：“这样的话，那么我希望休息下来去种田。”孔子说：“《诗》云：‘白天要去割茅草，夜里搓绳要搓好，急忙登屋修屋顶，又要开始播种了。’种田不容易，种田怎

Meek and reverent, morning and evening,
we perform our service with reverence.

Service to a lord is difficult, how could you expect to rest up by entering into service?"

"That being so, I would like to rest up in service to my parents."

Confucius responded: "An *Ode* says:

Filial sons have endless duties;
always giving you things perfect of their kind.

Service to parents is difficult; how could you expect to rest up in it."

"That being so, then I would like to rest up in the company of my wife."

Confucius replied: "An *Ode* says:

He was a model to his consort,
extended the example to his brothers,
and so governed his family and state.

Dealing with a wife is dificult, how could you expect to rest with her!"

"That being so, I would like to rest wih my friends."

Confucius said: "An *Ode* says:

Your friends are assisted,
assisted by your dignified demeanor.

Dealing with friends is difficult; how could you expect to rest with them!"

"That being so, then I would like to rest up being a farmer."

Confucius responded: "An *Ode* says:

In daylight gather the reed grass,
in evening make it into rope.
Quickly climb up to the rooftop
—soon we must begin our sowing anew.

A farmer's life is difficult; how could you expect to rest up being a farmer!"

【原文】

息者乎?”孔子曰:“望其圹,皋如也,嵿如也,鬲如也,此则知所息矣。”子贡曰:“大哉,死乎!君子息焉,小人休焉。”

27.96《国风》之好色也,传曰:“盈其欲而不愆其止 。其诚可比于金石,其声可内于宗庙。”《小雅》不以于污上,自引而居下,疾今之政,以思往者,其言有文焉,其声有哀焉。

27.97 国将兴,必贵师而重傅;贵师而重傅,则法度存。国将衰,必贱师而轻傅;贱师而轻傅,则人有快;人有快,则法度坏。

【今译】

么可以休息呢?”子贡说:“这样的话,那么我就没有休息的地方啦?”孔子说:“远望那个坟墓,高高的样子,山顶般的样子,鼎鬲似的样子,看到这个你就知道可以休息的地方了。”子贡说:“死亡嘛,可就大啦!君子休息了,小人也休息了。”

27.96《国风》爱好女色,解说它的古书说:“满足情欲而又不越轨。它的真诚不渝可以和金属石头的坚固不变相比,它的音乐可以纳入到宗庙中去。”《小雅》的作者不被腐朽的君主所用,自己引退而处于卑下的官位上,他们痛恨当时的政治,因而怀念过去,《小雅》的言辞富有文采,音乐具有哀怨的情调。

27.97 国家将要兴盛的时候,一定尊敬老师而看重师傅;尊敬老师而看重师傅,那么法度就能保持。国家将要衰微的时候,一定鄙视老师而看轻师傅;鄙视老师而看轻师傅,那么人就会有放肆之心;人有了放肆之心,那么法度就会破坏。

"That being so, then am I to be without any leisure in which to rest?"

Confucius replied: "Look into that grave pit and see how marsh-like it is, how precipitous its sides, and how it resembles the hollow legs of the *li* tripod. In that you will know what resting up really is!"

Zigong said: "How very great death is! The gentleman finds rest in it; the petty man his surcease."

27. 96

Of the eroticism of the *Airs of the States*, the *Commentary* says: "They give satisfaction to the desires men have but do not err in their stopping point. Their sincerity can be compared to metal and stone whose sounds are permitted within the ancestral temple."

The people of the period of the *Lesser Odes* would not be used by vile superiors, but withdrew of their own accord and dwelt among the humble people. Angry over the sick governments of their day, they were filled with remembrance of days gone by. Their language had such perfect expressive form, and their music such a plaintive air.

27. 97

When a country is on the verge of a great florescence, it is certain to prize its teachers and give great importance to breadth of learning. If it does this, then laws and standards will be preserved. When a country is on the verge of decay, then it is sure to show contempt for teachers and slight masters. If it does this, then its people will be smug. If the people are smugly self-satisfied, then laws and standards will be allowed to go to ruin.

【原文】

27.98 古者匹夫五十而士；天子诸侯子十九而冠，冠而听治，其教至也。

27.99 君子也者而好之，其人；其人也而不教，不祥。非君子而好之，非其人也；非其人而教之，赍盗粮、借贼兵也。

27.100 不自嗛其行者，言滥过。古之贤人，贱为布衣，贫为匹夫，食则馑粥不足，衣则竖褐不完，然而非礼不进，非义不受，安取此？

【今译】

27.98 古代平民百姓到五十岁才能做官；而天子与诸侯的儿子十九岁就举行冠礼，举行冠礼后就治理政事，这是因为他们受到的教育极好的缘故啊。

27.99 对于君子倾心爱慕的，就是那理想的学生；对这种理想的学生不施教，是不吉利的。对于并非君子的人也倾心爱慕的，就不是那理想的学生；对这种并非理想的学生去施教，就是把粮食送给小偷，把兵器借给强盗。

27.100 不自我意识到自己德行不足的人，说话往往浮夸过分。古代的贤人，卑贱得做个平民，贫穷得做个百姓，吃嘛连稀饭也不够，穿嘛连粗布衣也不完整，但是如果不按照礼制来提拔他，他就不入朝做官，如果不按照道义给他东西，他就不接受，哪会采取这种夸夸其谈的做法？

27. 98

In antiquity, commoners on their fiftieth birthday were given office, and the Son of Heaven and feudal lords at nineteen achieved their majority with the capping. When they were capped, they would hear the affairs of government, their education having been completed.

27. 99

When a person is fond of the ideal of the gentleman, he can become one. Where he would be a gentleman, but will not be instructed, there will be no auspicious result. Where he is fond of what is contrary to the ideal of the gentleman, he will not become one. Where he would not become one and he is taught, he will pilfer the stores of grain or become part of a gang of predatory bandits.

27. 100

Those who feel no dissatisfaction with the course of their life engage in wrongfully extravagant and exaggerated talk. In antiquity the worthy dressed so humbly that they appeared as poor as the common people. When they ate, it was congee and gruel in less than ample quantities, and when they dressed, they wore ragged short haircloth garments like workers. This being so, they would not advance without ritual principles being observed and would not accept any gain involved unless it was right. How could they engage in wrongfully extravagant and exaggerated talk!

【原文】

27.101 子夏贫，衣若县鹑。人曰："子何不仕？"曰："诸侯之骄我者，吾不为臣；大夫之骄我者，吾不复见。柳下惠与后门者同衣而不见疑，非一日之闻也。争利如蚤甲而丧其掌。"

27.102 君人者不可以不慎取臣，匹夫不可以不慎取友。友者，所以相有也。道不同，何以相有也？均薪施火，火就燥；平地注水，水流湿。夫类之相从也如此之著也，以友观人，焉所疑？取友善人，不可不慎，是德之基也。《诗》曰："无将大车，维尘冥冥。"言无与小人处也。

【今译】

27.101 子夏贫穷，衣服破烂得就像悬挂着的鹌鹑。有人说："您为什么不去做官？"子夏说："诸侯傲视我的，我不做他的臣子；大夫傲视我的，我不再见他。柳下惠和看守后门的人同样穿破烂的衣服而不被怀疑，这已不是一天的传闻了。争权夺利就像抓住了指甲而丢了自己的手掌。"

27.102 统治人民的君主不可以不慎重地选取臣子，平民百姓不可以不慎重地选择朋友。朋友，是用来互相帮助的。如果奉行的原则不同，用什么来互相帮助呢？把柴草均匀地铺平而点上火，火总是向干燥的柴草上烧去；在平整的土地上灌水，水总是向潮湿的低洼地流去。那同类事物的互相依随就像这样的显著，根据朋友来观察人，还有什么可怀疑的？选取朋友，和别人友好，不可以不慎重，这是成就德行的基础啊。《诗》云："别扶牛车向前进，尘土茫茫会脏身。"这是说不要和小人相处啊。

27. 101

Zixia was from a home so poor that his clothes looked like hanging quails. A man said:"Master, why do you not hold office?"

He replied:"I will not serve as minister to those feudal lords who treat me in an arrogant manner. I will not have a return audience with a grand officer who is haughty with me. Liuxia Hui wore the same clothing as the people at the Aft Gate, yet he encountered no suspicion and not a day went by but that he was heard. Competing for profits is like obtaining something no bigger than a flea's suit of armor at the cost of losing your hand."

27. 102

It is impermissible for a lord of men to be incautious in the selection of his ministers. It is improper for the common people to be careless in the choice of friends. Friends are those with whom one has mutual interests. If their Way is not the same, how can there be mutual interests?

When firewood is spread out and lit, fire seeks out the driest sticks; when water is poured out on level ground, it flows to the dampest places. It is evident that things of the same kind naturally come together; hence one reviews a man by looking at his friends. Could there be any doubt about this? To choose good men as one's friends—in this it is wrong to be incautious, for it is the foundation of inner power. An *Ode* says:

> Do not lean on the great carriage,
> the swirling dust will blind you.

This says that one should not live among ordinary men.

【原文】

27.103 蓝苴路作，似知而非。偄弱易夺，似仁而非。悍戇好斗，似勇而非。

27.104 仁、义、礼、善之于人也，辟之，若货财粟米之于家也：多有之者富，少有之者贫，至无有者穷。故大者不能，小者不为，是弃国捐身之道也。

27.105 凡物有乘而来。乘其出者，是其反者也。

27.106 流言，灭之；货色，远之。祸之所由生也，生自纤纤也。是故君子蚤绝之。

【今译】

27.103 对人狙伺欺诈，好像明智而并不是明智。软弱而容易被人强行改变主张，好像仁慈而并不是仁慈。凶狠鲁莽而喜欢争斗，好像勇敢而并不是勇敢。

27.104 仁爱、道义、礼制、善行对于人来说，打个比方，就像是钱财粮食和家庭的关系一样：较多地拥有它的就富裕，较少地拥有它的就贫穷，丝毫没有的就困窘。所以大事不会干，小事又不做，这是抛弃国家丢弃自己的道路啊。

27.105 所有的事物都是有所凭借才来临的。凭借自己出现的事，这就是那返回到自己的事。

27.106 流言蜚语，消灭它；钱财女色，远离它。祸患所赖以产生的根源，都发生于那些细微的地方。所以君子及早地消灭祸患的苗头。

27. 103

Wearing tattered clothes and sackcloth garments while acting in a grand manner may seem like knowledge, but it is not. Being weak and timid so that one is easily robbed may seem like humanity, but it is not. Being violent, stupid, and fond of brawling may seem like bravery, but it is not.

27. 104

Humanity, morality, ritual principles, and goodness belong in man the way valuables, goods, grain, and rice belong in the household. Those that have them in abundance are rich; those that have them in small quantities are poor. To be entirely without them is to be utterly impoverished. Thus, for the great to be incapable and the small to fail to act is the Way to abandon the state and damage the self.

27. 105

As a general rule, things come about because something occasioned them. For what occasioned them turn back to yourself.

27. 106

Put an end to the wayward doctrines you hear; keep your distance from wealth and sex. They are the causes that bit by bit produce misfortune. This is why the gentleman is quick to cut them off.

【原文】

27.107 言之信者，在乎区盖之间。疑则不言，未问则不言。

27.108 知者明于事，达于数，不可以不诚事也。故曰：“君子难说，说之不以道，不说也。”

27.109 语曰：“流丸止于瓯、臾，流言止于知者。”此家言邪学之所以恶儒者也。是非疑，则度之以远事，验之以近物，参之以平心，流言止焉，恶言死焉。

27.110 曾子食鱼有余，曰:“泔之。”门人曰:“泔之伤人，不若奥

【今译】

27.107 说话真实的人，存在于阙疑之中。疑惑的不说，没有请教过的不说。

27.108 明智的人对事情十分清楚，对事理十分精通，我们不可以不忠诚地去侍奉明智的人啊。所以说:“对于君子，是难以使他高兴的，不通过正当的途径去使他高兴，他是不会高兴的。”

27.109 俗话说:“滚动的圆球滚到凹坑就停止了，流言蜚语碰到明智的人就止息了。”这就是那些私家之言与邪恶的学说憎恶儒者的原因。是对是错疑惑不决，就用久远的事情来衡量它，用新近的事情来检验它，用公正的观点来考察它，流言蜚语便会因此而止息，邪恶的言论便会因此而消亡。

27.110 曾子吃鱼有吃剩的，说:“把它和别的菜搀和在一起。”他

27. 107

The words of a trustworthy person lie in between "cover and concealment." If he has reservations, he does not speak; if he has not yet been asked about it, he does not discuss it.

27. 108

The wise man is clear in regard to his tasks and comprehensively employs his calculations; so it would be impossible for him to be insincere in his undertakings. Therefore it is said:"The gentleman takes pains with his persuasions. A persuasion that cannot be used for guidance is no persuasion."

27. 109

There is the saying:"Balls rolling in every direction are stopped by bowls and pans. Wayward doctrines spreading in every direction are stopped by those who know."This saying is why schools with heterodox learning hate the Ru. If matters of right and wrong are in doubt, measure them with distant affairs, verify them with things nearby, and examine them with a tranquil mind. This is how wayward doctrines are stopped and evil words destroyed.

27. 110

Master Zeng ate some fish, but had leftovers. He said: "Put rice

【原文】

之。”曾子泣涕曰:“有异心乎哉!”伤其闻之晚也。

27.111 无用吾之所短遇人之所长，故塞而避所短，移而从所仕。疏知而不法，察辨而操僻，勇果而亡礼，君子之所憎恶也。

27.112 多言而类，圣人也。少言而法，君子也。多少无法而流喆然，虽辩，小人也。

27.113 国法禁拾遗，恶民之串以无分得也。有夫分义，则容天

【今译】

的学生说：“搀和起来会伤害人的身体，不如再把它熬一下。”曾子流着眼泪说：“我难道别有用心吗？”为自己听到这种话太晚而感到悲伤。

27.111 不要用自己的短处去对付别人的长处，所以要掩盖并回避自己的短处，迁就并依从自己的特长。通达聪明而不守法度，明察善辩而坚持的观点邪恶怪僻，勇敢果断而不合礼义，这是君子所憎恶的。

27.112 话说得多而合乎法度，便是圣人；话说得少而合乎法度，就是君子；说多说少都不合法度却还是放纵沉醉在其中，即使能言善辩，也是个小人。

27.113 国家的法令禁止拾取别人遗失的财物，这是憎恶民众习

water over it. ”

A disciple replied: “Putting rice water over it may harm you; it would be better to cook it. ”

Master Zeng wept, saying: “How could I have had so aberrant a mind as not to realize this!” He was hurt that he had heard this so late in life.

27. 111

Do not use your shortcomings to combat others' strong points. Thus, put to an end and leave behind your shortcomings; advance and follow your abilities. Knowing things comprehensively but not according to the model; scrutinizing and discriminating but holding on to perverse doctrines; acting with bravery and firmness but forgetting the requirements of ritual principles—these are what the gentleman hates for their evilness!

27. 112

A sage, though he speaks often, always observes the logical categories appropriate to what he discusses. A gentleman, though he speaks but seldom, always accords with the model. A petty man speaks frequently but in a manner that does not adhere to the model, his thoughts drowning in the verbiage of his idle chatter even when he engages in the disciplined discourse of formal discriminations.

27. 113

The laws of the state forbid picking up objects that have been left be-

【原文】

下而治；无分义，则一妻一妾而乱。

27.114 天下之人，唯各特意哉，然而有所共予也。言味者予易牙，言音者予师旷，言治者予三王。三王既已定法度、制礼乐而传之，有不用而改自作，何以异于变易牙之和、更师旷之律？无三王之法，天下不待亡，国不待死。

27.115 饮而不食者，蝉也；不饮不食者，蜉蝣也。

27.116 虞舜、孝己，孝而亲不爱；比干、子胥，忠而君不用；

【今译】

惯于不按名分去取得财物。有了那名分道义，那就能包揽天下而把它治理好；没有名分道义，那么就是只有一妻一妾，也会搞得乱糟糟。

27.114 天下的人，虽然各有独特的看法，却也有共同赞许的东西。谈论美味的都赞许易牙，谈论音乐的都赞许师旷，谈论政治的都赞许三王。三王既已确定了法度，制作了礼乐制度而把它们传了下来，如果不遵用而加以改变并自己重新搞一套，那和变更易牙的调味，变更师旷的音律有什么不同呢？如果没有三王的法度，天下不等片刻就会沦亡，国家不等片刻就会覆灭。

27.115 只喝水而不吃东西的，是蝉；不喝水又不吃东西的，是蜉蝣。

27.116 虞舜、孝己，孝顺父母而父母不爱他们；比干、子胥，

hind, since they condemn the people's practice of obtaining thereby things that do not belong to their social station. If there is apportionment of goods by social station and a sense for what is right, then the whole world will become orderly. If there is neither apportionment nor a sense for what is right, then a single wife and a single concubine will cause chaos.

27. 114

Although everyone in the world has his own individual ideas, there are nonetheless points of common agreement. When discussing matters of taste of food, the point of agreement is Yiya;for musical tones it is Master Kuang;for good government it is the Three Kings. Immediately after the Three Kings had fixed their laws and standards, regulated ritual and music and transmitted them, there were no further alterations made by individuals. How could one use something that would modify the blended flavors of a Yiya or revise the pitch pipes of Master Kuang!Since they do not observe the model of the Three Kings, the world awaits its impending doom and nations await their demise.

27. 115

What drinks but does not eat is the *chan* cicada. What neither drinks nor eats is the *fouyou* mayfly.

27. 116

Shun of the Yu dynasty and Filial Yi observed their filial duties, but their parents did not love them. Bigan and [Wu] Zixu were loyal subjects,

【原文】

仲尼、颜渊，知而穷于世。劫迫于暴国而无所辟之，则崇其善，扬其美，言其所长，而不称其所短也。

27.117 惟惟而亡者，诽也；博而穷者，訾也；清之而俞浊者，口也。

27.118 君子能为可贵，不能使人必贵己；能为可用，不能使人必用己。

27.119 诰誓不及五帝，盟诅不及三王，交质子不及五伯。

【今译】

忠于君主而君主不任用他们；孔子、颜渊，明智通达而在社会上穷困窘迫。被迫生活在暴君统治的国家中而又没有办法避开这种处境，那就应该崇尚他的善行，宣扬他的美德，称道他的长处，而不宣扬他的短处。

27.117 唯唯诺诺却导致死亡的，是由于他诽谤人；知识渊博而处境困厄的，是由于他诋毁人；澄清它而愈来愈混浊的，是由于他搬弄口舌。

27.118 君子能够做到可以被人尊重，但不能使别人一定尊重自己；能够做到可以被人任用，但不能使别人一定任用自己。

27.119 向下发布告诫的命令与誓言，追溯不到五帝；两国之间结盟誓约，追溯不到三王；君主互相交换自己的儿子作为人质，追溯不到五霸。

but their lords would not use them. Confucius and Yan Hui were wise, but their generation left them in dire poverty. When you find yourself detained and harassed in a cruel and violent land with no means of escape, then heap praise on its good qualities, disply its fine points, discuss its strengths, but do not mention its shortcomings.

27. 117

Despite "going along"with whatever they hear, they are doomed to perish, because they are malicious.

For all their breadth of knowledge, they are reduced to poverty because of their penchant for slander. For all their appearance of personal probity, they sink further into corruption because they revile others.

27. 118

The gentleman can do what is honorable, but he cannot cause others to be certain to show him honor. He can act so that he is employable, but he cannot cause others to be certain to use him.

27. 119

"Announcements" and "Speeches" do not extend back to the Five Di Ancestors!"Covenants" and "Oaths with Imprecations" do not reach back to the Three Kings. Relations based on pledges of goods and exchanges of hostages do not reach back to the Five Lords-Protector.

宥坐第二十八

【原文】

28.1 孔子观于鲁桓公之庙，有欹器焉。孔子问于守庙者曰："此为何器？"守庙者曰："此盖为宥坐之器。"孔子曰："吾闻宥坐之器者，虚则欹，中则正，满则覆。"孔子顾谓弟子曰："注水焉！"弟子挹水而注之。中而正，满而覆，虚而欹。孔子喟然而叹曰："吁！恶有满而不覆者哉？"

子路曰："敢问持满有道乎？"孔子曰："聪明圣知，守之以愚；功被天下，守之以让；勇力抚世，守之以怯；富有四海，守之以谦。此

【今译】

28.1 孔子在鲁桓公的庙里参观，看到有一只倾斜的器皿在那里。孔子问守庙的人说："这是什么器皿？"守庙的人说："这大概是君主放在座位右边来警戒自己的器皿。"孔子说："我听说放在君主座位右边的这种器皿，空着就会倾斜，灌入一半水就会端正，灌满水就会翻倒。"孔子回头对学生说："向里面灌水吧！"学生舀了水去灌它。灌了一半就端正了，灌满后就翻倒了，空了就倾斜着。孔子感慨地叹息说："唉！哪有满了不翻倒的呢？"

子路说："我大胆地想问一下保持满有什么方法吗？"孔子说："聪明圣智，要用笨拙来保持它；功劳惠及天下，要用谦让来保持它；勇敢有力而能压住世人，要用胆怯来保持它；富足得拥有了天下，要用

Book 28

The Warning Vessel on the Right

28. 1

When Confucius was inspecting the ancestral temple of Duke Huan of Lu [r. 711—694], there was a vessel that inclined to one side. Confucius questioned the temple caretaker about it: "What kind of vessel is this?"

The caretaker replied: "I believe it is the warning vessel that sat on the right."

Confucius said: "I have heard of such a warning vessel: if empty, it inclines; if half full, it is upright, and if completely full, it overturns." Turning to his disciples, he continued:"Pour some water in it."

His disciples drew off some water and poured it into the vessel. When it was half filled, it became upright; when it was completely filled, it overturned; and when empty, it again inclined.

Confucius sighed deeply and exclaimed:"Alas!How indeed could there be complete fullness and no overturning!"

Zilu said:"May I ask whether there is a way to maintain complete fullness?"

Confucius replied:{"The way of maintaining complete fullness is to reduce by ladling out."

Zilu said:"Is there a way to 'reduce by ladling out?'"

Confucius replied} : "Brilliant intelligence and sage-like knowledge should be guarded by the appearance of stupidity; meritorious achievements covering the whole empire should be guarded by an attitude of deference; courageous power comforting the age should be guarded by fear;

【原文】

所谓挹而损之之道也。”

28.2 孔子为鲁摄相，朝七日而诛少正卯。门人进问曰：“夫少正卯，鲁之闻人也。夫子为政而始诛之，得无失乎？”

孔子曰：“居!吾语女其故。人有恶者五，而盗窃不与焉：一曰心达而险，二曰行辟而坚，三曰言伪而辩，四曰记丑而博，五曰顺非而泽。此五者，有一于人，则不得免于君子之诛，而少正卯兼有之。故居处足以聚徒成群，言谈足以饰邪营众，强足以反是独立，此小人之桀雄也，不可不诛也。是以汤诛尹谐，文王诛潘止，周公诛管叔，太

【今译】

节俭来保持它。这就是所谓的抑制并贬损满的方法啊。”

28.2 孔子做鲁国的代理宰相，上朝听政才七天就杀了少正卯。他的学生进来问孔子说：“那少正卯，是鲁国的名人啊。先生当政而先把他杀了，该没有弄错吧？”

孔子说：“坐下!我告诉你其中的缘故。人有五种罪恶的行为，而盗窃不包括在里面：一是脑子精明而用心险恶，二是行为邪僻而又顽固，三是说话虚伪却很动听，四是记述丑恶的东西而十分广博，五是顺从错误而又加以润色。这五种罪恶，在一个人身上只要有一种，就不能免掉君子的杀戮，而少正卯却同时具有这五种罪恶。他居住下来就足够聚集门徒而成群结队，他的言谈足够用来掩饰邪恶而迷惑众人，他的刚强足够用来反对正确的东西而独立自主，这是小人中的豪杰，是不可不杀的。因此商汤杀了尹谐，周文王杀了潘止，周公旦杀

and riches encompassing all within the four seas should be guarded by frugality. This is what is called the Way of 'drawing off and reducing.'"

28. 2

When Confucius acted temporarily as prime minister of Lu, he had been at court but seven days when he executed Deputy Mao. His disciples came forward to ask him about it, saying:"Deputy Mao is a famous man in Lu. You, Master, have just begun to exercise the government, and as your first act of punishment you execute him. How will you not lose the support of the people?"

Confucius replied:"Sit there, and I will tell you the reason. Humans act in five ways that are detestable—and robbing and thieving are not among them. The first is called a mind of penetrating cleverness devoted to treachery. The second is called peculiar conduct engaged in with obstinate persistence. The third is called false teachings defended with discrimination. The fourth is called a memory that is comprehensive but recalls only wickedness. The fifth is called obediently following what is wrong while glossing over it. If even one of these characterizes a man, then he cannot avoid punishment by a gentleman. But Deputy Mao possessed all of them at the same time. Thus, in his private life he had sufficient means to gather about him followers who operated effectively as a group. In his speech and discussions he was good enough to gloss over his depravity and bedazzle the masses. His strength was such that he could turn against what was right and stand alone. For these reasons he became the 'swaggering hero' of petty men, and it was impossible that he should go unpunished. It was for just such reasons that Tang punished Yinxie, King Wen punished Panzhi, the Duke of Zhou punished

【原文】

公诛华仕，管仲诛付里乙，子产诛邓析、史付。此七子者，皆异世同心，不可不诛也。《诗》曰：‘忧心悄悄，愠于群小。’小人成群，斯足忧矣。”

28.3 孔子为鲁司寇，有父子讼者，孔子拘之，三月不别。其父请止，孔子舍之。季孙闻之，不说，曰：“是老也欺予，语予曰：‘为国家必以孝。’今杀一人以戮不孝，又舍之。”冉子以告。

孔子慨然叹曰：“呜呼！上失之，下杀之，其可乎？不教其民而听其狱，杀不辜也。三军大败，不可斩也；狱犴不治，不可刑也；罪不

【今译】

了管叔，姜太公杀了华仕，管仲杀了付里乙，子产杀了邓析、史付。这七个人，都是处在不同的时代而有同样的邪恶心肠，是不能不杀的。《诗》云：‘忧愁之心多凄楚，被群小人所怨怒。’小人成了群，那就值得忧虑了。”

28.3 孔子做鲁国的司法大臣，有父子之间打官司的，孔子拘留了儿子，三个月了也不加判决。他的父亲请求停止诉讼，孔子就把他的儿子释放了。季桓子听说了这件事，很不高兴，说：“这位老先生啊欺骗我，他曾告诉我说：‘治理国家一定要用孝道。’现在只要杀掉一个人就可以使不孝之子感到羞辱，却又把他放了。”冉求把这些话告诉了孔子。

孔子感慨地叹息说：“唉呀！君主丢了正确的政治原则，臣下把他们都杀了，那行么？不去教育民众而只是判决他们的诉讼，这是在屠杀无罪的人啊。全军大败，不可以统统斩首；监狱方面的事情没有治

Guan and Cai, the Grand Duke punished Huashi, Guan Zhong punished Fuliyi, and Prince Chan [of Zheng] punished (Deng Xi and) Shi He. These seven men, although they lived in different ages, shared a common frame of mind, so it was impossible that they should go unpunished. An *Ode* says:

My sorrowful heart is pained, pained,
I am hated by that herd of petty men.

When petty men congregate and work effectively as a group, this is cause enough for sorrow."

28. 3

When Confucius was director of crime in Lu, there was a father and son who had a legal dispute pending before the court. Confucius put the son in prison and for three months did not resolve the matter. When the father requested permission to stop the proceedings, Confucius released the son.

[The head of the] Ji family, hearing about the matter was displeased and remarked:"The venerable one has deceived me. He told me that one must use filial piety to govern the nation. Now when he should execute a single man in order to make an example of this unfilial conduct, he goes and releases him."

When [the disciple] Master Ran related this to Confucius, he sighed deeply and exclaimed:"Alas!When superiors fail to execute subordinates on account of it—is that proper!Not having instructed the people and yet to decide criminal prosecutions against them is to kill the innocent. Just as when the three armies have been disastrously defeated, it is improper to behead them, so too when matters of litigation that lead to imprisonment

【原文】

在民故也。嫚令谨诛，贼也；今生也有时，敛也无时，暴也；不教而责成功，虐也。已此三者，然后刑可即也。《书》曰：‘义刑义杀，勿庸以即，予维曰：未有顺事。’言先教也。

“故先王既陈之以道，上先服之。若不可，尚贤以綦之；若不可，废不能以单之。綦三年而百姓往矣。邪民不从，然后俟之以刑，则民知罪矣。《诗》曰：‘尹氏大师，维周之氐。秉国之均，四方是维。天子是庳，卑民不迷。’是以威厉而不试，刑错而不用。此之谓也。

【今译】

理好，不可以施加刑罚；因为罪责不在民众身上的缘故啊。放松法令而严加惩处，这是残害；那作物生长有一定的季节，而征收赋税却不时在进行，这是残酷；不进行教育却要求成功，这是暴虐。制止了这三种行为，然后刑罚才可以施加到人们身上。《尚书》上说：‘按照合宜的原则用刑，按照合宜的原则杀人，不要拿刑罚来迁就自己的心意，我们只能说：自己还没有把事情理顺。’这是说要先进行教育啊。

“所以古代的圣王已经把政治原则向民众宣布后，自己就先遵行它。如果不能做到这一点，就推崇贤德的人来教导民众；如果不能做到这一点，就废黜无能的人来畏慑民众。至多三年，百姓就都趋向于圣王的政治原则了。奸邪的人不依从，然后才用刑罚来等待他们，那么人们就知道他们的罪过了。因此刑罚的威势虽然厉害却可以不用，刑罚可以搁置一边而不实施。《诗》云：‘尹太师啊尹太师，你是周室的基石。掌握国家的政权，四方靠你来维持。天子由你来辅佐，要使民众不迷失。’于是，权威严正而不发作，刑罚设置而不施行。说的

are not well ordered, it is improper to apply the punishments because the real blame does not lie with the people. To issue orders in an offhand manner, but to be punctilious in matters of punishment is an outrage against the people. When all living things have their season, to make exactions without regard to the season constitutes oppression. Not to instruct the people, yet to require from them completion of allotted tasks constitutes cruelty. It is only when these three practices have been ended that punishments may be considered. One of the *Documents* says:

> Punishments should be just and executions just. Do not follow your own notions in this. Rather, say only:'I have not as yet achieved full obedience in my tasks.'

This says that instruction should precede."

Thus, the Ancient Kings, having proclaimed their Way before their subjects, led the way in attaining it. If it still could not be attained, they would honor the worthy in order to teach them. If it still could not be attained, they cast down those who were incapable in order to strike fear into them. When a full three years had passed, the Hundred Clans followed their transforming influence. If depraved people would not follow, only after all this has been done, did they apply the punishments, so that then the people would realize the nature of their crime. An *Ode* says:

> O Grand Preceptor Yin
> be the base of Zhou,
> be the balance of the nation,
> unify our Four Regions.
> Our Son of Heaven—you must support him
> so as to prevent the people from going astray.

For these reasons, Let your majestic authority be stern and fierce, but do not wield it. Let your punishments be established, but do not use them.

【原文】

"今之世则不然。乱其教，繁其刑，其民迷惑而堕焉，则从而制之，是以刑弥繁而邪不胜。三尺之岸而虚车不能登也，百仞之山任负车登焉，何则？陵迟故也。数仞之墙而民不逾也，百仞之山而竖子冯而游焉，陵迟故也。今夫世之陵迟亦久矣，而能使民勿逾乎？《诗》曰：'周道如砥，其直如矢。君子所履，小人所视。眷焉顾之，潸焉出涕。'岂不哀哉？"

28.4《诗》曰："瞻彼日月，悠悠我思。道之云远，曷云能来。"

【今译】

就是这个道理啊。

"现在的社会却不是这样。君主把教化搞得混乱不堪，把刑法搞得五花八门，当民众迷惑糊涂而落入法网，就紧接着制裁他们，因此刑罚虽然更加繁多而邪恶却不能被克服。三尺高的陡壁，就是空车也不能上去；上百丈的高山，有负荷的车也能拉上去，什么道理呢？是因为坡度平缓的缘故啊。几丈高的墙，人不能越过；上百丈的高山，小孩也能登上去游玩，这也是坡度平缓的缘故啊。现在社会上类似坡度平缓的现象也已出现好久了，能使人不越轨吗？《诗》云：'大路平如磨刀石，它的笔直像箭杆。它是贵人走的路，百姓只能抬头看。回头看啊回头看，刷刷流泪糊了眼。'这难道不可悲吗？"

28.4《诗》云："看那日子过得快，深深思念在我怀。道路又是那

This expresses my point.

Now in the present generation this is no longer so. So chaotic is the instruction and so abundant are the punishments, that the people are led astray and bewildered and they fall into error for which they are then to be punished. On account of this, although punishments are frequently and abundantly applied, evil is not overcome. A sheer obstacle only three feet high cannot be surmounted even by an empty carriage, whereas a hill a hundred rods high can be surmounted even by a heavily loaded one. Why is that?It is because of the slow ascent. People cannot climb a wall several rods high, but a mountain a hundred rods high, small boys will trample and play upon, and the reason for this is its gentle ascent. Now the slow erosion that we find in the present generation has also been going on a long time, so how could it not cause the people to "climb over"? An *Ode* says:

> The road to Royal Zhou is smooth like a whetstone,
> it is straight as an arrow.
> That is where the gentleman should tread;
> where the petty man should look.
> I look back toward it with longing,
> my tears streaming down.

How can one not be moved to pity by this!

28. 4

An *Ode* says:

> I gaze at that sun and that moon,
> brooding, brooding in thought of you.
> The road being so long, so long,
> when can you come?

【原文】

子曰："伊稽首不？其有来乎？"

28.5 孔子观于东流之水。子贡问于孔子曰："君子之所以见大水必观焉者，是何？"孔子曰："夫水大，遍与诸生而无为也，似德；其流也埤下，裾拘必循其理，似义；其洸洸乎不淈尽，似道；若有决行之，其应佚若声响，其赴百仞之谷不惧，似勇；主量必平，似法；盈不求概，似正；淖约微达，似察；以出以入，以就鲜洁，似善化；其万折也必东，似志。是故君子见大水必观焉。"

【今译】

么远，他又怎么能回来？"孔子说："她磕头了没有？他又回来了吗？"

28.5 孔子观赏向东流去的河水。子贡问孔子说："君子看见浩大的流水就一定要观赏它，这是为什么？"孔子说："那流水浩大，普遍地施舍给各种生物而无所作为，好像德；它流动起来向着低下的地方，弯弯曲曲一定遵循那向下流动的规律，好像义；它浩浩荡荡没有穷尽，好像道；如果有人掘开堵塞物而使它通行，它随即奔腾向前，好像回声应和原来的声音一样，它奔赴上百丈深的山谷也不怕，好像勇敢；它注入量器时一定很平，好像法度；它注满量器后不需要用刮板刮平，好像公正；它柔和地无处不到，好像明察；各种东西在水里出来进去地淘洗，便渐趋鲜美洁净，好像善于教化；它千曲万折而一定向东流去，好像意志。所以君子看见浩大的流水一定要观赏它。"

The Master said:"When they bow their heads to the ground, how could there not be a 'coming.'"

28. 5

Confucius was once gazing at the water flowing eastward. Zigong questioned Confucius about it, saying: "Why is it that whenever a gentleman sees a great stream, he feels the necessity to contemplate?"

Confucius replied: "Ah! Water—it bestows itself everywhere, on all living things, yet there is no assertion:in this it resembles inner power. Its direction of flow is to descend toward the low ground and whether its course is winding or straight, it necessarily follows its natural principle: in this it resembles morality. {Things float along on its surface and its depths cannot be fathomed: in this it resembles knowledge.} Its vast rushing waters are neither subdued nor exhausted: in this it resembles the Way. If there should be anything that blocks its course, its response will be to react against it, like a reverberating echo. It will travel through chasms a hundred rods deep fearlessly: in this it seems as though it had courage. Led to an empty place, it is sure to make itself level: in this it resembles the law. It will fill something completely and not require a leveling stick: in this it resembles rectitude. Indulgent and restrained while penetrating into the subtlest matters: in this it resembles scrutiny. As it comes and goes, it accommodates itself [to whatever impurities enter it], renewing and purifying them: in this it resembles the transforming power of the good. Through myriad turns and twists its course is certain to flow eastward: in this it resembles the mind with a sense of purpose. It is for such reasons that whenever the gentleman sees a great stream he feels the necessity of contemplating it."

【原文】

28.6 孔子曰："吾有耻也，吾有鄙也，吾有殆也。幼不能强学，老无以教之，吾耻之。去其故乡，事君而达，卒遇故人，曾无旧言，吾鄙之。与小人处者，吾殆之也。"

28.7 孔子曰："如垤而进，吾与之；如丘而止，吾已矣。今学曾未如肬赘，则具然欲为人师。"

28.8 孔子南适楚，厄于陈、蔡之间，七日不火食，藜羹不糂，弟子皆有饥色。子路进问之曰："由闻之：'为善者，天报之以福；为不善者，天报之以祸。'今夫子累德、积义、怀美，行之日久矣，奚居

【今译】

28.6 孔子说："我对有的事有耻辱感，我对有的事有卑鄙感，我对有的事有危险感。年幼时不能努力学习，老了没有什么东西可以用来教给别人，我以为这是耻辱。离开自己的故乡，侍奉君主而显贵了，突然碰到过去的朋友，竟然没有怀旧的话，我以为这是卑鄙的。和小人混在一起，我以为这是危险的"。

28.7 孔子说："成绩即使像蚂蚁洞口的小土堆一样微小，但只要向前进取，我就赞许他；成绩即使像大土山一样大，但如果停止不前了，我就不赞许了。现在有些人学到的东西还不如个赘疣，却自满自足地想做别人的老师。"

28.8 孔子向南到楚国去，困在陈国、蔡国之间，七天没吃熟食，野菜羹中不搀一点米，学生们都有挨饿的脸色。子路前来问孔子说："仲由我听说：'行善的人，上天用幸福报答他；作恶的人，上天用灾祸报复他。'现在先生积累功德，不断奉行道义，怀有美好的理想，

28. 6

Confucius said: "I hold some things shameful, others despicable, and still others dangerous. When young to be incapable of studying hard so that in old age one lacks the means to instruct others—this I hold shameful. When a person, having left his ancestral home, succeeds in the service of his lord, but when encountering old acquaintances does not exchange reminiscences about past relations—this I despise. To accommodate oneself to the life pattern of petty men—this I consider dangerous."

28. 7

Confucius said:"When a person's studies are progressing, like an anthill being raised, I offer my assistance. But if his studies have ceased, like hillock that is complete, I desist."

Now where one's study has not reached its conclusion, self-satisfiedly wanting to teach others is like the case of a tumor or excrescence.

28. 8

When Confucius was traveling southward toward Chu, he was reduced to straits between Chen and Cai. When after seven days he and his disciples had not eaten hot food, only a soup of goosefoot greens with not a single grain of rice, the disciples all had a hungry look. Zilu stepped forward and asked:"According to what I have been taught, Heaven bestows good fortune on those who do good and disasters on those who do what is not good. Now you, our Master, have for a long time aug-

【原文】

之隐也？”

孔子曰：“由不识，吾语女。女以知者为必用邪？王子比干不见剖心乎！女以忠者为必用邪？关龙逢不见刑乎！女以谏者为必用邪？伍子胥不磔姑苏东门外乎！夫遇不遇者，时也；贤不肖者，材也；君子博学深谋不遇时者多矣！由是观之，不遇世者众矣！何独丘也哉？且夫芷兰生于深林，非以无人而不芳。君子之学，非为通也，为穷而不困，忧而意不衰也，知祸福终始而心不惑也。夫贤不肖者，材也；为不为者，人也；遇不遇者，时也；死生者，命也。今有其人不遇其时，虽贤，其能行乎？苟遇其时，何难之有？故君子博学深谋，修身端行，

【今译】

行善的日子很久了，为什么处境这样窘迫呢？”

孔子说：“仲由你不懂，我告诉你吧。你认为有才智的人是一定会被任用的吗？王子比干不是被剖腹挖心了吗！你认为忠诚的人是一定会被任用的吗？关龙逢不是被杀了吗！你认为劝谏的人是一定会被任用的吗？伍子胥不是在姑苏城的东门之外被碎尸了吗！是得到君主的赏识还是得不到君主的赏识，这要靠时机；有德才还是没有德才，这是各人的资质了；君子博学多识而能深谋远虑却碰不到时机的多着呢！由此看来，不被社会赏识的人是很多的了！哪里只是我孔丘呢？再说白芷兰草长在深山老林之中，并非因为没有人赏识就不香了。君子学习，并不是为了显贵，而是为了在不得志的时候不至于困窘，在碰到忧患的时候意志不至于衰退，懂得祸福死生的道理而心里不迷惑。有德才还是没有德才，在于资质；是做还是不做，在于人；是得到赏识还是得不到赏识，在于时机；是死还是生，在于命运。现在有了理想的人才却碰不到理想的时机，那么即使贤能，他能有所作为吗？如果碰到了理想的时机，那还有什么困难呢？所以君子广博地学

mented your inner power through your daily conduct, accumulated acts of moral good, and cherished the beautiful. Why, then, do you live in obscurity?"

Confucius replied: "You, you have not remembered what I told you. Did you imagine that the wise are certain to be employed? But did not Prince Bigan have his heart cut out! Did you imagine that the loyal are sure to be used? But did not Guan Longfeng endure punishment! Did you imagine that those who reprove are always followed?But was not Wu Zixu slashed apart and put outside the eastern gate of Gusu! From this it can be seen that those who have not met with the right time are legion. How am I unique in this regard?

"Whether one meets with opportunity depends on the time;whether one becomes a worthy depends on innate ability. Gentlemen of broad learning and profound plans who did not meet with the right time are numerous.

"Further, consider the orchid and angelica that grow deep in the forest: that there is no one to smell them does not mean that they are not fragrant. The studies of the gentleman are not undertaken in order to be successful, but so that in poverty he will not be beset with hardship, that in times of anxiety his sense of purpose will not diminish, and that by knowing fortune and misfortune, ends and beginnings, his heart will not suffer illusions. Just as whether one is worthy depends on innate ability, whether one acts or not depends on the man; just as whether one meets with success depends on the right time, so too matters of death and life depend on fate. Now if a man has not met with the right time, even though he is worthy, how would he be able to put [his ideas] into practice? If he should chance to meet with the right time, what difficulties would he have? Thus, the gentleman broadens his studies, deepens his

【原文】

以俟其时。"

孔子曰:"由!居!吾语女。昔晋公子重耳霸心生于曹,越王句践霸心生于会稽,齐桓公小白霸心生于莒。故居不隐者思不远,身不佚者志不广。女庸安知吾不得之桑落之下?"

28.9 子贡观于鲁庙之北堂,出而问于孔子曰:"乡者赐观于太庙之北堂,吾亦未辍,还复瞻被九盖,皆继,彼有说邪?匠过绝邪?"孔子曰:"太庙之堂亦尝有说,官致良工,因丽节文,非无良材也,盖曰贵文也。"

【今译】

习,深入地谋划,修养心身,端正品行来等待时机。"

孔子又说:"仲由!坐下!我告诉你。从前晋公子重耳的称霸之心产生于流亡途中的曹国,越王勾践的称霸之心产生于被围困的会稽山,齐桓公小白的称霸之心产生于逃亡之处莒国。所以处境不窘迫的人想得就不远,自己没奔逃过的人志向就不广大,你怎么知道我在这叶子枯落的桑树底下就不能得意呢?"

28.9 子贡参观了鲁国宗庙的北堂,出来后问孔子说:"刚才我参观了太庙的北堂,我也没停步,回转去再观看那九扇门,都是拼接的,那有什么讲究吗?是因为木匠过失而把木料弄断的吗?"孔子说:"太庙的北堂当然是有讲究的,官府招来技艺精良的工匠,依靠木材本身的华丽来调节文采,这并不是没有好的大木头。大概是因为看重文采的缘故吧。"

plans, reforms his person, and corrects his conduct in order to await his right time."

Confucius said again: "Zilu, sit down, and I will tell you. In the past Chonger, the son of the duke of Jin, conceived his ambition to become lord-protector because of the events in Cao.King Goujian of Yue conceived his ambition to become lord-protector because of the events at Kuaiji.Xiaobai, the future Duke Huan of Qi, conceived his ambition to become lord-protector because of the events at Ju.One who does not live in obscurity does not reflect on distant prospects;one who does not endure personal hardship does not have goals with wide aims.In what way do you know that I am unsuccessful here by the Sangluo?"

28. 9

Zigong, having inspected the north pavilion of the ancestral temple of Lu, proceeded to go and ask Confucius about it:"Just a moment ago, I was inspecting the north pavilion of the great ancestral temple.Just as I was about to finish, I look a second time and noticed that the north doors were both cut off.Does that have some proper cxplanation, or did the carpenters simply saw off too much?"

Confucius responded:"Since it is the pavilion of the grand ancestral temple, of course, it has an explanation.The officers in charge employed the best craftsmen, who utilized their skill to make it beautiful and to regulate its design.It was not because of a lack of skilled craftsmen or of good materials.Probably I should say that it was a matter of prizing this design."

子道第二十九

【原文】

29.1 入孝出弟，人之小行也。上顺下笃，人之中行也。从道不从君，从义不从父，人之大行也。若夫志以礼安，言以类使，则儒道毕矣；虽舜，不能加毫末于是矣。

29.2 孝子所以不从命有三：从命则亲危，不从命则亲安，孝子不从命乃衷；从命则亲辱，不从命则亲荣，孝子不从命乃义；从命则禽兽，不从命则修饰，孝子不从命乃敬。故可以从而不从，是不子

【今译】

29.1 在家孝敬父母，出外敬爱兄长，这是人的小德。对上顺从，对下厚道，这是人的中德。顺从正道而不顺从君主，顺从道义而不顺从父亲，这是人的大德。至于那志向根据礼义来安排，说话根据法度来措辞，那么儒家之道也就完备了；即使是舜，也不能在这上面有丝毫的增益了。

29.2 孝子不服从命令的原因有三种：服从命令，父母亲就会危险，不服从命令，父母亲就安全，那么孝子不服从命令就是忠诚；服从命令，父母亲就会受到耻辱，不服从命令，父母亲就光荣，那么孝子不服从命令就是奉行道义；服从命令，就行为像禽兽一样野蛮，不

Book 29

On the Way of Sons

29. 1

Inside the home to be filial toward one's parents and outside the home to be properly courteous toward one's elders constitute the minimal standard of human conduct. To be obedient to superiors and to be reliable in one's dealing with inferiors constitute a higher standard of conduct. To follow the dictates of the Way rather than those of one's lord and to follow the requirements of morality rather than the wishes of one's father constitute the highest standard of conduct. When the inner mind finds contentment with ritual principles and when speech is closely connected to categories encompassed in ritual, then the Way of the Ru is fully realized. Even a Shun would be incapable of adding even so much as the breadth of a single hair to this.

29. 2

Of filial sons who do not follow the course of action mandated by their fathers, there are three types.If following the mandated course would bring peril to his family whereas not following it would bring security, then the filial son who does not follow his commission still acts with true loyalty. If following his mandated course would bring disgrace on his family whereas not following it would bring honor, then in not following the mandated course he still acts morally. If following the mandated course would cause him to act like a savage whereas not following it would

【原文】

也；未可以从而从，是不衷也。明于从不从之义，而能致恭敬、忠信、端悫以慎行之，则可谓大孝矣。传曰："从道不从君，从义不从父。"此之谓也。故劳苦凋萃而能无失其敬，灾祸患难而能无失其义，则不幸不顺见恶而能无失其爱，非仁人莫能行。《诗》曰："孝子不匮。"此之谓也。

29.3 鲁哀公问于孔子曰："子从父命，孝乎？臣从君命，贞乎？"三问，孔子不对。

孔子趋出，以语子贡曰："乡者，君问丘也，曰：'子从父命，孝

【今译】

服从命令，就富有修养而端正，那么孝子不服从命令就是恭敬。所以可以服从而不服从，这是不尽孝子之道；不可以服从而服从，这是不忠于父母。明白了这服从或不服从的道理，并且能做到恭敬尊重、忠诚守信、正直老实地来谨慎实行它，就可以称之为大孝了。古书上说："顺从正道而不顺从君主，顺从道义而不顺从父亲。"说的就是这个道理。所以劳苦憔悴时能够不丧失对父母的恭敬，遭到灾祸患难时能够不丧失对父母应尽的道义，即使不幸地因为和父母不顺而被父母憎恶时仍能不丧失对父母的爱，如果不是仁德之人是不能做到的。《诗》云："孝子之孝无穷尽。"说的就是这个道理。

29.3 鲁哀公问孔子说："儿子服从父亲的命令，就是孝顺吗？臣子服从君主的命令，就是忠贞吗？"问了三次，孔子不回答。

孔子小步快走而出，把这件事告诉给子贡说："刚才，国君问我，

cultivate and improve him, then in not following it he still acts with proper reverence. Hence, if it were possible to have followed the course, not to have done so would constitute not being a proper son.If it were impossible to follow the course, to have done so would be disloyalty. If a son understands the principles of when to follow and when not to follow and is able to be utterly respectful and reverent, loyal and honest, straightforward and diligent, so that he carefully attends his conduct, then he may properly be called "greatly filial." A tradition says:

> Follow the dictates of the Way rather than those of one's lord and follow the requirements of morality rather than the wishes of one's father.

This expresses my meaning.

Hence, if despite toil, suffering, injury, and weariness, you are able to act without losing an attitude of reverence, and if despite calamity, misfortune, disasters, and difficulties, you are able to act without losing your sense of what is right, then if by misfortune you meet with disappointment and are disliked, you will be able to act without losing their love for you.None but the humane man can so behave.An *Ode* says:

> A filial son never finishes his duty.

This expresses my meaning.

29. 3

Duke Ai of Lu questioned Confucius, saying: "Does a son by following the course of action mandated by his father behave filially? Does a minister by following the commands of his lord behave with integrity?" Three times he posed the question, but Confucius did not reply.

Confucius, with hastened steps, departed and discussed the matter

【原文】

乎？臣从君命，贞乎？'三问而丘不对，赐以为何如？"

子贡曰："子从父命，孝矣；臣从君命，贞矣。夫子有奚对焉？"孔子曰："小人哉，赐不识也！昔万乘之国有争臣四人，则封疆不削；千乘之国有争臣三人，则社稷不危；百乘之家有争臣二人，则宗庙不毁。父有争子，不行无礼；士有争友，不为不义。故子从父，奚子孝？臣从君，奚臣贞？审其所以从之之谓孝，之谓贞也。"

29.4 子路问于孔子曰："有人于此，夙兴夜寐，耕耘树艺，手足胼胝，以养其亲，然而无孝之名，何也？"

【今译】

说：'儿子服从父亲的命令，就是孝顺吗？臣子服从君主的命令，就是忠贞吗？'问了三次而我不回答，你认为怎样？"

子贡说："儿子服从父亲的命令，就是孝顺了；臣子服从君主的命令，就是忠贞了。先生又能怎样回答他呢？"

孔子说："真是个小人，你不懂啊！从前拥有万辆兵车的大国有了诤谏之臣四个，那么疆界就不会被割削；拥有千辆兵车的小国有了诤谏之臣三个，那么国家政权就不会危险；拥有百辆兵车的大夫之家有了诤谏之臣两个，那么宗庙就不会毁灭。父亲有了诤谏的儿子，就不会做不合礼制的事；士人有了诤谏的朋友，就不会做不合道义的事。所以儿子一味听从父亲，怎能说这儿子是孝顺？臣子一味听从君主，怎能说这臣子是忠贞？弄清楚了听从的是什么才可以叫做孝顺，叫做忠贞。"

29.4 子路问孔子说："这里有个人，早起晚睡，耕地锄草栽植播种，手脚都磨出了老茧，以此来赡养自己的父母，却没有孝顺的名

with Zigong. "Just now our lord asked me, Qiu, whether a son by following the course of action mandated by his father acts filially and whether a minister by following the commands of his lord acts with integrity. Three times he posed the question and three times I did not respond. What, Ci, do you think I should have done?"

Zigong said: "A son who follows his father's instructions is indeed filial and a minister who follows his lord's commands does indeed act with integrity. Why did the Master not reply thusly?"

Confucius rejoined: "Ci, you are a petty man! You do not grasp the point! In the past, when a state of ten thousand chariots possessed four remonstrating servants, the border territories of that state would not be encroached upon. When a state of a thousand chariots had three remonstrating servants, its altars of soil and grain were not imperiled. When a family of a hundred chariots possessed two remonstrating servants, its ancestral shrine was not overturned. When a father had a remonstrating son, then nothing in his conduct lacked ritual principles. When a knight had remonstrating friends, he did not act against the requirements of morality. Accordingly, if a son merely follows his father, how is that son behaving filially? And, if a minister merely follows his lord, how is he behaving with integrity? You must carefully judge the manner of his 'following' before it can be described as 'filial' or as marked by 'integrity.'"

29. 4

Zilu questioned Confucius, saying: "Consider the case of the man who gets up at dawn and goes to bed late at night, who plows and weeds, sows and plants, until his hands and feet are thickly calloused in order to

【原文】

孔子曰："意者身不敬与！辞不逊与！色不顺与！古之人有言曰：'衣与缪与，不女聊。'今夙兴夜寐，耕耘树艺，手足胼胝，以养其亲，无此三者，则何为而无孝之名也？意者所友非仁人邪！"

孔子曰："由，志之！吾语女。虽有国士之力，不能自举其身，非无力也，势不可也。故入而行不修，身之罪也；出而名不章，友之过也。故君子入则笃行，出则友贤，何为而无孝之名也？"

29.5 子路问于孔子曰："鲁大夫练而床，礼邪？"孔子曰："吾不知也。"

【今译】

声，为什么呢？"

孔子说："想来大概是他举止不恭敬吧！是他说话不谦虚吧！是他脸色不温顺吧！古代的人有句话说：'给我穿啊给我吃啊，若不恭敬就不靠你。'现在这个人早起晚睡，耕地锄草栽植播种，手脚都磨出了老茧，以此来赡养自己的父母，如果没有举止不恭敬、说话不谦虚、脸色不温顺这三种行为，那为什么会没有孝顺的名声呢？想来大概是他所交的朋友不是个仁德之人吧！"

孔子又说："仲由，记住吧！我告诉你。即使有了全国闻名的大力士的力气，也不能自己举起自己的身体，这不是没有力气，而是客观情势不许可。回到家中品德不修养，是自己的罪过；在外名声不显扬，是朋友的罪过。所以君子在家就使自己的品行忠诚厚道，出外就和贤能的人交朋友，怎么会没有孝顺的名声呢？"

29.5 子路问孔子说："鲁国的大夫披戴白色熟绢为父母进行周年祭祀时睡床，合乎礼吗？"孔子说："我不知道。"

care properly for his parents, yet this man lacks a reputation for filial conduct. Why should this be so?"

Confucius replied: "I surmise that he was personally not properly respectful in his relations with others, that his speech was not conciliatory, or that the expressions on his face indicated a lack of cordiality. The ancients had an expression that said:

You give us clothes, you provide us with everything, but still we can never depend on you."

[Zilu continued]: "But since the man I just mentioned who gets up at dawn and goes to bed late, who plows and weeds, sows and plants, until his hands and feet are thickly calloused to care for his parents lacks these three characteristics, why should he lack a reputation for filial conduct? Do you surmise that his friends are not humane men?"

Confucius replied: "Zilu, remember what I have told you. Even if a man has the strength of a stout warrior of state, he cannot lift his own body. This is not due to any lack of strength; it is the force of circumstances that makes it impossible. Hence, if when he comes home his conduct is not disciplined, then he is himself at fault; if when he is in public, his reputation is not proclaimed, it is the transgression of his friends. It is for this reason that when the gentleman comes home, he is sincere in his conduct, and when he goes out, he befriends worthy men. How then could he not have a reputation for filial conduct?"

29. 5

Zilu questioned Confucius, saying: "The grand officers of Lu wear the bleached mourning cap, but lie on their beds—is this in accord with ritual principles?"

【原文】

子路出，谓子贡曰："吾以夫子为无所不知，夫子徒有所不知。"子贡曰："女何问哉？"子路曰："由问：'鲁大夫练而床，礼邪？'夫子曰：'吾不知也。'"子贡曰："吾将为女问之。"

子贡问曰："练而床，礼邪？"孔子曰："非礼也。"

子贡出，谓子路曰："女谓夫子为有所不知乎？夫子徒无所不知。女问非也。礼，居是邑，不非其大夫。"

29.6 子路盛服见孔子，孔子曰："由，是裾裾，何也？昔者江出于岷山，其始出也，其源可以滥觞，及其至江之津也，不放舟，不避风，则不可涉也，非维下流水多邪？今女衣服既盛，颜色充盈，天下且孰肯谏女矣？由！"

子路趋而出，改服而入，盖犹若也。孔子曰："志之！吾语女。奋

【今译】

子路出来后，对子贡说："我以为先生没有什么不知道，先生却偏偏有不知道的。"子贡说："你问了什么呢？"子路说："我问：'鲁国的大夫披戴白色熟绢为父母进行周年祭祀时睡床，合乎礼吗？'先生说：'我不知道。'"子贡说："我将给你去问问这件事。"

子贡问孔子说："披戴白色熟绢为父母进行周年祭祀时睡床，合乎礼吗？"孔子说："不合礼。"

子贡出来，对子路说："你说先生有不知道的事吗？先生却偏偏没有什么不知道的。你问得不对啊。根据礼制，住在这个城邑，就不非议管辖这城邑的大夫。"

29.6 子路穿戴整齐后去见孔子，孔子说："仲由，这样衣冠楚楚的，为什么呢？从前长江发源于岷山，它开始流出来的时候，源头小得只可以浮起酒杯，等到它流到长江的渡口时，如果不把船并在一起，不避开大风，就不能横渡过去了，这不是因为下游水大的缘故么？现在你衣服已经穿得很庄重，脸上又神气十足，那么天下将有谁肯规劝你呢？仲由！"

子路小步快走而出，换了衣服再进去，不外乎穿得很宽松的样

Confucius replied: "I do not know."

Zilu went out and spoke to Zigong, saying: "I had assumed that there was nothing the Master did not know, but there is at least something that he does not know."

Zigong said: "What did you ask?"

Zilu replied: "I asked whether it was according to ritual principles that the grand officers should wear the bleached mourning cap but lie on their beds, and the Master said that he did not know."

Zigong responded: "I will pose your question," and so he asked: "Is it according to ritual to wear the bleached mourning cap yet lie on the bed?"

Confucius replied: "It is contrary to ritual."

Zigong went out and told Zilu: "Did you really say that there were matters the Master did not know about?It was not that he did not know but that you asked your question wrongly. It is a matter of ritual that one does not condemn the grand officers of the city in which one resides."

29. 6

Zilu appeared before Confucius in full dress. Confucius said: "You, why are you so elaborately dressed? Where it begins, the Yangtze issues from the Min Mountains, and its initial flow at the source can barely fill a goblet.When it reaches the Yangtze Ford, it cannot be crossed except with a raft or boat that avoids windy weather. Is this not because only in its lower course are the waters so abundant? Now in this attire you are so elaborately dressed and your manner so overstuffed and overblown, who in the world would be willing to remonstrate with you?"

Zilu departed with hastened steps and, having changed his attire,

【原文】

于言者华，奋于行者伐。色知而有能者，小人也。故君子知之曰知之，不知曰不知，言之要也；能之曰能之，不能曰不能，行之至也。言要则知，行至则仁。既知且仁，夫恶有不足矣哉？”

29.7 子路入。子曰：“由！知者若何？仁者若何？”子路对曰：“知者使人知己，仁者使人爱己。”子曰：“可谓士矣。”

子贡入。子曰：“赐！知者若何？仁者若何。”子贡对曰：“知者知人，仁者爱人。”子曰：“可谓士君子矣。”

颜渊入。子曰：“回！知者若何？仁者若何？”颜渊对曰：“知者自

【今译】

子。孔子说：“记住！我告诉你。在说话方面趾高气扬的人夸夸其谈，在行动方面趾高气扬的人自我炫耀。从脸色上就能知道他有才能的人，是小人啊。所以君子知道了就说知道，不知道的就说不知道，这是说话的要领；会做的就说会做，不会的就说不会，这是行动的最高准则。说话合乎这要领就是明智，行动合乎这准则就是仁德。既明智又有仁德，哪里还有不足之处了呢？”

29.7 子路进来。孔子说：“仲由！明智的人是怎样的？仁德的人是怎样的？”子路回答说：“明智的人能使别人了解自己，仁德的人能使别人爱护自己。”孔子说：“你可以称为士人了。”

子贡进来。孔子说：“端木赐！明智的人是怎样的？仁德的人是怎样的？”子贡回答说：“明智的人能了解别人，仁德的人能爱护别人。”孔子说：“你可以称为士君子了。”

颜渊进来。孔子说：“颜回！明智的人是怎样的？仁德的人是怎样

returned so that he appeared as before.

Confucius said: "Zilu, remember what I am going to tell you. A person who makes a display of his words is vainglorious, and one who makes a display of his actions flaunts himself. One who puts on the appearance of wisdom and ability is a petty man. Thus, the gentleman when he knows a thing will say that he knows it, and when he does not will admit that he does not—in speech this is the essential matter. When he is able to do something, he says that he can do it, and when he cannot, he admits that he is unable to do it—in action this is the highest standard. When speech is concerned with essential matters, there is wisdom, and when action attains the highest standard, there is true humanity. When there is true humanity as well as wisdom, how could there be any question of inadequacy?"

29. 7

Zilu entered, and the Master said: "Zilu, what is the wise man like and what is the humane man like?"

Zilu replied: "The wise man causes others to know him, and the humane man causes others to love him."

The Master said: "Zilu, you deserve to be called a scholar-knight."

Zigong entered, and the Master said: "Zigong, what is the wise man like, and what is the humane man like?"

Zigong replied: "The wise man knows others, and the humane man loves others."

The Master said: "Zigong, you deserve to be called a scholar and gentleman."

Yan Yuan entered, and the Master said: "Hui, what is the wise man

【原文】

知，仁者自爱。”子曰：“可谓明君子矣。”

29.8 子路问于孔子曰：“君子亦有忧乎？”孔子曰：“君子，其未得也，则乐其意；既已得之，又乐其治。是以有终身之乐，无一日之忧。小人者，其未得也，则忧不得；既已得之，又恐失之。是以有终身之忧，无一日之乐也。”

【今译】

的？”颜渊回答说：“明智的人有自知之明，仁德的人能自尊自爱。”孔子说：“你可以称为贤明君子了。”

29.8 子路问孔子说：“君子也有忧虑吗？”孔子说：“君子，在他还没有得到职位时，就会为自己的抱负而感到高兴；已经得到了职位之后，又会为自己的政绩而感到高兴。因此有一辈子的快乐，而没有一天的忧虑。小人嘛，当他还没有得到职位的时候，就担忧得不到；已经得到了职位之后，又怕失去它。因此有一辈子的忧虑，而没有一天的快乐。”

like, and what is the humane man like?"

Yan Yuan replied: "The wise man knows himself, and the humane man loves himself."

The Master said: "You deserve to be called an enlightened gentleman."

29. 8

Zilu questioned Confucius, saying: "Does the gentleman also have anxieties?"

Confucius responded: "{He does not.Having cultivated his conduct, } should the gentleman not obtain a position, then he takes pleasure in his aspirations.If he has already obtained one, then he takes pleasure that everything is in order with him.It is for this reason that throughout his life he is personally happy and that for not even a single day is he troubled with anxieties.Should the petty man not yet have obtained a position, then he frets over his not having it. If he already has obtained one, then he is consumed with fear that he will lose it.It is for this reason that throughout his life he is anxiety-ridden, and there is not single day he is happy."

法行第三十

【原文】

30.1 公输不能加于绳，圣人莫能加于礼。礼者，众人法而不知，圣人法而知之。

30.2 曾子曰："无内人之疏而外人之亲，无身不善而怨人，无刑已至而呼天。内人之疏而外人之亲，不亦反乎？身不善而怨人，不亦远乎？刑已至而呼天，不亦晚乎？《诗》曰：'涓涓源水，不雝不塞。毂已破碎，乃大其辐。事已败矣，乃重大息。'其云益乎？"

【今译】

30.1 公输班不能超越墨线，圣人不能超越礼制。礼制这种东西，众人遵循它却不懂其所以然，圣人遵循它而且能理解其所以然。

30.2 曾子说："不要疏远家人而亲近外人，不要自己不好而埋怨别人，不要刑罚降临才呼喊上天。疏远家人而亲近外人，不是违背情理了吗？自己不好而埋怨别人，不是舍近求远了吗？刑罚已经临头才呼喊上天，不是悔之已晚了吗？《诗》云：'涓涓细流源头水，不加堵截就不绝。车毂已经全破碎，这才加大那车辐。事情已经失败了，这

Book 30

On the Model for Conduct

30. 1

Gongshu [Ban] was unable to improve on the precision of the blackened marking line. No sage could improve on ritual principles. They are the model for conduct for the common lot of men, although they do not understand them, and are the model for sages, who do understand them.

30. 2

Master Zeng said: "Do not be distant with your close relatives while being intimate with the relatives of strangers. Do not bear resentments against others for your own lack of excellence. Do not call out to Heaven when you have already come to criminal punishment."

{Zigong asked: "How is that?"

Master Zeng replied:} "Being distant with your relatives while being intimate with strangers, is that not the reverse of the proper order? Bearing resentment against others for one's own lack of excellence, is that not preposterous? Calling on Heaven only after you have come to grief, is that not belated? An *Ode* says:

> The clear spring waters bubble up
> nothing can obstruct them, nothing stop them.
> Only when the chariot wheel has shattered
> will they enlarge its spoke.

【原文】

30.3 曾子病，曾元持足。曾子曰：“元，志之！吾语汝。夫鱼鳖鼋鼍犹以渊为浅而堀穴其中；鹰鸢犹以山为卑而增巢其上；及其得也，必以饵。故君子苟能无以利害义，则耻辱亦无由至矣。”

30.4 子贡问于孔子曰：“君子之所以贵玉而贱珉者，何也？为夫玉之少而珉之多邪？”孔子曰：“恶！赐！是何言也！夫君子岂多而贱之，少而贵之哉？夫玉者，君子比德焉：温润而泽，仁也；缜栗而理，知也；坚刚而不屈，义也；廉而不刿，行也；折而不桡，勇也；瑕适

【今译】

才深深长叹息。’这样做有益吗？”

30.3 曾子病得很厉害，曾元抱着他的脚。曾子说：“元，记住！我告诉你。那鱼鳖鼋鼍以为渊池还太浅而在那里面打洞才安身；鹰鸢以为山岭还太低而在那上面筑巢才栖息；它们被人捕获，一定是为钓饵所诱。所以君子如能不因为财利而伤害道义，那么耻辱也就无从到来了。”

30.4 子贡问孔子：“君子珍视宝玉而轻视珉石的原因，是什么呢？是因为宝玉少而珉石多吗？”孔子说：“唉！赐啊！这是什么话啊！君子怎么会因为多了就轻视它，少了就珍视它呢？这宝玉，君子用来比拟品德：它温柔滋润而有光泽，好比仁；它坚硬而有纹理，好比智；它刚强而不屈，好比义；它有棱角而不割伤人，好比行；它即使折断

Only when matters have gone amiss
will they once again increase their repose.
But of what benefit is this!"

30. 3

Once when Master Zeng was ill, Zeng Yuan held his feet.Master Zeng told him: "Yuan, remember well what I am going to tell you. Consider that although fish and turtles, tortoises and alligators, think the depths of water shallow, they dig their nests in their midst, and although wild geese and hawks consider the mountains to be low, they make their nests atop their summits. When men try to get them, they must use some kind of bait. Thus, if the gentleman is able to rid himself of any consideration of profit at the cost of morality, shame and disgrace will never come."

30. 4

Zigong questioned Confucius, saying: "Why does the gentleman prize jade and despise serpentine? Is it because of jade's rarity and the commonness of serpentine?"

Confucius replied: "Shocking, Ci! Why would you say that! Why, indeed, would a real gentleman despise something because it is common and prize something because of its rarity! Jade is a thing the gentleman compares to inner power. It is refined, pleasant, and beneficial, like the principle of humanity. Its veining has regular patterns and an orderly arrangement, like knowledge. It is hard and strong and will not be bent, like morality. It is sharply angular, as though punctili-

【原文】

并见，情也；扣之，其声清扬而远闻，其止辍然，辞也。故虽有珉之雕雕，不若玉之章章。《诗》曰：'言念君子，温其如玉。'此之谓也。"

30.5 曾子曰："同游而不见爱者，吾必不仁也；交而不见敬者，吾必不长也；临财而不见信者，吾必不信也。三者在身，曷怨人？怨人者穷，怨天者无识。失之己而反诸人，岂不亦迂哉？"

30.6 南郭惠子问于子贡曰："夫子之门，何其杂也？"子贡曰："君子正身以俟，欲来者不距，欲去者不止。且夫良医之门多病人，檃栝

【今译】

也不弯曲，好比勇；它的斑点缺陷都暴露在外，好比诚实；敲它，声音清越远扬，戛然而止，好比言辞之美。所以，即使珉石带着彩色花纹，也比不上宝玉那样洁白明亮。《诗》云：'我真想念君子，温和得就像宝玉。'说的就是这道理。"

30.5 曾子说："一起交游却不被人喜爱，那肯定是自己缺乏仁爱；与人交往而不受到尊敬，那必然是自己没有敬重别人；接近财物而得不到信任，那一定是自己没有信用。这三者的原因都在自己身上，怎么能怪怨别人？怪怨别人就会陷入困厄，怪怨上天就是没有见识。过失在于自己却反而去责备别人，岂不是太不切合实际了么？"

30.6 南郭惠子问子贡说："孔夫子的门下，怎么那样混杂呢？"子贡说："君子端正自己的身心来等待求学的人，想来的不拒绝，想走的

ous, yet does not cause injury, like proper conduct. It will break, but will not give way, like true courage. Its flaws and virtues are both visible, like the genuine thing. Strike it and its sounds will ring forth clearly and be heard in the distance, and when they cease, there is a sense of sadness, like modulated speech. Thus, although the serpentine is carved, the result does not equal the natural markings of jade. An *Ode* says:

> I am thinking of my gentleman,
> how refined he looks, like jade.

This expresses my meaning."

30. 5

Master Zeng said: "When I travel the same route as others but I am not loved by them, then I must not be genuinely humane.When I have close contact with others, but they do not respect me, then I must not be respectful of age.When in financial dealings I am not trusted, then I must not be genuinely trustworthy.If these three attributes lie within my own person, how can I bear resentments against others? Those who resent others are reduced to poverty;those who resent Heaven do not learn from experience. Neglecting their own self and resorting to others—is this not wide of the mark indeed!"

30. 6

Master Hui of Nanguo questioned Zigong, saying: "Why is there always such a motley crew at your Master's gate?"

Zigong replied: "The gentleman rectifies himself in order to be

【原文】

之侧多枉木。是以杂也。”

30.7 孔子曰：“君子有三恕：有君不能事，有臣而求其使，非恕也；有亲不能报，有子而求其孝，非恕也；有兄不能敬，有弟而求其听令，非恕也。士明于此三恕，则可以端身矣。

30.8 孔子曰：“君子有三思，而不可不思也。少而不学，长无能也；老而不教，死无思也；有而不施，穷无与也。是故君子少思长，

【今译】

不阻止。况且良医的门前多病人，整形器的旁边多弯木，所以夫子的门下鱼龙混杂啊。”

30.7 孔子说：“君子要有三种推己及人之心：有了君主不能侍奉，有了臣子却要指使他们，这不符合恕道；有了父母不能报答养育之恩，有了子女却要求他们孝顺，这不符合恕道；有了哥哥不能敬重，有了弟弟却要求他们听话，这不符合恕道。读书人明白了这三种推己及人之心，身心就可以端正了。”

30.8 孔子说：“君子有三种考虑，是不可以不考虑的。小时候不学习，长大了就没有才能；老了不教人，死后就没有人怀念；富有时不施舍，贫穷了就没有人周济。因此君子小时候考虑到长大以后的

ready.Those who desire to come are not kept away, and those who desire to leave are not stopped. Further, just as at the gate of a good physician there are many sick people and beside the press-frame there is crooked wood, this is the reason for the motley crew."

30. 7

Confucius said: "The gentleman has three standards for reciprocity. Where a person has a lord whom he is incapable of serving yet expects his own servants to serve him, this is contrary to the requirements of reciprocity. Where a person does not requite the affections of his own parents yet expects his son to strive to be filial toward him, this is contrary to the requirements of reciprocity. Where he has an elder brother whom he is incapable of respecting yet expects his own younger brother to strive to execute his commands, this is contrary to the requirements of reciprocity. If a knight-scholar clearly understands the requirements of reciprocity, then it is possible for him to correct himself."

30. 8

Confucius said: "The gentleman has three matters he reflects on, for it is impermissible that he not consider them. If he does not study when he is young, when he matures he will have no abilities. If when he has grown old he does not teach, then when he dies no one will reflect on his life. If when he has things he does not share them, then when he is in reduced circumstances no one will share with him. It is for precisely these reasons that the gentleman, when young, reflects on the time when

【原文】

则学；老思死，则教；有思穷，则施也。”

【今译】

事，就会学习；老了考虑到死后的景况，就会从事教育；富有时考虑到贫穷的处境，就会施舍。”

he will be mature and so he studies. When the gentleman is old, he reflects on his death and so he teaches. When the gentleman has things, he reflects that there may be times when he lives in reduced circumstances and so shares what he has."

哀公第三十一

【原文】

31.1 鲁哀公问于孔子曰："吾欲论吾国之士与之治国，敢问何如取之邪？"

孔子对曰："生今之世，志古之道；居今之俗，服古之服。舍此而为非者，不亦鲜乎？"

哀公曰："然则夫章甫、绚屦、绅而搢笏者，此贤乎？"

孔子对曰："不必然。夫端衣、玄裳、絻而乘路者，志不在于食荤；斩衰、菅屦、杖而啜粥者，志不在于酒肉。生今之世，志古之道；居今之俗，服古之服。舍此而为非者，虽有，不亦鲜乎？"

哀公曰："善！"

【今译】

31.1 鲁哀公问孔子说："我想选择我国的人才和他们一起治理国家，冒昧地问一下怎样去选取他们呢？"

孔子回答说："生在当今的世上，牢记着古代的原则；处在当今的习俗中，穿着古代式样的服装。做到这样而为非作歹的人，不是很少的吗？"

哀公说："这样的话，那么那些戴着商代式样的礼帽、穿着缚有鞋带的鞋子、束着宽大的腰带并在腰带上插着朝板的人，他们都贤能吗？

孔子回答说："不一定贤能。那些穿着祭祀礼服、黑色礼袍、戴着礼帽而乘坐祭天大车的人，他们的心思不在于吃荤；披麻戴孝、穿着茅草编成的鞋、拄着孝棍而吃稀粥的人，他们的心思不在于喝酒吃肉。生在当今的世上，牢记着古代的原则；处在当今的习俗中，穿着古代式样的服装。做到这样而为非作歹的人，即使有，不也很少吗？

哀公说："好！"

Book 31

Duke Ai

31. 1

Duke Ai questioned Confucius, saying: "I want to assess the qualities of the knight-scholar of my country and share with them governance of the state.May I presume to inquire how to go about selecting them?"

Confucius responded: "Born in the present generation yet aspiring to the Way of the Ancients, living amid the customs of the present yet dressing in the robes of antiquity. Would it not be a rare person indeed who would hold firmly to these things and yet act contrary to them!"

Duke Ai said: "Quite so, but then are those who wear the Zhangfu cap, shoes with corded ornaments on their toes, and a large belt with a *hu* writing table inserted in it, all worthy men?"

Confucius replied: "That is not necessarily the case.Those who wear the rectangular robe with dark lower garment and a ceremonial cap while riding in a carriage do not have their aspirations set on eating garlic. Those who wear unhemmed coarse robes, straw sandals, bamboo staff, and sip gruel do not have their aspirations set on wine and meat. Born in the present generation, yet aspiring to the Way of the Ancients, living amid the customs of the present yet dressing in the robes of antiquity, holding these things firmly and yet acting contrary to them, although there are some such men, are they not indeed quite rare!"

"Well said, "replied the Duke.

【原文】

31.2 孔子曰："人有五仪：有庸人，有士，有君子，有贤人，有大圣。"

哀公曰："敢问何如斯可谓庸人矣？"

孔子对曰："所谓庸人者，口不能道善言，心不知邑邑；不知选贤人善士托其身焉以为己忧；动行不知所务，止立不知所定；日选择于物，不知所贵；从物如流，不知所归；五凿为正，心从而坏。如此，则可谓庸人矣。"

哀公曰："善！敢问何如斯可谓士矣？"

孔子对曰："所谓士者，虽不能尽道术，必有率也；虽不能遍美善，必有处也。是故知不务多，务审其所知；言不务多，务审其所

【今译】

31.2 孔子说："人有五种典型：有平庸的人，有士人，有君子，有贤人，有伟大的圣人。"

哀公说："请问像怎样可以称之为平庸的人？"

孔子回答说："所谓平庸的人，嘴里不能说出好话，心里也不知道忧愁，不知道考虑选用和依靠贤人善士；出动时不知道去干什么，立定时不知道立脚点在哪里；天天在各种事物中挑选，却不知道什么东西贵重；一味顺从外界的事情就像流水似的，不知道归宿在哪里；为耳、目、鼻、口、心的欲望所主宰，思想也就跟着变坏。像这样，就可以称之为平庸的人了。"

哀公说："好！请问像怎样可以称之为士人？"

孔子回答说："所谓士人，即使不能彻底掌握治国的原则和方法，但必定有所遵循；即使不能尽善尽美，但必定有所操守。所以他了解知识不求多，而务求审慎地对待自己的知识；说话不求多，而务求审

31. 2

Confucius said: "There are five levels of deportment for men:that of the common man, the scholar-knight, the gentleman, the worthy, and the sage."

Duke Ai asked: "May I inquire what sort of person should be called a common man?"

Confucius responded: "Those who are called common men have a mouth that is unable to utter good words and a heart that is insensible to the need for concern. They are ignorant of the need to select worthy men and expert scholars and to rely on them to cure the causes of their distress. In acting, they do not know what they should devote their attention to; in rest, they do not know what to take as their standard. Day by day they select and choose among things, not knowing which are valuable. Being aimless, they are seduced by external things, and they do not understand what principles they should be committed to. Rather, they are governed only by the Five Passsions. Their minds follow the passions and are corrupted. Anyone who behaves thusly should properly be called a common man."

"Well said, "responded the Duke. "May I inquire what sort of person should be called a scholar-knight?"

Confucius replied: "Those who are called scholar-knights, although they may be unable to exhaust the full range of methods belonging to the Way, are certain to possess principles that they follow. Although they may be unable to encompass fully the beautiful and good, they are certain to possess principles to which they hold firmly. For these reasons their desire to know is not engrossed in many topics, for they are engrossed in

【原文】

谓；行不务多，务审其所由。故知既已知之矣，言既已谓之矣，行既已由之矣，则若性命肌肤之不可易也。故富贵不足以益也，卑贱不足以损也。如此，则可谓士矣。”

哀公曰：“善！敢问何如斯可谓之君子矣？”

孔子对曰：“所谓君子者，言忠信而心不德，仁义在身而色不伐，思虑明通而辞不争。故犹然如将可及者，君子也。”

哀公曰：“善！敢问何如斯可谓贤人矣？”

孔子对曰：“所谓贤人者，行中规绳而不伤于本，言足法于天下而

【今译】

慎地对待自己所说的话；做事不求多，而务求审慎地对待自己所经手的事。知识已经了解了，话已经说了，事已经做了，那就像自己的生命和肌肤一样不可能再加以改变了。所以富贵并不能使他增加些什么，卑贱并不能使他减少些什么。像这样，就可以称之为士人了。”

哀公说：“好！请问像怎样才可以称之为君子？”

孔子回答说：“所谓君子，就是说话忠诚守信而心里并不自认为有美德，仁义之道充满在身而脸上并不露出炫耀的神色，思考问题明白通达而说话却不与人争辩。所以洒脱舒缓好像快要被人赶上似的，就是君子了。”

哀公说：“好！请问像怎样才可以称之为贤人？”

孔子回答说：“所谓贤人，就是行为符合规矩法度而不伤害本身，言论能够被天下人取法而不伤害自己，富裕得拥有天下而没有私藏的

being careful about what they do know;their discourse is not devoted to numerous topics, for they are devoted to being careful about what they do discuss;their conduct is not devoted to numerous matters, for they are devoted to being careful about the principles upon which their actions rest.Thus, knowing what they ought to know, discoursing on what they ought, and conducting themselves according to their principles, it is no more possible to alter them than it would be to change the skin and flesh with which their inborn nature has endowed them.Thus, riches and eminent position do not improve them and poverty and humble position do not detract from them.If a person behaves thusly, then he may properly be called a scholar-knight."

"Well put, "commented the Duke."May I ask what sort of person should properly be termed a gentleman?"

Confucius replied: "Those who are called gentleman are in their discourse always loyal and trustworthy and in their hearts do not consider that they possess real inner power.Humane and moral principles reside in their person, yet they do assume a self-righteous attitude. Their thoughts and considerations are clear and comprehensive, but they do not advance their propositions to triumph over others. They behave inconspicuously as if they could be surpassed, {yet they can never be equaled}—such are gentlemen."

"Well said, "observed the Duke. "I venture to ask what sort of person should be termed a worthy?"

Confucius responded: "Those who are worthies behave in perfect accord with the compass and marking line, yet they do not impair their fundamental nature. Their discourse is equal to the task of being the model for the world, yet it does no injury to their own persons. They may be so rich as to possess the whole world, yet they do not accumulate

【原文】

不伤于身，富有天下而无怨财，布施天下而不病贫。如此，则可谓贤人矣。"

哀公曰："善！敢问何如斯可谓大圣矣？"

孔子对曰："所谓大圣者，知通乎大道、应变而不穷、辨乎万物之情性者也。大道者，所以变化遂成万物也；情性者，所以理然不取舍也。是故其事大辨乎天地，明察乎日月，总要万物于风雨，缪缪肫肫。其事不可循，若天之嗣；其事不可识，百姓浅然不识其邻。若此，则可谓大圣矣。"

哀公曰："善！"

31.3 鲁哀公问舜冠于孔子，孔子不对。三问，不对。哀公曰："寡人问舜冠于子，何以不言也？"

【今译】

财富，把财物施舍给天下人而不用担忧自己会贫穷。像这样，就可以称之为贤人了。"

哀公说："好！请问像怎样才可以称之为伟大的圣人？"

孔子回答说："所谓伟大的圣人，就是智慧能通晓大道、面对各种事变而不会穷于应付、能明辨万物性质的人。大道，是变化形成万物的根源；万物的性质，是处理是非、取舍的根据。所以圣人做的事情像天地一样广大普遍，像日月一样明白清楚，像风雨一样统辖万物，温温和和诚恳不倦。他做的事情不可能被沿袭，好像是上天主管的一样；他做的事情不可能被认识，老百姓浅陋地甚至不能认识和它相近的事情。像这样，就可以称之为伟大的圣人了。"

哀公说："好！"

31.3 鲁哀公向孔子打听舜所戴的礼帽，孔子不回答。哀公问了三次，孔子仍不回答。哀公说："我向您打听舜所戴的礼帽，您为什么不说话呢？"

goods. They distribute their bounty to the whole world, yet they suffer no poverty.If one behaves in this fashion, then he may properly be called a worthy."

"Excellent, "commented the Duke. "I would like to know what sort of person should be called a great sage."

Confucius responded: "Those who are called great sages are persons who have an awareness that extends to the Great Way, who are limitlessly responsive to every transformation, and who discriminate between the essential and inborn natures of each of the myriad things. The Great Way is what is employed to alter and transmute and then in consequence to perfect the myriad things. The essential and inborn natures of things provide the natural principles of order whcreby one determines what is so and what is not so of them and whether one should select or reject them.For this reason their undertakings are great and comprehensive like Heaven and Earth, brilliant and illuminating the truth like the sun and moon, and essential and important to the myriad things like the wind and rain.With their formless majesty and their profound and pure mystery, their activities cannot be grasped.It is as though they were the successor of Heaven whose undertakings cannot be recognized. The Hundred Clans in their stupid shallowness do not recognize that they are close at hand.If one is like this, then he should be called a Great Sage."

31. 3

Duke Ai asked Confucius about Shun's ceremonial hat, but he did not respond.Thrice he asked, and thrice Confucius did not reply.Duke Ai then said:"This Orphaned One asked you about Shun's ceremonial hat;why is it you have said nothing?"

【原文】

孔子对曰："古之王者有务而拘领者矣，其政好生而恶杀焉。是以凤在列树，麟在郊野，乌鹊之巢可俯而窥也。君不此问，而问舜冠，所以不对也。"

31.4 鲁哀公问于孔子曰："寡人生于深宫之中，长于妇人之手，寡人未尝知哀也，未尝知忧也，未尝知劳也，未尝知惧也，未尝知危也。"

孔子曰："君之所问，圣君之问也。丘，小人也，何足以知之？"

曰："非吾子，无所闻之也。"

孔子曰："君入庙门而右，登自胙阶，仰视榱栋，俯见几筵，其器存，其人亡，君以此思哀，则哀将焉而不至矣？君昧爽而栉冠，平明而听朝，一物不应，乱之端也，君以此思忧，则忧将焉而不至矣？君平明而听朝，日昃而退，诸侯之子孙必有在君之末庭者，君以此思

【今译】

孔子回答说："古代的帝王中有戴便帽并穿圆领便服的，但他们的政治却是致力于使人生存而厌恶杀人。因此凤凰栖息在成行的树上，麒麟活动在国都的郊外，乌鸦、喜鹊的窝可以低头观察到。您不问这个，却问舜戴的礼帽，所以我不回答啊。"

31.4 鲁哀公问孔子说："我出生在深邃的后宫之中，在妇人的哺育下长大，我从来不知道什么是悲哀，从来不知道什么是忧愁，从来不知道什么是劳苦，从来不知道什么是恐惧，从来不知道什么是危险。"

孔子说："您所问的，是圣明的君主所问的问题。我孔丘，是个小人啊，哪能知道这些？"

哀公说："除了您，我没有地方可问啊。"

孔子说："您走进宗庙的大门向右，从东边的台阶登堂，抬头看见椽子屋梁，低头看见灵位，那些器物还在，但那祖先已经没了，您从这些方面来想想悲哀，那么悲哀之情哪会不到来呢？您黎明就起来梳头戴帽，天亮时就上朝听政，如果一件事情处理不当，就会成为祸乱的发端，您从这些方面来想想忧愁，那么忧愁之情哪会不到来呢？你天亮时上朝处理政事，太阳偏西时退朝，而各国逃亡而来的诸侯的子

Confucius replied: "The kings of antiquity had helmets and tightfitting collars. Their government was such that good was produced and evil was destroyed. For this reason phoenixes were to be found in the rows of trees, unicorns in the suburban fields, and one could bend down and peer into the nests of crows and owls.My lord did not ask about this, but about Shun's ceremonial cap, which is why I did not respond."

31. 4

In a discussion with Confucius, Duke Ai said: "The Orphaned One was born in the inner recesses of the palace and grew up in the hands of women, so he has never directly experienced grief, anxiety, weariness, fear, or danger."

Confucius responded: "The problem posed my lord is that of a sage ruler.How should I, Qiu, a petty man, be competent to know of it?"

Duke Ai continued: "But for you who are my Master, I would find no one from whom to learn about them."

Confucius responded: "When my lord next enters through the gate of his ancestral temple, goes to the right, mounts the host stairs, let him look up and behold the pillars and rafters or look down and see the low sacrificial table with the offerings and notice that the vessels survive but their owner has perished.If my lord will take this and reflect on the sadness of it, then will he not be able to experience grief? At first light my lord rises, combs his hair, and dons his cap so that by dawn he is hearing court, where if a single thing is not properly attended to, it may be the first beginning of anarchy.If my lord would take this and reflect on the need to be anxious about it, then will he not be able to experience anxiety? While he is hearing court from dawn until he retires at sunset, there are certain

【原文】

劳，则劳将焉而不至矣？君出鲁之四门以望鲁四郊，亡国之虚则必有数盖焉，君以此思惧，则惧将焉而不至矣？且丘闻之：‘君者，舟也；庶人者，水也。水则载舟，水则覆舟。’君以此思危，则危将焉而不至矣？”

31.5 鲁哀公问于孔子曰：“绅、委、章甫有益于仁乎？”

孔子蹴然曰：“君胡然焉？资衰苴杖者不听乐，非耳不能闻也，服使然也。黼衣黻裳者不茹荤，非口不能味也，服使然也。且丘闻之：‘好肆不守折，长者不为市。’窃其有益与其无益，君其知之矣。”

【今译】

孙一定有等在您那朝堂的远处来侍奉您的，您从这些方面来想想劳苦，那么劳苦的感觉哪会不到来呢？您走出鲁国国都的四方城门去瞭望鲁国的四郊，那些亡国的废墟中一定有几处茅屋，您从这些方面来想想恐惧，那么恐惧之情哪会不到来呢？而且我听说过这样的话：‘君主，好比船；百姓，好比水。水能载船，水能翻船。’您从这个方面来想想危险，那么危险感哪会不到来呢？”

31.5 鲁哀公问孔子说：“束宽大的腰带，戴周代式样的黑色丝绸礼帽和商代式样的成人礼帽，有益于仁吗？”

孔子惊恐不安地说：“您怎么这样问呢？穿着丧服、拄着孝棍的人不听音乐，并不是耳朵不能听见，而是身穿丧服使他们这样的。穿着祭祀礼服的人不吃荤菜，并不是嘴巴不能品味，而是身穿祭服使他们这样的。而且我听说过这样的话：‘善于经商的人不使所守资财折耗，德高望重的长者不去市场做生意谋利。’束腰带、戴礼帽是有益于仁还是无益于仁，您大概知道了吧。”

to be the sons and grandsons of other feudal lords in his back court.If my lord would take their plight and reflect on the hardships of their exile, then will he not be able to experience weariness? When next my lord goes out from the Four Gates to gaze over the four suburban regions of Lu, he should notice the ruins of all the states that have been destroyed, for he is certain to reckon that this is the common fate of all.If he will reflect on the threat of this happening, then will he not be able to experience fear? Moreover, I have heard that the lord is the boat;his subjects the water.It is the water that sustains the boat, and it is the water that capsizes the boat. If my lord would take this saying and reflect on the danger it suggests, then will he not be able to experience danger?"

31. 5

Duke Ai questioned Confucius, saying: "Do the large belt, the Wei cap, and the Zhangfu cap have any benefit for true humanity?"

Confucius frowned uneasily and said: "Why does your lordship ask such a question? When the ear of one who wears coarse hempen garments and carries a grayish bamboo staff does not listen to music, it is not because the ear is incapable of hearing it; rather, his wearing these funeral things causes it.When one who is wearing a robe emblazoned with black and white axes and an embroidered ceremonial cap does not devour garlic, it is not because the mouth could not taste it, but because he is wearing such ritual clothing.Moreover, I, Qiu, have heard that people who are good at trading in the marketplace do not allow their stores to diminish in value and that those who have superior natures do not engage in commerce. By carefully examining which of these has advantages and which not, my lord will know it.

【原文】

31.6 鲁哀公问于孔子曰:“请问取人。”

孔子对曰:“无取健，无取诎，无取口哼。健，贪也；诎，乱也；口哼，诞也。故弓调而后求劲焉，马服而后求良焉，士信悫而后求知能焉。士不信悫而有多知能，譬之，其豺狼也，不可以身尔也。语曰:‘桓公用其贼，文公用其盗。’故明主任计不信怒，暗主信怒不任计。计胜怒则强，怒胜计则亡。”

31.7 定公问于颜渊曰:“东野子之善驭乎？”

颜渊对曰:“善则善矣。虽然，其马将失。”

定公不悦，入谓左右曰:“君子固谗人乎？”

【今译】

31.6 鲁哀公问孔子说:“请问怎样选取人才？”孔子回答说:“不要选取要强好胜的人，不要选取钳制别人的人，不要选取能说会道的人。要强好胜的人，往往贪得无厌；钳制别人的人，往往会犯上作乱；能说会道的人，往往会弄虚作假。所以弓首先要调好，然后才求其强劲；马首先要驯服，然后才求其成为良马；人才首先要忠诚老实，然后才求其聪明能干。一个人如果不忠诚老实却又非常聪明能干，打个比方，他就是豺狼啊，是不可以使自己靠近他的呀。俗话说:‘齐桓公任用逆贼，晋文公任用强盗。’所以英明的君主根据利害得失来选用人而不凭感情用事，昏庸的君主凭感情来选用人而不根据利害得失。对利害得失的计较超过了感情用事就会强盛，感情用事超过了对利害得失的计较就会灭亡。”

31.7 鲁定公问颜渊说:“东野先生车驾得好吗？”颜渊回答说:“好倒是好。虽然这样，他的马将要奔逃了。”

定公很不高兴，进去对近臣说:“君子原来是诽谤人的吗？”

31. 6

Duke Ai questioned Confucius, saying: "I would like to find out how one should select men."

Confucius responded: "Do not select clever, glib, or loquacious men.The clever are covetous, the glib are given to creating anarchy, and the loquacious are unreliable.Only when the bow has been adjusted does one test its strength;only when the horse has been broken does one try to determine its virtues So, too, only when a scholar-knight has proved trustworthy and guileless does one seek to determine his knowledge and ability.A scholar-knight who is not trustworthy and guileless yet possesses much knowledge and many abilities may be likened to a wolf, since one cannot approach him.A proverb says:

Duke Huan used his assailant; Duke Wen used his robber.

Thus, an intelligent ruler depends on calculation and does not trust wrath;the benighted trusts wrath and does not depend on calculation.If calculation triumphs over wrath, there is strength;if wrath triumphs over calculation, there is annihilation."

31. 7

Duke Ding asked Yan Yuan: "Is not Dongye Bi quite expert at driving the chariot?"

Yan Yuan responded: "He is good at what he is good at. That notwithstanding, the horses are going to bolt out of control."

Duke Ding was not pleased and going inside remarked to those about him that "that gentleman assuredly slanders the other man."

【原文】

三日而校来谒，曰："东野毕之马失。两骖列，两服入厩。"定公越席而起曰："趋驾召颜渊！"

颜渊至。定公曰："前日寡人问吾子，吾子曰：'东野毕之驭，善则善矣。虽然，其马将失。'不识吾子何以知之？"

颜渊对曰："臣以政知之。昔舜巧于使民，而造父巧于使马。舜不穷其民，造父不穷其马，是以舜无失民，造父无失马也。今东野毕之驭，上车执辔，衔体正矣；步骤驰骋，朝礼毕矣；历险致远，马力尽矣。然犹求马不已，是以知之也。"

定公曰："善！可得少进乎？"

颜渊对曰："臣闻之：'鸟穷则啄，兽穷则攫，人穷则诈。'自古及今，未有穷其下而能无危者也。"

【今译】

三天以后，养马的官员来拜见，说："东野毕的马逃跑了。两匹旁边的马挣断缰绳分别跑了，两匹中间的马回到了马棚中。"定公离开坐席站起来说："赶快套车去召见颜渊！"

颜渊来了。定公说："前天我问您，您说：'东野毕驾车，好倒是好。虽然这样，他的马将要奔逃了。'不知道您凭什么了解到这一点？"

颜渊回答说："我是根据政治上的原则来了解到这一点的。从前舜善于役使民众，造父善于驱使马。舜不使他的民众走投无路，造父不使他的马走投无路，因此舜没有逃跑的民众，造父没有逃跑的马。现在东野毕驾车，登上车子手握缰绳，马嚼子和马身都端正了；慢走快跑驱赶奔驰，朝廷所规定的礼仪全部达到了；经历各种险阻而到达了远方，马的气力也就用光了。然而他还是要求马不停步，因此我知道他的马会逃跑。"

定公说："好！您可以稍微再进一步说说吗？"

颜渊回答说："我听说过这样的话：'鸟走投无路了就会乱啄，兽走投无路了就会乱抓，人走投无路了就会欺诈。'从古到今，还没有使臣民走投无路而能没有危险的君主啊。"

Three days later, a stable keeper came to announce that Dongye Bi's horse had bolted out of control, the two outside horses of his team breaking away and the two inner horses entering their stalls.Duke Ding rose and stepped across his mat, saying:"Hurry and yoke a carriage to summon Yan Yuan."

When Yan Yuan arrived, Duke Ding said: "A few days ago this Orphaned One questioned you, Master, who replied that Dongye Bi as a charioteer was good at what he was good at, but that notwithstanding, his horses were going to bolt out of control.I do not understand how my Master knew this?"

Yan Yuan responded: "Your servant used the principles of governing to know it.Formerly, Shun was skillful at handling the people, and Zaofu was skilled at handling horses.Shun would not press his people to their limits, and Zaofu would not wear out his horses.For this reason, Shun never lost control over the people, and Zaofu never had his horses bolt out of control.Now in his charioteering, Dongye Bi mounts the chariot, takes hold of the reins, and pulls the bits so that the horses' bodies are correctly upright.In making them trot, canter, gallop, and race at full speed, he fully observes court ritual.But he makes the horses pass through dangerous areas to reach the distant parts, and then, although their strength has been exhausted, he urges the horses on without end. This is why I knew that they would bolt out of control."

"Well put, "said Duke Ding. "Would you develop your point a little more?"

Yan Yuan replied: "Your servant has heard that when pushed to the limit, a bird will peck, an animal bite, and a man deceive.From antiquity to the present day, there has never been a case of someone pressing his subjects to their limits and being able to encounter no danger."

尧问第三十二

【原文】

32.1 尧问于舜曰:“我欲致天下，为之奈何?”

对曰:“执一无失，行微无怠，忠信无倦，而天下自来。执一如天地，行微如日月，忠诚盛于内，贲于外，形于四海，天下其在一隅邪？夫有何足致也?”

32.2 魏武侯谋事而当，群臣莫能逮，退朝而有喜色。吴起进曰:“亦尝有以楚庄王之语闻于左右者乎?”

武侯曰:“楚庄王之语何如?”吴起对曰:“楚庄王谋事而当，群臣莫逮，退朝而有忧色。申公巫臣进问曰:‘王朝而有忧色，何也?’庄

【今译】

32.1 尧问舜说:“我想招引天下的人，对此该怎么办?”

舜回答说：“主持政务专心一意而没有过失，做细小的事也不懈怠，忠诚守信而不厌倦，那么天下人自会归顺。主持政务专心一意像天长地久一样，做细小的事像日月运行不息一样，忠诚充满在内心，发扬在外表，体现在四海之内，那么天下人岂不就像在室内的角落里一样啦？又哪里要去招引呢?”

32.2 魏武侯谋划政事得当，大臣们没有谁能及得上他，退朝后他带着喜悦的脸色。吴起上前说：“曾经有人把楚庄王的话报告给您了吗?”

武侯说:“楚庄王的话怎么说的?”吴起回答说:“楚庄王谋划政事得当，大臣们没有谁及得上他，退朝后他带着忧虑的神色。申公巫臣

Book 32

The Questions of Yao

32. 1

Yao asked Shun, saying: "I desire to cause the empire to come to me.How might this be accomplished?"

Shun responded: "Hold fast to unity and do not lose it.Act with subtlety and do not fall idle. Be loyal and honest and do not become tired.Then the empire will come to you of its own accord.In holding fast to unity, one behaves like Heaven and Earth. In acting with subtlety, one acts like the sun and moon.When loyalty and sincerity become complete within, they become apparent without.When this is visibly manifest to all within the four seas, the empire will be but a single corner;then indeed what more would be needed to cause them to come?"

32. 2

Marquis Wu of Wei [r.396—371] contrived a plan so perfectly suited to the circumstances that none of his assembled ministers could improve upon it.When court was concluded, the marquis had a pleased expression.Wu Qi advanced toward the throne and said: "In light of what has just transpired, I assume that you must have heard from all your assistants about the statement of King Zhuang of Chu [r.613—591]."

Marquis Wu said: "What was the statement of King Zhuang of Chu?"

Wu Qi replied: "King Zhuang of Chu contrived a plan so perfectly suited to the circumstances that none of his assembled ministers could

【原文】

王曰：‘不穀谋事而当，群臣莫能逮，是以忧也。其在中蘬之言也，曰：“诸侯得师者王，得友者霸，得疑者存，自为谋而莫己若者亡。”今以不穀之不肖，而群臣莫吾逮，吾国几于亡乎！是以忧也。’楚庄王以忧，而君以喜！”

武侯逡巡，再拜曰：“天使夫子振寡人之过也。”

32.3 伯禽将归于鲁，周公谓伯禽之傅曰：“汝将行，盍志而子美德乎？”

对曰：“其为人宽，好自用，以慎。此三者，其美德已。”

周公曰：“呜呼！以人恶为美德乎！君子好以道德，故其民归道。

【今译】

上前询问说：‘大王被群臣朝见后面带忧虑的神色，为什么呀？’庄王说：‘我谋划政事得当，大臣们没有谁能及得上我，因此我忧虑啊。那忧虑的原因就在仲虺的话中，他说过：“诸侯获得师傅的称王天下，获得朋友的称霸诸侯，获得解决疑惑者的保存国家，自行谋划而没有谁及得上自己的灭亡。”现在凭我这样的无能，而大臣们却没有谁及得上我，我的国家接近于灭亡啦！因此我忧虑啊。”楚庄王因此而忧虑，而您却因此而高兴！”

武侯后退了几步，拱手拜了两次说：“是上天派先生来挽救我的过错啊。”

32.3 伯禽将要回到鲁国去，周公旦对伯禽的师傅说：“你们要走了，你为什么不估量一下你所辅导的这个人的美德呢？”

伯禽的师傅回答说：“他为人宽大，喜欢靠自己的才智行事，而且谨慎。这三个方面，就是他的美德了。”

周公说：“唉呀！你把人家不好的东西当作美德啦！君子喜欢按照

improve upon it;so when court concluded, he had a worried expression.Wu Chen, the Duke of Shen, approached and asked: 'Why does Your Majesty have a worried expression after royal court?' King Zhuang said: 'This Unworthy One has devised a plan so perfectly suited to the circumstances that none of my assembled ministers can offer improvement.This is why I am worried.The sayings of Zhong Hui apply to this situation: He whom the feudal lords themselves seek for their leader will become king;he with whom the feudal lords seek friendly relations will become lord-protector;he whom they seek out as their equal will merely survive;and he who must lay plans on his own that none are able to surpass is doomed. Now, even with the lack of ability of this Unworthy One, none of my assembled ministers can improve upon my plan.My country faces imminent doom.This is why I am worried.'"

Marquis Wu drew back and made repeated obeisance, saying: "Heaven has caused you, Master, to shake the Solitary One from the error of his ways."

32. 3

When Boqin was about to take up residence in Lu, the Duke of Zhou addressed his tutors, saying:"Since you are about to set out on the journey, why have you masters not taught my son how to refine his inner power?"

They replied: "He is personally magnanimous toward others, is fond of acting on his own, and is cautious in all things.In these three characteristics lies the refinement of his personal inner power."

The Duke of Zhou said: "Alas!How can you consider what men all despise to be refinement of inner power? The gentleman delights in em-

【原文】

彼其宽也，出无辨矣，女又美之！彼其好自用也，是所以窭小也。君子力如牛，不与牛争力；走如马，不与马争走；知如士，不与士争知。彼争者，均者之气也，女又美之！彼其慎也，是其所以浅也。闻之曰：'无越逾不见士。'见士问曰：'无乃不察乎？'不闻，即物少至，少至则浅。彼浅者，贱人之道也，女又美之！"

"吾语女：我，文王之为子，武王之为弟，成王之为叔父，吾于天下不贱矣，然而吾所执贽而见者十人，还贽而相见者三十人，貌执之士者百有余人，欲言而请毕事者千有余人，于是吾仅得三士焉，以正吾身，以定天下。吾所以得三士者，亡于十人与三十人中，乃在百人与千人之中。故上士吾薄为之貌，下士吾厚为之貌。人人皆以我为

【今译】

道理去行事，所以他的民众也归顺正道。他对人一味宽大，那么赏赐就会不加分别了，你却还赞美它。他喜欢靠自己的才智行事，这是使他浅陋无知而胸怀狭窄的根源啊。君子气力像牛一样大，也不和牛较量气力；跑起来像马一样快，也不和马赛跑；智慧像士人一样高明，也不和士人比聪明。那较量竞争，只是把自己和别人等同的人的气量，你却还赞美它。他的谨慎，这是使他孤陋寡闻的原因。我听说过这句话：'不要过分地不会见士人。'见到士人就要问道：'不是我不明察吧？'不询问，那么事情就了解得少，了解得少就浅陋了。那浅陋，是下贱之人的为人之道，你却还赞美它。"

周公对伯禽说："我告诉你：我，对文王来说是儿子，对武王来说是弟弟，对成王来说是叔父，我在天下不算卑贱了，然而我拿着礼物去拜见的尊长有十个，还礼会见的平辈有三十个，用礼貌去接待的士人有一百多个，想要提意见而我请他把事情说完的人有一千多个，在这些人之中我只得到三个贤士，靠他们来端正我的身心，来安定天下。我得到三个贤士的办法，不是在十个人和三十个人之中挑选，而是在上百人和上千人之中挑选。所以对于上等的士人，我对他们的礼

ploying the Way and its Power so that he causes his people to turn to the Way as to home.That magnanimity of which you speak issues from a lack of discrimination, yet you would praise him for it! That fondness of acting on his own is the result of pettiness and smallness.Even though a gentleman had the strength of an ox, he would not compete in matters of strength with an ox. Even though he could gallop like a horse, he would not compete as a runner with a horse. Even though he had the knowledge of a scholar-knight, he would not compete in matters of knowledge with a scholar-knight. Competing in each of these contests requires an adjustment of his vital humours, yet you praise him for it.What you have considered caution is the result of his shallowness. I was taught that one should not for fear of lowering oneself be unwilling to give audience to scholars.When you give audience to scholars, you must ask: 'What is not as yet fully ascertained?' If you do not question, the advice you will be given on the true state of things will be trivialitics. If you are given but trivialities, there is shallowness. Such shallowness is the way of despicable men, yet you praise my son for it!

"I tell you this: I am the son of King Wen, the younger brother of King Wu, and the uncle of King Cheng. My position in the empire is not to be despised.Nonetheless, those to whom I offer introductory presents, as though they were superiors, and to whom I grant audiences number ten.Those with whom I exchange gifts and whom I receive number thirty.The scholars whom I treat with full ceremony number over a hundred.Those from whom I sought advice and who were requested to finish tasks number more than a thousand. From all of these, there are only three scholars who correct me personally and who settle the affairs of the empire. Those whom I so use came not from among the ten or thirty, but from the hundred and thousand.Hence, scholars of the highest

【原文】

越逾好士，然故士至；士至，而后见物；见物，然后知其是非之所在。戒之哉！女以鲁国骄人，几矣！夫仰禄之士犹可骄也，正身之士不可骄也。彼正身之士，舍贵而为贱，舍富而为贫，舍佚而为劳，颜色黎黑而不失其所，是以天下之纪不息，文章不废也。”

32.4 语曰：缯丘之封人见楚相孙叔敖曰：“吾闻之也：‘处官久者士妒之，禄厚者民怨之，位尊者君恨之。’今相国有此三者而不得罪楚之士民，何也？”孙叔敖曰：“吾三相楚而心愈卑，每益禄而施愈博，

【今译】

貌轻一些；对于下等的士人，我对他们的礼貌重一些。人人都认为我特别喜欢士人，所以士人都来了；士人来了，然后我才能看清事物；看清了事物，然后才能知道它们的是非在什么地方。要警戒啊！你如果凭借鲁国高傲地对待人，就危险了！那些依赖俸禄生活的士人还可以高傲地对待，而端正身心的士人是不可以高傲地对待的。那些端正身心的士人，舍弃高贵的地位而甘居卑贱，舍弃富足的待遇而甘愿贫穷，舍弃安逸而干劳苦的事，脸色黝黑也不丧失自己所选择的立场，因此天下的治国纲领能流传不息，古代的文献典籍能经久不废啊。”

32.4 民间传说云：缯丘的封人拜见楚国的丞相孙叔敖说：“我听说过这样的话：‘做官长久的人，士人就会嫉妒他；俸禄丰厚的人，民众就会怨恨他；地位尊贵的人，君主就会憎恶他。’现在相国具备了这三种情况却没有得罪楚国的士人民众，为什么呢？”孙叔敖说：“我三次任楚国相国而心里越来越谦卑，每次增加俸禄而施舍越来越广

rank I treat in a contemptuous manner, and scholars of the lowest ranks I treat in a generous fashion. All men believe that I am willing to lower myself because of my love of scholars. That being the case, scholars come. Only after scholars have come does one perceive the true state of things, and only after one has perceived the true state of things does one know where true right and wrong lie.

"Heed this well.If in governing Lu you behave arrogantly toward others, you will be in danger.With scholars who look only after their emolument, you can be arrogant, but with scholars who would rectify you cannot behave arrogantly.Those scholars who would rectify you forsake honors and act humbly, forsake riches and live modestly, forsake indolence and toil away, so that their complexions become pitch black, yet they never fail to accept their position. It is precisely for these reasons that the guiding norms of the empire are not broken and that culture and refinement are not cast aside."

32. 4

The story goes that once when the border warden of Zengqiu had an audience with Sunshu Ao, the prime minister of Chu, he said: "I have heard that anyone who occupies office for a long time incurs the jealousy of the knights, that one whose emolument is substantial excites resentment among the people, and that one who holds an eminent position incurs the animosity of his lord.Now, these three conditions are fulfilled in the case of the prime minister of a state, yet you have not incurred any blame rome the people or knights of Chu.How is that?"

Sunshu Ao replied: "I have three times been prime minister of Chu, yet my attitude has become more humble each time.Each time I have

【原文】

位滋尊而礼愈恭，是以不得罪于楚之士民也。”

32.5 子贡问于孔子曰：“赐为人下而未知也。”孔子曰：“为人下者乎？其犹土也。深扣之而得甘泉焉，树之而五谷蕃焉；草木殖焉，禽兽育焉；生则立焉，死则入焉；多其功而不得。为人下者，其犹土也。”

32.6 昔虞不用宫之奇而晋并之，莱不用子马而齐并之，纣刳王子比干而武王得之。不亲贤用知，故身死国亡也。

32.7 为说者曰：“孙卿不及孔子。”是不然。孙卿迫于乱世，鰌于

【今译】

泛，地位越尊贵而礼节越恭敬，因此没有得罪楚国的士人民众啊。”

32.5 子贡问孔子说：“我想对人谦虚却还不知道怎样做。”孔子说：“对人谦虚么？那就要像土地一样啊。深深地挖掘它就能得到甜美的泉水，在它上面种植而五谷就茂盛地生长；草木在它上面繁殖，禽兽在它上面生息；活着就站在它上面，死了就埋在它里面；它的功劳很多却不自以为有功德。对人谦虚嘛，那就要像土地一样啊。”

32.6 从前虞国不用宫之奇而晋国吞并了它，莱国不用子马而齐国吞并了它，商纣王将王子比干剖腹挖心而周武王夺取了他的政权。君主不亲近贤能的人，不任用明智的人，所以会身死国亡啊。

32.7 那些立说的人说：“荀卿及不上孔子。”这不对。荀卿被迫处

enjoyed increased emoluments, but have given them away all the more widely.My position has grown ever more eminent, yet the ritual forms I practice have become all the more respectful.It is for these reasons that I have not incurred any blame from the people or knights of Chu."

32. 5

Zigong questioned Confucius, saying: "I, Ci, would like to be more humble than others, but I do not yet know how."

Confucius replied: "Do you mean that you want to be lower than others, like the humble lowness of the ground? By digging deep into the ground, you will get sweet spring waters. When planted in the ground, the Five Grains will multiply;grasses and trees will thrive from it;and birds and beasts will prosper on it.While alive, we stand on it;when we die, we are entered into it.Multitudinous are its merits, yet it claims no Power.Does 'being more humble than others' mean you want to be like the ground?"

32. 6

Formerly the state of Yu did not employ Gongzhi Qi and was annexed by Jin. Lai did not use Prince Ma and was annexed by Qi.Zhou Xin disemboweled Prince Bigan, and King Wu obtained his kingdom. Not being intimate with worthy men and not using the wise are the reasons individuals meet with death and countries are destroyed.

32. 7

Those who offer persuasions say: Xun Qing was not the equal of

【原文】

严刑；上无贤主，下遇暴秦；礼义不行，教化不成；仁者绌约，天下冥冥；行全刺之，诸侯大倾。当是时也，知者不得虑，能者不得治，贤者不得使。故君上蔽而无睹，贤人距而不受。然则孙卿怀将圣之心，蒙佯狂之色，视天下以愚。《诗》曰："既明且哲，以保其身。"此之谓也。是其所以名声不白，徒与不众，光辉不博也。今之学者，得孙卿之遗言余教，足以为天下法式表仪。所存者神，所过者化。观其善行，孔子弗过。世不详察，云非圣人，奈何？天下不治，孙卿不遇

【今译】

在乱世，身受严刑钳制；上没有贤德君主，下碰上暴虐之秦；礼制道义不能推行，教育感化不能办成；仁人遭到罢免束缚，天下黑暗昏昏沉沉；德行完美反受讥讽，诸侯大肆倾轧兼并。在这个时代啊，有智慧的人不能谋划政事，有能力的人不能参与治理，有德才的人不能得到任用。所以君主受到蒙蔽而看不见什么，贤能的人遭到拒绝而不被接纳。既然这样，所以荀卿抱着伟大的圣人的志向，却又给自己脸上加了一层装疯的神色，向天下人显示自己的愚昧。《诗》云："不但明智又聪慧，用来保全他自身。"说的就是这种人啊。这就是他名声不显赫、门徒不众多、光辉照耀得不广的原因。现在的学者，只要能得到荀卿遗留下来的言论与残剩下来的教导，也完全可以用作为天下的法度准则。他所在的地方就会得到全面的治理，他经过的地方社会就会发生变化。看看他那善良的行为，孔子也不能超过。世人不加详细考察，说他不是圣人，有什么办法呢？天下不能治理好，是因为荀卿

Confucius. This is not so. Xun Qing was oppressed by a chaotic age and lived under the intimidating threat of stern punishments. On the one hand there were no worthy rulers, and on the other hand he faced the aggression of Qin. Ritual and moral principles were not observed. The transforming effects of teaching were not brought to completion. The humane were degraded and under constraint. The whole world was lost in darkness. Conduct that strove after completeness was ridiculed and derided. The feudal lords engaged in the greatest of subversions.

It was a time when the wise had no opportunity to reflect, when the able had no opportunity to govern, and when the worthy had no opportunity to serve. Hence, the lords elevated the blindly obsessed and had no vision of their own; worthy men were rebuffed and were not given office. Nonetheless, Xun Qing cherished in his heart the mind of a great sage, which had to be concealed under the pretense of madness and presented to the world as stupidity. An *Ode* expresses my meaning:

> Brilliant was he but shrewd as well,
> so he protects his own life.

This is why his fame and reputation are not plainly evident, why his followers are not legion, and why his glory and brilliance are not widely known.

Students of today can obtain the transmitted doctrines and remaining teachings of Xun Qing in sufficient detail to serve as a model and pattern, the paradigm and gnomon, that establish the standard for the whole world. His presence had an effect like that of a spirit, and wherever he passed by he produced transformation. If one closely inspects his good works, one would see that even Confucius did not surpass him. Because the age does not examine things in detail or judge matters carefully, so it says that he was no sage—how could it be otherwise? Since the world

【原文】

时也。德若尧、禹，世少知之；方术不用，为人所疑。其知至明，循道正行，足以为纪纲。呜呼！贤哉！宜为帝王。天地不知，善桀、纣，杀贤良。比干剖心，孔子拘匡；接舆避世，箕子佯狂；田常为乱，阖闾擅强。为恶得福，善者有殃。今为说者又不察其实，乃信其名；时世不同，誉何由生？不得为政，功安能成？志修德厚，孰谓不贤乎？

【今译】

没有遇到时机啊。他的德行像尧、禹一样，世人却很少知道这一点；他的治国方略不被采用，反被人们所怀疑。他的智力极其聪明，他遵循正道，端正德行，足以成为人们的榜样。唉呀！贤能啊！他应该成为帝王。天地不知，竟然善桀、纣，杀害贤良。比干被剖腹挖心，孔子被围困在匡地，接舆逃避社会，箕子假装发疯，田常犯上作乱，阖闾放肆逞强。作恶的得到幸福，行善的反遭祸殃。现在那些立说的人又不考察实际情况，竟然相信那些虚名；时代不同，名誉从哪里产生？不能执政，功业哪能建成？志向美好，德行敦厚，谁说荀卿没有德才呢？

was not well governed Xun Qing never met with a suitable opportunity. Men of moral authority like a Yao or a Yu were seldom recognized in that age. His methods and procedures went unused. What he did in the interests of others raised suspicions. Since his knowledge was the most perspicacious, since he followed the true Way and acted uprightly, he could be taken as the guiding norm and fundamental principle.

Alas! He was a true worthy, one fit to be a Di Ancestor or King. But the world did not recognize him, taking pleasure instead in the Jies and Zhou Xins of the age and killing the good and worthy. Bigan had his heart cut out; Confucius was seized in Kuang, Jie Yu was forced to flee the world, the Viscount of Ji had to feign madness, Tian Chang created chaos, and Helü seized power for himself. Those who behaved wickedly gained riches, whereas those who were good came to ruin. The persuaders of today further have not examined into his real value, but have merely put their faith in his common reputation. Since his time and today are not the same, what could give cause for praise? It was impossible for him to exercise control over the government so that his true merit might have been perfected. Yet, since his aspirations were truly cultivated and his moral worth was highly developed, who can say that he was not a worthy man!

译名对照表

Bilingual Table of Translated Nouns or Terms

本表收录人名、地名、书名、官职、典章制度和学术名词等专有名词,按汉语拼音字母次序排列,所有名词均在后面的括号里注明所出现的章。

A

哀公	Duke Ai	(31)

B

百里	Baili Xi	(25)
百王	the Hundred Kings	(18,19)
百姓	the Hundred Clans	(8, 13, 15, 16, 17, 18,19,25,26,31)
鲍叔	Bao Shu	(21)
北海	the Northern Sea	(9)
比干	Bigan	(8,13)
辟闾	Bilü	(25)
卞随	Bian Sui	(25)
亳	Bo	(11)
伯禽	Boqin	(32)
伯牙	Bo Ya	(1)

C

蔡	Cai	(28)
仓颉	Cang Jie	(21)
曹触龙	Cao Chulong	(13,15)
陈	Chen	(28)

陈仲	Chen Zhong	(6)
成王	King Cheng	(7,13,32)
乘杜	Chengdu	(21)
重耳	Chonger	(28)
处士	scholar-recluse	(6)
楚	Chu	(16,18,20,28,32)
楚王	the King of Chu	(17)
楚庄王	King Zhuang of Chu	(32)
倕	Chui	(21)
垂沙	Chuisha	(15)
《春秋》	*Annals*	(1,8,27)
春申	Chunshen	(25)

D

妲己	Daji	(21)
大儒	Great Ru	(8)
大神	Great Divine Order	(9)
大师	grand master	(9)
《大雅》	*Great Odes*	(8)
道	the Way	(11,15,17,21,22,29)
《道经》	*Classic of the Way*	(21)
德	inner power	(10)
邓析	Deng Xi	(3,6)
狄	Di	(18)
氐	Di	(27)
地	Earth	(17)
地利	the benefits of Earth	(10)
定公	Duke Ding	(31)
东海	the Eastern Sea	(9,18)
东野子	Dongye Bi	(31)

F

繁弱	Fanruo	(23)
飞廉	Feilian	(8,13,21,25)
《风》	*Airs*	(8)
奉阳	the Lord of Fengyang	(13)
夫差	King Fuchai	(13)
浮游	Fuyou	(21)
付里乙	Fuliyi	(28)
傅说	Fuyue	(5)

G

干将	Ganjiang	(23)
皋陶	Gaoyao	(5,25)
工师	master of craftsmen	(9)
公慎氏	Gongshen	(8)
公孙吕	Gongsun Lü	(5)
公孙子	Gongsun Zi	(16)
公行子之	Gonghang Zizhi	(27)
公子高	Prince Gao	(5)
宫之奇	Gongzhi Qi	(32)
共工	Gonggong	(15)
共头	Gongtou	(8)
勾践	King Goujian	(11,15,28)
关龙逢	Guan Longfeng	(21,28)
管仲	Guan Zhong	(7,13,21,27,28)
虢公	the Duke of Guo	(25)
《国风》	*Airs of the States*	(27)
国君	the lord of state	(8)
国贼	threat to the state	(13)

H

干	Han	(1)
韩	Han	(13)
鄗	Hao	(11)
阖闾	King Helü	(11,15,32)
横革	Heng Ge	(25)
闳夭	Hongyao	(5)
后稷	Houji	(21,25)
《护》	*Guarding*	(8,18,19,27)
华仕	Huashi	(28)
骅骝	Hualiu	(23)
桓公	Duke Huan	(13,23,24)
驩兜	Huan Dou	(15)
惠施	Hui Shi	(3,6)
霍叔	Huoshu	(8)

J

箕子	the Viscount of Ji	(8,13)
季	Ji Liang	(25)
祭社	the Altar of Soil	(18,19)
祭稷	the Altar of Grain	(18,19)
祭郊	the Suburban Altar	(19)
觙	Ji	(21)
坚白	hard and white	(2)
桀	Jie	(1, 9, 11, 13, 15, 16, 17, 18, 21, 23, 24,25,26)
接舆	Jie Yu	(32)
晋	Jin	(13,21,28,32)
晋文公	Duke Wen of Jin	(11)
井里	Jingli	(27)

九皋	the Nine Marshes	(19)
九州	the Nine Shepherds	(18)
咎犯	Uncle Fan	(13)
涓蜀梁	Juan Shuliang	(21)
君畴	Jun Chou	(27)
君子	the Gentleman	(2,6,8,17,18,20,21,24,25,26,27)

K

《康诰》	*The Announcement to Kang*	(10)
孔子	Confucius	(18,21,25,27,28,30,31,32)
会稽	Kuaiji	(28)
匡	Kuang	(32)
夔	Kui	(21,25)

L

莱	Lai	(32)
《礼》	*Rituals*	(6,9,17,21)
礼	ritual principles	(7, 10, 17, 18, 19, 27)
礼义	ritual and moral principles	(5,17,23,26)
李斯	Li Si	(15)
力父	Lifu	(26)
厉王	King Li	(25)
临武君	the Lord of Linwu	(15)
令尹子西	Premier Prince Xi	(5)
六畜	the Six Domestic Animals	(17)
鲁桓公	the Duke Huan of Lu	(28)
吕尚	Lü Shang	(11)
吕望	Lü Wang	(21)
闾娵	Lüqu	(26)

绿耳	Lü'er	(23)

M

蛮	Man	(18)
孟轲	Mencius	(6,21,23,27)
苗	Miao	(15)
缪虮	Miao Ji	(15)
闵王	King Min	(9,11)
鸣条	Mingtiao	(15)
莫邪	Moye	(15,23)
墨翟	Mo Di	(6,10,17,21,25)
貉	Mo	(1)
牟光	Mou Guang	(25)
穆公	Duke Mu	(25)

N

南郭惠子	Master Hui of Nanguo	(30)
南海	the Southern Sea	(9)
宁戚	Ning Qi	(21)

P

蜂门	Pengmen	(11,18)
彭祖	Patriarch Peng	(2)
平原君	the Lord of Pingyuan	(13)

Q

齐	Qi	(3, 11, 13, 18, 23, 27)
骐骥	Qiji	(23)
齐桓公	Duke Huan of Qi	(7,11)
启	Qi	(25)
羌	Qiang	(27)

秦	Qin	(3,11,13,25,28)
秦昭王	King Zhao of Qin	(8)
阙党	Quedang	(8)

R

冉	Master Ran	(28)
人和	the concord of humanity	(10)
仁义	the principle of humanity and morality	(11)
戎	Rong	(18)
儒	Ru	(8,19)

S

三公	the Three Dukes	(11)
三苗	the Three Miao	(25)
商	Shang Dynasty	(21,25)
少正卯	Deputy Mao	(28)
《韶》	*Succession*	(18,19,20,27)
庶人	commoner	(12)
社稷	altars of soil and grain	(10)
申生	Shensheng	(21)
申徒狄	Shentu Di	(3)
申子	Shen Buhai	(21)
沈犹氏	Shenyou	(8)
圣臣	sage minister	(13)
圣人	sage	(2, 17, 18, 21, 25, 27)
圣王	sage king	(13)
慎到	Shen Dao	(6,17,21,25)
慎溃氏	Shenhui	(8)
《诗》	*Ode*	(1,2,3,4,5,6,7, 8, 10, 11, 12, 13, 14,17,18,21,24,

		26,28,32)
史鳍	Shi Qiu	(3,6)
士	scholar	(2)
士君子	the scholar and gentleman	(2)
士大夫	knights and grand officers	(11)
《书》	*Documents*	(1,4,8,10,12,13,18,24,28)
竖子	immature lad	(7)
舜	Shun	(3,5,8,9,10)
司空	director of public works	(9)
司寇	director of crime	(8,9)
司马	director of the horse	(9)
司徒	director of the multitude	(9)
四海	the four seas	(8)
四夷	the Four Yi tribes	(2)
《颂》	*Ancestral Hymns*	(8,20)
宋	Song	(15,21,25)
宋钘	Song Xing	(6)
苏秦	Su Qin	(13)
燧人	Suiren	(18)
孙卿	Xun Qing	(16,32)
孙叔敖	Sunshu Ao	(5,13,32)

T

太公	the Grand Duke of the Zhou	(13,28)
太皞	Taihao	(18)
《泰誓》	*Great Oath*	(15)
汤	Tang	(3, 10, 11, 13, 15, 18,23,26,28)
唐蔑	General Tang Mie	(15)
唐鞅	Tang Yang	(21)
天子	the Son of Heaven	(5)

天地	Heaven and Earth	(6)
天时	the Heaven's natural seasons	(10)
田常	Tian Chang	(32)
田单	Tian Dan	(15)
田骈	Tian Pian	(6)
田仲	Tian Zhong	(3)
它嚣	Tuo Xiao	(6)

W

王道	the Way of the King	(20)
王良	Wang Liang	(11)
王梁	Wang Liang	(18)
微子	the Viscount of Wei	(15)
卫	Wei	(16,20)
卫灵公	Duke Ling of Wei	(5)
魏	Wei	(13)
魏牟	Wei Mou	(6)
卫鞅	Wei Yang	(15)
文王	King Wen	(12,15,17,21,23,25,27,28,32)
吴	Wu	(11)
吴起	Wuqi	(32)
五伯	the Five Lords-Protector	(7,11)
五帝	the Five Di Ancestors	(5)
五行	the Five Processes Theory	(6)
伍子胥	Wu Zixu	(24,28)
《武》	*Martial*	(8,18,19,20,27)
武	Wu	(3, 11, 13, 15, 18, 26)
务成昭	Wucheng Zhao	(27)
恶来	Wulai	(8,13)

X

西海	the Western Sea	(9)
西施	Xi Shi	(18)
先王	Ancient Kings	(6)
纤离	Xianli	(23)
乡师	master of rural communities	(9)
象	Xiang	(18)
《象》	*Imitation*	(8,18,19,27)
小白	Xiaobai	(28)
《小雅》	*Lesser Odes*	(8)
小人	petty men	(14, 17, 20, 21, 26, 29)
邪道	perverse Way	(8)
信	faithfulness	(8)
信陵君	the Lord of Xinling	(13)
徐偃王	King Yan of Xu	(5)
薛公	Duke of Xue	(11)

Y

燕	Yan	(11,27)
颜渊	Yan Hui	(27,29,31)
晏子	Yan Ying	(27)
杨朱	Yang Zhu	(11)
尧	Yao	(2, 3, 6, 8, 9, 10, 11, 15, 17, 23, 27, 32)
伊尹	Yi Yin	(5,11,13)
夷	Yi	(1)
义	moral principles	(11)
羿	Yi	(8,11,12,18,21)
益	Yi	(25)

《易》	*Changes*	(5,27)
尹谐	Yinxie	(28)
殷	Yin	(8,13,15,27)
阴阳	Yin and Yang	(9,17,18,19)
有厚无厚	dimension and dimensionless	(2)
有子	Master You	(21)
虞师	master of forests	(9)
禹	Yu	(2,3,8,9,10,11,12,17,23,26,27)
《乐》	*Music*	(1)
越	Yue	(1,3,18)

Z

宰爵	intendant of the noble ranks	(9)
造父	Zaofu	(8,11,23,31)
曾子	Master Zeng	(27,30)
张去疾	Zhang Quji	(13)
张仪	Zhang Yi	(13)
赵	Zhao	(11,13,15)
郑	Zheng	(20)
跖	Robber Zhi	(1,3)
治市	director of marketplace	(9)
治田	director of fields	(9)
中国	the Central State	(9)
忠	loyalty	(8)
冢宰	high intendant	(9)
仲尼	Confucius	(5,11)
周	Zhou	(13)
周公	the Duke of Zhou	(5,8,9,13,21,24,27,28,32)
周幽	King You of Zhou	(25)
纣	Zhou Xin	(3,4,8,9,11,13)

诸侯	feudal lords	(9)
子产	Prince Chan	(27,28)
子贡	Zigong	(6,27,28,29)
子家驹	Zijia Ju	(27)
子路	Zilu	(28,29)
子思	Zisi	(6)
子夏	Zixia	(6)
子胥	Wu Zixu	(13)
子游	Ziyou	(6)
子张	Zizhang	(6)

图书在版编目(CIP)数据

荀子:汉英对照/张觉 今译;[美]诺布洛克(J.Knoblock)英译

长沙:湖南人民出版社 1999.9

(大中华文库)

ISBN 7-5438-2086-2

Ⅰ.荀... Ⅱ.①张... ②诺... Ⅲ.荀子-汉、英

Ⅳ.B222.6

中国版本图书馆 CIP 数据核字(1999)第 42247 号

责任编辑:李 林 曹伟明

审　　校:蒋坚松

大中华文库

荀 子

[美]诺布洛克 英译

张 觉 今译

出版发行者:

湖南人民出版社

(湖南省长沙市展览馆路 66 号)

邮政编码 410005

外文出版社

(中国北京百万庄大街 24 号)

邮政编码 100037

http://www.flp.com.cn

制版、排版者:

湖南省新华印刷三厂(湖南新华精品印务有限公司)

印制者:

深圳佳信达印务有限公司印刷

开本:960×640 1/16(精装) 印张:67 印数:3001-5300

2003 年第 1 版第 2 次印刷

(汉英) ISBN 7-5438-2086-2/B·47

定价:123.00 元(全 2 卷)